The Time of Theory

The Time of Theory

A History of Tel Quel
(1960–1983)

PATRICK FFRENCH

CLARENDON PRESS · OXFORD
1995

Oxford University Press, Walton Street, Oxford OX2 6DP
Oxford New York
Athens Auckland Bangkok Bombay
Calcutta Cape Town Dar es Salaam Delhi
Florence Hong Kong Istanbul Karachi
Kuala Lumpur Madras Madrid Melbourne
Mexico City Nairobi Paris Singapore
Taipei Tokyo Toronto
and associated companies in
Berlin Ibadan

Oxford is a trade mark of Oxford University Press

Published in the United States
by Oxford University Press Inc. New York

British Library Cataloguing in Publication Data
Data available

Library of Congress Cataloging in Publication Data
Ffrench, Patrick
The time of theory: a history of Tel quel (1960–1983) / Patrick Ffrench.
Based on the author's thesis (Ph. D. University College London).
Includes bibliografhical references and index.
1. Tel quel (Paris, 1960–) 2. French periodicals—France—Paris—
History—20th century. 3. Periodicals, Publishing of—France—
Paris—History—20th century. 4. Avant-grade (Aesthetics)—France.
5. France—Intellecual life—20th century. I. Title.
PN5190. T44F47 1995
054'. 1' 09045—dc20
ISBN 0–19815897–1

1 3 5 7 9 10 8 6 4 2

Typeset by Pure Tech Corporation, Pondicherry, India
Printed in Great Britain
on acid-free paper by
Bookcraft Ltd.
Midsomer Norton, Avon

TO
my Father and Mother

Acknowledgements

Many thanks to the British Academy, for the Major State Studentship grant which enabled me to conduct research leading to the Ph.D. thesis of which this book is a transformation. Thanks also to University College London French Department for being a lively and vital context for research and for its support during the writing of this book. I am particularly grateful to Professor Malcolm Bowie and Dr Peter Collier for their support in the final stages of the Ph.D. and their suggestions for its reworking into a form suitable for publication. I owe much gratitude to Professor Michael Worton of University College French Department for his enthusiasm and unflinching support throughout and to Dr Roland-François Lack of the Department of European Studies at the University of Sussex for his help with word-processing problems and for general inspiration. Thank you to Philippe Sollers, Marcelin Pleynet and Professor Julia Kristeva for granting me interviews and for their openness and generosity towards the project.

Anita Phillips helped enormously at a crucial moment in the preparation of the book, dedicating much of her time to the reading of the manuscript and suggesting vital improvements. Without her generosity, abundant talent and inspiration the book would not have been possible. I am infinitely grateful to her for her practical and spiritual support.

Finally, the book owes its existence to the enthusiasm, talent, and dedication of Professor Annette Lavers, Fielden Professor of French at University College London, and supervisor of my Ph.D. Her exceptionally rigorous, exciting and broad intellectual style was and is an inspiration and an example.

Contents

Abbreviations

APF	Association psychanalytique de France
Cin.	*Cinéthique*
CPA	*Cahiers pour l'Analyse*
CPSU	Communist Party of the Soviet Union
Crit.	*Critique*
EFP	École freudienne de Paris
ENS	École normale supérieure
EPHE	École pratique des hautes études
FLN	Front de libération nationale
IPA	International Psychoanalytical Association
NRF	*Nouvelle Revue française*
OAS	Organisation armée secrète
PCF	Parti communiste français
PCI	Partito comunista italiano
SFP	Société française de psychanalyse
SPP	Société psychanalytique de Paris
TQ	*Tel Quel*

Introduction

In Ancient Greece, a group of people travel, in a procession, to consult the oracle. Having arrived, and heard the divine words, they sit down to contemplate, to speculate on what they have heard. From procession to speculation, through the experience of the divine voice, a dramatic change occurs. This movement is reflected by the two meanings of the word *théorie* in French: speculative thought, and procession. The time of *Tel Quel*, 1960 to 1983, exhibits both derivations; it is a time of speculation, an intense ferment of activity devoted to the elaboration of a theory of literature. It is also a time of procession, of a traversal or passage of people across spaces, spaces which were at the time those between the institutions of intellectual Paris, and are now those of the texts open to our readings. In this time of theory there is also a dramatic change, but in the opposite direction. After speculation, theory returns to its processionary mode. This procession, or *traversée* is not closed within the frame of a system, it is not a theory as structure, but a more sinuous, sensuous affair, a dance. *Tel Quel*'s history exhibits this move from the terroristic closure of theory as speculation, a terror before the divine voice, to a dance across space, incarnating the divine voice in the body. It is the history of a shift to a time after theory which is to a large extent that of the present.

What is the divine voice in this mythic, metaphoric story? For *Tel Quel* it is the voice of writing, divine in that it speaks through the body of the writer, not from his intentional ego, neither from his unconscious. It is language itself which is the oracle, giving rise to speculation and to dance.

The time of theory, its temporality, is complex. On the one hand it refers simply to a historical moment in the history of the French intellectual context of the 1960s when various anti-humanist, scientific discourses from different sites intersected with one another, mobilizing the French intelligentsia in favour of theory. These discourses are now attached to names: Lacan, Derrida, Foucault, Barthes, Althusser, Kristeva, Lévi-Strauss. *Tel Quel* is the site of their intersection. The time of theory is, then, the moment of a scientific discourse which in *Tel Quel* takes the literary text as its object.

On the other hand, historical temporality is a time of illusions, the illusion, for example, that *Tel Quel* is limited to the moment of this theoretical explosion. The temporality of theory is also that of its creation, and of its mutation from speculation into dance. Intellectual historians tend to assume that the creative moments of writing, whether fictional or theoretical, run on the same level as the history of events, giving rise to a view of intellectual history as invariably determined by social and political contexts. But the temporality of literary creation exists on a different level from history. It tends to puncture this level, to make unexpected traversals across history, establishing a time specific to itself. The time of theory is also undermined by the 'vertical' temporality of creativity, so that there is a consistent, insistent message enounced across the history of *Tel Quel*, while the context itself changes and the image of the review changes with it.

This book, as well as being an attempt to assess historically what is possibly the most important post-war literary review and movement, is also about the modalities and shifts in the language and style of theory in the French intellectual context. It seeks to rescue *Tel Quel* from the largely pejorative images of it in the English-speaking academic world by analysing the history of the review from the perspective of what is identified as a coherent and consistent theory of literature. This theory is specific to the review, particularly to its principal animator, Philippe Sollers. It is distinct from the work of Barthes, Lacan, Derrida, Foucault, and Althusser, while the work of Kristeva feeds into and off the activity of *Tel Quel*. The review is also distinct from Surrealism. It is not just a repetition of an old adventure, of literature as avant-garde promoting social change, although it may at times appear, despite itself, to echo the fortunes of the Surrealist movement. It is critical of Surrealism, reactivating interest in figures dissident from or tangential to it (Artaud and Bataille), while focusing on other figures celebrated by the Surrealists (Sade and Lautréamont), only in order to wrest them from that association and bring them into a different context. But Surrealism's limitations for *Tel Quel* do not prevent it from adopting some of the strategies of a radical movement prefigured in the history of the Surrealist periodicals.

This is an attempt to establish the specificity of *Tel Quel* and to address its terroristic difficulty, accounting for this terror without reducing the difficulty, showing how the difficulty is both functional and part of the nature of the ideas themselves. The book emphasizes the relevance in the present of *Tel Quel*'s ideas and texts, and its continuation in a different form with the current review *L'Infini*.

There is a problem of reference. 'Tel Quel' can refer to the review itself, as object, or to the group, or to the ideology proposed by both. It is used in all these senses throughout the book, giving rise to an apparent looseness in terminology. But *Tel Quel* was unlike most periodicals in committing every article and its author to the programme or project of the group. In this sense it is not just a review, but also a movement in literature and theory. At the same time, it is not just the sum of its contributors. Philippe Sollers speaks for *Tel Quel*, but cannot be identified with it exclusively. The review is also a site of contradictions, between moments of its history and between the different perspectives of its contributors. It is a mobile site in continual displacement.

The study is justified by the unacknowledged but enormous influence of the review in the French intellectual context and beyond. Whether positively or reactively, the context is still responding to the time of theory focused in *Tel Quel*. Although at the time the review sold only up to 8,000 copies per issue (up to 25,000 for special issues), its influence is wide and disparate. Many of the principal intellectual figures of the time passed across its pages. The review had a part to play in the launching of the careers of Michel Foucault and Jacques Derrida, certainly Julia Kristeva; it remained a vitally supportive site for Roland Barthes from 1964 until his death in 1980. *Tel Quel* also proposed a way of reading texts that influences literary criticism and theory, almost secretly, and it has brought writers like Sade, Lautréamont, Artaud, and Bataille, to a lesser extent Céline, out of *l'enfer des bibliothèques* and into the light of analytic enquiry. Its production contains a large and important body of fictional work, in the novel and in poetry, which seems to have been overshadowed by the paradoxical permanence of the Nouveau Roman and its perpetuation, the Nouveau-Nouveau Roman, and so on. Accounts of the time recall that scarcely a student or an intellectual could be found without the latest copy of the review in their possession. But there is a difference between its true and secret lesson and influence and its ideological inflation. This study attempts to read the texts in their original contexts and to redress the balance.

Finally, the book attempts to show that the experience of literature, of writing and reading, from which *Tel Quel*'s theory derives, is fundamental to literature, not limited to the moment of theory. The time of theory is not simply a historical moment but a trans-historical temporality, bringing to life a procession of literary ghosts from the past and projecting itself into a future proposed to be infinite, *infini*. This time is a punctuation of time as illusion, *punctum temporis,* and a rediscovery of the temporality of creation. Philippe Sollers writes of this moment: 'Là, pas de temps . . . ou alors le temps vraiment retrouvé.'[1]

---

[1] P. Sollers, *Théorie des exceptions* (Paris, 1986), 11.

1   The Ferment

Intellectual history is a question of the contextualization of reading or readings. Placing a reading in a context can mean placing it in relation to a network of texts, or of events. Of course, every text exists in a number of different contexts, not all of which are determined by history. A trans-historical context or intertext can be established that bears no relation to chronology or to events. However, in order for this context to exist across history, the historical context has first to be determined. That is what is undertaken here: the mapping of a series of intertexts or contexts for the reading of the review *Tel Quel*. The review itself, however, operates a rereading of intellectual history as part of its theoretical activity which brings out a hidden context behind the most immediate and apparent historical context. The following attempts to describe both the hidden context that will become relevant for the review, and the immediate context of its formation.

Marking out a context for a movement that existed over a twenty-year period is not straightforward. The context itself shifts and the movement affects it. This is more difficult in relation to the 1960s and 1970s, when, due to the intense cross-fertilization between what had been distinct areas, a single context for literary criticism, for example, is not identifiable. It is more pertinent to speak of contexts and their intersection; in this way the ferment of the period will be more accurately represented. Ferment signifies an intense, tumultuous activity. It also signifies the result of a process of fermentation. The time of *Tel Quel* can be seen as this result, or as the process, so that we would now be enjoying the fruits of this fermenting process, perhaps without knowing it.

Ferment and intersection are not simply a question of ideas or ideologies. The intellectual scene in France is centralized in Paris and then in a fairly small area south of the Seine that runs, let's say, from the start of the Boulevard Saint-Michel to the Jardin des Plantes and not further south than Montparnasse. In this small area, the passages of people, 'across a rather brief moment of time'[1] and space, and the intersection of their passages, form the historically lived aspect of what is now related as intellectual history. The ferment of the time, in this brief moment of time and space, results then from intersections, and the network they define, of groups and of persons. A contextualization of a review like *Tel Quel* is a question of the intersection of ideas as they are concretized in groups and the personal itineraries of individuals.

Meanwhile, the review itself is a microcosm of this, a ferment, a locus of the intersection of these passages or traversals. Only this intersection is not arbitrary, it is the deliberately engineered juxtaposing of disparate elements with a view to the promoting of a certain effect in the context. Philippe Sollers reports that the activity of the committee and its smaller groupings was to work out the disposition of the context, we could say the map of the passages of people across Paris or across texts, establish the fault lines and the areas of resistance, and to act pragmatically according to this map, with a view to promoting a certain strategy.[2] The nature of the strategy is part of the subject of this book.

It is necessary, then, to delineate the topography of this space, both in terms of ideas (textual passages) and persons (trajectories of individuals or groups) to be able to grasp the coherence and continuity of the review *Tel Quel* in its historical context.

Post-war

The contexts that determine *Tel Quel* and which *Tel Quel* seeks to affect are not limited to the period of its existence (1960–82). *Tel Quel* proposed, in fact, a reframing of the history of literature from the time of Dante, but that is beyond the scope of this project. The more immediate context for *Tel Quel*, ideologically, is the post-war period, hence our concentration on the trajectories and lines of force of French intellectual life since 1945. The period from 1945 to 1960 is also a time

---

[1] See the title of a film by Guy Debord, chief editor of the review *L'Internationale situationniste*. 'Sur le passage de quelques personnes à travers une assez courte unité de temps'. See also *Sur le passage de quelques personnes à travers une assez courte unité de temps* (Paris, 1989), catalogue of an exhibition held at the Centre Georges Pompidou in 1989.

[2] See interview with Philippe Sollers by author, Paris, 1989: 'c'est chaque fois des analyses, un recul, retour des vacances, puis des analyses, c'est très, très complexe; il y a l'histoire personelle, l'histoire tout court, son complément indéchiffré, incomplètement. Il y a des rapports de forces. Donc on met tout ça au tableau noir et on voit comment . . . c'est très très lié à la vie, à l'existence, ce n'est pas des théorèmes qui se passent comme ça, c'est simplement une mise en pratique des analyses.'

in which potential forces, in terms both of ideas and of individual biographies, are set in place.

During the Occupation the intellectual milieu in France was understandably polarized between the sanctioned and the clandestine. While the major pre-war literary review, the *Nouvelle Revue française* (*NRF*) was taken over by the Fascist Drieu la Rochelle, *Les Lettres françaises* was a focus for underground Resistance literature. The publishing house Éditions de Minuit was also founded in 1941 as a forum for Resistance writing. Gallimard, meanwhile, was allowed to continue to publish books by writers such as Sartre, Camus, Eluard, and Queneau. So as well as the polarized responses of outright collaboration (Drieu, Brasillach) or Resistance, associated, particularly in the case of *Les Lettres françaises*, with the Communist party (PCF), writers could publish with the apparent sanction of the occupying forces, while remaining sympathetic to the Resistance.

After the war, the ambiguity of that position defined the atmosphere of the time. The collaborationist elements were purged, and the Resistance and Communist party emerged heroically. The *Nouvelle Revue française* having (temporarily) disintegrated, a space was left for a non-affiliated literature. It was filled to a certain extent by the existentialist grouping around Jean-Paul Sartre, who had not been active in the Resistance and who had continued to publish during the war. The tension between the Resistance and Communist factions and the existentialist or 'ambiguous' writers would define the intellectual atmosphere for the next ten years.

The focus of the debate was the journal *Les Temps modernes*, founded in 1945.[3] It entered into a field of debate in which the other prominent reviews were the Communist *Les Lettres françaises* and the Catholic Marxist *Esprit*.[4] The latter had been created in 1932 by Emmanuel Mounier as the review of the ideology of 'personalism', which proposed a humanism based on the individual, but without conflict with Communism. In a slightly more marginal position was the review *Critique*, founded in 1946 by Georges Bataille and associates from pre-war projects such as the Collège de sociologie. The shifting forces between these periodicals reflect the movements of ideas in this period.

[3] For historical accounts of *Les Temps modernes*, see: H. Davies, *Sartre and 'Les Temps modernes'* (Cambridge, 1987); A. Boschetti, *Sartre et 'Les Temps modernes'* (Paris, 1985).

[4] For a historical account of *Esprit* see: M. Winock, *Histoire politique de la revue 'Esprit': (1930–1950)* (Paris, 1975).

While the slightly esoteric debates figured in *Critique* occupied a reserved space, the main debates of the time centred on the question of commitment. The Occupation could be said to have engendered a guilt about the crimes of the Right, which determined a will for renewal and reconstruction of political and moral values. A system of values had to be created that would resist the 'irresistible' rise of Nazism; for some it was Communism, for others existentialism, and this Manichean divide dominated the field of intellectual debate between 1945 and 1956.

For Sartre the philosophical basis of this renewal also had to be established. He proposed that existentialism was a humanism, in a pamphlet of 1947, affirming that existentialism was not a quietism, but a doctrine of action, that (existential) man was first of all a project.[5] At about the same time, Simone de Beauvoir published *Pour une morale d'ambiguité*, defending existentialism as a philosophy of ambiguity.[6] Existentialism's stance of ambiguity in action was in contrast to the strict adherence to Stalinism of the PCF. The relation between *Les Temps modernes* and the PCF critics such as Henri Lefebvre and Jean Kanapa would see various extremes and reversals, making problematic any elaboration of an existential Marxism, or delaying it until 1960, when Sartre would produce the monumental *Critique de la raison dialectique*.[7] Kanapa, for example, whose ghost writer was rumoured to have been Michel Foucault, wrote a reactive tract 'L'Existentialisme n'est pas un humanisme' in 1947.[8]

Within the camp of *Les Temps modernes*, disagreements over commitment to Marxism were a source of friction. Maurice Merleau-Ponty, disillusioned with the Communist role in Korea, left the review in 1953. Sartre had also quarrelled with Camus, who was not a member of the committee of *Les Temps modernes* but was involved with the review *Combat*, over Camus's book *L'Homme révolté* (1951), seeing it as an existentialism that refused the Marxist path and had to be resisted. Despite the lack of dialogue with the PCF, the existentialists never dissociated themselves, at this time, from a general affirmation of the USSR as the locus of proletarian revolution. Although aware of the existence of the labour camps in the USSR, Sartre and Merleau-

[5] J.-P. Sartre, *L'Existentialisme est un humanisme* (Paris, 1947).

[6] S. de Beauvoir, *Pour une morale d'ambiguité* (Paris, 1947).

[7] J.-P. Sartre, *Critique de la raison dialectique* (Paris, 1960). For an informative account of this period, see: M. Poster, *Existential Marxism in Post-war France* (Princeton, NJ, 1975).

[8] J. Kanapa, *L'Existentialisme n'est pas un humanisme* (Paris, 1947).

Ponty could still claim, in a 1950 editorial, that: 'Quelle que soit la nature de la présente société soviétique, l'URSS se trouve grosso modo située dans l'équilibre des forces du côté de celles qui luttent contre les formes d'exploitation de nous connues.'[9] From 1945 to 1956 the relation between *Les Temps modernes* and the PCF was to suffer numerous upsets. Sartre, although he never joined the party, was to remain, nominally at least, a *compagnon de route* of the PCF until 1956.

At the same time, but in an arena removed from the front line of political debate, and largely within universities, a Hegelian renaissance had taken place, due, originally, to the lectures of Alexander Kojève at the École pratique des hautes études (EPHE) between 1933 and 1938 and the teaching of Jean Hyppolite at the École normale supérieure (ENS). Before then, the teaching of philosophy in French universities had been limited to the Kantian rationalism of Brunschvicg and Alain, resisting any intrusion from 'Germany'. Kojève's lectures, attended by Sartre, Bataille, Lacan, Breton, Raymond Aron, Merleau-Ponty, and Raymond Queneau, were collected in the 1947 publication, edited by Queneau, *Introduction à la lecture de Hegel*, while Hyppolite, who taught Althusser, Foucault, Derrida, and Deleuze, among others, translated Hegel's *Phänomenologie des Geistes* in 1941, and wrote a number of commentaries on Hegel in the following years.[10] Kojève is particularly important as a filter for the thought of Hegel in France. His vision of Hegel is fundamentally Marxist but is also influenced by the thought of Heidegger.

A major focus for these questions was the periodical *Critique*, founded by Bataille with associates from the pre-war groupings of Acéphale and the Collège de sociologie. *Critique* published articles by Kojève, introductory essays on Heidegger by the philosopher Alexander Koyré, and important articles on Nietzsche.[11] The role of *Critique* as an ex-centric forum for questions removed from the existentialism–Marxism deadlock was crucial for the cross-fertilization of the 1960s, attracting figures such as Foucault, Barthes, and Derrida, who play an important part in the emergence of the review as a vital force.

---

[9] M. Merleau-Ponty and J.-P. Sartre, 'Les Jours de notre vie', *Les Temps modernes*, 51 (Jan. 1950), 1162.

[10] J. Hyppolite, *Genèse et structure* (Paris, 1947); id., *Introduction à la philosophie de l'histoire de Hegel* (Paris, 1948; repub. 1988).

[11] A. Koyré, 'L'Évolution philosophique de Heidegger', *Crit.* 1–2 (June–July 1946); A. Kojève, 'Hegel, Marx et le Christianisme', *Crit.* 3–4 (Aug.–Sept. 1946); G. Bataille, 'Nietzsche', *Crit.* 34 (May 1949).

The Break-up

A number of events determine 1956 as a decisive turning-point. In February, at the twentieth Congress of the Communist Party of the Soviet Union (CPSU), Krushchev denounced Stalinism and began the programme of de-Stalinization and 'peaceful co-existence' that was to characterize the next few years. In November, Soviet tanks entered Hungary and the Hungarian uprising was crushed.

The invasion of Hungary led directly to Sartre's break with the Soviet Communist party and indirectly to *Les Temps modernes*'s support of the Algerian Front de libération nationale (FLN) and its embracing of revolutionary causes outside the USSR. The Krushchevite doctrine of de-Stalinization, meanwhile, was met with dismay by many previously Stalinist PCF members, and this led eventually to their resignations or exclusions and to a new theoretical geography. Within France this created the possibility of the emergence of a leftism not affiliated to the PCF and not in agreement with *Les Temps modernes*. Outside France, the twentieth Congress led indirectly to the Sino-Soviet split of 1960 and the eventual emergence of Maoism as an alternative for left-wing intellectuals. The possibility of Maoism as an alternative for the Left is a major factor in the tumult of 1968 and the break-up of the Left in the late 1970s, a drama in which *Tel Quel* plays a large part.

The new space for leftism was occupied by groups such as Socialisme ou barbarie, involving Cornelius Castoriadis, Claude Lefort, Jean Laplanche, and later Jean-François Lyotard, criticizing Stalinism from a Trotskyist perspective that evolved into a 'critique of everyday life'.[12] Revolution was not only political but had to affect the totality of experience; ideological and cultural revolution became paramount. The notion of cultural revolution is obviously very seductive for cultural movements and groups who seek to articulate art with a revolutionary politics. It also partly explains the explosion of Maoism in France after 1966.

The Arguments group was a more sober forum for leftism. With Barthes and Edgar Morin on its founding committee, it would act as a corridor for works of the Western Marxists, but also for more creative sociological enquiries, in works by Henri Lefebvre and Jean Duvignaud among others.[13] The influence of Heidegger could also be felt here

---

[12] See H. Lefebvre, *Critique de la vie quotidienne* (Paris, 1947).

[13] Id., *Fondements d'une société de la quotidienneté* (Paris, 1961). There were special issues of *Arguments* on 'Le Problème de l'amour' (Jan.–Mar. 1961) and 'Le Problème de la cosmologie' (Oct.–Dec. 1961). See also Poster, *Existential Marxism*.

through the activity of Kostas Axelos.[14] Barthes's involvement suggests the review to be less dogmatic and more free-thinking than others of the time, open to articles on literature, for example, such as Barthes's own championing of Robbe-Grillet and structuralism.[15]

Both the Socialisme ou barbarie and the Arguments groups would have a profound but contested influence on the situationist group and their review, the *Internationale situationniste*, which also developed a critique of everyday life that would evolve into a critique of the 'spectacle'.[16] The spontaneous creation of situations to counter the alienation of the spectacle would be an explosive ideology for the students of 1968, but this also parallels *Tel Quel* in certain ways. Sollers's present celebration of the work of Guy Debord, *Tel Quel* having not once referred to the situationists, is evidence of a proximity and a blind spot that will prove telling in the history of the review.[17]

If intellectual debate from 1945 to 1956 had been paralysed by the Manichean deadlock of the PCF and *Les Temps modernes*, the fracturing and dispersal of groups after 1956 may have contributed to the emergence of disciplines that were previously more marginal. *Arguments* and *Critique*, for example, published work by academics from university institutions such as the École pratique des hautes études or the Centre national de recherche scientifique. *Critique* also acted as a forum for a generation of students from the École normale supérieure influenced by the Hegelian and Heideggerian teaching of Kojève, Hyppolite, and Jean Wahl, as well as the radical epistemology of Bachelard and Canguilhem. The fracturing and dispersal launches a review like *Critique* into a more prominent position, and is a condition for the rise to prominence of certain individuals who will become the 'stars' of the period of the 1960s and 1970s.

So while the general, ideological movement of the fracturing of the 'existentialism or Marxism' question, the dispersal of interests, and the emergence of new areas create the conditions of possibility

[14] K. Axelos arranged the publication of a discussion between Jean Beaufret, the Heidegger expert, and Heidegger, 'Dialogue avec Heidegger' and an article by Heidegger, 'Les Principes de la pensée' for *Arguments* (1960). The review also published the proceedings of a conference on Heidegger.
[15] R. Barthes, 'Écrivains et écrivants', *Arguments* (1960), and 'L'Imagination du signe', ibid. (1962), both repub. in id., *Essais critiques* (Paris, 1964).
[16] See *L'Internationale situationniste* (Paris, 1958–69); G. Debord, *La Société du spectacle* (Paris, 1967).
[17] See P. Sollers and M. Clavel, *Délivrance* (Paris, 1977), 51.

for what is called 'structuralism', its realization, in texts and in history, depends on a series of personal itineraries which we will now examine.

Althusser

A number of the names with which this history is partly concerned have in common institutional ties with the École normale supérieure, situated in the Rue d'Ulm in Paris. The ENS is a respected institute which trains prospective teachers; to have studied or taught there is a precondition, it seems, to being taken seriously by the intellectual world and particularly the academic context in France. Many of the names of the time of *Tel Quel* emerge from the ENS, and in particular from the field of philosophy. It is the inner temple of French philosophy. In the period we are concerned with it will appear as a magnetic pole towards which philosophical faith is drawn, but also as an élite which resists any pretension to its throne. The distinction between a *normalien* and a non-*normalien* is a telling difference in the ferment of the time of *Tel Quel.*

In 1949, having been taught at the ENS by Georges Canguilhem, whose Bachelardian epistemology resonates in much structuralist and post-structuralist thinking, Louis Althusser took up a lecturing position at the ENS. He would teach, at different times in his career, Michel Foucault, Jacques Derrida, Étienne Balibar, Jacques Rancière, Pierre Macherey, Jacques-Alain Miller, Michel Tort, and many others. He would remain there until November 1980, when he strangled his wife, Hélène, in the same building in the Rue d'Ulm and committed himself to psychiatric treatment of the depressive illness that had haunted him throughout his life. His legacy at the ENS affects an entire generation of French intellectuals, but it is also his adherence to the PCF after 1948 and his attempt to re-establish the philosophy of Marxism within these limits that make for the inestimable importance of Althusser and of his intellectual biography for the history of the time. Once more, it is in 1968 that the tensions set in place by Althusser's life and work will be unleashed into 'everyday life'.

It is necessary, in order to understand Althusser's intervention, to have some notion of the theoretical geography of Marxism at the time. Althusser became a Marxist in 1948, after an active engagement with Catholicism, finally abandoned in 1952. But it is not until the early 1960s that Althusser will begin to publish the articles that establish his philosophy. It is in response to the events of the 1950s that he writes.[18]

Until the twentieth Congress of the CPSU in 1956, the International Communist Movement had been marked by a strict theoretical adherence to the deterministic materialism put forward by Stalin, the PCF following this line to the letter. However, at the twentieth Congress, Krushchev detailed a programme of de-Stalinization which effectively meant a dedication to the doctrine of 'peaceful co-existence' and also to that of the 'peaceful transition' to socialism. After the initial shock, this doctrine was in turn followed by the PCF and most other European Communist parties. Later in the same year came the Soviet invasion of Hungary, which led in particular to the expulsion of leading PCF intellectuals Henri Lefebvre and Jean-Toussaint Desanti, and the alienation of former fellow-travellers.[19] In 1960 came the decisive split with the Communist Party of China (CPC), which saw the Krushchevite de-Stalinization as revisionist, betraying the principles of Marxist-Leninist political theory. Within the PCF the Krushchevite de-Stalinization resulted in a theoretical formulation which advocated a return to the young Marx as an antidote to the dogmatism of Stalinism. The return to the young Marx stresses the Hegelian aspects of Marxism, and it was also exercised in the name of a rigorous humanism. Krushchev declared at the twenty-second Congress that everything was 'in the name of Man, for the benefit of Man'.[20]

The return to the Hegelian Marx was also accompanied, outside the PCF, by the continuation, or the renewed legacy, of the tradition of Western Marxism. Texts by Western Marxists of the 'first wave' (Lukaçs, Karl Korsch) were republished or translated in France at this time, and translations of the work of later 'Western Marxists' such as Marcuse were also published.[21] In 1947 Sartre had also declared his philosophy to be a 'humanism'. The most striking aspects of this renaissance of Marxist theory were its humanism, its Hegelianism, and its historicism.

It is within this context that Althusser started to develop his original contribution to Marxist philosophy. Seeing the Krushchevite line as a

[18] For a historical and theoretical account of Althusser's life and work, see G. Elliott, *Althusser: The Detour of Theory* (London, 1987).

[19] J.-T. Desanti will later be interviewed by Julia Kristeva in *Tel Quel* as part of an investigation of the limits of science. See *TQ* 58 (summer 1974).

[20] See Elliott, *Althusser*, 10.

[21] Marcuse's works, *Eros and Civilisation*, *One Dimensional Man*, and *An Essay on Liberation* were pub. by the Arguments group through their collection at Minuit.

right-wing critique of Stalinism, and prompted to write by the twentieth Congress and the Sino-Soviet split, he hinted, in articles of the late 1950s, that this return to the young, Hegelian Marx was at the expense of Marx's fundamental discovery—of historical materialism as the science of history. His critique of Krushchev's de-Stalinization programme implied an allegiance to the Maoist, anti-CPSU position, for which Althusser was arraigned in 1963 and 'was obliged to affirm the correctness of the PCF's own line'.[22]

Althusser's critique of the return to the younger Marx was a result of two beliefs: first that it implied a regression to German idealist philosophy, which remained within bourgeois ideology; and secondly that this return necessitated a deliberate blindness to the 'epistemological break' effected by Marx and Engels in *The German Ideology*, which left behind the 'speculative philosophy of history'[23] to formulate the science of history that was historical materialism. The accompanying humanism of Sartre, Garaudy, and others was likewise suspect as concomitant with right-wing bourgeois ideology, a barrier to any true formulation of historical materialism on a scientific basis. Althusser's project was to restructure the science of historical materialism as it was proposed by the later, mature Marx (of *Das Capital*); a project of 'critique, reconstruction and defence'[24] which ran against the official line of the PCF.

While Althusserian Marxism was enounced from within the PCF, it was not its 'official' philosophy. Althusser's work always occupied an uneasy place within the PCF, being more sympathetic to Maoism, for example, while not opting for it explicitly. Althusser's position 'inside' the party, while tending towards elements extrinsic to it, is a crucial element in the pre- and post-1968 ferment of the Left and its extremes. *Tel Quel* is irresistibly knotted into this affair.

Althusser's importance derives not only from his philosophy of Marxism, his obstinate adherence to the party, and his status at the ENS, but also from the degree to which his work established cross-currents between disciplinary boundaries. Althusser's concept of reading elaborated in *Lire le Capital* (1965) owes much to Freud's *The Interpretation of Dreams*, and his article 'Freud et Lacan' of 1963 laid down a basis for interchanges between Marxism and psychoanalysis that would result in the ugly term 'Lacano-Althusserianism' being applicable to a generation of ENS students who studied under Althusser. The *Cahiers pour l'analyse* group is such a phenomenon; it will be instrumental in certain ways in

---

[22] Elliott, *Althusser*, 35.   [23] Ibid. 41.   [24] Ibid. 67.

the history of *Tel Quel*. The cross-fertilization pioneered in a sense by Althusser could be seen to engender the encounter between psychoanalysis and politics as the crucial issue of the period. In some ways the encounter does not work out; the history of *Tel Quel* is the history of this failure.

Foucault

An articulation of the psychological and the philosophical of an entirely different kind was the project of another ENS graduate and an ex-student of Althusser's, Michel Foucault, in his monumental *Histoire de la folie à l'âge classique* (1961). Foucault's career was not, like Althusser's, dedicated to the establishment of a system, but traversed multiple and disparate areas, from the history of madness to an 'archeology' of the human sciences, and then studies of the discourses of the clinic, of the penal system, and of sexuality. Foucault's intellectual personality resists identification, but the archeological imperative to analyse the history of a discourse or of discourses, to establish the 'space of knowledge' or its conditions of possibility could, risking generalization, be said to be constant. Foucault's disparate interests intersect at a number of points with the history of *Tel Quel*. His early work, *Maladie mentale et psychologie* (1955) and the introduction to Ludwig Binswanger's *Rêve et existence* of 1954 are major references for *Tel Quel* writers in an early period of interest in pre-analytical psychology and in dreams. The problematization of a dialectical relation between subject and object in extreme or liminal states such as madness or dreams which Foucault's studies underlined is an important moment in the development of *Tel Quel*'s view of literature as transgressive of the space of subject–object relations. Foucault's essays on literature in the early 1960s, on Bataille, Blanchot, Klossowski, Hölderlin, influenced by Blanchot and Bataille, are an important parallel to *Tel Quel*'s thinking, which has similar influences but is subtly different. The two intersect briefly in 1963, only to diverge from one another and to remain incommensurate from then on. Despite this difference, Foucault's trajectory is an important part of the context for the review, the conflict of interests after the brief encounter betraying a more fundamental intellectual desire not to be identified and classified on the part of both parties.

Foucault was also involved with the review *Critique*, invited on to the advisory committee by the editor Jean Piel, to join his illustrious colleagues Barthes and later Derrida in the shadow cast by Bataille, who

died in 1962. The obituary issue of *Critique* after Bataille's death was a
good indication of the already established network that linked *Tel Quel*
to *Critique* and to figures like Foucault and Derrida, including articles by
Barthes, Foucault, and Sollers, among others.[25] Another figure of
influence on Foucault was Maurice Blanchot, also one of the contributors to the *Critique* obituary issue on Bataille. Blanchot's view of the
silence engendered by literature mirrors Foucault's vision of unreason
as the unspoken other of Western rationality. *Tel Quel*'s relation to
Blanchot, as will be discussed later, is ambiguous, partly unacknowledged, and undeniably critical. The difference between Foucault's
thinking on literature and that of the review perhaps rests on the
influence of Blanchot, which *Tel Quel* wished to resist and which
Foucault wished to perpetuate.

Foucault's itinerary in the 1960s and 1970s is a major part of the
context not only for *Tel Quel* but more generally. The sound and fury
of the two decades which his history of madness opened did not fail to
end in tragedy, like the story of his teacher Althusser, when Foucault
died of the AIDS virus in 1985, leaving his history of sexuality
incomplete.

Derrida

Jacques Derrida's relations with *Tel Quel* were more intense and
prolonged, but became equally distant. Derrida had also emerged from
the ENS, having studied with Althusser and Foucault. He would
eventually become a lecturer at the ENS, where he would stay until
1984. His association with *Tel Quel* begins in 1965 with his first article in
the review, on Artaud. He had previously published work in *Critique* (on
the critic Rousset[26]) and was a colleague of Gérard Genette, so he was
potentially close to *Tel Quel* on those levels. But it was his 1962
introduction to Husserl's *L'Origine de la géometrie* (1962), which earned him
the prestigious Prix Jean Cavaillès, that made him most interesting for
Sollers and *Tel Quel*. Sollers refers to his enthusiasm on reading a
passage in this book where Derrida mentions Joyce.[27] Derrida proposes
that there are two responses to the equivocation that science or
philosophy must overcome and which is an inevitable and essential

---

[25] *Crit.* 195–6 (Aug.–Sept. 1963).
[26] J. Derrida, 'Forme et signification', *Crit.* 194 (July 1963).
[27] Sollers, interview with author, Paris, 1989.

aspect of language. Husserl's response is to impoverish language until only the univocal and translatable remains. Joyce's option, Derrida affirms, is a language that celebrates equivocation and 'settles into the labyrinthine field of culture' (surely a veiled allusion to Robbe-Grillet's 1959 novel *Dans le labyrinthe*, the scope of which is thereby suggested as being restricted with relation to Joyce), opting for the greatest historical distance possible, as opposed to its reduction to sterility.[28] The writing Derrida describes is one of play and extension, rather than of reduction and stasis, offering *Tel Quel* the vision of writing as an envelopment of the languages of science and philosophy and hinting at writing as a concept that could unhinge metaphysics and institute a generalized critique of the Western ideology of presence. Literature, celebrated equivocation, would evidently become the privileged locus of such an unhinging. The possibilities of Derrida's vision, visited on Sollers, were extremely promising.

Derrida's relentless deconstructive vigilance, his rigour and ruthlessness in the exposure of 'logocentrism' (not sparing Foucault[29]) would make him an extremely seductive figure for *Tel Quel* and Sollers. The affair would be tempestuous.

While the ENS harboured and produced most of the philosophical references and 'stars' of the 1960s and 1970s which *Tel Quel* has recourse to or comes up against, part of the intense cross-flow of intellectual currents derives from the emergence of other institutions and disciplines.

Despite the difference of the disciplines of, for example, anthropology, psychoanalysis, sociology, the emergence of 'structuralism' in these fields can be traced to a common denominator or even perhaps to a historical event. The common denominator is the emergence of linguistics and the proposition of language as a model for other sciences. This emergence itself might have been the result of developments within linguistics, or of influences upon it by 'harder' sciences such as cybernetics, but the explicit evidence in the discourses of the humanities, although this term begins to tremble, was the rise of linguistics. Paul de Man suggests that the advent of what is called 'theory' results from the introduction of linguistic terminology into the discourse of literary criticism.[30] It enables a turn from the aesthetics of the literary text to the modalities of its production. At the same time, the turn to rhetoric undermines the pretension of theory to closure and universality, since

[28] J. Derrida, introd. to E. Husserl, *L'Origine de la géométrie* (Paris, 1962).
[29] See J. Derrida, 'La Mythologie blanche', in id., *Marges de la philosophie* (Paris, 1972).
[30] P. de Man, *The Resistance to Theory* (Manchester, 1986), 8.

rhetoric involves moments of resistance to theory.[31] The history of *Tel Quel* can be seen as the adventure of theory and its subsequent undoing by the literary text, a pattern historically mapped out over the twenty-year period. Perhaps only now is it possible to stand outside this history and trace the undoing of theory. Its conception, meanwhile, is locatable in the turn to linguistics, generally in the human sciences and specifically within literature.

Lévi-Strauss

If linguistics is the common denomimator, the historical event of the turn to linguistics in the human sciences is perhaps the meeting of the anthropologist Lévi-Strauss and the linguist Roman Jakobson in New York in 1945. In the same year, Lévi-Strauss contributed to Jakobson's linguistics journal *Word* the article 'L'Analyse structurale en linguistique et en anthropologie', where he laid out the basis of the use of linguistics as a model for the analysis of kinship systems, showing four operations: the shift to infrastructure, to relations between terms, to system or structure, and the intention to uncover basic laws.[32] His main references were to Jakobson and Troubetzkoy of the defunct but still influential Prague School of Linguistics.

However, the use of linguistics as a model had been suggested before, although perhaps not in such a systematic way. Lévi-Strauss's acknowledged precursor was the anthropologist Marcel Mauss. Introducing the latter's work in 1950, Lévi-Strauss underlines Mauss's recognition that societies were symbolic systems and that language was not only a tool for their analysis, but also an analogous structure, in that 'symbols are more real than what they symbolize, the Signifier precedes and determines the signified'.[33] The necessity of system, structure, and 'combinatorial analysis' (structuralist analysis of relations between terms) is extracted by Lévi-Strauss from Mauss's *Essai sur le don*, but while he warns against reading it in isolation, he does not take from it the same lesson as Georges Bataille, seventeen years earlier, who refers to Mauss as having recognized that exchange was based on a notion of expense

[31] P. de Man, op. cit., 16.

[32] C. Lévi-Strauss, 'L'Analyse structurale en linguistique et en anthropologie', *Word, Journal of the Linguistic Circle of New York*, 2 (Aug. 1945). Repub. in id., *Anthropologie structurale* (Paris, 1958).

[33] Id., *Introduction à l'œuvre de Marcel Mauss* (Paris, 1950), trans. F. Baker as *Introduction to the Work of Marcel Mauss* (London, 1987), 36.

as absolute loss or destruction.[34] While Lévi-Strauss builds structure and exchange out of Mauss's gift, Bataille recognizes negativity as an archaic principle before any system or structure (of exchange), which is incommensurable with it. *Dépense*, a radical negativity, is already present before the structure of exchange, which it will come to trangress later, in the work of Derrida, Kristeva, and J.-J. Goux. Through the foreclosure of this negativity the structuralism of Lévi-Strauss appears as a system erected in order that it be undermined by what it represses, which in fact it already knows. The structure is erected so that the pain of its subversion can be experienced, a masochistic pattern that seems equally to apply to theory in general.

Lévi-Strauss's main adversary in the intellectual context of the time was not Bataille, however, but the humanism of Sartre. The publication of Lévi-Strauss's *Anthropologie structurale* (1958) and *La Pensée sauvage* in 1962 was crucial to the transition from existentialism to structuralism. Writing in a chapter entitled 'Histoire et dialectique', directed specifically against Sartre's 'synthetic anthropology' of the *Critique de la raison dialectique*, that: 'le but dernier des sciences humaines n'est pas de constituer l'homme, mais de la dissoudre',[35] Lévi-Strauss was laying down the precepts of a scientific, anti-humanist perspective in the human sciences. Structuralism had overtaken and confronted existential anthropology before it had even had the time to enounce its new and total vision.

Lévi-Strauss's structural anthropology was the condition of possibility for the cross-over of linguistics to other disciplines and the rise of a broad front across the human sciences. If the existentialists could have accused structuralism of eliding the dimension of subjectivity, a factor in favour of the latter was the development and emergence of a psychoanalysis that took partial inspiration from the linguistics of Saussure and Jakobson. However, psychoanalysis, with its models and terms, plays the same role of cross-fertilization across the disciplines, and especially in literary theory, as did linguistics. The 1960s and 1970s is also the time of the psychoanalytic revolution. *Tel Quel* plays a large but critical role in this cross-over. The intersection of these signifiers in different disciplines may be disparate and fragmentary, but the name that 'upholsters' them is Lacan.[36]

---

[34] G. Bataille, 'La Notion de dépense', *La Critique sociale*, 7 (Jan. 1933) and in id., *Oeuvres complètes*, i (Paris, 1970).

[35] C. Lévi-Strauss, *La Pensée sauvage* (Paris, 1962), 326.

[36] See Lacan's use of the metaphor of the *point de capiton* in *Écrits*, i (Paris, 1970).

Lacan

The implantation of psychoanalysis as a separate discipline in the French academic world was preceded by its engagement with literature and art in Surrealism. Psychoanalysis was already enmeshed with literature, and this is perhaps true in a wider sense, since Freud's theoretical models frequently reveal a debt to literature. As Surrealism had already annexed Freudian theory, the main thrust of the critique of Surrealism of *Tel Quel* is that Breton's reading of Freud was a misreading; the Surrealist engagement with Freud is the major historical paradigm of the articulation of literature with psychoanalysis, hence its importance as an obstacle to be overcome.[37] *Tel Quel*'s critique of Surrealism underlines the necessity of reading Freud 'through' Lacan; Surrealism is historically disadvantaged by coming 'before' Lacan. Yet this blindness caused by history is accompanied by an equal blindness to history on the part of *Tel Quel*, since Lacan's early work as a psychiatrist was undertaken in close proximity to the Surrealist movement.[38] Lacan was to publish in the art journal *Minotaure*, for example, and his thesis on 'le cas Aimée' is inextricable from the Surrealist cult of the hysterical, ecstatic woman, as David Macey has shown in his *Lacan in Contexts* (1988). Before developing the theory for which he is perhaps more notorious, which does not really become widely known until after the publication of *Écrits* in 1966, Lacan was also in close contact with Georges Bataille, whose ex-wife he would marry. So Lacan was already part of a network in which mutual exchanges between psychoanalysis and literature were common. This prehistory will be essentially forgotten in the period of theory. The intervening years see psychoanalysis becoming institutionally established and then emerging as a separate discipline. It is Lacan's relations with the institution of psychoanalysis itself that provide the possibility of the theoretical ferment that would emerge in the 1960s.[39]

The Société psychanalytique de Paris (SPP) was formed in 1926. Lacan was to join it in 1934, having trained as a psychiatrist under Clérambault and been analysed by the ego psychologist Rudolf Lowenstein. Having started work at the Sainte-Anne hospital in 1927, he

[37] See *TQ* 46 (summer 1971), for a critical assessment of Surrealism and neo-Surrealism in the review.

[38] For an account of Lacan's debt to Surrealism, see D. Macey, *Lacan in Contexts* (London, 1988).

[39] For an intellectual biography of Lacan, see E. Roudinesco, *La Bataille de cent ans. Histoire de la Psychanalyse en France*, ii (Paris, 1986).

published his doctoral thesis, 'De la psychose paranoïaque dans ses rapports avec la personnalité', in 1932. In the late 1930s Lacan would attend Alexander Kojève's lectures on Hegel, with many other notable figures of the time. This encounter would revolutionize Lacan's thought and result in a psychoanalytical account of the infant's formative years articulated with a philosophical, Hegelian vision of desire. Freudian desire is reread as a desire for recognition. Desire is desire for the Other. Later this reading will itself be reread and transformed by Saussurean and Jakobsonian linguistics, but also by an encounter with Heidegger, whom Lacan would meet in 1951. The development of theory, which here is suggested as resulting from the importation of Hegelian philosophy into psychoanalysis, was not without costs. The SPP was becoming increasingly polarized into medical and academic factions, the struggle between which resulted eventually in the schism of 1953, when a number of analysts split off from the SPP to form the Société française de psychanalyse (SFP). Lacan was prominent among them. While courting the International Psychoanalytical Association (IPA) for institutional recognition, this society would be the basis of a theoretical flowering which established psychoanalysis as a discipline with the same intellectual respectability as philosophy. A number of students from the ENS, for example, became psychoanalysts in this society; analysts of a philosophical, academic formation emerged among those of a medical foundation. An example of the possibilities of passages across these disciplines is the figure of Jean Laplanche, an ENS student who had studied under Hyppolite, and who was one of the founding members of the Socialisme ou barbarie group. The philosophical background of Lacanian analysts is a further prerequisite for the explosion of theory.

The period of existence of the SFP from 1953 to 1964 also saw Lacan, in his 'Discours de Rome' and other texts, elaborating a psychoanalytical theory via the structural linguistics of Saussure and Jakobson. Lacan insisted, as had Lévi-Strauss, on the predeterminative nature and function of the signifier, language as such, and the repressive bar that separated it from the signified, meaning.[40] The 'passion of the signifier' was an aspect of what Sollers would see as a materialist theory of language, but not until much later, in the late 1960s.[41] The theoretical groundwork was undertaken in the 1950s.

---

[40] See J. Lacan, 'Fonction et champ de la parole et du langage en psychanalyse' and 'L'Instance de la lettre dans l'inconscient depuis Freud', *Écrits*, i (Paris, 1970).
[41] See P. Sollers, 'Survol/Rapports(Blocs)/Conflit', *TQ* 36 (winter 1969), 6.

The 'Discours de Rome' of 1953 was published in a periodical of the SFP titled *La Psychanalyse*. This journal functioned as the major site of the theoretical expansion of psychoanalysis and its infiltration by and into philosophy and linguistics. Lacan published articles on Hegel and Heidegger in the review, as well as the seminar on 'The Purloined Letter', where a literary text was used as a parable for psychoanalytic theory in a way that was later to provoke much debate about the relations between literature and psychoanalysis.[42] The review would also publish work by Jean Hyppolite, the Hegel specialist, and Émile Benveniste, the linguist, who elaborated a critique of Saussure focused on the subject and subjectivity that would be crucial for theorists like Kristeva in the move away from structuralism, precisely towards a more psychoanalytic perspective on language.[43] *La Psychanalyse* was the major forum for a cross-fertilization of disciplines by psychoanalysis. On the side of its reception it was also the site for the encounter of Lacan's work and more generally of Freud by people like Althusser, who would have been attracted by the inclusion of names such as Hyppolite.[44] In the 1950s, then, psychoanalysis emerged into philosophical respectability and took on board the influence of linguistics. Lacan's work became more and more central and known outside the walls of the psychoanalytic institution. People of non-medical backgrounds began to attend Lacan's regular seminar at the Sainte-Anne hospital in Paris.

It would be misleading to suggest, however, that Lacan was solely responsible for the rise to prominence of psychoanalysis as a theoretical discipline, although he was the scapegoat and champion of this tendency. In the late 1950s and early 1960s a number of writers in different areas spread the word of Freudian theory in ways not always fully in accord with Lacan's thought. In *Les Temps modernes*, the stalwart of Sartrean existentialism, Lacanian psychoanalysis had a powerful voice in the articles of J.-B. Pontalis, an ex-student of Sartre.[45] Any implied compatibility between Sartre and Lacan soon waned, however, in favour of the latter (Pontalis would cease to publish in *Les Temps modernes* after 1963), while in Pontalis's articles there was the suggestion that a closer ally to Lacan was Merleau-Ponty, in fact acknowledged as such

---

[42] J. Lacan, 'Introduction au commentaire de J. Hyppolite sur la "Verneinung" de Freud', *La Psychanalyse*, 1 (1956) and 'Le Séminaire sur "La Lettre volée" ', *La Psychanalyse*, 2 (1957). Heidegger would contribute an article entitled 'Logos' to issue 1.

[43] Roudinesco's book (*La Bataille*) offers an extended account of this period.

[44] Ibid. 378.

[45] Articles collected in the book *Après Freud* (Paris, 1968).

by Lacan in his seminar of 1964.[46] Merleau-Ponty's importance seems to have been elided from the theoretical skeleton of Lacanian theory, extracted for the sake of theory. Emphasizing a phenomenological irreducibility in what Lacan would term the Real, Merleau-Ponty's work would influence that of Lyotard on the figure,[47] but the structuralist insistence on the ubiquity of the symbolic, le discours, would remain blind to it.

Meanwhile, Althusser's seminars at the ENS had also become a fertile site of cross-influence. ENS pupils like Jacques-Alain Miller, later to become Lacan's son-in-law, and Michel Tort, later to be involved with the Tel Quel issue on Sade, gave seminar papers on Lacan at the ENS.[48] With other colleagues they would later form the review Cahiers pour l'analyse, the site of an epistemological synthesis of Lacanian and Althusserian theory, and a major reference for Tel Quel.[49]

Lacanian analysis had also not ignored literature in the 1950s and early 1960s. While Pontalis had written a psychoanalytical study of Leiris in Les Temps modernes[50] his colleague at the SFP, Jean Laplanche, would write the important Hölderlin et la question du père in 1961. The book would be a critical focus of Derrida's in an important article on Artaud published in Tel Quel.[51] There is a context for psychoanalytic enquiries into literature that prefigures Tel Quel's engagement with Lacan.

So in the early 1960s psychoanalysis was a theory in proliferation, with many articles being written under the influence of, or in response to, the burgeoning thought of Lacan. The 1960 Bonneval colloquium, attended by Lacan, Laplanche, Pontalis, André Green, Merleau-Ponty, Althusser, Henri Lefebvre, Jean Hyppolite, was a showcase for this panoply of forces, and it led to some inevitable fissures. Laplanche and Pontalis, for example, produced papers critical of Lacan in certain ways and established a tension that would come to the crunch four years later. In 1964, under pressure from the IPA, the SFP underwent an internal crisis that led to its splitting into two separate groups. One group, named the École freudienne de Paris (EFP), consisted of Lacan

[46] See J. Lacan, Le Séminaire, xi: Les Quatre Concepts fondamentaux de la psychanalyse (Paris, 1973).

[47] See J.-F. Lyotard, Discours, figure (Paris, 1971).

[48] See Roudinesco, La Bataille, 378.

[49] See Sollers, 'Survol/Rapports', TQ 36. 10–11. Sollers refers to articles by A. Badiou and J.-A. Miller.

[50] J.-B. Pontalis, 'Michel Leiris ou la psychanalyse sans fin', repub. in id., Après Freud.

[51] J. Derrida, 'La Parole soufflée', TQ 20 (winter 1965), repub. in id., L'Écriture et la différence (Paris, 1967), 253.

and analysts loyal to him. The other, the Association psychanalytique de France (APF), was made up of Lacanians who could no longer stand such close proximity to their 'master' and his dominance. Laplanche, Pontalis, and Michel Tort were among this group. The split was perhaps more productive than harmful for Lacan, since he now had a school all of his own, and his seminar shifted location from Sainte-Anne to the École normale supérieure, where he could influence a larger and more diverse audience. With the establishment of 'Le Champ freudien' collection at Le Seuil with Lacan as editor, the Lacanian empire was ready to reap the rewards of its conquest of theory.

As well as the EFP, the two main groups in 1964 were the APF and the more sober SPP. However, both of these groups, pulled by the influence of Lacanian theory, were also promising ground for the intellectual expansion of psychoanalysis. Laplanche and Pontalis, in the APF, were to publish in 1964 their *Vocabulaire de la psychanalyse*, which, through explanation of Freudian terms filtered through Lacan's reading, rendered psychoanalysis more readily accessible to non-analysts. In 1970 Pontalis would launch the *Nouvelle Revue de psychanalyse*, which was a crucial forum for psychoanalytic studies of all persuasions. The SPP's review, the *Revue française de psychanalyse*, set up in 1927, was still an important organ. A principal ally of Lacan, and one who had much to say about literature, was André Green, who wrote on narcissism in the *Revue* and also organized a seminar at the SPP-affiliated Institut de psychanalyse. Green would develop a critique of Lacan as having left out of his theory an account of the affect, a perspective not unlike the Merleau-Pontyan critique of Lyotard focused on the figure.[52] The theoretical dominance of Lacan and the silence of *Tel Quel* on writers like Green is all the more surprising in that Green was more sensitive to literature (he would also give a seminar in Barthes's course at the EPHE) and the fact that Derrida's article on Freud, published in *Tel Quel*, originated in a seminar of Green's at the Institut.[53] *Tel Quel* also published work by Michel de M'Uzan, a member of the SPP, on psychosomatic phenomena.[54] *Tel Quel*'s initial interest in Freud is thus non-Lacanian and institutionally distinct from Lacan. This is evidence of how the proliferation of psychoanalysis in the early 1960s goes further

[52] See A. Green, *Le Discours vivant* (Paris, 1973).

[53] See Derrida, *L'Écriture et la différence*, 293.

[54] M. de M'Uzan 'Aperçus psychanalytiques sur le processus de création littéraire', *TQ* 19 (autumn 1964). See also J.-L. Baudry's review of his *Investigations psychosomatiques* in *TQ* 18 (summer 1964) and his early fictional piece 'Richesse' in *TQ* 4 (winter 1961).

than the circle and person of Lacan, while it may derive its notoriety and prestige from him. The proliferation was such that the publication of Lacan's *Écrits* in 1966 fell on ground already fertile for the explosion of theory and the full importation of psychoanalysis into literary theory.

The itineraries of Althusser, Foucault, Derrida, Lévi-Strauss, Lacan, and others around them and in their wake open up the possibility for the convergence and intersection of disciplines towards what we have called theory and its ferment. With *Tel Quel* the primary concern is literature. Theory is always a theory of literature and the review is the site of the intersection and appropriation of these theoretical trajectories for literature, with varying degrees of success or felicity. Within the field of literature itself, and of literary criticism, there are important precursors who create part of the context for the review. If in philosophy the major triumvirate consists of three Hs (Hegel, Husserl, Heidegger), in this field the three resonant names begin with B: Bataille, Blanchot, Barthes.

Bataille

The importance of Bataille for *Tel Quel* is all the more decisive for the fact that Bataille was always tangential to Surrealism and at times openly in conflict with André Breton. Bataille was never part of the Surrealist group and cannot be considered even as a dissident from Surrealism, far less as an ex-Surrealist, although the review *Documents* did involve some ex-Surrealists like Leiris and Desnos. Bataille will play an important role in the distancing of Surrealism by *Tel Quel*; Bataille's difference never ceases to be affirmed by the review.[55] The violent polemics with Breton that arose through Bataille's review *Documents* and Breton's second manifesto show Bataille to be critical of the idealist and romanticizing tendencies of Surrealism, and *Tel Quel*'s publication of Bataille's article 'La "vielle taupe" et le préfixe *sur* dans les mots *surréaliste* et *surhomme*' is a reactivation of this polemic, at the crucial moment of 1968.

Tangential to the Surrealist group dominated by Breton, Bataille's projects for reviews and groups are also exemplary for *Tel Quel*. Through *Documents*, *Acéphale*, and the Collège de sociologie, Bataille sought to found a community based on what he will call later *l'expérience intérieure*, an experience of the excess or *dépense* he saw as primary.

---

[55] See J.-L. Houdebine, 'L'Ennemi du dedans', in P. Sollers (ed.), *Bataille* (Paris, 1973).

Evidently the experience in question, being interior and transgressive, tended to fracture the community itself.[56] The groups were determined by the contradiction of their public, political interventions in the reviews, and the violence and tension of their private relations, in the case of *Acéphale* founded in a secret society. The relations of the founders of the more public Collège de sociologie, Leiris, Caillois, and Bataille, bear witness to the transgressive relation to any community, particularly of 'science', that Bataille's projects embodied.[57] This imperative is also present in *Tel Quel*, the Groupe d'études théoriques, founded in 1968 as a public forum for the review's work, explicitly sought a reformulation of the aims of the Collège in its effect on a wider public, outside institutional walls. The fractured community, of which the review was the expression, in a state of 'permanent dissolution', as Sollers puts it,[58] was the result of the transgressive and contradictory logic of the text that could not remain within an enclosed, homogeneous collective. Sollers and Pleynet 'realized' this strategy, in the sense of not hindering the effects on the committee that the logic of transgression demanded, according to their interpretation.[59] How much the affective tensions within the committee were determined by this 'logic' and how much engineering by Sollers towards a certain strategy played a part is a matter for discussion. What may be more interesting, however, is the extent to which the strategy itself follows the transgressive movement of literature or veers into ideological blockages. At any rate, ostensibly and actually, Bataille's projects of community are exemplary for *Tel Quel*.

The 'fractured community' itself is interesting from the point of view of the history of literature. Jean-Luc Nancy, in his *La Communauté désœuvrée* traces the notion of 'literary communism' to the German Romantic *Athenaeum*.[60] In an elliptical way he suggests that *Tel Quel* was a reformulation of the myth of a literary community.[61] To what extent

---

[56] This is moreover a subject of specific interest in *Tel Quel* itself, through the publication of articles by Michel Fardoulis-Lagrange, a colleague of Bataille at the time of the abortive Collège socratique. See M. Fardoulis-Lagrange, 'C'est en 1942', *TQ* 81 (autumn 1979) and 'Un art divin: L'oubli', *TQ* 93 (autumn 1982).

[57] See D. Hollier (ed.), *Le Collège de sociologie* (Paris, 1979).

[58] P. Sollers, 'Le GSI', *TQ* 86 (winter 1980), 11.

[59] Interviews by author with Sollers, Pleynet, Paris, 1989–92. Pleynet: 'Le groupe produit, dans ce qui différencie fondamentalement les éléments, quelque chose qui rend la vie intenable à un des éléments. La machine tourne . . . et ils sont naturellement démis.'

[60] J.-L. Nancy, *La Communauté désœuvrée* (Paris, 1986), trans. (and ed.) Peter Connor as *The Inoperative Community* (Minnesota, 1991), 64.

[61] Nancy, *The Inoperative Community*, 64: 'Blanchot has insisted that "community, in its very failure, remains linked in some way to writing" and has referred to the "ideal

the review was the presentation of the exposure and fracture, the excess, of its community in a work and how much it was itself in its written form that exposure, is perhaps the crucial question for any study of the review. It might be a question of reading the exposure of literature of *Tel Quel* against its insertion into theory or system, of reading *Tel Quel* against the tautological connotations of its title, 'as such', or it might be a question of revealing how the 'as such' is always subjected to displacement, to the exposure at its limits. The relation to Bataille is part of the stakes in this debate.

The importance of Bataille in this question, and more generally for *Tel Quel*, also rests on the ambiguous tension of his work 'between' Nietzsche and Hegel.[62] The Marxism and Maoism of the review will be shown to rest on this ambiguity, which is also resonant in the work of a writer like Foucault. Is the excess of *l'expérience intérieure* reinsertable into a dialectic, while ruining any synthesis, or does it portray a Nietzschean dance or *gai savoir*? *Tel Quel*'s history lives out this ambiguity, which is essentially the drama of the possibility of getting beyond Hegel.

But Bataille's example cannot be limited or enclosed by this philosophical question. It also operates in his thinking of the body and sexuality, not only in books like *L'Érotisme* but also in his fiction, a more secret part of his influence, revealed more in the poetry of Pleynet than in the theory of *Tel Quel*, which it outlasts and undermines.[63] The vision of sexuality as overdetermined by death is fundamental to *Tel Quel*'s thought. Bataille's vision of femininity is a strong influence on that of Souers, and on Lacan's. Femininity as excessive and virulent in relation to masculine phallocentricity, femininity as *jouissance*, predetermines any relations with feminism both Lacan and *Tel Quel* might have.

---

community of literary communication". This can always make for one more myth, a new myth, and not one even as new as some would believe: the myth of the literary community was outlined for the first time (although in reality it was perhaps not the first time) by the Jena romantics and it has filtered down to us in various different ways through everything resembling the idea of a "republic of artists" or, again, the idea of a communism (of a certain kind of Maoism, for example) and revolution inherent, *tels quels*, in writing itself.'

[62] See D. Hollier, 'De l'au-delà de Hegel à l'absence de Nietzsche', in Sollers (ed.), *Bataille*.

[63] Interview by author with Pleynet, Paris, 1991: 'Ma lecture de Bataille a été certainement beaucoup plus empirique, de toute façon mon attitude est beaucoup plus empirique que celle des autres membres du groupe, mais Bataille a joué un rôle considérable. C'est à dire, au fond j'ai toujours été davantage attiré par la production romanesque, littéraire, poétique, entre guillemets, de Bataille, que par sa production théorique.'

These questions are part of the continuity of Bataille's work in *Tel Quel*. Historically, Bataille's influence resides more in the marginality of his position and the relations he entertained with figures like Sartre. For example, Bataille's opposition to Sartre, who had castigated Bataille in the essay 'Un nouveau mystique', on Bataille's side was more subtly mediated through the position of *Critique* in relation to *Les Temps modernes* after the war. The essays collected in *La Littérature et le mal*, some of which respond specifically to Sartre, also functioned as a useful reference-point for writers like Foucault, Barthes, and Derrida, reading 'against' Sartre. In *La Littérature et le mal* Bataille takes issue with Sartre's readings of Baudelaire and Genet, arguing that literature could not be used as a basis for action. Neither Baudelaire nor Genet were guilty of abdicating moral or existential responsibility, for 'La littérature n'est pas innocente, et, coupable, elle devait à la fin s'avouer telle. L'action seule a les droits.'[64] Literature could not be judged according to morality, it was a 'hypermorality'. Sartre's argument for the 'commitment' of literature was therefore inadmissible. Literature was all or nothing. This would be an important influence for Barthes in his *Le Degré zéro de l'écriture* (1953), and for *Tel Quel* in its opening 'Déclaration'. *Critique*, in the late 1940s and 1950s, where many of these articles were published, sets out in many ways the hidden programme for the next decade.

Blanchot

While Bataille is the acknowledged hero of *Tel Quel*, Blanchot is the precursor it would like to forget. His work is also partitioned between fiction and criticism or theory, although Blanchot still writes in the tradition of the literary essay rather than of theory. Blanchot's fiction, a persistent, haunting but marginal voice since the war (*Thomas l'obscur*, 1941 and 1950; *Aminadab*, 1942; *L'Arrêt de mort*, 1948; *Celui qui ne m'accompagnait pas*, 1953; *Le dernier homme*, 1957; *L'Attente, l'oubli*, 1961) informs and prefigures the *nouveau roman* and the novelistic experiments of *Tel Quel*. Blanchot's criticism is perhaps more important than the fiction. In *La Part du feu*, *L'Espace littéraire*, and *Le Livre à venir* not only does Blanchot map out the territory at the limits that *Tel Quel* will later explore, in essays on writers like Lautréamont and Sade (in a book of 1947), Artaud, Kafka, and especially Mallarmé, but he proposes, for example, that literature is 'a question posed to language by literature

[64] G. Bataille, *Oeuvres complètes* ix (Paris, 1979), 171.

become language'.[65] Blanchot's notion of literature is premised on the same rhetorical, transgressive strategy as that of *Tel Quel*. The proximity of Blanchot's thought and *Tel Quel*'s theory is worrying, particularly as there is no confrontation of the problematic except in asides, in passing. Sollers proposes, for example, that Blanchot's thought was determined by a 'fundamental Hegelianism' and was 'une problématique de l'essence du langage fondée sur la négativité hégélienne'.[66] It is difficult to determine, fundamentally and essentially, in what ways *Tel Quel*'s theory differs from this. If Blanchot's thought is idealist and Hegelian, as Sollers suggests, and that of *Tel Quel* materialist as it professes itself to be, then the often reiterated notion that dialectical materialism results from an exacerbated Hegelian idealism pushed to its limit and over-turned,[67] is crucial in the Blanchot-*Tel Quel* relation. The confrontation with Blanchot, as the idealist summit before *Tel Quel*'s materialism, would be an essential aspect of *Tel Quel*'s textual materialism. The lack of a confrontation and analytic distinction results in an ambiguity and indistinctness over this question. The fact that Blanchot's thought is not closed 'before' *Tel Quel*, but continues in *L'Entretien infini* (1969) makes the lack of an analysis of Blanchot all the more telling.

While the fundamental and essential relation to Blanchot is unclear, there are evident differences. Blanchot's enquiries are those of a 'literary anthropologist' who 'reflects on the human condition while ostensibly writing literary criticism or theory'.[68] It may not be forcing the issue to say that Blanchot's enterprises fall uncomfortably within the closure of a philosophical, metaphysical enterprise, which asks 'what is literature?' or 'what is man, given that literature exists?' While Blanchot asks what the text is, in its essence, *Tel Quel* enquires into its process; what it does and how. There is an incommensurability between the two projects that perhaps explains their mutual lack of engagement.

Blanchot's work is nevertheless crucial in the context in marking out the territory of literature's limits, where it puts itself in question, and in focusing on the text itself as essential, as Bataille had also affirmed, rather than on its ideological or political value. With Bataille, Blanchot is part of a network of individuals which includes Pierre Klossowski (the Catholic Nietzschean), and Roger Caillois, both of whom will intersect

---

[65] See M. Blanchot's works during this period: *La Part du feu* (Paris, 1949); *L'Espace littéraire* (Paris, 1956); *Le Livre à venir* (Paris, 1959).

[66] See P. Sollers in J. Ristat (ed.), *Qui sont les contemporains?* (Paris, 1975), 150–3.

[67] See P. Sollers, *Sur le matérialisme* (Paris, 1974).

[68] A. Lavers, *Roland Barthes: Structuralism and After* (London, 1982), 62.

with *Tel Quel* at various moments,[69] and who are both prominent among contributors to *Critique* (Blanchot was on the committee). Blanchot and Caillois and another important writer, Jean Paulhan, director of the *Nouvelle Revue française*, are also both associated with the reading committee at Gallimard, the prestigious publishing house which published both Blanchot's and Bataille's principal works. Through Bataille, *Tel Quel* also has a connection with Gallimard.

Barthes

Barthes's thought is also marked fundamentally by that of Blanchot, and in his later works by that of Bataille. But it is not simply a question of influence. Barthes's first book *Le Degré zéro de l'écriture* (1953), crucial for the context of *Tel Quel*'s vision of literature, is held in a network of other works investigating the nature of literature. Sartre's *Qu'est ce que la littérature?* had appeared in 1947, and Barthes's 1953 publication is partly a response to that book. Articles by Bataille in *Critique* in the late 1940s had criticized Sartre's biographical essays on Baudelaire and Genet.[70] A further important text for Barthes was Jean Paulhan's *Les Fleurs de Tarbes ou la terreur dans les lettres* (1941), to which Blanchot wrote a short response entitled 'Comment la littérature est-elle possible?'[71]

Barthes's *Le Degré zéro* is part of a series of reflections on the nature of literature, its possibility or impossibility, which appear in the post-war period and implicitly inform *Tel Quel*'s eventual theory of literature. The debate is complex, and not easy to paraphrase, but Barthes's argument proposes that, in a historically defined period, literature has become an object and undergone a 'progressive solidification'.[72] That is to say that while it was thought to be mere ornament or instrument, from Chateaubriand onwards it has become self-conscious and taken itself as its own object. It undergoes the 'concretion' of a look (Chateaubriand), a 'fabrication' (Flaubert), then to disappear through annihilation or murder with Mallarmé, and ends as absence, in the neutral or degree-

---

[69] P. Klossowski, 'Sade ou le philosophe scélérat', *TQ* 28 (winter 1967). Klossowski's article was orig. a paper given at a conference on 'Signe et perversion chez Sade' in 1966. See also a review of Klossowski's novel *Le Baphomet* J.-P. Faye, 'Gnose blanche, roman noir', *TQ* 22 (summer 1965). R. Caillois, 'Puissances du rêve', *TQ* 8 (winter 1962); Jorge Luis Borges, 'Degrés' (trans. by Caillois), *TQ* 11 (autumn 1962); Caillois, 'Le Démon de l'analogie', *TQ* 14 (summer 1963).

[70] Bataille, *Oeuvres complètes*, ix, 199–202, 287–316.

[71] See M. Blanchot, *Faux pas* (Paris, 1975), 92–101.

[72] R. Barthes, *Le Degré zéro de l'écriture* (Paris, 1953).

zero writing of Camus, Cayrol, Blanchot, Queneau.[73] This movement of negation, Barthes suggests, also parallels the crisis of the bourgeois conscience.[74] The notion of literature as negation, as destruction, obviously reveals a debt to Blanchot and Bataille, and more fundamentally to Mallarmé, perhaps the key to all these contemporary debates, and it also has a subtle influence on the theory of *Tel Quel*.

The other sub-text for Barthes, Paulhan's work, proposed that when rhetoric (a law specific to literature) is replaced by terror (a law outside it) the search for authenticity often turns into a purifying destruction of language. In the discourse on literature this is a recourse to extra-literary values.[75] Blanchot's response is to locate the terror, the destructive will, at the heart of literature as such.[76] This move is an important part of the context for both Barthes and *Tel Quel*, for if all literature is terror, this leaves the way open for a terrorism, an avant-garde which takes literature itself as its ultimate value. The insistence on rhetoric, on literature's own laws, becomes equally terroristic, rather than conservative. While Blanchot's vision of literature is essentially synchronic, Barthes's addition to the debate is to establish the negation as 'progressive' and to link it to history. For *Tel Quel* this will make possible the view of texts as situated in a historical intertextuality of progressive negations, and enable the later link between textuality and Marxist theory. It will also pose the problem of finitude, for if the writings of Blanchot, Camus, and others are a literature of absence, what could come after the end?

Paulhan's affirmation of rhetoric as an antidote to terror looks forward to the introduction of linguistic terminology in criticism, largely pioneered in *Tel Quel*. Rhetoric itself, in the case of *Tel Quel*, could become terror. Annette Lavers has suggested how the same imperative of a denial of ideological justification and a recourse to rhetorical forms was present in Barthes's *Mythologies* (1957), especially in the last chapter 'Le Mythe aujourd'hui', which refers to Saussure's nascent project for semiology and to linguists such as Jakobson.[77] The linguistic and semiological enterprise, the search for an all-embracing 'science of signs'

---

[73] Ibid. 9.

[74] Ibid. 8.

[75] J. Paulhan, *Les Fleurs de Tarbes ou la terreur dans les lettres* (Paris, 1941).

[76] Blanchot, *Faux pas*, 97: 'elle [la Terreur] est la littérature, ou du moins son âme'.

[77] A. Lavers, 'France: The End of the Terreur? The Evolution of Contemporary Critical Attitudes', *The Human Context*, 2 (1970).

which would be the new rhetoric is also evident in Barthes's work of the early 1960s, up to 'Éléments de sémiologie' of 1964.

If there is a coherence behind Barthes's various endeavours, the proliferation of his activities and their difference is nevertheless important in forming the context for *Tel Quel*. Barthes published articles in *Critique*, for example, and so was a valuable connection to that network. He was a founding member and contributor to *Arguments* with Edgar Morin, who would later join him on the committee of the semiology review *Communications*. He was also a critical champion of the *nouveau romancier* Alain Robbe-Grillet, whose textual perspective *Tel Quel* will seek to overcome. Straddling the contemporary literary avant-garde, the non-affiliated Left, the earlier community around Bataille, and the forum for linguistics and semiology at the EPHE, Barthes enables a series of links and cross-overs which will make the review with which he was closely associated a juncture of many discourses. His *vertige du déplacement*[78] will inform and inspire that of *Tel Quel*.

Perhaps the most important of these connections is the review *Communications*, founded in 1960, and the organ of a group of researchers at the EPHE, the main forum for structuralist linguistics and semiology. Barthes joined colleagues such as Edgar Morin the sociologist, Christian Metz the semiologist of film, Greimas and Ducrot the linguists. Tzvetan Todorov and Gérard Genette, who will be important contributors to *Tel Quel*, also come out of this context.

While Todorov and Genette produced works that can be associated with structuralism and the EPHE context, a further current of importance in criticism in the late 1950s was the *nouvelle critique*, as it was known. The label *nouvelle* distinguished it from the more traditional modes of criticism of the academic world, influenced by the important work of Lanson. In fact, *nouvelle* covered a variety of disparate approaches to the text. Barthes, in the article 'Les Deux Critiques' would characterize the difference in terms of ideological justification.[79] While the *nouvelle critique* explicitly acknowledged its ideological derivation from existentialism, Marxism, psychoanalysis, and so on, *la critique lansonienne*, in Barthes's terms 'refuse toute idéologie et ne se réclame que d'une méthode objective'.[80] The polemical conflict between *les deux critiques* would erupt in 1964 around Barthes's *Sur Racine*, but the ground had already been shifted towards structuralism by that time. Among the

[78] See S. Heath, *Le Vertige du déplacement* (Paris, 1974).
[79] R. Barthes, 'Les Deux Critiques', in id., *Essais critiques*.
[80] Ibid. 246.

works referred to as *nouvelles critiques* a number of distinct approaches are identifiable. Jean Starobinski's work is influenced by existentialism in its study of the modalities of self-reflection in literature, for example in *La Transparence et l'obstacle*, on Rousseau's autobiographies.[81] Charles Mauron's *psychocritique* is influenced by psychoanalysis in its study of the 'personal myth' of an author.[82] Lucien Goldmann's work is influenced by that of Lukaçs in the relation of the novel to sociological and historical change.[83] These currents, which were explicitly linked to certain ideologies, were not of special interest for *Tel Quel*, whose initial approach was anti-ideological, paradoxically joining with the reactive criticism attacked by Barthes. This apparent proximity will soon be displaced. A less explicitly ideologically determined criticism was the work of Jean-Pierre Richard, reviewed in *Tel Quel* by Genette.[84] Richard's criticism looks at the poetics of a particular writer with a view to establishing a phenomenology of the use of images specific to the writer. It is fundamentally influenced by the work of Bachelard on the phenomenology and psychology of the elements.[85] Although it focuses on literary creation and its genesis, its relevance for *Tel Quel* is limited because of the turn away from the text and towards phenomena that it privileges.

The *nouvelle critique* is initially important for the review as a new and innovative moment in criticism. However, the interest in Barthes, Bataille, and, in a more ambiguous way, Blanchot, is more fundamental. The *nouvelle critique* current will moreover be criticized, in the pages of *Tel Quel*, by the structuralist-influenced work of Genette and Todorov.

The Literary Context in 1960: The Novel

The context of intellectual Paris in the late 1950s is structured around institutions such as the ENS, the EPHE, the PCF, the EFP, SPP, and SFP. The passages of individuals between these institutions will make possible the ferment of theory and its explosion in the mid-to late 1960s.

---

[81] J. Starobinski, *La Transparence et l'obstacle* (Paris, 1958). See also id., *L'Oeil vivant* (Paris, 1961).

[82] C. Mauron, *Des métaphores obsédantes au mythe personnel: Introduction à la psychocritique* (Paris, 1961).

[83] L. Goldmann, *Le Dieu caché* (Paris, 1956) and *Pour une sociologie du roman* (Paris, 1964).

[84] J.-P. Richard, *Littérature et sensation* (Paris, 1954) and *Poésie et profondeur* (Paris, 1955). See G. Genette, 'Bonheur de Mallarmé', *TQ* 10 (summer 1962).

[85] G. Bachelard, *La Psychanalyse du feu* (Paris, 1938).

Within and across these institutions there is also the context of ideologies. The two important factors we have identified are the demise of existentialism and the turn to literature 'as such'. These aspects form the broad, ideological context for *Tel Quel*, which it will come to inherit after a period of development. However, *Tel Quel* emerges into a context of literature and its reception in reviews that also needs to be taken into account.

Any literary context can be characterized by writers who seek to establish themselves in conflict with tradition and those who belong to an earlier tradition or perpetuate it. In terms of contextualization, the former are evidently more important. Consequently, works that appeared after the war by writers like Gide, Breton, Aragon, Giraudoux, Giono, although they may be important works, do not enter into the immediate context. Having said this, given that *Tel Quel* essentially seeks to reactivate a context from before the war, certain writers who continue to produce works after the war are important. Céline, for example, wrote *Féerie pour une autre fois* in 1952, *D'un château l'autre* in 1957, *Nord* in 1960; a large part of his output comes after the Occupation. Artaud, incarcerated in a lunatic asylum until just before his death in 1948, wrote his *Van Gogh* in 1947, but a large part of his work written after the war would not appear until much later, with the publication of his *Œuvres complètes*. Céline and Artaud both write at the limit of both form and content, and both are to an extent marginalized during the post-war period. They are part of a hidden history that *Tel Quel* will seek to recall.

As concerns the literature that sought to establish itself against tradition, the ideology of commitment and responsibility affected, at least thematically, a series of novels produced before and after the war. Malraux's *La Condition humaine*, Sartre's *La Nausée* and the *Chemins de la liberté* trilogy, Camus's *L'Étranger* and *La Peste*, Simone de Beauvoir's novels thematically address the responsibility of the individual, placed 'in situation' in a world without pre-given meaning. Although style is fundamental to these writers, the ideological imperative tended to overdetermine the reception of the works. Commitment was the key term. In the 1950s Sartre and Camus both turned towards the theatre as a more popular and direct form of committed writing. Camus's *La Chute* (1953) is the exception to this tendency.

As if in response to the existential seriousness of this movement, a literature of *désinvolture* emerged in the mid-1950s in which a stylistic lightness of tone and theme was prevalent. The *hussards* and their leader

Roger Nimier rejected the ideology of commitment and opted instead for an indifference, even a cynicism, that veered dangerously towards the right. Ostensibly, the pleasure of writing, of style, was paramount. The works of Françoise Sagan, Roger Vailland, and Christiane Rochefort could also be attributed to this literature of *désinvolture*.

Other responses to the Occupation that did seek innovation included a retreat into naturalism, in the novels of Hervé Bazin and Henri Troyat, or into the fantastic, in the work of André Dhôtel and Henri Bosco. Meanwhile, if the responses of commitment and indifference can be characterized as a confrontation and a refusal of history, other novelists sought responsibility and engagement in other ways. The fiction of writers like Blanchot, Bataille, Klossowski, puts the individual in the context of an absurd universe, but here the response is not the commitment of revolution or meaning in art, but the fracture of the subject unable to respond, and a corresponding difficulty at the level of the language itself. With the novelistic experiments of Queneau and the language play of Michel Leiris, recalling that of Raymond Roussel and Surrealism, these writers are the most immediate precursors to the *nouveau roman* and to *Tel Quel*'s innovations. Bataille's *L'Abbé C* (1950) and *Le Bleu du ciel* (1936, republished in 1957) present a writing and a subject fractured by the experience of an excess present thematically in the novel. The fracturing takes place mostly at the level of theme rather than of style, while in the work of Blanchot, the reduction of plot and characterization to an absolute minimum leaves the way clear for a writing of infinite hesitation and struggle for identity and meaning. Both are fundamental influences on *Tel Quel* in their thematic and stylistic effects. The novels of Klossowski (*Roberte ce soir*, 1953; *Le Bain de Diane*, 1956; *La Révocation de l'Édit de Nantes*, 1959) and Queneau (*Zazie dans le métro*, 1959) and the writing of Leiris (*Fourbis* 1956, part of the autobiographical series *La Règle du jeu*) are equally important examples of innovative writing in this period, but less obviously influential for *Tel Quel*. All can be said to refuse the false dichotomy of commitment or cynicism and opt for a responsibility at the level of form. Although Blanchot and Queneau are included in Barthes's list of 'degree zero' writers, these innovations can be said to inject new possibilities into literature, after its turn to 'absence', by pushing back the limits of form and experience in the novel. They are important historically for *Tel Quel*, despite the review's evident lack of acknowledgement of this fact.

The most immediate movement of innovation in the novel relevant for *Tel Quel* was the *nouveau roman*. The term itself was not used

until 1957,[86] so it is established as a movement just before the foundation
of *Tel Quel*. Many of the key works were published before this date,
however. Robbe-Grillet's *Les Gommes* and *Le Voyeur* came out in 1953 and
1955 respectively. *La Jalousie* and *Dans le labyrinthe* appeared in 1957 and
1959. The latter novel is the object of *Tel Quel*'s immediate scrutiny and
will be the focus of its discourse on the *nouveau roman* to begin with.[87]
Nathalie Sarraute's short *Tropismes* had appeared before the war, but the
series of novels which established her as part of the *nouveau roman* group
were *Martereau* (1953), *Le Planétarium* (1959) and *Les Fruits d'or* (1962).
Michel Butor had already written *L'Emploi du temps* (1956) and *La
Modification* (1957) before the term *nouveau roman* was properly established.
The other writers associated with the *nouveau roman*, Robert Pinget,
Claude Simon, and Claude Ollier, produced their most important
works around the time of *Tel Quel*'s formation and after, so the *nouveau
roman* is very much the literary movement in the ascendance during *Tel
Quel*'s first years of existence.

The ideology of the *nouveau roman*, which *Tel Quel* will confront, is itself
an illusory phenomenon since the creative practice of each writer was
different, as Barthes had underlined in a 1958 article in *Arguments*, 'Il n'y
a pas d'école Robbe-Grillet'. However, Barthes himself was to an extent
responsible for the view of Robbe-Grillet's writing, for example, as an
'objective' literature that through a 'radical formalism' sought to refuse
anthropomorphism.[88] Common characteristics could be found in the
formalistic experimentation with narrative and the reduction of the
traditional elements of character and psychology. This could not,
however, be said so easily of Sarraute's work. In fact the *nouveau roman*
presented a series of different responses to novelistic experimentation.
Tel Quel enters a context of innovation in the novel labelled under an
ideology it must confront in order to establish its own practice as
distinct. This will be the first dramatic moment of the review's history.

Poetry since 1945

The situation of poetry after the war was understandably difficult.
Adorno's questioning of the ethics of writing poetry after Auschwitz

---

[86] The term was first used in the review *Esprit* in an issue of July–Aug. 1958 entitled 'Le
Nouveau Roman'. An issue of *Arguments* on the phenomenon, in Feb. of the same year,
called it 'le roman d'aujourd'hui', including Duras and Cayrol in the list.

[87] See P. Sollers, 'Sept points sur Robbe-Grillet', *TQ* 2 (summer 1960).

[88] See the article by Barthes: 'Littérature littérale', in id., *Essais critiques*, 63–9.

comes to mind.[89] Yet certain traditions and voices continued. Surrealism had by then become a part of tradition, losing its earlier radicalism. The immediate post-war years see the publication of works by Aragon, Eluard, Desnos, Soupault, and Reverdy, but the exciting developments were elsewhere. It seems that poetry of the post-war period sought some kind of response to an absence, to the loss of an object. Rather than the pure, self-sufficient vision of Valéry, its antecedents were Baudelaire and Rimbaud. What emerged was a search for something lost, in an open form, with a consciousness of human alienation and the artifice of language.

In some cases this led to extremities of form and vision, for example in the work of Michaux (*Épreuves, exorcismes*, 1945; *L'Infini turbulent*, 1957; *Connaissance par les gouffres*, 1961; *Vents et poussières*, 1962) and Ponge (*Poèmes*, 1948; *Le Grand receuil*, 1961), enormously influential on the poetry of the 1960s. Either through the turbulence of imagery, threatening rational consciousness, or the undermining of the latter through an extreme rhetorical self-awareness, Michaux and Ponge, in the wake of Surrealism, were powerful voices. Also in this lineage was the poetry of Leiris (*Haut mal*, 1943) and Queneau (*Si tu t'imagines*, 1952), constituting a decisive current of post-Surrealist poetry which was nevertheless freer, less determined by Surrealism's formulas and poetic ideology.

Outside the epic character of the poetry of Saint John Perse (*Vents*, 1946; *Amers*, 1957) or the *poésie brute* of Reverdy (*Plupart du temps*, 1945; *Main d'œuvre*, 1949), a dominant voice was that of René Char (*Les Feuillets d'Hypnos*, 1946; *Fureur et mystère*, 1948; *Recherche de la base au sommet*, 1955; *La Parole en archipel*, 1962). His was a poetry which sought, after the war and the Resistance, some kind of re-establishment of the value of humanity, through a striving towards the sacred, or Being, in the Heideggerian sense. Char was a powerful influence on a group of poets who emerged gradually in the 1950s and established themselves in the early 1960s; Yves Bonnefoy (*Du mouvement et de l'immobilité de Douve*, 1953; *Hier régnant désert*, 1958; *Pierre écrite*, 1965), Philippe Jaccottet (*L'Ignorant*, 1957; *Éléments d'un songe*, 1961), Jacques Dupin (*Cendrier du voyage*, 1951; *L'Épervier*, 1960; *Gravir*, 1963), and André du Bouchet (*Dans la chaleur vacante*, 1961). These poets will form the current that is most immediate in the context of *Tel Quel*.

The poetic context of 1960 is a multiplicity of different voices, some traditional, some older yet unrecognized, some younger and representative

[89] See T. Adorno, *Negative Dialectics* (London, 1973), 361.

of new trends. Some poetic voices fall out of the description of the context in terms of currents, such as Guillevic, Jabès, Supervielle, Emmanuel, Jouve, no less important for the history of poetry in the period. *Tel Quel* in its early years will publish work from a variety of sources, by Eluard, Michaux, Ponge, Jaccottet, Dupin, du Bouchet, before establishing its own poetic voices with Marcelin Pleynet and Denis Roche.[90] Excerpts from the work of poets Michel Deguy and Jean-Pierre Faye would also appear in the early years. *Tel Quel* essentially continues and develops the current of writing in the wake of Surrealism resonant in the work of Ponge and Michaux, rather than the Heideggerian current influenced by Char. However, alongside this activity an interest developed that to some extent stepped outside the French context to appeal to a more radical and iconoclastic current of poetry from the USA. Pleynet and Roche translate and appeal to work by Pound, Cummings, Charles Olson, and John Ashbery.[91] A fundamental influence, not easily identifiable in the context, was also the writing of Artaud. Pleynet, for example, had just emerged from a detailed reading of Artaud before joining the committee of *Tel Quel*.[92] It was the novel, however, which was the ascendant literary form of the time, the *nouveau roman* tending to push poetry into the shadows. The conflict between this interest and the underlying tension towards a more poetic language will lead to interesting developments in *Tel Quel* in its first few years.

Geography of the Context

The map of the intellectual milieu of Paris in the 1960s, the space across which passages are traced and in which intersections are effected, is to a large extent determined by the disposition of publishing houses and the reviews which reside in them, the academic milieu forming a parallel world. In the late 1950s and early 1960s the context is determined by three publishers, Seuil, Gallimard, and Minuit. The intellectual distance between each of them is in contrast to their proximity in space; only a few hundred yards separates Gallimard, in the Rue Sébastien Bottin, from Seuil in the Rue Jacob, and Minuit, the

[90] An important moment is Pleynet's article 'Poésie '61' *TQ* 8 (winter 1962).

[91] See E. Pound, 'Canto IV', *TQ* 6 (summer 1961); id., 'L'Art de la poésie', *TQ* 11 (autumn 1962); D. Roche, 'Pour Ezra Pound' and 'E. E. Cummings', *TQ* 11; M. Pleynet, 'Charles Olson, poète et critique', *TQ* 12 (winter 1963); id., 'Notes sur le "projective verse"' *TQ* 19 (autumn 1964); John Ashbery, 'Poèmes français', *TQ* 27 (autumn 1966).

[92] See M. Pleynet, 'La Matière pense', *TQ* 52 (autumn 1972) and in P. Sollers (ed.), *Artaud* (Paris, 1973), 135–6.

other side of the Boulevard Saint-Germain, in the Rue Bernard Palissy. However, while the sociological perspective which would see *Tel Quel* as determined ideologically by this 'field' may be accurate in its own terms, it is entirely unable to account for anything that transcends its structure, specifically literary creation.[93] With this reservation in mind, it is pertinent in a restricted sense that at the time of *Tel Quel*'s formation, the publisher of Sollers's first novel *Une curieuse solitude* (1958), Seuil, is seeking to establish a review to rival the *Nouvelle Revue française* of Gallimard, and a literary movement to rival the *nouveau roman*, which for the most part came out of Minuit. Gallimard was certainly the dominant publisher for literature: the works of most of the figures valorized in *Tel Quel*—Bataille, Artaud, Ponge—to begin with, were published by Gallimard. The *NRF* was dominant in the area of 'literary quality', with its directors, Jean Paulhan and Marcel Arland, assuming the aesthetic reins of the review in 1953. Minuit, meanwhile, had been associated with the Resistance during the war and apparently perpetuated this stance in its championing of the *nouveau roman*. Its director, Jérôme Lindon, was militant in favour of any cause which affirmed the value of literature against censorship. *Critique* was also published by Minuit; its role as a forum for the emerging currents in the human sciences and in literary criticism (it published Barthes, Starobinski, and Richard) was a factor that made Minuit the principal locus of innovation at the time. Seuil, meanwhile, had been formed by Catholic Marxists in the post-war period. Its principal review was *Esprit*, founded by Emmanuel Mounier as the review of his philosophy of personalism. *Esprit* was taken over by Seuil after the war to become a committed review, sympathetic to Marxism but also emphasizing the individual. *Esprit*'s left, humanist approach defined the character of Seuil before the 1960s. Sollers would caricature the publishers in his novel *Portrait du joueur* as 'chrétiens progressistes, spiritualistes de progrès'.[94] While Seuil had a financial success with *The Little World of Don Camillo*, it was able to publish more politically radical material by writers such as Franz Fanon, Léopold Sédar Senghor, and the leftist film-maker Chris Marker. Through Francis Jeanson it had links with Sartre and *Les Temps modernes*. Its will towards innovation in the discursive field was assured by the publication of Barthes's early works, written from a leftist

[93] See N. Kuappi, *Tel Quel: La Constitution sociale d'une avant-garde* (Helsinki, 1990), and L. Pinto, 'Au sujet des intellectuels de parodie', *Actes de la recherche en sciences sociales* (Oct. 1991).
[94] P. Sollers, *Portrait du joueur* (Paris, 1984), 125.

perspective: *Le Degré zéro de l'écriture*, *Mythologies*, and *Michelet*. In the literary field, Seuil had an important figure in Jean Cayrol, who ran a review and collection, '*Écrire*', devoted to the launching of new writers, both novelists and poets. Most of the writers associated with *Tel Quel* were launched by Cayrol's collection.

In addition to the triangle Gallimard-Minuit-Seuil and the reviews *NRF-Critique-Esprit* there was Sartre's *Les Temps modernes*, published by Julliard, which also brought out *Les Lettres nouvelles*, set up in 1953 by Maurice Nadeau. *Les Temps modernes* was an 'engaged' review, never a literary review in any sense, although it did publish literary work; Sartre's play *Les Séquestrés d'Altona* was published at this time. The review was specifically committed, after 1956, to left-wing causes in the struggle against colonialism. *Les Lettres nouvelles* was run by Maurice Nadeau, who, despite his links with Barthes, was particularly antipathetic to Sollers. Nadeau's aesthetic tastes in *Les Lettres nouvelles* favoured experimental work, by writers such as Sarraute and Beckett. The review would also publicize foreign literature through translations. Other literary reviews of the time included some which had an established place; the *Mercure de France* was particularly important. *Cahiers du Sud* and *Action poétique* favoured poetry and originated in Marseille. *L'Arc* (from 1957), *Preuves*, and *L'Herne* (taking over from *Preuves* in 1963) were less influential, but still important. *Les Lettres françaises*, run by Aragon and Pierre Daix, was the literary organ of the PCF. Publication there essentially meant endorsement by and of Marxism and the party. It would become particularly important in the mid-1960s, first as a site favourable to writers such as Sollers, Pleynet, Henric, and Guyotat, then as a site resisted and resistant to *Tel Quel* in the later period. Its editors, Pierre Daix and then Jean Ristat, would interact with *Tel Quel* at certain moments.[95] Non-literary or philosophical reviews, *La Nouvelle Critique* and *La Pensée* for the PCF, the leftist *Arguments*, *Socialisme ou barbarie*, and the more marginal *Internationale situationniste* were less immediately important for the context of *Tel Quel*.

Across the space formed by these sites and the differences between them, intersections and alliances could be made. The context was not

---

[95] See P. Daix, *Nouvelle critique et art moderne* (Paris, 1968) in the 'Collection Tel Quel'. See also articles by Günter Grass, Antonin Liehm, and Pavel Kahout, presented by P. Daix, in *TQ* 58 (summer 1974). For J. Ristat see J. Ristat, 'L'Entrée dans la baie', *TQ* 44 (winter 1971) and id., *Qui sont les contemporains?*, which contains interviews with Sollers, Denis Roche, J.-L. Baudry, and others. *Les Lettres françaises* would come to an end in 1972, when Aragon and Daix's affirmative response to the Czech uprising and Czechoslovak dissidence would meet disfavour with the Party authorities.

a static structure. Barthes, for example, was friendly with Nadeau, Cayrol, and also the Minuit-*nouveau roman* context. Cayrol was associated with Francis Ponge and Jean Paulhan at the *NRF*. So, in 1960, there is a network of intersections which *Tel Quel* will fall into, but transform fairly rapidly.[96] The 1960s saw the very rapid rise of Seuil as the spearheading publisher of the new structuralism, promoting Barthes, the *Communications* team and review, *Tel Quel*, and eventually the work of Lacan. François Wahl, in charge of the human sciences section at Seuil, was an important individual figure in this advance. The role of *Tel Quel* itself as a site of publication and intersection is inestimable.

The structuralist and post-structuralist trends in the human sciences of the 1960s, although to a large extent carried in already existing reviews such as *Critique*, will lead to the creation of new periodicals, such as *Communications*, *Cahiers pour l'analyse*, *Scilicet*, and *Change*, all of which were published by Seuil. In 1970 the structuralist and semiology-inspired currents in linguistics and criticism around Todorov and Genette would gain their own platform with the creation of the review *Poétique*. While *Poétique* is a vital forum for the introduction of new critical approaches (Paul de Man, Jauss and reception theory), it is seen by Sollers as a review created by Seuil in order to displace *Tel Quel* from its ascendant position, where it had a certain independence.[97] The review's position within Seuil is subject to various shifts. If at the beginning the review is intended as a 'mast-head', this function is soon adumbrated by the interest in writers published by Minuit, and in Ponge, Bataille, and Artaud, published by Gallimard. The formalist and structuralist period establish *Tel Quel* as the leading factor in Seuil's spearheading publication of structuralist work. The militant period diverts this back into politics, but this was not at all out of place within Seuil. The final period, however, sees the review establishing links with Grasset and Gallimard and moving away from the field of Seuil; at this point *Tel Quel* is a kind of enclave within its publishing house.[98] After the deaths of Barthes and Lacan, the two figures that assured the review's position at Seuil through Sollers's amicable links with both,[99] the break is

[96] For a limited account of this network, see J.-L. Calvet, *Roland Barthes* (Paris, 1990).

[97] See Ristat *Qui sont les contemporains?*, 166. See also interview by author with Sollers, Paris, 1989: 'Le Seuil a donc créé *Poétique* et *Change* pour essayer de torpiller *Tel Quel*, et *Tel Quel* devenait plus fort'.

[98] Sollers, interview with author: 'un état dans un état'.

[99] Ibid.: 'Je crois que Le Seuil était lassé déjà depuis longtemps, de cet espèce de cyste au sein; or il y avait des gens qui trouvaient que ce cyste était nécessaire, c'étaient Barthes et Lacan'.

precipitated by Sollers's writing of *Femmes*, in which Barthes and Lacan are thinly disguised and parodically inserted in a humorous narrative that does not spare their privacy. *Tel Quel* does not, therefore, act as a mouthpiece of Seuil, although at times it publishes excerpts from forthcoming works, but operates independently of the publisher, also with a minimum amount of financial pressure. This independence undoubtedly determines the review's effect of displacement in the context and its ability to determine its own trajectory.

During *Tel Quel*'s existence, it engages in polemics and interchanges with a number of other reviews, created during the period. Among reviews opposing *Tel Quel*, in competition with it, were *La Quinzaine littéraire*, *L'Arc*, *L'Herne*, as well as *Change* and *Poétique*. None of these, with the exception of *Change*, is the vehicle of a project, a group, or a movement. *Tel Quel* occupies a quite specific place as a review with a defined project and theory, intersecting perspectives from numerous disciplines towards the furtherance of this project. Other reviews are more eclectic, journalistic sites. Apart from *Critique*, and the PCF reviews, a number of satellites to *Tel Quel* will appear during its existence: *Promesse*, *Peinture, cahiers théoriques*, *Cinéthique*, *Art press*, and to a lesser extent the music theory review *Musique en jeu*. Their interaction with *Tel Quel* forms part of its history. The period of *Tel Quel*'s existence also sees the formation of a number of reviews which are directly or indirectly modelled on its example. These would include *Change*, *Littérature*, *Po&sie*, *Digraphe*, *Textuel*, *TXT*, *Première livraison*, and others. None of them, however, aspire to the breadth and influence of *Tel Quel*, nor do they come close to it.

This geography of the context, the institutional structure of the time, is none the less transformed by the existence and movement of *Tel Quel*. Because it was an ever-shifting, mobile site of intersection, the context it enters into is affected by it profoundly, in ways which it is the task of this history to assess.

The Political Context in 1960

The immediate political context in which *Tel Quel*'s first issue appears is one of relative instability.[100] Although economic prosperity in France was increasing, the country faced a major crisis in Algeria. Despite independence having been granted to Morocco and Tunisia and

---

[100] For an account of the political history of the time, see: A. Cobban, *A History of Modern France*, iii (Harmondsworth, 1965).

enabled in other African colonies, in 1956, France was less ready to give up its hold on Algeria. The nationalists were in open revolt. The adoption of terrorist tactics led the government of Guy Mollet to make tentative moves towards negotiation, but, encountering violent resistance on the part of the *colons* and the army, the policy was radically reversed. There followed a violent and bloody confrontation between the nationalists, the government, and the Right, principally the army, whose counter-terrorist squad, the Organisation armée secrète (OAS), adopted violent underground tactics itself. In 1958, the Fourth Republic government was unable to function, a crisis leading to the swift accession to the presidency of General de Gaulle, who had been expecting such an eventuality. De Gaulle introduced a new constitution, the Fifth Republic, in 1958. He favoured negotiation and independence for Algeria, which was finally granted in 1962, but not without an increase of violence from the Right. The right-wing opposition continued its terrorist activity, which spilled over into metropolitan France and in to its capital. The climate in Paris is one of violence, principally against to the left wing. Despite its inability to consolidate its electoral support, the PCF was still a powerful political force.

The intellectual milieu was mobilized by this situation. Sartre's *Les Temps modernes* militated on behalf of the Algerian FLN, while publishers such as Minuit and Seuil, favourable to the Left and to anti-colonialism, suffered several *plastiquages* (bombings) by the OAS. The situation inevitably favoured commitment to the Left among intellectuals. In September 1960 the 'Manifeste des 121', a petition against the Algerian war, created a schism between the committed group of Sartre, Nadeau, Jérôme Lindon, with some of the *nouveaux romanciers*, and the emerging structuralist *réseau* of Barthes, Morin, and the *Critique* group, who did not sign. The context is thus polarized around the question of commitment, 'for or against'.

Tel Quel's entry into the context and its position is not as simple as it first appears. The title and the declaration, suggesting a conservatism and a distrust of commitment, would have alienated, and did alienate, intellectuals sympathetic to the Left. However, *Tel Quel*'s affiliation with Minuit makes this stance ambiguous. Textually, Sollers's first text in the review, 'Requiem', a formalistic and tragic account of the funeral of a friend (in fact Pierre de Provonchères, killed in Algeria) leads to a notion of commitment at the level of form that displaces the polarization of the commitment debate. It is also pertinent that at this time many of the writers involved in *Tel Quel* were at the age when they were forced to

undertake their military service. There was a real sense of the imminence of violence underlying such texts as Sollers's 'Requiem' and
Faye's *Battement*. At the same time, the lack of any consideration of the
situation of Francophone literature or the colonial or neo-colonial
question (except indirectly, in the texts of Guyotat) makes *Tel Quel*
appear a specifically French, Parisian phenomenon.

The political crisis of Algeria and the governmental crisis of the
Fourth Republic have a direct effect in the mobilization of intellectuals
for a cause. However, the displacement of the focus of intellectual
enquiry and artistic practice away from the question of commitment—
the waning of the dominance of Sartre and the rise of structuralism in
more dispersed milieux—led to a shift in the relation of intellectual
activity to politics. The link was not as direct. The 1960s is a time when
thought was concerned with the inherent structure of knowledge or
creativity rather than action. 1968, of course, will catastrophically alter
this situation. But the early 1960s, after the displacement of the
intellectual context away from politics, is also a time of innovation, both
in the emerging human sciences in the university, and in creative
practice, signalled by the proliferation of the 'new': *nouveau roman,
Nouvelle critique, Nouvelle vague* in the cinema. This suggested an atmosphere of innovative enquiry into form, which *Tel Quel* will accelerate
and transform. The intellectual climate is a mixture of decline and
innovation, ending and beginning. The incidence in the same year of
the tragic death of Camus and the appearance of Godard's casual film
A bout de souffle, with the launch of *Tel Quel*, subtly indicates this duality.

2 Intersections

THE FORMATION OF *TEL QUEL*

Biography or Myth?

The biography of Philippe Sollers (Philippe Joyaux),[1] is undoubtedly a crucial condition for the formation and the survival of *Tel Quel*. He was born in 1936 in Talence, near Bordeaux, the son of a minor industrialist and anarchistic liberal and a Catholic mother. However, biography is complicated by its implication in the writer's own version of his life. To some extent, the biography has become a myth, reinvented in the writing (in *H*, *Paradis*, and the novels from *Femmes*) and for the purposes of an intellectual strategy. The myth of Sollers in fact serves both sides; Sollers's own parodic occupation of the status of the intellectual, his constant displacement of this function, and the contextual resistance to this function, which has also projected a certain image of the writer. Certainly, elements may be picked out of the biography of Philippe Joyaux which have a relevance for the writing: his mother's Catholicism affects his later turn to religion, which was scandalous with regard to the ideologies of the time. The dominance of his two elder sisters might explain his vision of a repressed matriarchy at work in a society that refuses femininity, and his embracing of femininity in the writing. His precocious sexuality might determine his professed insight into this area of social discourse. His childhood in Bordeaux might suggest an affinity for 'the South', a closer connection to England, and so on. These are all aspects, however, which the writing reactivates; they are not unconsciously determinative factors. The biographical imperative of criticism is short-circuited by the writer's own adoption and interpretation of his 'life', particularly in such books as *Vision à New York* and *Carnet*

---

[1] There are various interpretations of the name 'Sollers' given by the writer himself: 'tout entier intact' (from *H* (Paris, 1973), 11) is the Latin definition, 'possessed entirely of an art, hence, skilful, clever, adroit' (*Cassell's Latin Dictionary*). It is also 'le surnom d'Ulysse' (also *H*, 11). It is linked to the Greek 'holos', thus to 'holocauste', 'sacrifice sans reste' (interview with Sollers by author) and to 'hologramme', suggesting a writing 'en trois dimensions' (voice-image-text).

de nuit.[2] The 'mythobiography' of Sollers has more to do with the literary strategy, the place and function of Sollers as a writer and intellectual, than with the history of *Tel Quel* and the life of Philippe Joyaux. To take the latter at face value would be to miss the point.

The early history of Sollers as a writer is more instructive. The publication of 'Le Défi' in Cayrol's collection 'Écrire' and the award of the Prix Fénéon are vitally important.[3] 'Le Défi' won the approval of François Mauriac, another Catholic from Bordeaux, in his regular column, 'Bloc-notes' in *Le Monde*, and of Louis Aragon in *Les Lettres françaises*.[4] Mauriac saw in Sollers a promising young writer who would continue the tradition of stylistic, autobiographical *belles-lettres* in the line of Proust and Radiguet. Sollers was also in contact with Jean Paulhan at Éditions Gallimard, through the person of Francis Ponge, whom he had met at a lecture at the Alliance française, opposite his flat in the Boulevard Raspail. Gallimard refused the scurrilous 'Introduction aux lieux d'aisance', but accepted the short 'Images pour une maison' for the *NRF* in 1960.[5] Ponge, had, however, given 'Le Défi' to Jean Cayrol at Seuil. Sollers's full-length novel *Une curieuse solitude* was published shortly afterwards by Seuil, in 1958. It would be a relative success. It is the story of a *rite de passage* with obvious autobiographical elements, but it is certainly no indication of the direction Sollers would subsequently take.

The Accidents of History

Tel Quel's formation had an economic motive. The promise of Sollers's *Une curieuse solitude* was ostensibly the reason why Seuil agreed to the formation of a literary review around Sollers, as a good investment. Seuil sought to establish a literary review of the same form and status as the *NRF*, from its own stable of writers. *Tel Quel* would initially fulfil this promise. So the publisher's motives are determined by the disposition of the context, by financial considerations; the formation of the review is not initially determined by any kind of will to innovate or to

---

[2] See P. Sollers, *Vision à New York* (Paris, 1981) and *Carnet de nuit* (Paris, 1989).

[3] *Écrire*, 3 (1958); it can also be found in *The Penguin French Reader* (Harmondsworth, 1967).

[4] See F. Mauriac, *Nouveaux bloc-notes* (Paris, 1961), 63, 132; L. Aragon, 'Philippe Sollers', *Les Lettres françaises* (20 Nov. 1958).

[5] See P. Sollers, 'Images pour une maison', *Nouvelle Revue française*, 151 (1960). Sollers's early texts, including 'Introduction aux lieux d'aisance' and 'Images pour une maison', are included in his book *L'Intermédiaire* (Paris, 1963).

create a new literary movement. In terms of the review's orientation and
the history of ideas, it is an accident. The development of Sollers's
writing and the review from then on will turn this accident into a
literary movement with precise aims that conflict with those of the
publisher, establishing it as an independent enclave within Seuil. The
contractual agreement was such that the publisher was co-owner of the
name 'Tel Quel', so that little financial pressure could be exerted and
the review itself had some kind of independence. From Sollers's
perspective, much later, it is only an accident of this sort that could have
set the innovative and transgressive mechanism of the review in motion,
since the context would have not permitted the foundation of a
'machine' that would reinterpret and transform it.[6]

Apart from Sollers, the first committee of the review is made up of
writers of the same potential and approach. Jean-René Huguenin,
Jean-Edern Hallier, and Renaud Matignon had met at college and had
all published work in Cayrol's collection 'Écrire'. Huguenin could
perhaps have developed as Seuil would have liked Sollers to. His novel
La Côte sauvage was also very successful.[7] However, historical accident
was to intervene: Huguenin was killed in a car crash in 1962. Hallier
was a vital personality who seems to have been something of a dandy.
His attempt to take over the committee as director in 1962[8] and the
subsequent complete reformulation of the committee almost led to the
early demise of the review, but, largely due to the strategy of Sollers,
the new committee launched the review in a fresh direction that would
prove vital and radical.

The first issue of the review appears very much as a platform for Seuil
while at the same time appropriating elements from the prominent
Gallimard publishing house. It contains a new poem by Francis Ponge,
'La Figue (sèche)' as well as an older 'Proème' which dated from 1924.
Jean Cayrol is represented by a short prose piece.[9] The six members of
the editorial committee were all represented in the contents of the first
issue, five of them by short prose pieces; Sollers would contribute the
short 'Requiem', Matignon a short critical piece on 'Flaubert et la

[6] Cf. Sollers, interview with author, Paris, 1989: 'la revue n'a pu avoir lieu que parce
que j'avais publié un livre qui avait eu énormément de succès, qui est *Une curieuse solitude*.
L'éditeur s'est dit qu'il allait faire un investissement rentable, en créant une revue littéraire
autour de moi'.

[7] See also Huguenin's *Journal* (Paris, 1964), and his *Une autre jeunesse* (Paris, 1961) for brief
accounts of the early years of *Tel Quel* and Huguenin's involvement.

[8] See J.-E. Hallier, *La Cause des peuples* (Paris, 1973).

[9] J. Cayrol, 'La Presqu'île', *TQ* 1 (spring 1960).

sensibilité moderne'.[10] However, the extracts 'La Poursuite' by Claude Simon and 'L'Attentat' by Jean Thibaudeau indicate an orientation towards the *nouveau roman* and Éditions de Minuit.

The opening editorial statements of the review show a certain orientation which will be the basis for its more innovative deviations. The issue opens with a 'Déclaration', while at the centre of the review is an 'Enquête sur le don de l'écrivain' in which the question 'Pensez-vous avoir un don d'écrivain?' was put to many contemporary writers. The 'gift of the writer' questionnaire further suggests the desire to return to the ground of 'literary quality', which the 'Déclaration' expands on, but the mostly negative responses by the *nouveaux romanciers* given there make this suggestion slightly ambiguous.[11] A published reply by Céline shows a reluctance to bow to political motives in editorial choices.[12] At the end of the issue there are some 'Notes de lecture', in which books recently published are given marks out of twenty by each of the committee members.[13] The questionnaire and the last device deliberately recall the Surrealist reviews, and a desire for literary revolt. This is also shown by the indication that the next issue would include unpublished work by Eluard and a debate on Surrealism. This would unfortunately not appear, due to Breton's lack of response to a questionnaire.[14]

The most noticed and discussed elements of the first issue were the title, the 'Déclaration', and the opening epigraph. While the title *Tel Quel* may have called to mind the title of the book of aphoristic fragments by Valéry,[15] the epigraph derives from Nietzsche:

[10] The committee members were: Philippe Sollers, Jean-Edern Hallier, Jean-René Huguenin, Boisrouvray, Jacques Coudol, Renaud Matignon. Their contributions to issue I were as follows: P. Sollers, 'Requiem'; J.-E. Hallier, 'Un visage à part'; J.-R. Huguenin, 'Adieu'; Boisrouvray, 'Une vallée sous les nuages'; Jacques Coudol, 'Le Voyage d'hiver'; Renaud Matignon, 'Flaubert et la sensibilité moderne'.

[11] See *TQ* I. 40. Answers to the question: 'Pensez-vous avoir un don d'écrivain?': Claude Simon, 'Peut-être vaudrait-il mieux parler d'une certaine disposition de l'esprit'; A. Robbe-Grillet: 'Non'; N. Sarraute: 'Je croyais en avoir un quand j'écrivais en classe mes devoirs de français'.

[12] See *TQ* I: 40: 'On écrit parce qu'on est malheureux. Votre monde dévore tout le reste.'

[13] Ibid. 93. Robbe-Grillet's *Dans le labyrinthe*, Sarraute's *Le Planétarium*, Blanchot's *Le Livre à venir* get the highest marks from all the committee members.

[14] Cf. Sollers, interview with author, Paris, 1989: 'une des premières idées a été d'envoyer un questionnaire assez détaillé à André Breton. Alors la façon dont il parle, dont se manifeste son intérêt pour une nouvelle revue est tout à fait étonnante, c'est vraiment très chaleureux.'

[15] P. Valéry, *Tel Quel* (2 vols.; Paris, 1941).

Je veux le monde et le veux tel quel et le veux encore, le veux éternellement, et je crie insatiablement: bis! et non seulement pour moi seul, mais pour toute la pièce et pour tout le spectacle; et non pour tout le spectacle seul, mais au fond pour moi, parce que le spectacle m'est nécessaire, parce qu'il me rend nécessaire, parce que je lui suis nécessaire et parce que je le rends nécessaire.[16]

The affirmation of the state of things implicit here differs from the Valéry title, where the emphasis is on a raw, unchanged state. Although Valéry is a reference the review would be likely to welcome, suggesting a stylistic self-consciousness and a valorization of literature above all else, a celebration of poetry as *édifice enchanté*,[17] the potential conservatism of this position is to be set against its optimism.

The title 'Tel Quel' is, however, justified and qualified by the 'Déclaration' as an apology for literature, without an ideological derivation:

Les idéologues ont suffisamment regné sur l'expression pour que celle-ci se permette enfin de leur fausser compagnie, de ne plus s'occuper que d'elle-même, de sa fatalité et de ses règles particulières.[18]

The call for *la qualité litteraire* and an end to the rule of literature by ideology, the Manichaeism of committed or non-committed literature, in this declaration exhibits most of the characteristics of a literary aestheticism. This aestheticism affirms writing and poetry above all, as a privileged contact with the world, rather than as an 'art for art's sake' which denies reality. *Tel Quel*'s aestheticism, in the context, would have been a scandalous refusal of responsibility, but history shows that it is an aestheticism that is susceptible to develop into a formalism, a commitment at the level of form.

The first issue of the review indicates the coexistence of a number of currents. First, a purely aesthetic current concerned with the reduction to a pure vision of literature's powers. This tends towards a second current, which is the more formally experimental tendency of the *nouveau roman* and Ponge, and a third, emphasizing the experience of the subject of writing. If the first current was the necessary paean to 'literary quality' that would rival the *NRF* and give a jolt to the ideology of literary commitment, it is soon purged, and the other currents develop

---

[16] *TQ* 1: 2. The epigraph is taken from Nietzsche's *Beyond Good and Evil*.

[17] 'Déclaration', *TQ* 1: 4: 'Vouloir le monde, et le vouloir à chaque instant, suppose une volonté de s'ajouter la réalité en la ressaisissant, et, plus qu'en la contestant, en la représentant. Alors, l'œuvre pourra vraiment devenir, selon le mot de Valéry, un "édifice enchanté" '.

[18] Ibid. 3.

more fully. The conflict between them will result in a certain turmoil in the committee as the distinct character of the review is established. The instability of the committee and the lack of distinction determine the 'aesthetic ambiguity'[19] of the early period. The recourse to 'literary quality' means that no distinct critical perspective is established. Although texts by Sollers, Hallier, and other committee members use language in a very self-conscious way, as if questioning always the notion of creativity as such, this speculation on language is not thought critically. The emergence of a distinctive critical discourse on literature is due, intially, to the *nouveau roman* and the review's dissociation from it. Also, Barthes's reminder in a 1961 interview that literature *tel quel* was itself an ideology, not natural, is a decisive moment.[20]

The Nouveau Roman *and Minuit*

Tel Quel deviates from the path of aestheticism and the traditional role of the *NRF* through support of the *nouveau roman* and the Éditions de Minuit. Association with Minuit is to some degree a gesture of resistance to orthodoxy. It is through this alliance that *Tel Quel* will mark out a place for itself at the forefront of literary innovation. The strategy put into practice is to establish the alliance by publishing extracts from the work of the *nouveaux romanciers*, affirmative critical reviews of their work, and to introduce into the editorial committee individuals who have a particular connection with Éditions de Minuit and the *nouveau roman*.[21] At the same time, the *tactical* nature of this support is indicated by an emphasis on other, parallel, interests, specific to the review, in areas which could come to conflict with the ideas and practice of the *nouveau roman*. There is also a support of elements from which a possible systematic critique could emerge. The critical distance is also attained through increasing qualification of affirmative criticism with reminders of these other elements.

The first two years see a proliferation of extracts from the work of *nouveaux romanciers*, accompanied by critical reviews of their work, including an affirmative review of *Dans le labyrinthe* by Sollers in issue 2.[22]

---

[19] Cf. P. Sollers, 'Le Réflexe de réduction', *Théorie d'ensemble* (Paris, 1968), 391: 'La "déclaration" de 1960—année de fondation de *Tel Quel*—est en effet un exemple d'ambiguité esthétique.'

[20] R. Barthes, 'La Littérature aujourd'hui', *TQ* 7 (autumn 1961); also in id., *Essais critiques* (Paris, 1964), 161–2.

[21] Jean Thibaudeau and Jean Ricardou.

[22] P. Sollers, 'Sept points sur Robbe-Grillet', *TQ* 2.

Very soon the novelists and critics Jean Thibeaudeau and Jean Ricardou enter the committee. Both are associated with Minuit and had written critical articles on the *nouveau roman* in *Critique*.[23] Thibaudeau and Ricardou's entry into the committee cements the alliance, while a critical discourse begins to emerge through the 'La Littérature aujourd'hui' series of interviews and articles by the critics Barthes and Genette.[24] The following years will see the development of this criticism and an explicit statement of the review's critical position in Sollers's review of *Pour un nouveau roman*.[25] The novelistic trend of the review is also checked by the entry into the committee in 1962 of the poets Michel Deguy (who would leave very soon), Marcelin Pleynet, and Denis Roche. The publication of work by Ponge, Bataille, and Artaud also tends to mark a distance from the formalistic tendencies of the *nouveau roman* through an insistence on the experience of the subject.

A major factor in the development of a critical perspective, generally and specifically, on the *nouveau roman* is the review's publication of articles by Genette and Barthes. The former's article 'Vertige fixé' sounds the first note of adverse criticism of Robbe-Grillet, while Barthes's responses to questions posed enables a thinking of the review's position in the context of criticism. Despite publications which indicate the review's sympathy with the *nouvelle critique* of Jean-Pierre Richard, for example, it soon becomes evident that *Tel Quel* separates itself from the *nouvelle critique* as such, and is more sympathetic to the emerging structuralist criticism of Barthes and Genette. This sympathy will prove efficient in allying the review with an innovative criticism which identifies language or rhetoric as the main field of enquiry, and in associating the review with the structuralist milieu of *Communications*.

Outlining a Canon

The early period sees the tentative development of a canon or a series of privileged texts. Beyond the interest in the *nouveau roman*, this moves

[23] See J. Thibaudeau, 'Un théâtre de romanciers', *Crit.* 159–60 (Aug.–Sept. 1960); 'La Leçon de l'école' (on Ricardou), *Crit.* 173 (Oct. 1961); 'Un écrivain averti en vaut deux' (on Sollers), *Crit.* 177 (Feb. 1962). J. Ricardou, 'Un ordre dans la débâcle' (on Claude Simon), *Crit.* 163 (Dec. 1960).
[24] See 'La Littérature aujourd'hui' I: R. Barthes, *TQ* 7 (autumn 1961); II: N. Sarraute, *TQ* 9 (spring 1962); III: L.-R. des Forêts, *TQ* 10 (summer 1962); IV: M. Butor, *TQ* 11 (autumn 1962); V: J. Cayrol, *TQ* 13 (spring 1963); VI: A. Robbe-Grillet, *TQ* 14 (summer 1963). See also G. Genette, 'Sur Robbe-Grillet', *TQ* 8 (winter 1962).
[25] P. Sollers, 'Pour un nouveau roman', *TQ* 18 (summer 1964).

towards the establishment of the review's specific character. The canon is still fairly fluid, however. The publication of *inédits* by Artaud and Bataille emphasizes an experience of excess that will later become the basis of a theory.[26] It also marks out poetic language as of more interest for the review than the rationalism of the *nouveau roman*. The continuing celebration of Ponge partakes both of this poetic orientation and of an interest in a self-referential and rhetorical use of language.[27] Other texts of the early canon, Pound, Hölderlin, Borges, reveal more specific interests and associations.[28] Pound's texts are present essentially because of the input of Denis Roche, their translator. The interest in Hölderlin seems to have been dropped because of the association with the excessively metaphysical, Heideggerian orientation of Michel Deguy, briefly a member of the committee. This tendency is resisted and, as a result, Hölderlin will not appear as part of the canon.[29] If the affirmation of Artaud and Bataille establishes a continuity of interest in the limits of literature and experience, the publication of work by Virginia Woolf, T. S. Eliot, Defoe, and Borges is more limited to the aestheticism of the review's initial appearance.[30]

The Committee

Before developing any kind of specific approach, however, the committee would undergo fundamental changes. After the earlier purging of the heroic moral tendency of Huguenin and the Heideggerian tendency of Deguy, the main shift occurs in 1963, when the first major split in the

[26] See A. Artaud, 'Chiotte à l'esprit', *TQ* 3 (autumn 1960) and 'Notes sur la peinture', *TQ* 15 (autumn 1963). G. Bataille, 'Les Larmes d'Éros', *TQ* 5 (spring 1961), and 'Conférences sur le non-savoir', *TQ* 10 (summer 1962). The latter text was a lecture given personally to the review by Bataille in 1962.

[27] After issue 1, see F. Ponge, 'L'Asparagus', *TQ* 4 (winter 1961); id., 'Pour Fenosa', *TQ* 6 (summer 1961); id., 'L'Objet c'est la poétique', *TQ* 10 (summer 1962); id., 'Ardens organum', *TQ* 13 (spring 1963); id., 'Le Pré', *TQ* 18 (summer 1964). See also P. Sollers's monograph on Ponge, orig. pub. in *La Mercure de France* as 'Francis Ponge ou la raison à plus haut prix': *Francis Ponge* (Paris, 1963).

[28] See E. Pound, 'Canto IV', *TQ* 6 (summer 1961); F. Hölderlin, 'Retour', *TQ* 6 (summer 1961); J. L. Borges, 'L'Art narratif et la magie' (trans. by Sollers), *TQ* 7 (autumn 1961) and 'Degrés' (poems trans. by R. Caillois), *TQ* 11 (autumn 1962).

[29] 'Fragments inédits' by Hölderlin will appear much later, *TQ* 68 (winter 1976), after a renewal of Sollers's interest, as evinced in the novel *H*, and after an article by J.-L. Houdebine (see *Excès de langages* (Paris, 1983)). Pleynet reports (interview with author) that the committee at one moment 'democratically' decided not to publish a text by Hölderlin on Sophocles.

[30] See V. Woolf, 'Le Moment: Soir d'été', *TQ* 1; T. S. Eliot, 'Goethe ou la sagesse', *TQ* 2; D. Defoe, 'Histoire de fantômes', *TQ* 7; J. Donne, 'Poèmes', *TQ* 2.

editorial committee takes place, leaving Sollers and the much-absent Boisrouvray as the only two remaining members of the original committee. Jacques Coudol leaves at the same time as Hallier. Hallier's departure is due ostensibly to his attempt to take over the exclusive direction of the review. However, aesthetic differences between the formalistic tendencies of the group around Sollers and the less serious and less analytical approach of Hallier can be cited as further reasons.

With Hallier, Coudol, Huguenin, and Matignon now gone, the committee is entirely restructured under Sollers's initiative, when Marcelin Pleynet, Jean-Louis Baudry, and Denis Roche enter the committee at issue 13 (spring 1963). Marcelin Pleynet immediately becomes the *secrétaire de rédaction*, and the committee is restructured as a group rather than a committee with a *directeur* (Hallier was nominally the director of the review). The new members of the committee change the orientation of the review. Pleynet had been a *lecteur* at the Éditions du Seuil and had published poetry in the collection 'Écrire', *Botteghe oscure*, and the review *Locus Solus*, run by John Ashbery.[31] He had sent some of his work to Philippe Sollers in 1961 and the latter had replied very positively, inviting publications in *Tel Quel*.[32] The liaison led to Pleynet's eventual entry into the committee and activity as *secrétaire de rédaction*. Pleynet's position at Seuil evidently made this possible, another instance of how arbitrary, coincidental factors set in place an analytic force—the productive dialogue between Sollers and Pleynet—that will become crucial to the review and perhaps the condition of its survival. Pleynet's moderating role as secretary is a very important factor in this survival; it also has repercussions on his poetic activity which will become evident later.[33]

Denis Roche had also published poetry, alongside Pleynet's in *Locus Solus*, and then in 'Écrire'.[34] His entry, with Pleynet, into the committee in 1962 after publishing texts on Pound or translations of his work represents a decisive step towards the poetic, and towards a poetry which appealed to a different tradition than the French; Roche's principal critical references are the US poets Pound, Cummings, Carlos

---

[31] See M. Pleynet, *Premières poésies* (Montpellier, 1987).

[32] The letter is reprinted in J. Risset, *Marcelin Pleynet* (Paris, 1988), 44.

[33] Cf. Pleynet, interview with author, Paris, 1991: 'je n'ai réussi à mon avis à maintenir l'activité qui était la mienne dans la revue qu'à ne jamais faire intervenir dans la revue les conséquences que la revue pouvait avoir sur moi'. He describes the relation between his activity as *secrétaire de rédaction* and poet as 'complètement schizée'.

[34] Denis Roche, 'Forestière amazonide', *Écrire*, 11 (Paris, 1962) and 'Trois poèmes', *Locus Solus*, 3–4 (winter 1961–2).

Williams, and Charles Olson, the mentor of the Black Mountain College. The same could be said of Pleynet to a lesser extent. The typographic, 'iconic'[35] fragmentation of both works immediately focuses attention on their formal, linguistic experimentation instead of the metaphysical bias of poets such as Deguy. Roche's work also represents an iconoclastic element in *Tel Quel*'s panoply of forces, associating it with the avant-garde. The appeal to a fresh tradition invests the review with a radical edge.

Jean-Pierre Faye's entry into the committee in autumn 1963, is not part of the same influx of poetic approaches, despite the fact that Faye is a poet as well as a novelist. Faye was in fact better known as a novelist, having already published a novel, *Entre les rues* in 1958. By 1962 he had published a second novel, *La Cassure*, and a third, *Battement*, reviewed favourably by Sollers in the *NRF*. He had also published work in 'Écrire'. He was slightly older than the other committee members, and had a more philosophical training. Faye's original input would tend towards Russian formalism and towards a critique of totalitarian discourses, with a commitment to the Left.[36] These specific interests and Faye's different background are factors which determine the eventual conflict between himself and Sollers, and his departure from the committee in 1967. Jean-Louis Baudry had been involved with the earlier grouping around Sollers and Hallier. He had published critical articles in the review and a novel, *Le Pressentiment*, in 1962 with Seuil.

With Pleynet, Denis Roche, Baudry, and Faye's arrival the committee is as it will stay for quite some time, until the departure of Boisrouvray and the arrival of other new members, Pierre Rottenberg and Jacqueline Risset. The constitution of the committee is another accidental factor that enables the review to function as it does. It may not be so accidental, however, if we consider the eventual committee to be made up of individuals favoured by Sollers, and Sollers as the motivating force of the review. Sollers does objectively force the exclusions of Hallier, Faye, Thibaudeau, and others, but he does not create the situation in which the exclusions are made possible. There is a part of the functioning of the review which is that of the mechanism, and a part which is the precipitation of crises by a will, aware of this mechanism. Through this functioning, the history of ideas intersects with that of individuals.

[35] Cf. V. La Charité, *Twentieth Century Avant-garde French Poetry* (Kentucky, 1992).
[36] See J.-P. Faye, *Le Récit hunique* (Paris, 1967) for a collection of his critical articles from this period.

The subsequent history of *Tel Quel*, from 1963 to 1967, follows the development of the review from the inception of the new committee and the exclusion of Hallier to its intersection with the scientific currents that emerge in the mid- to late 1960s, to transform the space of the avant-garde in the review into a space of science. This period sees the elaboration of both a textuality proper to the review in the practice of both novelists and poets, and a coherent theory of textuality. This implies a disengagement from the *nouveau roman*, the emergence of poetic language as an important force, and the introduction into the review of currents from linguistics and formalism which develop into a powerful critical tool. The review also functions in this period as a melting-pot or site of intersections of the avant-garde in literature and other areas, which can be seen as paralleled by the critical exploration of 'limit texts' (Ponge, Artaud, Dante, Bataille, Sade, Mallarmé, Lautréamont) from which a theory of literature is built up that forms the basis of *Tel Quel*'s radical vision of the text, and which is affirmed throughout the existence of the review in various forms. This period sees *Tel Quel* establishing its specificity and beginning to emerge as the important site for publications concerned with a radical textuality associated with the new emerging discourses of literary theory, psychoanalysis, and philosophy. It is also the time of *Tel Quel*'s initial associations with the major intellectual figures of the time, Michel Foucault, Roland Barthes, and Jacques Derrida. These intersections provide the basis of the moment of synthesis, into theory, of the latter half of the decade. Adopting a metaphor favoured by the writers of *Tel Quel*, the time sees the assembly of the constituent parts of a mechanism, a machine, that will remain the same throughout the history of the review, despite its shifts in the context.

THE EMERGENCE OF FICTIONAL SPACE

Critique of the Nouveau Roman

In the early 1960s the *nouveau roman* was the ascendant movement of the literary avant-garde. A succession of works were published in the early part of the decade that established the group after the earlier work of Robbe-Grillet, Sarraute, and Butor. Claude Simon, Robert Pinget, and Claude Ollier would all publish important works in this period. A crucial moment, however, was the publication of Robbe-Grillet's *Pour un nouveau roman* in 1963, which established the *nouveau roman* as an ideological phenomenon as well as a creative practice. This tendency was strengthened with Jean Ricardou's 1967 *Problèmes du nouveau roman* and *Pour une théorie du nouveau roman* in 1971, and especially by the 1971 conference at Cérisy, 'Nouveau roman, hier, aujourd'hui'.[37] The *nouveau roman* is a phenomenon that continues, both ideologically and creatively, up to the end of the decade and beyond.

The *nouveau roman* has in fact fared better than the fiction of the *Tel Quel* writers in terms of popularity. Writers like Robbe-Grillet, Sarraute, and Simon are continuing to produce work which, while it may turn to autobiography at certain moments, is not absolutely dissociable from the earlier work.[38] From one perspective, Sollers has abandoned the formal experimentation of his earlier work, (see Chapter 4), while other *Tel Quel* novelists, Baudry, Scarpetta, Henric, and Rottenberg, have either ceased to publish novels or opted for different strategies.[39] This is perhaps to some extent due to the difficulty of the *Tel Quel* novels, their risk, in their writing and reading. It may also be because the *Tel Quel* novel tends towards the dissolution of the novel form, while the *nouveau roman* retains elements of narrative, plot, character, and realism. On another level the theoretical naïvety of the *nouveau roman* has played a part in its survival. The inter-relationship of theory and fiction in the writings of *Tel Quel* is a fundamental aspect of the writing, and of its finality. The novel's theorization of its own practice leaves little place for the reader, except the place of subjection to the mechanisms or play of writing itself. A lack of commitment to this dangerous subjection on the part of readers, more willing to retain the position of spectators outside the writing, can explain the finality or the dead end of the *Tel Quel* novel. To an extent the *nouveau roman* lives off the theoretical advances of *Tel Quel*, through the critical input of Ricardou. Despite this, *Tel Quel*'s theory and practice of fiction is distinct from the *nouveau roman*, and the relationship is fairly complex.

Tel Quel is initially very positive towards the *nouveau roman* and Éditions de Minuit, with which it is largely associated. Excerpts from the work

---

[37] See J. Ricardou (ed.), *Nouveau roman: Hier, aujourd'hui* (2 vols.; Paris, 1972).

[38] See A. Robbe-Grillet, *Le Miroir qui revient* (Paris, 1985) and *Angélique ou l'enchantement* (Paris, 1988); N. Sarraute, *Enfance* (Paris, 1983) and *Tu ne t'aimes pas* (Paris, 1989); C. Simon, *L'Acacia* (Paris, 1989).

[39] P. Rottenberg and G. Scarpetta have not pub. works of fiction since their *Tel Quel* novels. J. Henric has pub. poetry through Grasset (*Walkman*, 1988); J.-L. Baudry has recently pub. a novel, *Personnages dans un rideau* (Paris, 1991), in Denis Roche's 'Fiction et Cie' collection at Seuil, formally similar to his earlier work.

of Butor and Ollier are published in the review until a fairly late moment.[40] A text by Simon appears as late as 1970.[41] On one level, therefore, the creative practice of the novelists concerned is viewed positively. The presence of Ricardou in the committee is undoubtedly a major element of support. Ricardou's engagement with both *Tel Quel* and the *nouveau roman* is, however, ambiguous. On one side Ricardou's critical assessment of the *nouveau roman* is a positive aspect for the review. On the other, his creative practice is associated more with the *nouveau roman*. His novels are not published in the *Tel Quel* collection.[42] Ricardou's theoretical mastery over the other *nouveaux romanciers* is also undoubtedly due to his involvement with the *Tel Quel* group, while his theoretical input to the review is never fully consistent with the theory of literature proposed by other writers such as Sollers, Baudry, Kristeva, and Pleynet. It seems more accurate to see Ricardou on the side of the *nouveau roman*, while benefiting from the theoretical advances made in *Tel Quel*.

It is undoubtedly the ideological presuppositions of the *nouveau roman* that are most suspect for *Tel Quel*. In order to establish its own theory and practice as distinct, the review needed to separate itself critically from the *nouveau roman*. It is also overtaken textually, in the fiction. Sollers's *Le Parc* was in certain ways reminiscent of the work of Robbe-Grillet. As Foucault had suggested in 'Distance, aspect, origine', its objects, its 'look' had the same resonance as elements in Robbe-Grillet's fiction.[43] *Le Parc* presents a narrator who, in his room overlooking the park, recalls memories and projects fantasies, but this narrative is continuously doubled by the 'other' narrator, who sits at the table in the room and writes the narrative we are now reading. The space or scene of writing enfolds that of representation and imagination within its frame, while in Robbe-Grillet the realist and meta-textual elements work on the same level as the narrative, creating an ambiguity between the two. *Le Parc* can be read as an intertextual enfolding of Robbe-Grillet's writing, while Sollers's next novel, *Drame*, goes beyond the necessity of this anxiety of influence. A major aspect of the fiction of *Tel Quel*, the mechanism by which it attempts to go beyond the objectivism

[40] M. Butor, 'Dans les flammes', *TQ* 24 (winter 1966); C. Ollier, 'Murnau' (a film review), *TQ* 23 (autumn 1965).

[41] C. Simon, 'Propriété des rectangles', *TQ* 44 (winter 1971).

[42] See J. Ricardou, *L'Observatoire de Cannes* (Paris, 1961), *La Prise de Constantinople* (Paris, 1965); and *Les Lieux-dits* (Paris, 1969), the first two pub. by Minuit, the latter by Gallimard.

[43] See M. Foucault, 'Distance, aspect, origine', *Crit.* (Nov. 1963) and in *Théorie d'ensemble*, 11.

of Robbe Grillet or the expressionistic writing of Sarraute, is the focus on the 'scene of writing' itself.

The *nouveau roman* is also confronted in other critical concerns. It seems that the main target for *Tel Quel* in the ideology of the *nouveau roman* is the notion of realism that it implies. *Tel Quel* begins to develop a textuality in which the old problematic of real/unreal is redundant, as well as that of objective/subjective. This strategy is an enclosing of oppositions within a larger space, the displacement of dualities by a third position. This is a movement that will become characteristic for the review, perhaps the principal aspect of its transgressions. The wider space, or the arch-ispace in Derrida's terms, in this case is the space of language, so that the review's critique of the *nouveau roman* engages with the linguistic focus of many of the structuralist debates of the time.

Foucault–Roussel: Textual Space

A moment of intersection is Sollers's review of Michel Foucault's book *Raymond Roussel*.[44] Foucault's 1963 book is one of a series of texts written in the early 1960s, on Hölderlin, Bataille, Blanchot, *Tel Quel* itself, and Klossowski, which elaborate a specific vision of literature very close to that of *Tel Quel*, but distinct on important points. Roussel was a writer who had not been given much critical acknowledgement. Apart from an article in *Critique* by Michel Leiris, Foucault's book is inaugural of a critical assessment of Roussel. Echoing the title of Foucault's *Naissance de la clinique*, Sollers recognizes its inaugural qualities by referring to it as 'Naissance de la critique'.[45] His article shifts the perspective from a debate around the question of realism to more radical questions of textual space, auto-referentiality and infinity, a space closer to Blanchot than to Robbe-Grillet. He stresses in Foucault's account how textual space envelops questions of objectivity or subjectivity. If the debate on the *nouveau roman* is a question of objectivity or realism, the whole question is shifted by relocating the space of fiction as a textual space rather than a phenomenal space, a move beyond the phenomenal that will become characteristic. So while Robbe-Grillet emphasizes the objective qualities of Roussel's work, Foucault and Sollers focus on the linguistic reality of the text:

[44] P. Sollers, 'Logicus Solus', *TQ* 14 (summer 1963); M. Foucault, *Raymond Roussel* (Paris, 1963).

[45] Sollers, 'Logicus Solus', *TQ* 14; 50.

il faut accepter [la] réalité [de Roussel], c'est à dire une pratique vertigineuse du langage (incessament confronté à son origine et au hasard qu'il implique aussitôt).[46]

This suggests a fundamental disparity between the two approaches. Robbe-Grillet sees in Roussel a reduction of language to a pure descriptive function. Sollers and Foucault see in Roussel a vertiginous, that is to say, risky, transgressive language which confronts its own origin. For Sollers the equation has to be rethought from the point of view of language as the space within which the text operates. In this sense Robbe-Grillet remains on the other side of the limit that enables a text such as Roussel's to be read as a text. Robbe-Grillet remains a prisoner of the distinction between subjective and objective, real and imaginary, interior and exterior, that is dissolved once the text is seen as a space interior to language, resulting primarily from the productivity of language.[47]

In the same way, Roussel can only be said to be a writer of the imaginary or the fantastic, as for the Surrealists, if a reality is posited as a basis for the view of the world implied in the text. Sollers repeats and affirms Foucault's analysis that Roussel's texts do not represent a pre-given reality but construct a new, linguistic reality and are 'cette fabrication en acte'.[48] As an inventor of an *espace linguistique*,[49] Roussel is disengaged from the problems of realism that Robbe-Grillet in his emphasis on objective description and the imaginary had focused on, and which Surrealism implied. The move towards textual space is something like a paradigm shift both in the history of fiction and theoretical apprehensions of it, and in *Tel Quel*'s history. Textuality is not any longer a question of ambiguity with relation to reference to the real, nor does it preclude reference; reference is precisely to a reality seen as textual.

An Imaginary Book

The delineation of textual space in a more theoretical, abstract framework continues in Sollers's important essay 'Logique de la fiction'.[50]

---

[46] Ibid. 46.
[47] Cf. J. Kristeva's article on Roussel, 'La Productivité dite texte', in ead., *Séméiotiké, Recherches pour une sémanalyse (Paris,* 1969).
[48] Sollers, 'Logicus Solus', *TQ* 14 ; 47.
[49] Ibid.
[50] P. Sollers, 'Logique de la fiction', *TQ* 15 (autumn 1963). Reprinted also in id., *Logiques* (Paris, 1968), but with certain changes, for example, the elision of a ref. to Jung.

Bypassing the *nouveau roman*, Sollers describes an imaginary book that would inhabit this space. In doing so he both creates a tradition, referring to precursors, and a project, the writing of novels like the book he has projected. In fact, while *Le Parc* related in certain ways to the *nouveau roman* and superseded it, *Drame*, the first of a series of texts up to *Paradis*, is this imaginary book projected into existence.

Sollers begins characteristically with a distancing of the present ideology of the novel. Implicitly, this includes the *nouveau roman*. The representational novel as a reflection of reality or as a decoration, from which the reader remains separate and detached, is related to a Platonic idealism of forms and ideas. The text of fiction, as Sollers terms what we have called textual space, implicates its reader. As the representational text is exterior to the reality it purports to represent, the reader is exterior to the text. The text of fiction situates all three elements within the same interior, immanent space.

In order to delineate this space, Sollers has recourse to a Husserlian *epoché* or reduction. Robbe-Grillet's work is also a reduction, to the objective, but he goes too far and not far enough in this reduction, eliding subjectivity. He remains a prisoner of the Cartesian *cogito* that is implicit in any objectivism. Sollers recognizes subjectivity as a kind of basis: 'Quoi que je fasse, il y a toujours la présence obscure du reste que j'étais.'[51] *Je* is here and now, neither absent nor omnipresent. This phenomenological gesture does not go as far as existentialism, however, in seeing this subjectivity as a basis for action. As opposed to the existentialist credo 'I am because I do' or 'I am constituted by what I do', Sollers situates the *je* inside a current, a process of thought, 'I am thought' (*Je suis pensé*). The *je* is not in a position of control over the current he inhabits, but nevertheless he attempts to understand his position. This understanding, *la compréhension*, derives from a source of contestation of the current and an attempt to follow it:

C'est pourquoi je définirai la 'compréhension' que j'attends comme une opération assez souple, pour suivre ses propres phénomènes, se placer à leur côté lorsqu'ils se font 'langage' . . . le mouvement que j'évoque tient de la danse, de la nage, de tout ce j'appelle une chance en marche. La mobilité délivre le chant, le chant se fait immobilité sans frein (courant dans un courant).[52]

Fiction is a question of the attempt to swim with the current of thought, to contest it, but not to control it or to step outside it, both illusory possibilities. Fiction is a dance without pause or break, an

---

[51] Id., 'Logique de la fiction', *TQ* 15; 5.   [52] Ibid. 7.

affirmation of the current of thought in language. Moreover, the current defined here can be recognized as a continuity, in the Bataillean sense:

Nous sommes ainsi conduits à reconnaître un milieu porteur de continuité, un champ où s'exerce périodiquement la faculté d'identification, un espace ni intérieur ni extérieur, susceptible d'être englobé par une combinatoire neuve et mathématiquement fondée.[53]

Identification exists periodically within this field, as a situation of the subject in the current. Reader, writer, subject and object, conscious and unconscious are not opposed here but within the same space of continuity. The aleatory and combinatorial potential of this space is realized by the oscillating structure of *Drame* and the 'combinatoire neuve et mathématiquement fondée' of the next novel, *Nombres*, more explicitly based on a numerical structure. It also prefigures the later interest in mathematics and Chinese philosophy (see below).

On this basis a number of formulations that remain constant throughout the passage of *Tel Quel* are set in place: fiction as a *redoublement* or doubling of a subjectivity that is within a current infinitely in movement, and an aleatory quality that is emphasized as *une chance en marche*. While Sollers's essay is important beyond its implicit critique of the *nouveau roman*, the criticism is present in the elaboration of a continuous space and the critique of representative fiction. While the *nouveau roman*'s auto-referentiality (as in Robbe-Grillet's *Dans le labyrinthe*, recognized by Sollers) is close to the notion of *redoublement*, the theory of the subject that is outlined by Sollers is absent from Robbe-Grillet's theoretical formulations, as is the philosophical basis in Bataille's notions of continuity and transgression.

In his review of Robbe-Grillet's *Pour un nouveau roman* Sollers develops the Bataillean critique of the *nouveau roman* as a critique of rationality. The modern novel, for Sollers, places itself at the level of an interrogation, or a contestation, as was proposed in 'Logique de la fiction', of meaning or thought. Sollers stresses how *la déraison* or *le non-savoir* is also part of this thought, part of the continuity of which Robbe-Grillet's rationality is a restricted area. The contestation of thought must of necessity go by way of a recognition of *le non-savoir*. Foucault's work on the limit between reason and unreason is crucial here. Sollers is recognizing how the rationality of the *nouveau roman* is undermined by the *non-savoir* recognized in or by Artaud, Bataille, or Foucault.

[53] Ibid.

Sollers also attacks the opposition of subjective and objective, the author, and the notion of the text as spectacle, all from a perspective that we can define as one of transgressive continuity. This is the application of a logic of transgression that is applied at other moments. It is also a logic of the precipitation of crises in *Tel Quel*'s strategy. The third space, of continuity, operates both strategically and textually. The resistance to reading *Tel Quel*'s fiction is perhaps a resistance to enter this space, while the resistance to *Tel Quel*'s strategy in the context also suggests a resistance to the recognition of the current of thought which envelops social discourse.

Une littérature nouvelle? *Cérisy 1963*

In 1963 *Tel Quel* organized a conference at the colloquium centre Cérisy-la-Salle on the question 'Une littérature nouvelle?'[54] Ideally, this would have established the new fictional space, but it appears as a failure to apply its logic. The discussion, chaired by Foucault, comes up against the obstacle of the necessity of referring every point to Robbe-Grillet and realism. However, where the conference is useful for the evolution of the review is in the presence of Michel Foucault, who defines for the review its own status and direction. His comments are pertinent for a discussion of the difference between *Tel Quel* and other fictional perspectives.

Foucault significantly suggests the differences between the approach of *Tel Quel* and the Surrealists, voicing a distinction that was latent in such articles as 'Logique de la fiction'. The distinction, as Foucault presents it, is twofold; while the Surrealists treat various spiritual experiences such as dreams, madness, transgression, as aspects in a psychological space, positing a beyond (*au-delà* or *en deçà*) to the operation of thought, Sollers and *Tel Quel* treat these experiences as taking place within the space of thought seen as language. Foucault cites the importance of Blanchot and Bataille, especially of the latter, whose importance for the review results partly from his having brought such experiences as eroticism and *la folie* out of the psychological space of the Surrealists and on to the level of thought as such. While for the Surrealists, Foucault clarifies, language was only 'un instrument d'accès' or a 'surface de refléxion' of the psychological processes pushed forward

---

[54] The contributions by Pleynet, 'La Pensée contraire', and Faye, 'Une nouvelle analogie?' were pub. in *TQ* 17 (spring 1964), as were the 'Débat sur le roman' and the 'Débat sur la poésie'. Sollers's contribution, 'Logique de la fiction', had already been pub.

by the *au-delà*, into the space of language, language for Sollers and *Tel Quel* is the element in which these operations take place.[55] As we saw in 'Logique de la fiction', language is a space of continuity, into which its exterior is merged. It therefore makes no sense to talk of a beyond, a non-linguistic space in which psychological operations could take place. The main difference between a psychological approach and one which situates itself on the level of continuity is the difference of relation to language. Psychology postulates the existence of operations of the mind that are exterior to language, in that they are independent and generative of motives that are revealed or expressed in language (as the Surrealists would postulate). Sollers's emphasis on language as interior space places itself in direct opposition to what Foucault calls 'psychologism': 'Tout l'anti-psychologisme de la philosophie contemporaine, c'est bien dans cette ligne là que Sollers se place.'[56]

Foucault proposes how Soller's enquiries address themselves to the area of correlation of thought and language, to the intermediary space which links *penser et parler*. He would also take sides in the debate against the Italian novelist Sanguineti, who argued for a kind of realism committed to social issues. However, the debates on the novel and on poetry, published in the review, excepting Foucault's interventions, tend more to reveal the obstacles to *Tel Quel*'s new literature rather than developing innovative responses. The innovative elements are more present in the fictional and poetic practice of the review.

Fictional Space

Between 1963 and 1967 a series of texts emerge which define *Tel Quel*'s specific fictional space. The 'Collection Tel Quel', run by Sollers, here exerting a direct control, is the platform for these works, which are recognizable by their covers, white with a brown edging, as opposed to the orange edging of Le Seuil's other fictional publications. They also define a continuous space, in the sense that the texts correlate with each other in certain ways; the same structures are repeated, the same experience is present, the same images often recur. The fictional and poetic works are moreover recognized as being specific to *Tel Quel* in two landmark articles: Foucault's 'Distance, aspect, origine'[57] and

---

[55] See 'Débat sur le roman', *TQ* 17: 13.
[56] Ibid.
[57] Foucault, 'Distance, aspect, origine, *Théorie d'ensemble*.

Barthes's 'Drame, Poème, roman' on Soller's *Drame*.[58] Both are significantly republished in 1968 in *Théorie d'ensemble*, theoretically recasting *Tel Quel*'s fictional practice up to that point.

A first series of texts by *Tel Quel* novelists relates more to the *nouveau roman*, while sometimes including elements transgressive of its frame of reference. Sollers's *Le Parc* and Jean Thibaudeau's *Une cérémonie royale* (1961) can be seen in this light. The latter novel owes much to Robbe-Grillet, but also hints at the future development of Thibaudeau's work in the contamination of the objective descriptions by emotive connotations which imply a subjective point of view, nevertheless not reducible to the identity of a narrator. Ricardou's '*L'Observatoire de Cannes* (1961) is closer to the *nouveau roman*. As in Robbe-Grillet's writing, description is multiplied and problematized through shifts in perspective. The novel is a clinical analysis of the problems associated with observation and vision in their relation to writing. The focus on description and observation implies that Ricardou remains within the representational framework of the *nouveau roman*. Jean-Louis Baudry, who joined the committee in 1963, also having published in *Écrire*, had previously published the novel *Le Pressentiment* (1962), approaching from the direction of Proust rather than Robbe-Grillet. Its first-person narration significantly features moments of subjective tension which intervene in the text in the form of blanks rupturing the narration and the typographic disposition of the text. The narration is deformed by subjective excess; its silence enters the text and becomes an element to be read. The texts of Jean-Pierre Faye, although also interesting from the point of view of the fracturing of the narration, relate this to a psychological rather than textual perspective. *Battement*, published in 1962 but not in the 'Collection', features aspects of what will become the characteristic *Tel Quel* text in its oscillation of point of view from *je* to *il*, but this is related not to the aleatory effects of language but to the psychological disturbance of the narrator. The later *Analogues* (1964), which was published by *Tel Quel*, is more interesting in its intertextual enfolding of the trilogy of previous texts, *Entre les rues*, *La Cassure*, and *Battement*. Faye's subsequent development as a novelist with the group Change, which he set up with the poet Jacques Roubaud, implies, however, that his association with *Tel Quel* was not the sign of a true community of interests (see Chapter 3).

---

[58] R. Barthes, 'Drame, poème, roman', *Crit.* 222 (Oct. 1965). and *Théorie d'ensemble*.

We have already suggested how in Sollers's *Le Parc* the subjective experience of the scene of writing exceeds the narrative frame which could pertain to a Robbe-Grilletian space. The first series of texts and the extracts from them in *Tel Quel* are prefatory to the fiction specific to the review, and generally can be ranged either under the dominance of the *nouveau roman* or within the context of literature seen as expression or representation. The entry into a textual space depends both on the development of elements in the fictional practice of the writers concerned, but also on the theoretical input of the criticism, for example in Sollers's projective article 'Logique de la fiction'.

Foucault's article 'Distance, aspect, origine' is nominally a review of Sollers's *Le Parc* (1961) and *L'Intermédaire* (1963), Marcelin Pleynet's second collection of poetry *Paysages en deux* suivi de *Les Lignes de la prose* (1963), and Baudry's novel *Les Images* (1963). Thibaudeau's *Une cérémonie royale* is also mentioned. Foucault recognizes certain distinctions between the texts and Robbe-Grillet, a central reference, and proposes tools for the definition of the new fictional space the texts inhabit. Objects, for example, are not isolated, but refer to each other; identity is not stable but *buissonnante*, in a space of simulation, a word which recalls the fiction of Klossowski and of Bataille.[59] Identity incessantly doubles itself. The space of doubling is moreover at a distance, Foucault affirms, which enables a continuity between subject and object, placed in the same space. This is in contrast with the objective gaze of the narrator in Robbe-Grillet's writing. Time, in this space, does not flow in a linear fashion but is superimposed on itself, in a series of blocks, which are figured by the typographically separated blocks of the writing itself. The temporality of the book is anchored in the temporality of the reading process; the spatialization, or shift from reference to a real time to the time of reading is a crucial aspect, which Foucault does not insist on, of *Tel Quel*'s fiction. The structure of superimposition is, however, easily recognizable in Baudry's novel *Les Images*, where it is figured as a series of reflections on a window, seen by the narrator, where the typography of the book is related to images in the phenomenal world. Again, the description of phenomena is doubled and enveloped by a scene of writing.

Foucault's article recognizes a space of continuity, which he calls fiction. Certain of his references, to Klossowski, and to *le Même* as this space of continuity, seem, however, to belong to an essentialist

---

[59] Foucault, 'Distance, aspect, origine', in *Théorie d'ensemble*, 13–14.

perspective. The Derridean terms of difference and deferral, trace and effacement, will take the discussion of textuality out of this Blanchotian frame. At the same time, Foucault's article does launch a theoretical discourse on the texts in their specificity, while suggesting interesting links, which are not analysed, between *Tel Quel*'s fiction and the earlier novels of Blanchot, Bataille, and Klossowski.

Foucault's article had addressed texts which were ambiguously at the initial limit of *Tel Quel*'s specific fictional space. Only Baudry's *Les Images* and Pleynet's *Paysages en deux* can be said to inhabit fully this space. A subsequent series of texts develop its frontiers. Sollers's 1965 *Drame* is a key text in this respect, but other texts of importance include *Le Livre partagé* (1965) by Pierre Rottenberg, who joins the committee in 1967, and *Ouverture* by Thibaudeau (1966). From outside the committee, but in the 'Collection Tel Quel' Eduardo Sanguineti's *Capriccio italiano* (1964) was translated from the Italian by Thibaudeau. Maurice Roche's *Compact* (1966) is an interesting annexe to the textual innovations of the review. It extends the radicalism of the text into a subversion of typography and to a polyphony of textual voices. The work of Severo Sarduy, translated from Spanish and commented by Barthes, is also of interest.[60] Its striking features are a parodic and humorous treatment of the language, in which the latent formalism of *Tel Quel* is replaced by a more hedonistic and playful, baroque textuality.

Drame, Les Images, Le Livre partagé, and *Ouverture* present a fictional space in which the notions of identity and of narrative temporality are replaced by a continuity between writing and reading. The only space the reader can choose to inhabit, or to read from, is the moment of the writing being read. There is no possibility, essentially, of a distance with regard to the text which would allow its judgement. The temporality of narrative is superseded by the physical mechanism of reading, which is figured in the texts as a continual consuming and effacement of the writing behind the point of reading. Writing and reading become almost indistinguishable. As the writing is a process that effaces the text behind it from the point of the pen upon the page, the reading is also a creative process undertaken in the text itself, by itself. So in a sense, the texts read themselves. Narrative temporality is replaced by a different

---

[60] See S. Sarduy, *Écrit en dansant* (Paris, 1965), and R. Barthes's review of it, 'La Face baroque', pub. in *La Quinzaine littéraire* in 1967 and in R. Barthes, *Le Bruissement de la langue* (Paris, 1984). See also S. Sarduy, 'Pages dans le blanc', *TQ* 23 (autumn 1965), poems based on paintings by Franz Kline, trans. from the Spanish by the author and P. Sollers, and a critical article, 'Sur Gongora', *TQ* 25 (spring 1966).

temporality of consuming and effacement, a movement continuous across the different texts. Baudry's metaphor of the superimposition of images, of both text and reality becomes in *Drame* an internal effect of reading and is figured also in *Le Livre partagé*, as a burning, a sacrifice, or a loss of vital body-fluids. The subject of literature finds him- or herself consumed, a subject of loss and of sacrifice, and this is figured in the texts as a dispersal and fragmentation of the body, and its *dépense* in excreta. This figuration of the movement or structures of textuality poses problems, since figuration is a relation of mimesis between writing and some kind of real. Mimesis, as a variant of representation, does not sit easily within *Tel Quel*'s textual ideology of the anti-representative text.[61] Mimesis, as a relation of the text to something outside it, is further problematized, however, by the operations of permutation that the texts favour. The subject of the text, for example, goes through various permutations across a series of pronoun positions as he or she is written by the tracing and effacement of the novel. The I of the narration is far from stable, often split between *je* and *il*, a tendency fully realized in Baudry's *Personnes* (1967), where pronoun permutations structure the novel itself as a multiplicity of viewpoints. Due to the importance of reading as a figure of the text itself, which it programmes itself, and the permutational structure, typography becomes an important element. In Maurice Roche's work this tendency is taken to its extreme in the contamination of the writing by figures, musical scores, different levels and sizes of typeface. The reading process becomes non-linear, so that again the reader is obliged to read the text at the letter, in its materiality and at its moment of inscription.

These innovations are theoretically far more complex than those of the *nouveau roman*, where the ambiguity between realism or expression remains the focal point. The *nouveau roman*'s innovations exist more at the level of narrative and representation as opposed to the level of reading at which *Tel Quel*'s texts operate. But certain common aspects may be found between these works and the fiction of writers such as Perec and the Oulipo group; although the ludic elements there are less connected to a textual ideology, less inhabited by a theoretical consciousness or strategy, and lie more comfortably on the level of linguistic deviations and play than the deeper implications of *Tel Quel*'s fictional space. In the context, the texts that defined this fictional space must

---

[61] For a revalorization of mimesis in this sense, see P. Lacoue-Labarthe, 'Typographie' in S. Agacinski, J. Derrida, S. Kofman, P. Lacoue-Labarthe, J.-L. Nancy, and B. Pautrat, *Mimesis des articulations* (Paris, 1975).

have appeared as fairly terroristic in their firm rejection of the traditional structures of narration, including the *nouveau roman*, and in their confident innovations and magnetic pull of the reader to a place already programmed by the text and the theory of the text. Theoretical fiction, which theorizes itself, produces theory, and is strategically informed by theory, is largely the specific and proper domain of the review and its writers.

In poetry, books by Denis Roche and Pleynet present startling innovations which are as fresh and iconoclastic as those in the novel. Denis Roche published *Récits complets* in 1962 and *Les Idées centésimales de Miss Elanize* in 1964. *Éros énergumène* would follow in 1968. Extracts from all these works appear in the review itself throughout this period.[62] Roche's critical interests as represented in the review are rather more eclectic than those of other members, ranging from Michaux to Finnish mythology to Kandinsky, alongside the continual interest in Pound and Cummings.[63]

The poetry itself is of subversive intent. Roche sees poetry as a vestige of an idealist conception of literature, and sets out to destroy this edifice. This destruction is, however, a subversion in that it works from within the edifice of poetry; to the eye the writing looks like poetry. It displays all the visual signs: lines of unequal length, each line beginning with a capital letter, surrounded and eroded by the empty spaces of the page, set in its centre. Yet often the subject-matter is perversely non-poetic; obscene, scatalogical, or simply banal. Where poetic themes are present, they are deliberately subverted by the typographic disposition of the poem, by the fixed lozenge-shape of the poem, or the ending of the line in mid-phrase or word, or in false *enjambements* between lines.

Récits complets presents in fact a multiplicity of *récits* which are far from complete, but fragmented and internally fractured. The 'idées' of Miss Elanize, which is a deviated anagram of *miscellanées*, are 'centésimales', not unified. With *Éros énergumène* it becomes more apparent that the force that fragments and subverts the idealist edifice of poetry is the pulsional energy of the sexual drive, more often than not figured as perverse.

[62] D. Roche, 'La Poésie est question de collimateur', *TQ* 10 (summer 1962); id., 'Les Idées centésimales de Miss Elanize', *TQ* 14 (summer 1963); id., 'La Bibliothèque du Congrès', *TQ* 18 (summer 1964); id., 'Éros énergumène', *TQ* 22 (summer 1965); id., 'Éros énergumène: Théâtre', *TQ* 27 (autumn 1966).

[63] Id., 'Pour Ezra Pound', 'E. E. Cummings', and 'Vents et poussières de Henri Michaux', *TQ* 11 (autumn 1962); id., 'Kandinsky à venir', *TQ* 14; id. 'Les Religions arctiques et finnoises', *TQ* 22.

Roche's internal subversion of poetry also has effects in theory; since the position of critical distance with regard to the text is not so stable, the critique being undertaken from within, in the text, the position of theory is made increasingly untenable, leading to the abdication of this critical voice by the poet.[64] Because of this abdication, and because of the singular mechanisms of the subversion of poetry, it seems that Denis Roche occupies an extraneous, marginal position within *Tel Quel*. But the radical vitality of his voice gives the review a certain force.

Marcelin Pleynet's experience of poetic language is of a radical subjection. It is experienced as a *battement de sens* that subverts identity, authorship, and the name.[65] In the first text, *Provisoires amants des nègres* (1962), there is a *mise en scène* of the conflict, induced by this experience, between a Heideggerian nostalgia for a lost origin and the radical alienation writing entails. In the later works this nostalgia is no longer present, so that there is a definite movement towards a more fundamental subjection to the writing, a more radical experience of alienation. This experience of loss of identity is what defines poetic language, at first, for Pleynet. The presence of such writing in *Tel Quel* is an excess compared to the rationality of the *nouveau roman*, which can be said to attempt to foreclose this question of subjectivity through a fetishistic attention to detail. As Sollers had emphasized, the subjection to language could also be accompanied by a critical consciousness that would run alongside this current. In Pleynet's work the motif of doubling is particularly productive. In the second work it is figured as a *paysage en deux*, the doubling itself referring to language's ability to refer either to itself or to the real. The doubling is then between language as *chant*, simple unmediated sound, and *critique*, consciousness of itself.[66] This is further complicated by the duality of poetry and prose. Typographically, verticality and horizontality come into play as signifying elements. The title of the work itself is a double: *Paysages en deux* suivi de *Les Lignes de la prose*. Each is in fact a separate work but they are

[64] There are no more critical articles by D. Roche after summer 1965. The text in *Théorie d'ensemble*, 'La Poésie est inadmissible, d'ailleurs elle n'existe pas', stages this abdication of the voice of theory, or its subversion, by titling a prosaic, critical section 'Théorie I', and a second section, typographically 'poetic', 'Théorie II', suggesting that 'Theory' is henceforth continued within the subversive activity of the writing.

[65] See M. Pleynet, *Les Trois Livres* (Paris, 1984), a republication of the first three books, *Provisoires amants des nègres*, *Paysages en deux* suivi de *Les Lignes de la prose*, and *Comme*, prefaced by Pleynet, p. 7: 'L'inspiration, l'emportement poétiques ne vivent ici que de ce battement de sens qui touche le cœur avec force et livre, en rythmes, la présence sensible des réussites et des échecs de la création.'

[66] A duality signalled by Risset in *Marcelin Pleynet*, 9.

presented in the same text, as dual versions of the same experience of a subjection to language. In the next text, *Comme*, the prose/poetry division is also present, this time under the same title. Here the division or duality is figured as emerging from the point of the *comme*, the moment where language turns either outwards or back upon itself. The *as* is seen as both the internal and external limit of language. Wittgenstein is a key reference for this text, particularly the dictum that language exists between the limits of contradiction and tautology. A more formal level of experimentation has been reached. The poetics of nostalgia for some kind of absent meaning is dropped. Fragmentation is seen not in a melancholy sense, as in the poetry of du Bouchet, for example, but as a source of meaning and eroticism.[67] Already in *Paysages en deux* Pleynet had written 'Fragmentation est la source'.[68]

Pleynet and Roche's poetry represent two very different but equally radical approaches to language that correlate with many of the innovations in the novel proposed by other writers of the group. Their influence seems to have been as diffuse as that of the *Tel Quel* novel, but the effect in the context is one of a terroristic shift of textuality on to the level of form and its theoretical analysis, within the text itself.

INTERSECTIONS IN THE AVANT-GARDE

In the early 1960s the burgeoning movement of what is known as structuralism was in fact a number of distinct currents or moments, preparing for the theoretical explosion of the middle of the decade. In 1965 Althusser published his *Pour Marx* and *Lire le Capital*, proposing a structural reading of Marx's works that purported to do away with the baggage of humanism. In 1966 Lacan and Foucault both produced their key works, respectively, the *Écrits* and the archaeology of the human sciences *Les Mots et les choses*. Almost immediately they became best sellers and the writers were projected into a kind of intellectual stardom. The works themselves provided the possibility for new syntheses of the kind which *Tel Quel* produced, and this theoretical expansion would very soon become politicized in the wake of May 1968.

[67] Cf. e.g. A. du Bouchet, *Dans la chaleur vacante* (Paris, 1961). See also Pleynet, interview with author, Paris, 1990: 'Au lieu de le verser au compte d'une complainte nostalgique il est emporté par un dynamisme érotique'; 'Pour moi Du Bouchet est typiquement un phénomène de rétention.'
[68] Pleynet, *Les Trois Livres*, 119.

The picture is far from complete, however, without an account of less obviously structuralist currents or those which were in fact attempting to move beyond the limits of structure; these currents and their intersections lead up to and feed into the atmosphere of theory of the mid-decade. Barthes, Derrida, and Deleuze were highly active in this period, producing work which has an influence on and through the time of theory. While Barthes was very close to *Tel Quel*, Derrida's work will become relevant in this time as an articulation with a critique of metaphysics. The work of Deleuze, although reviewed affirmatively in the review, evolves independently of it.[69]

The Quarrel of the Critics

A major moment was the Barthes—Picard debate of 1964–6, which neatly threw into distinction the new critical perspectives on literature, as against the more traditional and academic forms of literary criticism. After Barthes published the radical *Sur Racine* in 1963, showing how even the classic texts could be treated structurally and psychoanalytically, R. Picard, a lecturer at the Sorbonne, took him to task in the pamphlet 'Nouvelle critique ou nouvelle imposture'.[70] Barthes, in his *Critique et vérité* (1966), seems to have gained from the crisis, presenting a reformulation of critical aims and perspectives which points towards the later development of literary theory in *Tel Quel*.

The Barthes–Picard debate would also reveal a potential distinction between what was known as the *nouvelle critique* and the more linguistics-oriented perspective of writers like Barthes, Genette, and Todorov. While the first, in the work of writers like Jean-Pierre Richard, Jean Starobinski, and Georges Poulet aimed at a definition of the 'creative core of the work',[71] the second was more taxonomic and structural. While the first could have been accused of sentimentality and of being unscientific by the second, the second could have been accused of positivism by the first. Such an impasse seems to have been the starting-point for the later work of Barthes, and the work of Kristeva. *Tel Quel* is the forum for both kinds of criticism, but criticism with a basis in linguistics soon superseded the early interest in the *nouvelle critique*. The

[69] See P. Sollers, 'Proust et les signes', *TQ* 19 (autumn 1964); G. Deleuze works predomimantly within philosophy; see *Nietzsche et la philosophie* (Paris, 1962) and *La Philosophie de Kant* (Paris, 1963).

[70] R. Picard, *Nouvelle critique ou nouvelle imposture?* (Paris, 1965).

[71] A. Lavers, *Roland Barthes; Structuralism and After* (London, 1982), 12.

apparent limitations of the structuralist or formalist approach nevertheless soon became evident, after the publication of *Théorie de la littérature*,
a collection of work by the Russian formalists, introduced to France by
Todorov in a 'Collection Tel Quel' publication of 1965. The recognition
of the limitations of formalism is the starting-point for *Tel Quel*'s
development of a theory of literature specific to itself. The quarrel of
the critics produced interesting and vital distinctions and processes into
the development of criticism, with which *Tel Quel* was directly involved.
It precedes the moment of theory as such.

A further crucial element in the superseding of these limits was the
work of Derrida. After the Husserl introduction of 1962, Derrida
published a number of decisive articles, some of which appeared in *Tel
Quel* itself, and which are for the most part collected in the 'Collection
Tel Quel' publication *L'Écriture et la différence*.[72] The key work, however,
was *De la grammatologie*, which had first appeared in *Critique* in 1965.[73]
Here he elaborated the notion of a general writing, or *archi-écriture*,
a structure of difference and deferral that undermined any posing of a
presence, presence to self of the subject of speech, presence of truth or
meaning. Analysing in considerable depth Rousseau's *Essai sur l'origine
des langues*, through comparison with Lévi-Strauss's work, Derrida would
show how the notion of structure was underpinned by the notions of
truth and presence it sought to displace.[74] The notion of a generalized
writing, posed before the phenomenon of writing itself, could open up
the limits of structuralism and formalism to the process of generation of
meaning; the focus on meaning as a process rather than a structure or
an expression entailed a focus on the text in its production of meaning.
This *before*, which is more spatial than temporal, enables the emphasis
on the text and its production in the latter half of the decade. *Tel Quel*'s
reference and mutual exchanges with Derrida link the group's theory of
literature to a critical approach to metaphysics, while individual
developments within the review, in the criticism of Sollers, for example,
parallel Derrida's work without depending exclusively upon it. The
moment when these currents form a kind of synthesis is in 1968, with
the publication of *Théorie d'ensemble*.

[72] Derrida's articles in *Tel Quel* from *L'Écriture et la différence* (Paris, 1967): 'La Parole
soufflée', *TQ* 20 (winter 1965); 'Freud et la scène de l'écriture', *TQ* 26 (summer 1966).
[73] Id., 'De la grammatologie', *Crit.* 223–4 (Dec. 1965–Jan. 1966).
[74] See also the article, 'Structure, signe et jeu dans le discours des sciences humaines',
in *L'Écriture et la différence* (Paris, 1967), orig. a paper at a 1966 conference in Baltimore, also
attended by Lacan, Barthes, and Todorov, among others.

Critique

The intersections of ideas and individual itineraries in this period are usefully represented by the relations between the reviews *Tel Quel* and *Critique*. Early in the decade, *Critique* had provided support for *Tel Quel* with the publication of articles around the *nouveau roman* by Jean Thibaudeau and Jean Ricardou.[75] The *nouveau roman* having been dropped fairly early on as a privileged reference for *Tel Quel*, the common denominator shifted to the influence of Georges Bataille, the founder of *Critique*, who died in 1962. The special obituary issue of the next year was a crucial site of intersection; writers from an earlier generation such as Klossowski, Leiris, and Blanchot were represented there, along with the more contemporary perspectives of Barthes, Foucault, and Sollers.[76] The issue is important in linking the new structuralist approaches to the thinking of excess and negativity of an older generation. It is also a moment where the structure is opened up to non-structural energetic forces. The moment of intersection is also a moment of diversion, however, since Foucault's article 'Préface à la transgression' reveals a possible divergence over the question of whether the relation between the limit or the law and its transgression is a dialectical one.[77] *Tel Quel*'s elaboration of transgression into a dialectical movement that could provide a hinge with the Marxist dialectic differed from Foucault's anti-dialectical thinking on the matter. Foucault becomes a less pertinent reference for *Tel Quel*, especially with the later Marxism of the review.

Beyond the issue on Bataille but in its wake, *Critique* is a site of productive interchange with *Tel Quel*. Sollers, Pleynet, and Jean-Pierre Faye all publish important articles in the review, while Barthes and Derrida will be elected on to the advisory board of *Critique*, establishing a firm link between the two reviews that lasts up to the end of the decade.[78] This link is fruitful in the opportunity it provides for the

---

[75] See n. 23.

[76] 'Hommage à Georges Bataille', *Crit.* 195–6 (Aug.–Sept. 1963).

[77] M. Foucault, 'Préface à la transgression', ibid. 757: 'Nul mouvement dialectique, nulle analyse des constitutions et de leur sol transcendental ne peut apporter de secours pour penser une telle expérience où même l'accès à cette expérience.'

[78] The articles by *Tel Quel* members or associates in *Critique* during the 1960s are: P. Sollers, 'De grandes irrégularités de langage' (on Bataille), 195–6 and 'Critique de la poésie' (on Pleynet), 226; J.-P. Faye, 'Le Théâtre et ses décors', 226; J. Ricardou, 'L'Histoire dans l'histoire', 231–2; J. Kristeva, 'Bakhtine, le dialogue et le roman', 234 and 'Le Sens et la mode' (on Barthes), 247; J.-L. Houdebine, 'Figures en regard' (on Guillevic), 247; Ricardou, 'Le Caractère singulier de cette eau . . .' (on Poe), 243–4; Sollers, 'La

encounter of other work published in *Critique*. Gilles Deleuze, who wrote important works on Nietzsche and Proust during this time, would publish a series of articles there.[79] It is also a vital forum for both Lacanian and non-Lacanian psychoanalysis. Lacan himself would publish the essay 'Kant avec Sade' in the review, but there are also important articles by André Green.[80] In the general context *Critique* is a useful intersection for specialized work from many different areas of the human sciences. The serious and scientific approach of the review, together with the Bataillean influence which makes this scientific community problematic, is a decisive example for *Tel Quel*.

Problems and Currents of the Avant-Garde

Tel Quel itself also functions as a site of intersection of a number of disparate currents of the avant-garde, although this notion itself will be criticized and displaced into theory and analysis by Pleynet in an important article 'Les Problèmes de l'avant-garde'.[81] These currents derive mostly from extraneous sites, in the sense of being either from outside France or in areas other than literature. In this way *Tel Quel* functions as a corridor for new and fresh artistic practices. Translation is an important activity in the review, from the Italian in the case of Thibaudeau and Jacqueline Risset, from the English in the case of Pleynet and Denis Roche.[82] Links with the Italian neo-avant-garde, for

Science de Lautréamont', 245; M. Pleynet, 'La Poésie doit avoir pour but . . .' (on Denis Roche), 253; J.-J. Goux, 'Dérivable et indérivable', 272; Ricardou, 'La Bataille de Pharsale' (on C. Simon), 274; J. Henric, 'Une profondeur matérielle' (on Artaud), 278; J. Risset, 'C. E. Gadda ou la philosophie à l'envers', 282; Kristeva, 'Objet, complément, dialectique', 285; Sollers, 'La Matière et sa phrase' (on Guyotat), 290; Houdebine, 'Lectures d'une refonte' (on Kristeva), 295; Kristeva, 'L'Éthique de la linguistique', 322; Risset, 'La Poétique mise en question', 322 (special issue on Jakobson). After the early 1970s, the contributions will be more sparse, although ex-associates of *Tel Quel* such as H. Damisch, M. Deguy, J.-L. Schefer, and newer contributors such as L. Dispot and G. Scarpetta, will contribute articles. J.-L. Baudry contributes articles in the late 1970s.

[79] See G. Deleuze, 'Pierre Klossowski ou les corps-langage', *Crit.* 214 (mar. 1965); id., 'Une théorie d'autrui' (on M. Tournier), *Crit.* 241 (June 1967); id., 'Le Schizophrène et le mot' (on Artaud, L. Wolfson, L. Carroll), *Crit.* 255–6 (Aug.–Sept. 1968); id., 'Un nouvel archiviste' (on M. Foucault), *Crit.* 274 (Mar. 1970); id., 'Faille et feux locaux' (on K. Axelos), *Crit.* 275 (Apr. 1970).

[80] J. Lacan, 'Kant avec Sade', *Crit.* 191 (Apr. 1963); A. Green, 'Du comportement à la chair. L'Itinéraire de Maurice Merleau-Ponty', *Crit.* 211 (Nov. 1964).

[81] M. Pleynet, 'Les Problèmes de l'avant-garde', *TQ* 25 (spring 1966).

[82] Translations during this period include: *TQ* 1: V. Woolf; 2: T. S. Eliot, J. Donne; 3: R. Musil, G. Trakl; 4: D. Thomas; 6: F. Hölderlin, M. Heidegger (by M. Deguy), E. Pound; 7: J. L. Borges (by P. Sollers), D. Defoe; 8: G. Ungaretti (by F. Ponge); 9: C. E.

example, were forged with the review's publication of work by the Italian writers Eduardo Sanguineti, Nanni Balestrini, and Umberto Eco, the latter also associated with the critical perspectives of structuralism.[83] While the Italian literary avant-garde has certain limitations in terms of the more pervasive influence of Marxist-inspired realism, it enables links with the Italian context that will remain strong in *Tel Quel*.[84] The texts themselves, *Cappriccio italiano* (1964) by Sanguineti and *Tristan* (1972) by Balestrini present interesting applications of the textuality of *Tel Quel*. From the English, Denis Roche has a privileged place as a translator of Ezra Pound, but Marcelin Pleynet's translation and introduction of work by the US poet and critic Charles Olson is a vital hinge into a contemporary American context that will also prove a permanent interest for the review. (See Chapter 4)

With Pleynet the review gains also a vital and long-lasting critical perspective that encompasses literature, painting, dance, and music. The common element can be seen as a critique of the experience of poetic language. Painting, dance, and music are seen as an excess in relation to language, which produce an experience in the subject which he attempts to analyse. The problems of the avant-garde which Pleynet underlines were linked to the projection of the notion of rupture on to history; the avant-garde tended to become a succession of ruptures with regard to the past, for the sake of rupture, in fact functioning as a deviation from the limit, a guarding of the limit, rather than a transgression of it.[85] The approach Pleynet affirms is that of analysis and a concentration of the materiality of artistic practice, referring to the work of Barthes, Lacan, and Derrida; this approach is put into practice in Pleynet's articles on the avant-garde. He is a key figure in the

Gadda; 11: J. L. Borges (by R. Caillois), E. Pound, (by Denis Roche); 12: P. Klee (by M. Deguy, J. Beaufret), 15: G. Ungaretti (by P. Jaccottet); 19: C. Olson (by M. Pleynet); 20: J. Ashbery (by D. Roche); 21: R. M. Rilke; 22: J. Joyce; 23: Schelling, Vico (by J. Risset), Sarduy (by Sollers and S. Sarduy); 25: N. Balestrini (by Risset); 27: W. Burroughs; 30: J. Joyce.

[83] See E. Sanguineti, 'Capriccio italiano' (trans. by J. Thibaudeau), *TQ* 15 (autumn 1963); id., 'Inf. VIII' (on Dante) (trans. by J. Thibaudeau), *TQ* 23 (autumn 1965); id., 'Pour une avant-garde révolutionnaire', *TQ* 29 (spring 1967); and id., *Capriccio italiano* (Paris, 1964); N. Balestrini, 'Premier plan' (trans. by J. Risset), *TQ* 25 (spring 1966); U. Eco, 'Le Moyen Age de James Joyce', *TQ* 11–12, (autumn 1962–winter 1963). The latter is an excerpt from Eco's work *L'Oeuvre ouverte* (Paris, 1965).

[84] J. Risset contributes an article on Gramsci, 'Lecture de Gramsci' for *TQ* 42 (summer 1970). During the 1970s the review will publish work by Sanguineti, Balestrini, Maria-Antonietta Macciocchi, and the psychoanalyst Armando Verdiglione. See Ch. 4.

[85] See Pleynet, 'Les Problèmes de l'avant-garde', *TQ* 25 (Spring 1966).

introduction of a critical perspective in France on abstract expressionist painting, such as the work of Kline, Rothko, Rauschenberg, while Sollers writes on James Bishop.[86] Pleynet also writes on the dance and music of Merce Cunningham and John Cage.[87] The difference of the American context seems to reflect the excessive status of these arts with regard to language, an interest which will be revived in the late 1970s with the emergence from theory and the 1977 issue on the United States. This permanent interest is a crucial aspect of the review's history and its relation to history. Given that the contemporary artistic practices in the United States are determined by the 'grafting' of Surrealism into a different tradition in the post-war years, its critical return in France is a deviated rereading of Surrealism and its influence.[88] *Tel Quel*'s tense relation with Surrealism, rather than being worked out in a direct confrontation, is mediated through the interest in non-verbal artistic practices that emanate largely from the States. If a justification of this interest in terms of a critical approach to art can be found, it is perhaps in the attention to process and the production of meaning, 'l'image du sens' as Pleynet will term it in an article in *Tel Quel*.[89] Pleynet's interest is in the way the image, or the non-verbal in general, relates to language, and more specifically to poetry, since poetry is already, in some senses, an experience of the non-verbal, of what lies beyond the limits of language if such limits exist. Pleynet's work on painting represents a critical hinge into the avant-garde in terms of its extraneous relation to language and to French culture, to the French language as such.[90] Outside the review, Pleynet would also develop his highly original art-criticism in articles published in *Les Lettres françaises*.[91] In France *Tel Quel* would also gain a certain prestige through association with the avant-garde from its publication of an article and books by the

[86] Id., 'Exposition Mark Rothko', *TQ* 12; id., 'La Peinture de Robert Rauschenberg', *TQ* 13; id., 'Franz Kline et la tentative post-cubiste', *TQ* 19; id., P. Sollers, 'La Peinture et son sujet', *TQ* 20.

[87] Id., 'La Compagnie de Merce Cunningham', (introd. to J. Cage and M. Cunningham, 'L'Art impermanent'), *TQ* 18.

[88] See J. Kristeva, M. Pleynet, P. Sollers, 'Pourquoi les États-Unis?', *TQ* 71-3 (autumn 1977).

[89] M. Pleynet, 'L'Image du sens', *TQ* 18.

[90] Cf. id., interview with author, Paris, 1990: 'Le non-dit va apparaître aussi vite, notamment un des non-dits du Surréalisme et de ses conséquences, aujourd'hui mondiales, un des non-dits si vous voulez de l'avant-garde américaine post-dadaiste, au fond, c'est la langue même dans laquelle nous nous exprimons. C'est à dire la langue française et la culture française en tant qu'elle est née à un moment donné de l'histoire'.

[91] *Tel Quel* also pub. an important book on modern art by Pierre Daix, editor of *Les Lettres françaises: Nouvelle critique et art moderne* (Paris, 1968).

composer Pierre Boulez.[92] The emphasis on the process of meaning, in any artistic process, is a common denominator. The focus on form, or content as form, is moreover coupled with the elaboration of a critical language to account for it. This focus and elaboration are the necessary step before a commitment of form, with the Marxist period of the latter half of the decade.

Contre *Blanchot*

The relations with the context of *Tel Quel* up to the synthesis of 1968 appear as a drawing together of the work of a number of writers outside the review, such as Barthes, Foucault, and Derrida, coupled with the internal development of the theory of literature in the review, principally in articles by Sollers (see below: Logics of the Limit). These relations are focused in institutional relations such as those with *Critique* or with the *Communications* team. Before the formalist and structuralist influences in the review, and the activity of Barthes can be discussed, however, the ideological differences between the approaches to literature of *Tel Quel* and Foucault, which also seem to carry the differences with Blanchot, need to be elucidated, in order to identify the points of convergence and of difference.

Around the same time as his chairing of the Cérisy debate and the productive article on some *Tel Quel* texts, 'Distance, aspect, origine', and contemporary with the article on Bataille in *Critique*, Foucault published an article in *Tel Quel* entitled 'Le Langage à l'infini', which presents a view of literature similar but subtly distinct from that developing in the review.[93] The isomorphism between the two approaches is present in the emphasis on literature as *l'œuvre de langage* which identifies language as the space of literature, but also sees the latter as a critical doubling or contestation of the former.[94] The turn to language, however, is presented by Foucault as a response to the death of God, or the absence of a stable locus of symbolic meaning. It is over the insistence of this question that divergences can be recognized. The essentially modernist question of what literature can do once the gods have departed, in their absence, determines Foucault's arguments, influenced by the work of Blanchot. Hölderlin is a crucial reference-point for both critics, hence perhaps *Tel Quel*'s hesitation to introduce Hölderlin into its canon. The

---

[92] P. Boulez, 'Le Goût et la fonction', *TQ* 14–15; id., *Relevés d'apprenti* (Paris, 1964).

[93] M. Foucault, 'Le Langage à l'infini', *TQ* 15.

[94] Ibid. 45.

question for Foucault remains: what function can literature have in the absence of God? *Tel Quel*'s response to this loss seems to be somehow beyond the modernist frame; although the question does not so much become irrelevant as side-stepped in a more precise focus on the process of textual production. This focus soon turns into a science of the text, in which linguistics and psychoanalysis become the two poles of scientific authority. For *Tel Quel*, therefore, science displaces the question of the absence of divine authority. When the scientific references are eventually evacuated by the very process of the elaboration of a theory of the text in the 1970s, the reference to religion returns, but on very different ground (see Chapter 4). The divergence in question turns around the permanent insistence on absence in Foucault and Blanchot's literary thought, and *Tel Quel*'s turn to science. While the latter approach is perhaps self-destructive, the application of science to an element that subverts its principles and leads to an affirmation of the transcendent, the former reveals its limitations in an inability to proceed beyond the dichotomy of absence and presence; while *Tel Quel*'s literary theory develops into something that falls neither within modernism nor within post-modernism, Foucault's texts on literature are limited to the first half of the 1960s. The same divergence is pertinent in the present, between the emphases of Sollers and *L'Infini* and the philosophy-oriented literary criticism of Derrida and writers such as Jean-Luc Nancy.[95]

Formalism

The eclectic intersections in the avant-garde effected in *Tel Quel* in the period from 1963 to 1967 are made less diffuse by the emphasis on form and analysis in the review. In this sense the formalism of the review displaces any association with the avant-garde through which the review might have become fixed in a predictable place. A key moment is the importation and introduction into the French context, by *Tel Quel*, of the work of the Russian formalists from the 1920s and 1930s. The conjunction with the Russian formalists is exhibited both in the publication of articles in *Tel Quel* and by references to them by the writers of *Tel Quel*.[96] The major event in this conjunction, however, is the publication, in the 'Collection Tel Quel', of texts by the Russian

[95] See J.-L. Nancy, *Une pensée finie* (Paris, 1990) and *The Birth to Presence*, ed. W. Hamacher and D. E. Wellbery (Stanford, Calif., 1993).
[96] e.g. Pleynet, in 'L'Image du sens', *TQ* 18.

formalists, entitled *Théorie de la littérature*, collected and translated by Tzvetan Todorov in 1965.

Todorov's publication and the consequent publicizing of the work of the Russian formalists is an event of extreme importance not only for *Tel Quel* but also for French literary theory as such. While Roman Jakobson, a leading member of the formalists and of the Prague School of Linguistics, was publishing material in France[97] and had been specifically important in providing the generative seeds of structuralism in his interaction with Lévi-Strauss and in introducing important concepts such as the distinction between the two axes of linguistic signification and the poetic function of language, the Russian formalist school as an entity is unknown (in France; it was already familiar to anglophone readers) until Todorov's publication. The importance of the conjunction with Russian formalism more specifically for *Tel Quel* is evident in a number of ways. Philosophical, psychological, and sociological approaches to the text are rejected in the name of an approach which concentrates on the immanent structure of the text or on the system of literature. In the context of the specific history of Russian formalism this approach largely resulted negatively from opposition to the traditional approach of Potebnia and Vesilovsky and of the symbolists. The approach which relies upon extra-literary phenomena, according to the formalists, results in a mass of conflicting opinions and confusion, notions of decoration and realism, all resulting from a primary lack of distinction between the language of literature and the language of ordinary discourse.[98]

The most important aspect of the Russian formalist approach for *Tel Quel* is the advocacy of an approach to literature as a system with its own laws. This emphasis catalyses a tendency already present in the review. Resulting from this primary distinction, between literary discourse and ordinary discourse, Russian formalism and its French counterpart present themselves as a research into *litterarité*.[99] This research is carried out on a synchronic level, by the comparison of literary discourse with ordinary discourse. Linguistics, particularly Saussurean linguistics, is an important asset. The distinction between synchrony and diachrony, between system and incidence (*langue* and

---

[97] Jakobson contributed articles to *Tel Quel*: 'Du réalisme artistique', *TQ* 24; 'Glosso-lalie', *TQ* 26; 'Une microscopie du dernier spleen dans Les Fleurs du Mal', *TQ* 29.

[98] This is Jakobson's thesis in 'Du réalisme artistique'.

[99] See Eikenbaum, 'La Théorie de la méthode formelle', in T. Todorov (ed.), *Théorie de la littérature: Textes des formalistes russes* (Paris, 1965), 37.

parole) were efficient in clearing up a lack of clarity in criticism. This imperative also conditioned an enquiry into the difference between prose and poetry, the inner laws of genre, and the relation of works to each other. Concerning the latter question the formalists would introduce the concept of the series and of correlation, which Foucault had already hinted at in 'Distance, aspect, origine', and which Kristeva would replace with the notion of intertextuality. The positivistic limitations of formalism, which did not seek to elaborate a theory of literature and, despite the climate of revolution, was not a projective, radical criticism, were fairly soon superseded by the development of the work of Roland Barthes, and the arrival of Kristeva.

Roland Barthes

The character of Barthes's early interaction with *Tel Quel* is shown in two interviews conducted with him, the first in 1962, the second in 1964.[100] While the first sees Barthes pointing out the limitations of aestheticism, the second stresses literature as signification, an aspect of Barthes's semiological orientation of the moment. It is underlined that literature is a second-order sign-system, made with language, but different from language in that it does not purport to signify a real, but rather the fact that it is literature.[101] While this refers back to Barthes's earlier *Le Degré zéro de l'écriture*, the semiological emphasis points to further developments; it is after this interview that the relations between Barthes and *Tel Quel* begin to become more mutually beneficial. *Tel Quel* offers to Barthes a suitably mobile site for a continuous mutual friendship and a welcome place of publication, but if Barthes's nausea for hysteria seems contradicted by his interaction with the review, it must also be remembered that there is in Barthes's work a continual tendency towards militancy, a tendency that *Tel Quel* allows him to continue without committing himself. Rather than, as is usual, to stress the idiosyncrasies of the review's influence on Barthes, it is perhaps more illuminating to underline that Barthes sets an example of singularity important for *Tel Quel*. Barthes's interaction with the review soon emerges as a strong support and a parallel articulation of the experience of writing which associates it with the academic context. This articulation takes place in articles in *Critique* and in the seminar at the EPHE.

[100] Barthes, 'La Littérature aujourd'hui', *TQ* 7 and 'Littérature et signification', *TQ* 16 (Winter 1964), both repub. in id., *Essais critiques*.
[101] See Barthes, *Essais critiques*, 263.

The seminar constitutes not only a vital site of exploration but also a meeting-place between the project of *Tel Quel* and of semiology. Sollers's essay on Mallarmé, 'Littérature et totalité' was originally given as an exposé in this seminar in November 1965. It is also through the space of this seminar that Julia Kristeva first encounters Sollers and *Tel Quel*. In 1966 she will introduce Bakhtine into France through this space.[102]

Barthes's work is also influenced in its development by his interaction with the review. The passage 'from the work to the text', away from structure and towards process and play, is traced with sensitivity in Annette Lavers's book *Roland Barthes: Structuralism and After*.[103] It is in evidence in the development of Barthes from the structurally utopian *Éléments de sémiologie* (1964) and *Système de la mode* (1967) to the more ludic and subjectively oriented *S/Z* (1970) and *L'Empire des signes* (1970). It is carried through, meanwhile, by the focus on Sollers's texts, on other writers associated with the review such as Sarduy and Guyotat, and by the force of Kristeva's rereading of semiology. For the purposes of the relations with *Tel Quel*, however, the key text is the 1968, footnoted version of the article 'Drame, poème, roman', originally published in 1965, concerning Sollers's novel *Drame*.

The relation between the first version of the essay and its 1968 annotations illustrates well the move towards a less formalist or structuralist perspective. Barthes recognizes, for example, the limitations of structuralism's anthropological basis: 'poser un horizon anthropologique, c'est fermer la structure, donner, sous le couvert scientifique, un arrêt dernier aux signes'.[104]

Barthes moves towards a less enclosed approach to the text, for which signs are not indices of a structure but disseminated and infinitely dispersed. The activity of the reading of the text, and the way the subjectivity of the reader is engaged by the text, become more important. At the same time, the text appeals to or subverts the codes of ideology, which will be the focus of *S/Z*. While the movement towards ideology is a mark of the politicizing climate of the time, the engagement of the subjective shows a certain reaction against structuralism, which reflects a more general trend in the context. From now on, with Barthes established as an ally of the group, his contributions will occupy this uneasy space between the ideological, demystifying imperative and the engagement of the subjectivity of the critic, and of his singular tastes.

---

[102] See J. Kristeva, 'Mémoire', *L'Infini*, 1 (winter 1983).
[103] Lavers, *Roland Barthes*.
[104] Barthes, 'Drame, poème, roman', in *Théorie d'ensemble*, 27.

Psychoanalysis

The problems of the avant-garde, particularly any association with an exploitation of the erotic, are also displaced through the development of a reference to psychoanalysis in the review. However, this approaches the moment of theory from a quite specific ground. From 1960 to 1966, psychoanalysis had been gaining ground as a privileged reference-point for literary criticism or theory. When Lacan's *Écrits* were published in 1966 there was a veritable explosion of theory around his work, generated also by the seminar and the work of Althusser and his pupils at the ENS. Freudian psychoanalysis of a different orientation was not, however, eclipsed, and in the years leading up to the *Écrits* there was a proliferation of psychoanalytical perspectives, some represented in *Critique*, such as the work of André Green. *Tel Quel* showed itself reluctant at first to take on the Lacanian monument, but increasing references to his work in the mid-decade lead up to the annexing of Lacanian theory to a *théorie d'ensemble* in 1968.[105] The crucial possibility for this synthesis was Lacan's use of the structural linguistics of Jakobson and Saussure, and a focus on the signifier, on language as such, as structure of the unconscious or as the inevitable mediating grid of human symbolic activity. Language seen in its materiality became a definite focus for psychoanalysis, engaging with literature. The proximity of the two enquiries, analysis and literary criticism, leads to intense and fraught relations in the next decade. Initially, however, *Tel Quel* is resistant to the potential psychological implications of psycho-analysis, and its engagement is more with the literature of dreams.

The first couple of years show a marked interest in the non-rational, *le non-savoir* in Bataille's terminology, and it is in this sense that it is of interest for *Tel Quel*. Texts by Bataille, Caillois, Borges, and Michaux bear out this interest and approach. It is not yet informed by a reading of Freud; the main reference is to Foucault's introduction to Bin-swanger's *Rêve et existence*, an existential psychology filtered through a philosophical perspective.[106] This emphasis on the non-rational, which in the texts of Caillois and in some of the novels of the group tends to concentrate exclusively on dreams, is elaborated as a specific interest in the following years.

[105] See 'Division de l'ensemble', in *Théorie d'ensemble*, 8: '[Les noms de] Lacan et d'Althusser seront retrouvés, dans leurs positions de leviers, à l'intérieur des différentes études.'

[106] Cf. Sollers, 'Logique de la fiction', *TQ* 15; Pleynet, 'La Pensée contraire', *TQ* 17: 58, 64.

Baudry's review of 'Investigations psychosomatiques' by Michel de M'Uzan, Pierre Marty, and Christian David of the non-Lacanian SPP focuses on dreams.[107] The theoretical or scientific value of this investigation is not, however, underlined, which leads to the inference that the interest here is less in psychoanalysis than in dreams as a text, suggesting a proximity with Surrealism. The language of dreams is also the subject of Sollers's review of Hervey de Saint-Denys's *Les Rêves et les moyens de les diriger*.[108] Parallels with the Surrealists are again suggested by this emphasis on a non-Freudian, non-scientific, and non-analytic approach to dreams. However, dreams are presented by Sollers as a thought that exceeds rationality, and therefore as a language, and he criticizes the writer for his lack of insight into dreams as a language. Here Sollers at the same time points to future developments and indicates the limitations of the non-analytic approach by proposing that dreams be seen as signs. Sollers's formulation awaits a fertilization, as it were, by a scientific reading of Freud's *The Interpretation of Dreams*, or by a Lacanian theory of the unconscious as 'structured like a language', an encounter that will take place in 1965, when Sollers and Baudry attend the seminar.

The interest in pre-Freudian or non-Freudian psychology is continued with a review of Groddeck's *Le Livre du ça*, while in his review of Marthe Robert's biography of Freud, Thibaudeau also affirmatively recognizes Surrealism's involvement with Freud.[109] A more specifically psychoanalytical interest is indicated with Baudry's review 'Le Rêve de la litterature', a critical review of a 'Choix de rêves' by Jean Paul, the eighteenth-century German writer.[110] The perspective on dreams as treated in literature is informed by the same readings as Sollers's 'Logique de la fiction', as Baudry notes: 'les ordres du subjectif et de l'objectif semblent se dissoudre dans le milieu onirique, s'il est vrai que le rêveur habite et anime les objets qui lui sont proposés'.[111]

The dream world is a milieu of continuity parallel to the text. It is this parallel that characterizes *Tel Quel*'s approach to psychoanalysis, Baudry extending the parallel to describe the dream as an intermediary space, which is theoretically the same as the interior or continuous space of the text. It is a space in which contradiction is not annulled but thought through as a figure of thought crucial to both literature and the

---

[107] J.-L. Baudry, 'Investigations psychosomatiques', *TQ* 18 (summer 1964).
[108] P. Sollers, 'Les Rêves et les moyens de les diriger', ibid.
[109] Id., 'Le Livre du ça', ibid. Jean Thibaudeau, 'Freud', ibid.
[110] J.-L. Baudry, 'Le Rêve de la littérature', ibid.
[111] Ibid. 86.

oneiric world. Baudry's parallel between the text and the dream is a critical nexus for the theory of *Tel Quel*:

Le rêve, la situation du rêveur à l'interiéur de son rêve, fait songer à un livre qui racontait au lecteur, dans l'instant même où il le lit, sa propre lecture et cette lecture serait la vie. En fait, nous vivons nos rêves mais nos rêves nous lisent.[112]

The emphasis on life as a text, to be read, indicates the semiological orientation of the review, but the corresponding emphasis on the *mise en abîme* and on the productivity of reading, as a writing, at the same time prefigures the specific theory of the text of *Tel Quel* as *écriture-lecture* and process. This will be the foundation for the more theoretically framed analogies of *Théorie d'ensemble*.

With Derrida's essay on Freud in 1965 *Tel Quel* annexes a specifically non-Lacanian psychoanalysis. At the same time, however, Lacanian analysis becomes increasingly important as a strategic reference in articles by Sollers, Pleynet, and Baudry, and in articles contributed by Michel Tort and by Hubert Damisch to the special issue on Sade, for example.[113] The references are predominantly affirmative, but at the same time suggest a certain reluctance to apply this theory to the literary text wholesale. A reading of Lacan with relation to literature will not be engaged until much later, suggesting that there is an unresolved tension here behind the strategic support.

In the period in question *Tel Quel* functions to bring together diverse currents: from structuralism, formalism, psychoanalysis, the avant-garde in painting and other arts. These are reviewed in a spirit of analysis which focuses on the formal level of the creative practice and the production of sense. The disparate elements do not, however, form a coherent theory in the precise sense of the term; the elaboration of a theory specific to the review is more present in the articles of Sollers on a series of texts, identified as the limits of literature. These texts are collected in the book *Logiques*, published in 1968.

LOGICS OF THE LIMIT

It is largely due to the efforts of Sollers and *Tel Quel* that writers such as Artaud, Bataille, Sade, and Lautréamont have become the focus of theoretical and textually oriented criticism. Sollers's work, part of an

---

[112] J.-L. Baudry, 'Le Rêve de la littérature' 87.
[113] 'La Pensée de Sade', *TQ* 28 (winter 1967). See below.

ongoing critical and literary project that continues with *L'Infini*, defines the specificity of *Tel Quel*'s theory of literature. It does not, however, operate in a vacuum. It is closely connected to the work of Marcelin Pleynet and other members of the group, and later to the work of Kristeva particularly. It is also very much part of the context of the review and more generally of the growing interest in the margins of literature and culture that had been prefigured in the work of Bataille, Blanchot, Barthes, and Foucault, whose *Histoire de la folie* (1961) emphasizes the idea of the margin as an index of what has been excluded or repressed. The gesture these and Sollers's enquiries follow is to reassess culture from the perspective of the limit, whence the appellation the 'limit text'.

The Experience of Writing

The experience of writing that is celebrated and analysed in Sollers's book *Logiques*, in *Tel Quel* generally throughout its career, and since then in *L'Infini*, is fundamentally the same; it defines the continuity of the thirty-four-year existence of *Tel Quel* and *L'Infini*. It is fundamentally a sacrificial view of literature, such that the author is sacrificed to the writing; this is the sense in which Barthes's 'death of the author' is relevant. Writing involves an experience of alienation and subjective death, and this experience, through a kind of transference, is also that of the reading process. This is explicitly visible in the texts Sollers identifies initially as the limits of literature.

Artaud writes in his letters to Jacques Rivière: 'Je souffre d'une effroyable maladie de l'esprit. Ma pensée m'abandonne à tous les degrés.'[114] Sollers interprets this alienation from thought as the figure of a double, or a duality, between thought and language, in which it is the body that is fundamentally at stake: 'Ce qu'il décrit, ce qu'il crie, c'est justement l'absence de corps que devrait être cette pensée, sa déperdition, et la torture qu'elle lui fait subir.'[115]

For Sollers, Artaud lives and writes the bodily experience of alienation which derives from the insight that language speaks through and across, without the body.

Dante tranfers the sacrifice in question vicariously to Beatrice. Sollers writes: 'la mort de Béatrice est la clef du langage de Dante, car bien

---

[114] A. Artaud, *Œuvres complètes*, (Paris, 1970), 50.
[115] P. Sollers, 'La Pensée émet des signes', *TQ* 20 (winter 1965), also in id., *Logiques*, 135.

plus que la mort d'un autre, elle est la seule façon qu'il a de vivre la sienne et de la parler'.[116]

Dante then finds himself lost in the middle of life's passage ('Nel mezzo cammin di nostra vita'[117]) to then traverse its underworld and its after-life in the Divine Comedy. Mallarmé would echo Dante's loss in his phrase: 'La destruction fut ma Béatrice.'[118] More explicitly, he would write: 'Je viens de passer une année effrayante. Ma pensée s'est pensée, et est arrivée à une Conception pure ... mais, heureusement, je suis parfaitement mort.'[119] The realization involved is that 'la pensée', manifested in language, has its own rules and intentions, 'que la raison ne connait pas'. Thought is a current that the subject is situated within, not outside as its author. The links with 'Logique de la fiction', which begins *Logiques*, are evident. The autonomy of thought and language, the sacrifice of identity and of the body to this current, is the first stage of the experience Sollers is concerned with, and which he, as a writer, is implicated in.

The writer does not, because of this sacrifice, fall into silence. Writing traverses thought, doubling it, attempting to run with it, to contest it. In some cases this leads to psychosis, as in the cases of Hölderlin and Artaud. Artaud's apparently psychotic multiple personalities, Hölderlin's signing under obscure names, are signs of the occupation of the writing by the memory of language, by other voices. Lautréamont's list of 'Grandes têtes molles' in the *Poésies* put this in a more logical frame. Dante's traversal of the *Inferno*, *Purgatorio*, and *Paradiso* is read by Sollers as a traversal of the strata of language, which he calls an 'archéographie'.[120] In some senses this project mirrors Foucault's attempt to write an 'archaeology of the human sciences', to traverse the system of discourses, but the epistemological basis is different.

There is, still, a subjectivity of the writer. Subjectivity, being sacrificed, is reinvented in the writing. In one sense it is multiple and fragmented; Proust's *A la recherche du temps perdu* is a paradigmatic text in this respect. The experience of fragmentation in writing that is so evident in the poetry of Pleynet and—a major influence—Hölderlin, is an experience of the multiple subjectivities language affords. Not only every punctual incidence of *je* but also its structural opposites, *tu* and *il*

[116] Id., 'Dante et la traversée de l'écriture', *TQ* 23 (autumn 1965) and id., *Logiques*, 59.
[117] Dante, *La Divine Comédie i: L'enfer*, trans. J. Risset (5 vols.; Paris, 1992), 24.
[118] Cf. Sollers, *Logiques*, 98.
[119] S. Mallarmé, *Correspondance de Mallarmé*, 1862–1871 (Paris, 1959), 240.
[120] Sollers, *Logiques*, 66.

or *elle*. Rimbaud's dictum 'Je est un Autre' could be reformulated 'Je est Autres' to represent this experience of subjective fragmentation. It is an awareness that the individual voice is populated by infinite voices. In literature this is an awareness of the porousness of the writing with regard to literary history. Hence the importance of the notion of intertextuality. It is an 'anxiety of influence'[121] which recognizes the voices of multiple ghosts emanating from a past to which the subject has no immediate, authorial access.

The experience is of the sacrifice of identity, authorship, the body, and of becoming in the writing, becoming through the writing. It is essentially an existentialist ethic of becoming with which Sollers is concerned. In 'Le Roman et l'expérience des limites' he had presented the question in these terms: either we live according to some external representation, which we might postulate as nature or humanity, or we live according to the signs produced by thought.[122] Literature is a privileged experience of this productivity; the writer experiences his thought to an often life-threatening degree. Thought produces signs, moreover. Sollers's essay on Artaud misquotes Mallarmé in its title: 'La Pensée émet des signes'. The limit is approached and traversed when the writer attempts not to repress or to block this emission, but to swim with its current and to allow the current to determine life. Or, since this determination implies a fairly radical position, it is perhaps more often a question of a conflict between the' phenomenal, societal aspects of the writer's experience, and the experience of language or thought as autonomous and infinite, transgressive, with regard to this level. Biography is far from irrelevant. The writer's life is indicative of how the experience is lived. At moments this life enters into conflict with the social, at its limit points of madness (Artaud, Roussel) and of eroticism and violence (Sade, Bataille). It is also reappropriated within a view of literature as decoration or representation, or as poetry (Dante), or it may be dismissed as obscurantist (Mallarmé and Lautréamont). The limits of literature with which Sollers is concerned are determined by the conflict between an experience of writing and social discourse.

---

[121] See H. Bloom, *The Anxiety of Influence* (New York, 1973). Bloom's perspective is, however, more linked to intersubjectivity, to an inter-psychological notion of influence, than to intertextuality.

[122] Sollers, *Logiques*, 234.

Why Theory?

Sollers's essays in *Logiques* are largely executed without reference to the apparatus of criticism around the works in question. This is often due simply to the lack of such an apparatus, for example, in the cases of Lautréamont, Artaud, and Bataille. Obviously the two major precursors, here, and for Sade and Mallarmé, are the Surrealists and Blanchot. These other discourses are recognized, dismissed briefly, but not confronted, leaving serious aporias in Sollers's work in terms of its situation in the history of criticism.[123] In the case of Dante, for example, Sollers's interpretation is so far removed from the normal scholarship that it does not enter the frame at all, although Sollers's essay was accompanied by essays by Schelling, Vico, and a Dante scholar with a semiological approach.[124]

In fact, these are essentially close readings of texts, elaborating a theory of literature through identification of a common, but singular, experience. In elaborating this theory, however, Sollers does make various appeals and references to theoretical apparatuses, which link his readings to the theoretical expansions of the time. The historical figures Sollers refers to are Nietzsche, Marx, and Freud, their contemporary interpreters Barthes, Lacan, Derrida, Althusser. After 1967 Kristeva would join this illustrious company.

Some of Sollers's essays are very much linked to this developing context of theory, as this context is carried by the development of the review *Tel Quel* itself and since some of these figures publish work in *Tel Quel*. Derrida's essay on Artaud in *L'Écriture et la différence* accompanied that of Sollers in a special issue on Artaud, including a piece by Artaud's emissary Paule Thévenin.[125] Barthes's essay on Sade, 'L'Arbre du crime' was part of the 1967 special issue on Sade which also appealed to an older generation with a text by Pierre Klossowski and to a contemporary psychoanalytical and philosophical context with the articles by Michel Tort and Hubert Damisch.[126] Sollers's essay on Mallarmé was given as a seminar paper at Barthes's course at the École pratique. The

[123] cf. Sollers, *Logiques*. 250–1.

[124] See *TQ* 23 (autumn 1965), including: F. W. J. von Schelling, 'Dante dans la perspective philosophique'; P. Sollers, 'Dante et la traversée de l'écriture'; E. Sanguineti, 'Inf. VIII'; Bernard Stambler, 'Trois rêves'; G. Vico, 'Dante et la nature de la vraie poésie'.

[125] P. Thévenin. 'Antonin Artaud dans la vie', *TQ* 20 (winter 1965).

[126] See *TQ* 28 (winter 1967), 'La Pensée de Sade', including: P. Klossowski, 'Sade ou le philosophe scélérat'; R. Barthes, 'L'Arbre du crime'; P. Sollers, 'Sade dans le texte'; H. Damisch, 'L'Écriture sans mesures'; M. Tort, 'L'Effet Sade'.

Lautréamont essay was published in *Critique*,[127] while the essay on Bataille, 'Le Toit', was refused for the special issue of *L'Arc* on Bataille.[128] Sollers's essays appear in places that tie them into the context of *Tel Quel* and other currents.

They link the experience of the writing at the limit to the theoretical systems in development, through the use of terms and the vocabulary of linguistics-oriented criticism. Derrida's *écriture* has obvious links to the *pensée qui émet des signes* Sollers identifies in Artaud, and the concordance between the two approaches is evident in the Artaud issue. Barthes's vision of writing as an intransitive verb is again very close to the recognition of writing's autonomy, leading to the phrase perhaps emblematic of *Tel Quel*'s perspective at this stage: *ça s'écrit*.[129] As concerns the relation to structuralist criticism and linguistics, Sollers tends to use the terminology of signifier/signified and *énoncé/énonciation* in order to supersede it, since it is too static and binary to correlate with the transformative movement of writing Sollers is concerned with.[130] This leads to a complex terminology and a neologizing tendency which gives the writing an over-complex appearance. The terms more often than not are justified by a common sense of traversal. The terms *translinguistique, transfini* suggest the way the writer experiences or is subjected to the past, biographical, historical, or literary, then reads it, interprets it, and adds him- or herself to it at its limit.[131] Other terms relate to a thematics of negation and contradiction: *désénonciation, négativité, oui-non, contrascription* (all in the Lautréamont essay which is the most theoretically complex) suggest how literature comes into being as a negation, written across and against its pretexts.[132]

The neologizing tendency and its explanation here beg the question: why theory? This is especially pertinent since Sollers's later writing is far less theoretically complex, written in a more popular, less abstruse French. It is, though, fairly difficult to understand, implying that the subject in question is by its nature complex, or that it resists common sense. The appeal to theory may be due to the climate of the moment, which favoured proliferating theoretical systems to such a degree that the terms themselves were never fixed, becoming, in Lacan's

---

[127] P. Sollers, 'La Science de Lautréamont', *Crit.* 245 (Oct. 1967). Also in id., *Logiques*.
[128] See Sollers, *Logiques*, 164. It was eventually pub. in *TQ* 29 (spring 1967) and *Logiques*.
[129] See Sollers, *Logiques*, 98.
[130] Ibid. 254.
[131] Ibid. 258.
[132] Ibid. 254, 286, 291.

terminology, 'floating signifiers'. The floating signifiers of theory were fixed and unfixed at every incidence of their use, and quite often would be relevant only for the short time of their eventuality in an article or a book. Theory provides analogical models that enable links between disparate areas such as literature, political economy, and psychic economy, leading to the broad syntheses of *Théorie d'ensemble* and later, but tends to inject into discourse an exuberance and proliferation of conceptual innovation which subverts its own fixity and structure.

The terrorism of theory is due partly to its flotation, but this terror can easily be remedied by more detailed reading. There is perhaps a more fundamental terrorism, as in order to think the space with which Sollers is concerned, a radical leap over the limit has to be made. It is necessary to be able to see the space of discourse, social discourse, from a point at its limit. This point or limit is the space of literature and of its theory. Being outside social discourse and presenting a reinterpretation of it, theory is paranoiac. Theory as paranoia returns on the reader as terror, first, because it requires a leap outside the security of social identity and myth, secondly, because it proposes phenomena as essentially false. This last factor links theory in this case to a certain religious view of the world, and to a politics which appears as revolutionary. These aspects will become increasingly relevant in the course of *Tel Quel*'s history.

So the theory of what is in fact an experience present in literature enables syntheses with politics and psychoanalysis. This makes possible the articulation of the experience of writing with social discourse seen as spectacle and the economy of the subject. The theoretical front, across literature, politics, and psychoanalysis, will be the climactic adventure of theory of *Tel Quel*. Both the political and psychoanalytical encounters will fail, while the experience of literature will remain constant, later to be linked to the sacred.

Logic, Mathematics, Chinese Thought

The complexity and often the impenetrability of Sollers's writing in *Logiques*, which tends also to determine that produced by other writers in the review[133] is in some part conditioned by the reorganization of logic that is proposed. Essentially, Sollers is suggesting that literature

[133] Such as J.-L. Baudry, and later J.-L. Houdebine and G. Scarpetta. Not in the sense that they are repeating Sollers's voice, but in the sense that they are informed by the same theoretical references.

transforms the basis of thought and knowledge. The literary text, its creation and its apprehension, is a transformation at these most basic levels. While there is a certain continuity between the different texts analysed, such that there is a consistent logic of literature, each text proposes a different reordering of its universe, hence the title *Logiques*.

Logique in this sense has different connotations from the word *logic* in English, which in philosophy is associated with the analytic approach of, for example, Russell and Wittgenstein. Despite the apparent difference, however, Sollers does propose alternative conceptions of, for example, negation and contradiction. This reordering of conceptual logic was very much part of the atmosphere of the time. Lacan, in his seminars, was moving towards the complex and some would say irresponsible theory of knots, Möbius strips, and interconnected loops that proliferated in the baroque style of his work in the 1970s. He had already proposed a number of diagrammatic representations of the unconscious and its structures in the articles in *Écrits*.[134] They were collected by J.-A. Miller of the *Cahiers pour l'analyse* group, in whose periodical appeared a number of articles bearing on logic, by Quine, the mathematicians Boole and Cantor, and on Wittgenstein.[135] Julia Kristeva, having arrived in 1965 from Bulgaria, produced work of an almost oppressive complexity, referring to mathemetics and logic and structuring her articles numerically, as Wittgenstein's *Tractatus*.[136] The logical imperative is very much part of the climate. The title *Théorie d'ensemble* was an explicit echoing of a work of the group of mathematicians who published under the name Bourbaki, writing in France at this time.[137]

In *Tel Quel*, however, the references to mathematics, to the set theory of Cantor, for example,[138] function perhaps more radically, since they are in a space where literature is the focus. The reference to this 'other scene' appears as a terroristic affront to the sentimental or romantic approach to literature and its mystery. The suggestion was that the mystery of literature could and should be open to analyses of the most radical and formalizable nature.

---

[134] See J. Lacan, *Écrits*, ii (Paris, 1971), 176.
[135] See *Cahiers pour l'analyse*, 1–10 (Paris, 1966–9).
[136] See e.g. J. Kristeva, 'Pour une sémiologie des paragrammes', *TQ* 29 (spring 1967).
[137] Nicolas Bourbaki, *Éléments de mathématique: Théorie des ensembles* (Paris, 1968).
[138] See e.g. P. Sollers, 'Réponses à la nouvelle critique', in *Théorie d'ensemble*, 389: 'Lautréamont, Mallarmé et Cantor, par exemple, sont réellement contemporains.' See J.-L. Houdebine, 'L'Expérience de Cantor', *L'Infini*, 4 (autumn 1983).

It is not perhaps desirable or necessary in a book of this sort to go into the complexities of the references to logic and mathematics that Kristeva and Sollers effect. Their function and character can, however, be suggested. In Sollers's case the essay on Lautréamont is the most complex in this context, coming after and referring to Kristeva's 'Pour une sémiologie des paragrammes'.[139] The points Sollers summarizes from her article can serve as a useful suggestion of the essential aspects of the transformation of logic in question.

First, 'le fait de décrire le mécanisme des *jonctions dans une infinité perpétuelle*'[140] (Sollers's emphasis) refers to the permutative, combinatorial movement of language, which is potentially infinite. If language is thought as infinite, capable of 'saying everything' ('tout dire'[141]), then literature can be seen as the realization of this potential. It opens closed structures, such as that of communication, to an infinite process of the engenderment of meaning. This opening to *l'infini* is from a point or limit referred to as 'transfinite'.[142]

Secondly, Sollers refers to 'la nécessité de penser la contradiction et la négation selon une autre logique'.[143] Here Kristeva had proposed that contradiction is logically possible and significant in the literary text. Ducasse's generation of contradictions in the *Poésies*, for example, points to an intertextual parodic envelopment of apparent contradictions, good and evil, for example, in the 'higher' system of a new text. Negation is determinative, that is, it is not a denial or a repression.[144] On the same subject Pleynet refers in his book on Lautréamont to the linguist Benveniste's statement that linguistic negation has to enounce what it negates to begin with, so that the text itself is a contradictory site of negativity.[145] Kristeva sees literary texts as fundamentally negative in their relation to language, literary history, society. But as well as a destruction, this is at the same time a creation. In this sense negativity is a creative movement. Contradiction and negation are in fact, for Sollers, Kristeva, and Pleynet, the two basic elements of the philosophy of Marxism, as well as its materialism. The investigation of the philosophy of Marxism will focus on these elements (see Chapter 3), so that as well as proposing a logic at odds with that of rationality, in which

[139] Kristeva, 'Pour une sémiologie des paragrammes', *TQ* 29.
[140] Sollers, *Logiques*, 255.
[141] See Damisch, 'L'Écriture sans mesures', *TQ* 28 (winter 1967), 54.
[142] Sollers, *Logiques*, 258.
[143] Ibid. 255.
[144] Cf. Kristeva, 'Pour une sémiologie des paragrammes', *Tel Quel*, 29, 63.
[145] M. Pleynet, *Lautréamont* (Paris, 1967), 135–6.

the law of non-contradiction holds (Yes is the opposite of No, while Sollers refers to the *oui-non* of literature[146]) this aspect hinges into the dense philosophical arguments around dialectical materialism.

The third of the logical transformations Sollers footnotes is 'la mise en connection de la pensée mathématique et du *texte*'[147] (Sollers's emphasis). This proposes simply to look at the text as a relation of signifiers, that is, without reference to a pre-given meaning, at its formal relations and its productivity. Mathematical relations, as Derrida had remarked, do not refer to a signified and have no referent, as mathematical notation is an arbitrary and hieroglyphic system.[148] Looking at writing in this way allows a liberation from interpretation and a focus on the process by which meaning is generated.

Fourthly, the text is a 'zero path' (*voie zéro*).[149] This suggests that it is self-destructive. To see the text as essentially negative is to see it as a *dépense*, not producing meanings that can be exchanged in an economy of value. It also suggests the status of the subject involved in literature, as non-subject, or a subject of sacrifice.

The references to logic and mathematics are an 'other scene' or another rationality. Literature, at its limits, proposes, according to this theory, a different rationality from that upon which the system of knowledge of the Western world is based. This itself gives an impetus to another powerful strain in Sollers's, Kristeva's, and *Tel Quel*'s theoretical writing in general, which is the reference to non-Western philosophies or traditions. The references are predominantly to Chinese thought, although Indian philosophy also comes into question.[150] This gives *Tel Quel* an effect of radicality and strangeness; it is also at the same time innovative and related to a tradition in literature. It is innovative in its explicit and serious relation to historical scholarship on this subject, particularly the work of Marcel Granet[151] and Joseph Needham[152] and Maspero's *Le Taoisme*.[153] It follows a certain tradition of literary interest in Chinese life and thought, on the part of Ezra Pound,

---

[146] Sollers, *Logiques*, 286.
[147] Ibid. 255.
[148] J. Derrida, *De la grammatologie* (Paris, 1967), 12.
[149] Sollers, *Logiques*, 255.
[150] See id., 'Survol/Rapports(Blocs)/Conflit', *TQ* 36, ref. to the Indian scholar Louis Renou; id., 'La Science de Lautréamont' in *Logiques*, refs. to Benveniste's work on Sanskrit; id., *Sur le matérialisme* (Paris, 1974), ref. to Indian atomist philosophy.
[151] M. Granet, *La Pensée chinoise* (Paris, 1934) and *La Civilisation chinoise* (Paris, 1929).
[152] J. Needham, *Science and Civilisation in China* (6 vols.; Cambridge, 1954–86)
[153] H. Maspero, *Le Taoisme* (Paris, 1950).

Paul Claudel, and André Malraux, for example. The first two writers are, however, criticized as idealist in their relation to China.[154] More respect is given to Artaud and Bataille, who both made reference to oriental philosophy and religion. In his essay on Bataille, for example, Sollers refers to Chinese Taoism as a religion which, in contrast to Christianity, has a productive relation with science.[155]

It is in the essay on Lautréamont by Sollers, where it appears there is a definite shift in theoretical complexity, that the references to Chinese philosophy are most abundant, at this stage. Sollers refers, through Needham, to Tshai Chen, to justify the notion of 'une pensée numérologique'.[156] The idea is that a thought of permutation, or of language as a permutation of signifiers, opens reality to knowledge. Language in its materiality is a privileged access to the real. Sollers quotes the phrase: 'Si on connait les commencements, alors on connait les fins.'[157] This is an anti-Platonic philosophy which sees language as infinite and material. The phrase itself will later be used by Pleynet as a structural motif in *Stanze*.[158] This numerological thought is also at the basis of Sollers's novel *Nombres*, published simultaneously with *Logiques*, which contains many unattributed *prélèvements* (samples) from Chinese writings, as well as Chinese ideograms. Its structure is loosely based on numerological thought as presented in Granet's *La Pensée chinoise*.

Other references to Granet and Needham in the essay on Lautréamont are the first instances of an interest that accelerates up to the Maoist shift of 1971 and the issue on 'La Pensée chinoise' of 1972.[159] In this area *Tel Quel* functions innovatively to bring a whole area of knowledge into theoretical prominence. It is the philosophical and aesthetic aspects of the Chinese question that are of interest, more than the political. The desire to see both welded together is what fuels the Maoist persuasion of the review.

Mathematics and Chinese thought are the 'other scenes' which are introduced into theory in Sollers's *Logiques*, particularly in the essay on Lautréamont and via Kristeva. The terroristic aspects of this theoretical otherness are to be weighed against the innovation and contribution to a thinking of literature they afford. Sollers's writing is often terroristic

---

[154] See Sollers, 'Survol/Rapports', *Tel Quel*, 36. 14, and later: 'Pourquoi j'ai été chinois', *TQ* 88 (summer 1981), and in id., *Improvisations* (Paris, 1991), 77.

[155] Id., *Logiques*, 190.

[156] Ibid. 266.

[157] Ibid.

[158] See M. Pleynet, *Stanze* (Paris, 1973), 155–6.

[159] See *TQ* 48–9, 'La Pensée chinoise' (Spring 1972).

or provocative at least, and deliberately so, but at the same time it offers a *savoir* which it is difficult to ignore or to dismiss.

The Body

The experience of writing alienates, fragments, and finally annihilates the body. Artaud is a very evident paradigm of this corporeal alienation and sacrifice. Derrida's article, 'La Parole soufflée' emphasizes the writer's feeling of his spirit having been eroded, 'soufflée' by some other, anterior presence, identified or projected as divine.[160] In the essay on Bataille, Sollers outlines a vision of an 'écriture corporelle' which would be tied not to the whole body, the personal body, but to its contours, orifices, and organs. If the body is sacrificed to writing, the syntax of the body comes into play: the rhythm of pulsions across and through organs and the ingestion and expulsion, or *dépenses*, through the body's holes. The body in writing is therefore a fragmented body; since identity is in question, the whole body is not a unifying principle. Its economy becomes more important. In the writers concerned, there is a denigration or a removal of any principle of corporeal unification, or capitalization, such as the head or the phallus. This decapitation or castration is figured in Sollers's novel *Nombres*, to enable the play of the writing across the organic body. The writings of Sade and Bataille are evidently resonant with this perspective. This also implies that the psychoanalytical framework of the Oedipus complex, based on the fear of castration and the centrality of the phallus, becomes less relevant to literature, or to this writing that approaches the limit, than the pre-Oedipal, anal and oral stages described by Freud. The relevance of psychoanalysis for *Tel Quel* will lie in these pre-symbolic areas and their interaction with the symbolic, which Kristeva's psychoanalytical work will investigate. Derrida's article on Artaud suggests but does not follow up this line, mentioning the work of Melanie Klein, of whose work Derrida's wife was the translator. Sollers's article on Guyotat's novel *Éden, Éden, Éden*, 'La Matière et sa phrase', presents a complex analysis of the relation of writing to these oral and anal pulsions in the pre-Oedipal phase.[161]

The body in writing is a body inhabited by language and by its economy; this is the opposite of a view which would hold that the body

---

[160] J. Derrida, 'La Parole soufflée', in id., *L'Écriture et la différence*, 262: 'Soufflée: entendons du même coup *inspirée* depuis une *autre* voix, lisant elle-même un texte plus vieux que le poème de mon corps, que le théâtre de mon geste.'

[161] Sollers, 'La Matière et sa phrase', *Crit.* 290 (June 1971).

is expressed in writing, for example, that there could be a gendered writing which would reflect or express the feminine body. Instead, the body is sacrificed in the writing process. It becomes a *chair* rather than a *corps*, entirely subjected to the writing, and reinvented, as an organic body of pulsions, in the writing.[162] The process is captured by the phrase, which Sollers will quote and focus on in his later work: 'Au commencement était le Verbe, et le verbe s'est fait chair'.[163] Essentially, it is a question of a sacrifice of the body and its occupation by language, or its incarnation (see Chapter 5).

The experience of writing, as it implicates the body, also implicates sexuality. A discourse on sexuality is a major aspect of *Tel Quel*'s contribution to the thought of the post-war period. The subject emerges as a focus mainly in the essays on Sade and Bataille by Sollers, but also in the special issue on Sade and in a more fragmented way throughout the theoretical activity of the review, for example in the work of J.-J. Goux and J.-L. Baudry.[164] It is also present in the fiction, particularly in the work of Guyotat. In the late 1970s, sexuality emerges as a subject of fundamental importance, particularly in so far as it relates to the experience of the writer: Joyce, Sade, or Guyotat, for example, and in so far as it is studied by psychoanalysis. Sexuality, literary sexuality, one might say, becomes the contested ground in a debate between psycho-analytic theory and *Tel Quel*. Sollers in particular will address this question, and in his later novels push this interest still further. It is not, however, an interest in the erotic for its own sake, since the perspective adopted is analytic. The elaboration of a *savoir* on *jouissance* is, however, proposed by Sollers to be a far more problematic discourse than any kind of perversity in relation to a stable norm.[165] The kitsch eroticism that was in vogue in the 1960s, through such publishers as Pauvert and Eric Losfeld, and such writers as Klossowski or Pieyre de Mandiargues, is precisely avoided by *Tel Quel* through the emphasis on *le savoir* and through reference to psychoanalysis. The permissive climate of the 1960s is probably illusory, given the censure of Guyotat's novel *Eden, Éden, Éden,* (see Chapter 3). At the same time, the valorization of sexuality as natural or as free is implicitly criticized through *Tel Quel*'s

[162] Cf. id., *Logiques*, 179–80.

[163] See id., 'Le Sexe des anges', *TQ* 75 (spring 1978).

[164] J.-L. Baudry, 'Le Texte de Rimbaud', *TQ* 35–6 (autumn 1968–winter 1969), and 'Pour une matériologie', *TQ* 44–5 (winter 1971–spring 1971); J.-J. Goux, 'Numismatiques', *TQ* 35–6 (autumn 1968–winter 1969).

[165] See P. Sollers, 'Je sais pourquoi je jouis', *TQ* 90 (winter 1981), id., and in *Théorie des exceptions* (Paris, 1986).

approach to it as a profoundly cultural phenomenon, with an emphasis on the perverse and obscene countering society's supposed neurosis over the question.

A major emphasis of *Tel Quel*'s enquiry is the relation of sex to writing, and Sade is the principal focus. The special issue 'La Pensée de Sade' underlines precisely the analytic approach and appears as the first instance of such a perspective on *le divin marquis*.[166] The essays all underline the textual nature of Sade's transgressions, suggesting that the experience of writing alters the experience of sexuality, and that it is this written sexuality that is of most interest. Barthes, for example, distinguishes Sade's writing from modern eroticism, which functions allusively, through metaphor and suggestion. In Sade the sexual is permutative, functioning as a *combinatoire*, logically articulated.[167] Sadean sexuality is obscene, consequently, as it is subjected to the combinatory logic of language. Both Pierre Klossowski and Michel Tort see Sade's novels as subversive through this repetitive structure, a subversion of the code, functioning metonymically as opposed to allusively. Barthes had recognized the subversive and radical potential of language as permutation, predominantly metonymic, in an earlier essay on Bataille's *Histoire de l'œil*, which must be one of the most scandalous modern texts dealing with sexuality, precisely through its rigorous subjection of human desire to the arbitrary play of signifiers, a 'développement de signes', as Bataille writes, cited by Sollers.[168]

Consequently, to read Sade mimetically, as representation, rather than textually, is to misread.[169] The censure of Sade depends on this misreading, both Barthes and Sollers affirm.[170] So that Sade is a crucial text tying together a certain view of sexuality on the part of a neurotic culture, and a view of literature as representation. Sade is a hinge, for *Tel Quel*, between a critical approach to literature and a critique of culture as neurotic.

The reasons why Sade performs this function are perhaps due to the ambiguous status of sexuality, between nature and culture. The demystification of the natural, prefigured in Barthes and in Marxism, is taken by *Tel Quel* into the areas of sexuality and writing. The conclusion: that

---

[166] The focus on Sade of the previous decade, e.g. in de Beauvoir's *Faut-il brûler Sade* (Paris, 1951) and the Pauvert trial of 1958 is more explicitly moral. See Pauvert (ed.), *L'Affaire Sade* (Paris, 1958).

[167] Barthes, 'L'Arbre du crime', *TQ* 28, 30.

[168] Sollers, *Logiques*, 183.

[169] Ibid. 37.

[170] Ibid. 79.

there is no natural sexuality, or that, in Sollers's words, 'la nature est un phantasme de la culture',[171] is the scandalous lesson Sade's texts teach. Sexuality as cultural, moreover, is opened to the play of language; it becomes perverse. Perversity is revalorized as polymorphous and transgressive, potentially liberating.

One could object: if sexuality is already cultural, where does desire come from? Desire has been a specific focus of the debates on sexuality largely informed, as if secretly, by *Tel Quel*'s explorations. *Écriture féminine* has focused on this question. What is the relation of writing to desire, given that sexuality is written? *Tel Quel*'s response ambiguously seems to open up a new area of debate which brings into the enquiry the question of the death drive, which has again fuelled a large amount of critical enquiry.

Given that by now *Tel Quel*'s textual theorizations are informed by the Derridean notion of an original writing or *archi-écriture* (complicating the idea of origin itself), desire is proposed as a writing the differential structure of which precludes any notion of an original libidinal substance. Desire is 'ce qui se trouve écrit en moi'.[172] The notion of cause is undermined and desire becomes 'l'effet sans cause'.[173] Sexuality and text become inextricably bound as an *écriture* which society attempts to canalize and repress by positing a cause. But sexuality is proposed still as posterior to culture, in so far as it is linguistic: 'Le refoulement sexuel est d'abord un refoulement du langage.'[174] However, where a causal process is introduced is in the idea that writing and sexuality are a detour, a deferral. The question is posed: a detour from what? a deferral induced by what? The death drive, the tendency to return to inanimacy, is brought into play as the energetic but negative force which desire and writing must delay and defer. Kristeva's psychoanalytic work and the whole debate around negativity derive from this recognition.

The link between sexuality and death is, however, not original, being the basic premise of Bataille's work *L'Érotisme*. This makes Bataille of fundamental interest, specifically in coming after Sade, both in terms of his readings of Sade and in terms of the chronology of *Tel Quel* and Sollers's readings of 'limit texts'. The erotic, for Bataille, we can recall, is 'the affirmation of life to the point of death'.[175] The linking of sexuality

[171] Sollers, *Logiques*, 80.
[172] Ibid. 81.
[173] Ibid. 79.
[174] Ibid. 81.
[175] G. Bataille, *L'Érotisme* in *Œuvres complètes*, (Paris, 1987), 17.

to mortality short-circuits the cultural detour away from the death drive and, in literature, produces violence and subversion. The association of sexual pleasure with death and horror ruptures the screen of representation language is normally seen as, to produce an infinite *développement de signes*, which can be recognized textually, in Sade, Bataille, Sollers, and Guyotat. The erotic for *Tel Quel* is far different from the allusive or phantasmic eroticism celebrated in culture. It is scandalous in its analytic, permutative structure and in its link to death. *L'Infini* continues to promote such a scandalous view of sexuality, suggesting that the debate on the question is as alive today as thirty years ago.[176]

Neurotic Culture/Perverse Theory

Sollers's *Logiques*, as well as the elaboration of a literary theory and a project, is a cultural critique. The commentaries on the texts are related to the society which has misread or repressed these texts. The theory produces a theoretical project linked to a social and cultural criticism that, since it attacks the basis of social and cultural organization, can be termed revolutionary. That this critique, in the later essays and in the text 'Programme', which opens the book but which was written after most of the essays, invests in Marxism, and then in Maoism, might be seen as an effective strategic gesture of the moment, but also as essentially a diversion, since the critique is from the point of view of literature. It is fundamentally a transformative vision of society enounced from the point of view of the exception of the writer. That this focus does not emerge specifically until later does not detract from the consistency of *Logiques* with the later work. In fact, Sollers was to link the titles of his two main theoretical works in 1968, stating that *Logiques* was 'un appareil, une sorte de machine de lecture destinée à mettre en place, historiquement, une *théorie des exceptions*.'[177]

While in 'Logique de la fiction' and 'Le Roman et l'expérience des limites'[178] the critique was directed more specifically at the ideology of literature as representation, the essays on Sade, Artaud, Bataille, Mallarmé, and Lautréamont all introduce an articulation with a critique of culture, taken here to refer to the symbolic organization of the social—the social itself.

---

[176] See *L'Infini*, 15 (summer 1986).
[177] P. Sollers, 'Écriture et révolution', in *Théorie d'ensemble*, 70.
[178] Id., 'Le Roman et l'expérience des limites', *TQ* 25 (spring 1966).

Mallarmé's critique of literature is related by Sollers to a critique of the economy of circulation: 'les phénomènes sont ramenés à leurs chiffres et aux cycles qui éclairent leur réciprocité',[179] which literature both comprehends and transgresses. *Tel Quel*'s Marxism, and to an extent its psychoanalytical interests, are determined by this economic consideration, which will generate much theoretical enquiry. In the essay on Artaud the critique is directed more specifically against the fundamental dualism of social discourse: 'Pensée sans corps; corps privés de pensée.'[180] But the most radical propositions are in the essays on Sade and Bataille. The first concerns the notion of cause, the second the notion of discontinuity.

For Sollers, society is neurotic in its repression of its foundation.[181] Society projects as natural the cultural objects it invents in order to channel or repress desire, or desire as a writing. The cultural becomes natural in a movement Sollers, following Barthes, calls 'hypostatic'.[182] Religion is, of course, the most apparent form of this instituted neurosis, but behind this is the notion of cause, of the cause. Society is neurotic in its postulation of a cause, which in psychoanalytic theory would appear as a symptom, which is taken as divine when it is founded in language:

Que le monde se résorbe finalement en discours, que la nature soit ainsi montrée comme étant depuis toujours la création la plus irréductible de la culture, qu'il soit donc possible d'affirmer (un moment) calmement: la nature est un fantasme de la culture—voilà—sans doute—l'intolérable lui-même.[183]

Freud noted that the perversions were the negative of the neuroses. Sade's cataloguing of perversions is in fact widened by Sollers to take in both literature and theory. Perversion can include neurosis; it is not a reversible polarity. Given that theory comprehends and analyses society as neurosis, and this is the stance of *Tel Quel* in general: 'La perversion, c'est la pensée théorique elle-même.'[184] Given that Freud identifies in infantile sexuality a polymorphous perversity which normat-

---

[179] Id., *Logiques*, 113.
[180] Ibid. 133.
[181] This view, fundamentally the same as that of Freud, is also pertinent in the work of René Girard (*Des choses cachées depuis la fondation du monde*, (Paris, 1978)), which will be celebrated in *Tel Quel* in the late 1970s.
[182] Sollers, *Logiques*, 80.
[183] Ibid.
[184] Ibid. 82.

ive, phallic sexuality derives from, the perversions seem to be the ground on which neuroses exist. Perversion is also linked, in Sade, to permutation and combination, and thus to the fictional operations of *Tel Quel*. Writing as permutation becomes the equivalent of a generalized perversity, while theory, which attempts to uncover the ground on which social and cultural symptoms exist, analyses the ground of perversity on which culture is built.

So while culture is seen as neurotic in its repressive, defensive stance, writing and theory are seen as perverse. Seeing *Tel Quel*'s theory as perverse in this sense enables a liberation from the serious discourse normally associated with the theoretical, and an understanding of the shifts effected by the review. Perverse theory is a perspective which acts according to the disposition of the context, to effect a strategic unsettling of the context, paying no attention to the norms of intellectual discourse, and more attention to its own pleasure. If theory is seen as a closed system, necessarily involving some exclusion in order to define its own laws, then a perverse theory is a theory which undermines itself, a theory in continual permutation or dissolution. This explains, if we agree with it, the resistance to *Tel Quel*. It also institutes the potential for a generalized annexing of Freudian thought to the textual theory of the review, but it will ensure that this annexing is only expedient in so far as it serves the perverse, that is, critical, ends of textual theory.

The History of Literature

As emphasized above, Sollers's and *Tel Quel*'s vision of literature is trans-historical. The experience of writing is not limited to a historical period. However, initially, the project of *Tel Quel* is to identify and analyse the limits of literature in texts that for one reason or another have been censored, misread, or simply obscured. This misreading is the index of a resistance to the experience of writing and its transformative qualities. Initially, a canon of texts is elaborated: Dante, Sade, Mallarmé, Lautréamont, Artaud, Bataille. To this can be added others which are a focus for theoretical articles: Rimbaud, Proust, Roussel, Ponge, Hölderlin.[185] Joyce is always a major element, but an

---

[185] See Baudry, 'Le Texte de Rimbaud', *TQ* 35–6; Sollers, 'Proust et les signes', *TQ* 19; 'Logicus Solus', *TQ* 14, and 'La Poésie, oui ou non?', *Logiques*. Sollers refers to Hölderlin in *Logiques* on pp. 15, 61, 149, 217, 223.

extended exploration of his texts on the part of the review does not come until the 1970s.[186] After the time of theory in fact, the canon is opened up, and the limit becomes inherent in the literary experience as such, rather than being derived from the response to the text. All literature becomes potentially open to this vision of its transformative qualities. The later period of *Tel Quel* and *L'Infini* will include analyses of writers as diverse as Dostoevsky, Hemingway, Céline, Shakespeare, Hopkins, Bossuet, Voltaire, with an exploration also of texts relating to theology and religion. So, although history is of importance, in the situation of the writer in his national, political, and biographical context, writing transcends this historical temporality to engage in a different temporality, of creation. This should be taken into account if *Tel Quel* is often associated with a restricted canon of limit texts. Although the review is undoubtedly responsible for the bringing of these texts into prominence, the canon became a kind of orthodoxy, which is the recuperation of *Tel Quel*'s enquiries into a fixed frame. Resistance to this orthodoxy and recuperation in the later years and in *L'Infini* shows the critical canon to be less dogmatic and more a forceful entry into the arena of literature and its limits.

Despite the trans-historical temporality which is essentially in question, a certain view of literary history is proposed. It is not, Sollers suggests, linear, but 'monumental', describing how literary texts relate to language.[187] Until the end of the nineteenth century, the 'limit text' attempted a total and complete traversal and transformation of language. Dante is read by Sollers as a panoramic traversal of the history of the signifier, from its 'usury' in the *Inferno* to its plenitude in the *Paradiso*. Dante's *œuvre* is fundamental also in its inaugural relation to the Italian language. *De Vulgari eloquentia*, Dante's Latin treatise on the 'common tongue', was in this sense a necessary prefatory stage before the inauguration and transformation of the language in the *Commedia*. Jacqueline Risset's recent translation of the *Commedia* into a popular

---

[186] Although Sollers does refer to Joyce in *Logiques*, on pp. 50, 98, 226, 236–40. There are also articles on Joyce in *Tel Quel* by Eco, 'Le Moyen âge de James Joyce', *TQ* 11–12, and a concentration in issue 30 (summer 1967), based on the translation of P. Lavergne, with texts by J.-P. Faye, J. Paris, and a translation from *Finnegans Wake*. Pub. just before the split with Faye, this emphasis relates more to the perspective developed in *Change*.

[187] Sollers, *Logiques*, 11: 'La théorie de l'histoire de l'écriture textuelle peut être appelée "histoire monumentale" dans la mesure ou elle "fait fond" de façon littérale, par rapport à une histoire "cursive", figurée (téléologique), ayant servi à constituer en le dissimulant un espace écrit/extérieur.'

modern French is resonant with this perspective.[188] Sade, also, in his project to 'say everything' ('tout dire') produces a total reformulation of the language of sexuality.

With Hölderlin as a different moment, involving a fundamental experience of the fragmentation of language and thought, after Mallarmé and Lautréamont the transformative experience of literature only arrives 'in fragments'. The valorization of space and silence in Mallarmé, specifically in the final projects, is partly explained by the consciousness that language as totality escapes the writer. Mallarmé's utopian project, for 'un texte enfin réel qui serait l'explication permanente du monde'[189] only arrives fragmented, while the poetry attempts to conquer the arbitrary and the fragmentary through the 'guarantee' of a rigid, polyvalent syntax and an insertion of *le blanc* into the text. Mallarmé's experience of the totality of language, like that of Dante or Sade, and his failure to account for it, but his attempts to do so, are a moment of decisive change, making Mallarmé exemplary for the textual revalorization of literature effected by *Tel Quel*.

While Lautréamont's *Poésies* are seen as a dialectical *appareil*,[190] enveloping and negating literature and rhetoric and a specific moment at which literature becomes self-conscious and takes itself as an object, with Artaud and Bataille the experience comes to the reader fragmented. Artaud's writing is in its typography and its style fragmented, as is his experience of his own thought. Bataille's dispersal is explicit in the proliferation of his activities and his heterogeneous career.

However, the fragmented nature of twentieth-century literature makes the attempt at totality of Joyce, and his position in relation to literary history, exceptional. Sollers's *Paradis* and the encyclopaedic project of *L'Infini* and Sollers since *Tel Quel* also share this exceptional status. The exception is the focus of the later period of *Tel Quel*, as opposed to the movement towards theory of *Logiques*: the focus on Joyce and the writing of *Paradis* are understandable within the context of the history of the review and the evolution of its view of the history of literature.

Mallarmé is also exemplary and inaugural for *Tel Quel* in that he produces a self-consciousness in literature. As Barthes had proposed, with a slightly different chronology, literature 'becomes an object' around the middle of the nineteenth century. This self-consciousness,

[188] Dante, *La Divine Comédie*, (trans. J. Risset. See also J. Risset, *Dante écrivain* (Paris, 1982).
[189] Sollers, *Logiques*, 110.
[190] Ibid. 95.

and the elaboration of a critical perspective on literature, is situated by Sollers as contemporary with the scientific mutation of Marx and Freud.[191] It is termed an 'epistemological break', borrowing the term from Bachelard through Foucault and Althusser, who use it to refer to a leap in knowledge, whereby the basis on which thought rests is shifted. In *Tel Quel* this break relates to a critical bracketing, whereby literature, for example, takes as its sole object of reference itself and its own production. This historical vision prefigures and permits the Marxist theory of the review, in its focus on production. It also parallels Freud's focus on the work of the unconscious prior to fixed meaning, *le sens*. In literature this bracketing is most explicit with Lautréamont's tranformative treatment of rhetoric and literary history in *Maldoror* and the *Poésies*, making these texts programmatic and exemplary for *Tel Quel*.

The review's synthetic theory that brings together Marxism, Freud, and semiology in its focus on the production of signification depends on a vision or version of history, situating a break or shift in knowledge at a precise point. It is undoubtedly true that profound shifts in knowledge occurred at this time, but the attempt at synthesis does tend to impose a strait-jacket on the trans-historical temporality of literature. The relation between this version of cultural history and creativity, and their respective temporalities will make for a tension that will run underneath theory to push it to its limits and its dissolution. The history of *Tel Quel* appears to an extent as the development of a synthetic theory related to a fixed historical moment, which is then dissolved, making theory more permeable to the time and modalities of creative writing.

The areas we have separated in a discussion of Sollers's crucial book *Logiques* feed into one another at numerous levels. The critique of culture is, in the Sade essay, articulated with the theory of desire and sexuality, which implicates the body, the experience of writing. The theoretical style of the writing, perverse in its play and its effect, still tends towards a synthesizing moment in its liminary text 'Programme'[192] and the book of the same year, *Théorie d'ensemble* (1968). The next period of the review, from 1968 to 1971, sees this moment of synthesis mature and then begin to develop into a less static and more fluid style of thought, as its excessive or subversive elements are affirmed. Theory's auto-destructive, masochistic quality is also determined by the historical circumstance of the profound disturbance, for society and theory, of 1968.

[191] Sollers, *Logiques* 98.
[192] Id., 'Programme', *TQ* 31 (autumn 1967) and in id., *Logiques*.

3 The Time of Theory

It has been suggested that the time of theory was prepared for by the ferment of thought in the post-war period, and by the intersections of the context. *Tel Quel* acted as a forum for these intersections, pulling them together into a synthesis after the explosion of theory of 1967. The time of theory is a time of synthesis, of the articulation of different and disparate theories with the view of literature proposed in the review. This moment of theoretical proliferation is also more generally reflected in the context, and it coincides with a moment that appears as anti-theoretical in its spontaneity: the events of May 1968. The time is extremely tense in the contrasting pull of different temporalities. The time of theory, the temporality of its creation, also involves a tension between the structural and synthetic tendency of theoretical thought, and the more dynamic, punctual time of literary creation, the object of theory. The time of theory is one of extreme tension, both historically and in terms of its internal organization.

Historical temporality, which is not necessarily the same as the temporality of thought or theory, runs at an alarming pace. In 1966 the Chinese Cultural Revolution brought a new revolutionary movement on to the map; a new revolutionary reference in countries like France. In France in 1966 there was, we have proposed, an explosion in theory with the publication of Foucault's *Les Mots et les choses* (1966), Lacan's *Écrits* (1966) and a number of seminal works by Derrida. Closer to *Tel Quel*, it was the year of Kristeva's first publications. Whether connected to this explosion or not, student unrest began to spread, specifically from Strasbourg, where the situationists had disseminated the tract 'De la misère en milieu étudiant'.[1] 1967 also saw the publication, by the marginal publisher 'Champ Libre', of Guy Debord's *La Société du spectacle* and Vaneighem's *Traité du savoir-vivre à l'usage des jeunes générations*, both elaborating a critique of contemporary culture as alienated spectacle, and both arguing for spontaneity, drift (*dérive*), the creation of 'situations'. The spontaneous creation of the situation of May 1968 would have unforeseen consequences. But in the meantime, after the

[1] See also *L'Internationale situationniste*, 11 (Oct. 1967), 23–31, 'De nos buts et nos méthodes dans le scandale de Strasbourg'.

explosion, theoretical time had accelerated, producing another intense ferment of theory for which we have already described the conditions.

Tel Quel, rather than being an eclectic site of intersection, of texts and persons, now becomes a site of synthesis. Its publications are more related to a project, which a number of texts set out.[2] This moment of theory makes the review appear rather more as a movement or a group. It restricts both the scope and number of presentations, but it intensifies their complexity and the level of their implications, while the review also diversifies and engages in other activities. It is this time of theory which lasts until the mid-1970s, when things open out more, that defines the intellectual climate in which the events of 1968 occur. The time of the event also conflicts with the time of theory.

1968 appears as exorbitant and embarrassing with regard to the theory of the structuralist or post-structuralist theoretical orthodoxy, particularly that which had a political engagement. Only the situationists, whose review dissolved a few years after the events, escape this distance.[3] The figures of *Tel Quel* are neither involved, nor positive towards the students' revolt. However, the fact of the events did mean a sudden emergence of the political on to the scene of theory, and vice versa, since the revolt was deemed to be cultural. The theoretical, in *Tel Quel*, becomes increasingly linked to the political, and it also moves from the orthodox, but crucial, frame of theoretical Marxism towards a more popular, less abstruse language, to the point of its breakdown. 1968 produced an acceleration in theory's demise, under the pressure of what might be termed desire in language. It also produced a fracturing of the Left. The PCF came out of 1968 discredited in the eyes of many intellectuals and artists, who desired a more culturally aware politics. Theoretical Marxism of the Althusserian mould would also be left standing. So if the events of May 1968 are not relevant to the history of *Tel Quel* in terms of any influence of theory on the students, its effects are catastrophic.

---

[2] P. Sollers, 'Programme', *TQ* 31 (autumn 1967); id., 'Survol/Rapports(Blocs)/Conflit', *TQ* 36 (winter 1969); and, in the book *Théorie d'ensemble*, id., 'Division d'ensemble', 'Écriture et révolution', and 'Réponses à *La Nouvelle Critique*'.

[3] Of the dissolution, Guy Debord writes: 'Les avant-gardes n'ont qu'un temps; et ce qui peut arriver de plus heureux, c'est, au plein sens du terme, d'avoir fait leur temps. Après elles, s'engagent des opérations sur un plus vaste théâtre. On n'en a que trop vu, de ces troupes d'élite qui, après avoir accompli quelque vaillant exploit, sont encore là pour défiler avec leurs décorations, et puis se retournent contre la cause qu'elles avaient défendue. Il n'y a rien à craindre de semblable de celles dont l'attaque a été menée jusqu'au terme de la dissolution.' *Im girus imus nocte et consumimur igni* (Paris, 1990), 61. In an interview conducted with Sollers by the author, Sollers declared that this could apply equally to the dissolution of *Tel Quel*.

They are also slow to emerge. The next ten years, possibly more, is the time-span in which they are felt in *Tel Quel* and in the French intellectual scene in general. The history of *Tel Quel* in this time is inevitably determined by events with which, at the time, it had little contact.

TEL QUEL MARXISM

Since the early 1960s theoretical Marxism in France had suffered a variety of mutations. Sartre's totalizing project of the *Critique de la raison dialectique* had been criticized by Lévi-Strauss and overtaken by the work of Althusser. After the reviews *Arguments* and *Socialisme ou barbarie* folded, having produced critiques of Soviet bureaucracy (by Castoriadis, for example[4]) which went unnoticed, Western Marxist texts by Marcuse and Adorno were published in France, proposing a cultural Marxism very seductive for the students of 1968. The Marx-Freud synthesis of Reich was also extremely influential in this context.[5] The situationists, for their part, were critical of Marxism, while their work is fundamentally based on the notion of alienation. Althusser's more theoretically abstruse structural Marxism was distinct from these currents. Foucault's *Les Mots et les choses*, however, seemed to suggest that Marxism was not the radical science it was proposed to be by Althusser, that history was a myth. Foucault had already, in the article on Bataille 'Préface à la transgression', doubted the relevance of the dialectic and suggested its abandonment.[6] Other, more explicit critiques of Marxism, such as the early work of Baudrillard,[7] emerging from the context of *Les Temps modernes* and the work of Jean-Marie Benoist,[8] from outside the Left, perpetuate a current of thought critical of Marxism while not falling into an outright rejection. The influence of Western Marxism was continued in the work of Henri Lefebvre,[9] while a distinctive perspective based on the notion of class emerged in the work of Nicos Poulantzas.[10] There are a number of disparate currents in Marxist thought at this time, and

---

[4] See C. Castoriadis, *Le Socialisme bureaucratique* (Paris, 1973), a republication of articles in *Socialisme ou barbarie*.

[5] The journal *Arguments* largely made this possible through articles on Reich and its celebration of the work of Marcuse, also promoting a 'Freudo-Marxism'.

[6] See M. Foucault, 'Préface à la transgression', *Crit.* 195–6 (Aug.–Sept. 1963).

[7] J. Baudrillard, *Le Système des objets* (Paris, 1968).

[8] J.-M. Benoist, *Marx est mort* (Paris, 1970).

[9] H. Lefebvre, *La Révolution urbaine* (Paris, 1970).

[10] N. Poulantzas, *Pouvoir politique et classes sociales* (Paris, 1968).

this fragmentation suggests a tendency towards the pluralization and fracture of the structure of Marxism itself. Althusser's continuing work appears as an obstinate will to hold on to Marxism as a structure, from within the PCF, making Althusser's theory part of the essential stakes of a coherent theoretical Marxism at this time.[11] In some senses, theoretical, structural Marxism stands or falls with Althusserian theory. However, outside the PCF the development of psychoanalysis, the events of 1968, and the critique of structuralism will lead to the emergence in the 1970s of desire as an energetic force that fractures and dissipates the Marxist frame. The work of Deleuze and Guattari,[12] of Lyotard,[13] and of the 'Nouveaux philosophes'[14] in the next decade can be seen in this light. *Tel Quel* is also caught up in this epistemic change.

The tendency towards Marxism marked in Sollers's *Logiques* was principal among the motives which led the review to engage in 1967 in an adventure which is to some extent a repetition of history. The Surrealists, led by Breton, had engaged in a dialogue with the Communist Party, only later to diverge from it towards Trotskyism.[15] Gide, after visiting the USSR, would publish a critical renouncement of his previous faith.[16] In effect the relation to the PCF seems to have been a privileged reference-point which literary movements struggle over. *Tel Quel*'s adventure with the party is the last of such conflicts, and marks in this sense the end of an era.

With the 1968 collective publication *Théorie d'ensemble, Tel Quel* synthesizes aspects deriving from literary criticism into a comprehensive theory. Marxism is annexed into this project. This context replaces the structuralist, formalist, and avant-garde contexts of the previous years;

[11] After *Pour Marx* (Paris, 1965) and *Lire le Capital* (Paris, 1965), Althusser's major texts of this period were: *Lénine et la philosophie* (Paris, 1969) and 'Idéologie et appareils idéologiques d'État' *La Pensée*, 151 (June 1970).

[12] G. Deleuze and F. Guattari, *Anti-Œdipe: Capitalisme et schizophrémie* (Paris, 1972).

[13] J.-F. Lyotard, *Discours, figure* (Paris, 1971); id., *Dérive à partir de Marx et Freud* (Paris, 1973); id., *Des dispositifs pulsionnels* (Paris, 1973); id., *Economie libidinale* (Paris, 1974).

[14] The 'Nouveaux philosophes' were in fact a loose grouping of writers, a number of whom, (André Glucksmann, Christian Jambet and Guy Lardreau, Bernard Henri-Lévy) had emerged from the extreme-left groups in the wake of 1968. Other figures (Maurice Clavel and J.-M. Benoist) were less associated with the Left. The first major text of the movement was Glucksmann's *La Cuisinière et le mangeur d'hommes* (Paris, 1975), while Benoist and Clavel had already produced texts critical of Marxism as a totalitarian system.

[15] The reviews *La Révolution surréaliste* and *Le Surréalisme au service de la révolution* are paradigmatic for *Tel Quel* in this sense. Sollers reports (interview with author, Paris, 1989) that, before the formation of *Tel Quel*, he had spent much time reading these periodicals in the Bibliothèque de l'Arsenal in Paris. For a historical account of Surrealism and its political shifts, see M. Nadeau, *L'Histoire du Surréalisme* (Paris, 1964).

[16] A. Gide, *Retour de l'URSS* (Paris, 1936).

its intersections, and more frequent dissociations, become the vital productive context for the review. The theory has its own life, however, and it is complex and profound. *Tel Quel*'s linking of literary theory to Marxist theory is crucial in opening up a wide area of debate. The links with Althusser are particularly telling. It is essentially a very ambitious but flawed project, which throws up questions that have influenced literary theory since.

The turn to an overt dialogue with Marxism was prepared for by elements within literary theory, evident in Sollers's *Logiques*. The presence of Jean-Pierre Faye, closer to the context of the Left, was also determining in the shift. The chronology of the turn indicates, however, elements of tension within *Tel Quel*'s Marxism that will have repercussions at the end of the decade. In 1966, Marcelin Pleynet was in the United States, at Northwestern University in Chicago, lecturing on Lautréamont. His book on the author of *Les Chants de Maldoror* and the *Poésies* appeared in the same year. The analysis of the texts of Lautréamont, in Pleynet's own account, led to a realization that an analytic treatment of the rhetorical bases of an ideology could enable a political engagement.[17] In a sense *Tel Quel* adopts the rhetoric of Marxism, only to undermine its basis and push it out of its ideological frame. On his return, Pleynet finds Sollers fascinated with the recent event of the Cultural Revolution in China. However, the committee, run democratically, opts for a dialogue with the PCF. In Pleynet's account, it was not the right moment for 'la rhétorique chinoise'.[18] There is at the heart of *Tel Quel*'s Marxism a tension towards Maoism, coming principally from Sollers, which makes the engagement with the PCF highly unstable.

The engagement with the PCF is first initiated in 1967, through dialogues in the PCF cultural review *La Nouvelle Critique* with PCF intellectuals (Christine Glucksmann, Antoine Casanova, A. Gisselbrecht and Claude Prévost), and through other links with writers such as Jacques Henric and Pierre Daix, and the editors of the poetry review *Promesse*, Jean-Louis Houdebine and Guy Scarpetta.[19] *La Nouvelle Critique* was a context favourable to an extent to Althusser's work, and also towards psychoanalysis, through the efforts of Catherine Backès-

---

[17] Pleynet, interview with author, Paris 1989.

[18] Ibid.

[19] While *Tel Quel* members Sollers, Baudry, Faye, and Pleynet would publish articles or respond to questions in *La Nouvelle Critique*, there is no input into *Tel Quel* by its interlocutors. However, Pierre Daix, editor of *Les Lettres françaises* with Aragon, would publish a book, *Nouvelle critique et art moderne*, in the 'Collection Tel Quel' in 1968, and Henric, Houdebine, and Scarpetta would become regular contributors to the review.

Clément, attenuating the usual rejection of Freud by the party. Most of the articles resulting from the interchange with *Tel Quel*, or originally published in *La Nouvelle Critique*, are published in *Théorie d'ensemble*.[20] There followed a 1968 conference at Cluny, on 'Littérature et linguistique', organized by *La Nouvelle Critique* and attended by *Tel Quel* and other groups.[21] The articles and contributions to *Tel Quel* determined by this interchange attempted an articulation of the theory of literature with Marxism, particularly with Althusserian theory.

Critique of Exchange

Initially, the mode of this articulation is analogical. Jean-Louis Baudry and Jean-Joseph Goux both propose an analogy between an emphasis on literature as the production of meaning and Marx's emphasis on work.[22] The opposing ideology is premised on exchange, of meaning in language, and of the commodity in the economy. Literature, in its focus on the production of meaning in language, is able to demystify the ideology of exchange and value. A new method of reading, which recognizes the signifier in its productivity and materiality, its inscription, behind the effacing effects of exchange and of value, is necessary.

Goux makes an interesting step in stabilizing the above opposition as that between use value and exchange value. The use value, or *dépense*, of literature is related to Derrida's *différance* (the 'a' is added to underline its deferring movement and to affirm the specificity of writing), as it deviates meaning from exchange and value towards a deferral, an infinite loss. Goux's work would eventually deviate contextually from *Tel Quel*; he would go on to elaborate a more complex theory based on this critique of exchange. In the later article 'Numismatiques' in *Tel Quel* Goux would extend this critique of the equivalent to the realms of sexuality and the family structure, leaning heavily on Lacanian psychoanalytic theory.[23] The positive sides of the equation are not so well sketched out, but polymorphous perversity, a permutative sexuality is

[20] Cf. *Théorie d'ensemble*: J.-L. Houdebine, 'Première approche à la notion du texte'; P. Sollers, 'L'Écriture fonction de transformation sociale' and 'Réponses à *La Nouvelle Critique*'.

[21] The proceedings were pub. in a special issue of *La Nouvelle Critique*, 'Littérature et linguistique' (Nov. 1968), while the contributions by Sollers, Baudry, Pleynet, and Houdebine were repub. in *Théorie d'ensemble*.

[22] J.-L. Baudry, 'Écriture, fiction, idéologie', *TQ* 31 (autumn 1967), and in *Théorie d'ensemble*; id., 'Linguistique et production textuelle', *Théorie d'ensemble*; J.-J. Goux, 'Marx et l'inscription du travail', *TQ* 33 (spring 1968) and in *Théorie d'ensemble*.

[23] J.-J. Goux, 'Numismatiques', *TQ* 35–6 (autumn 1968—winter 1969).

suggested to replace the dominance of the phallus. An acephalic materialism is an approach suggested by Goux which we can see as covering a period of *Tel Quel*'s literary and cultural critique, linking it to Bataille.[24] The headless, valueless play of text and sexuality is a very powerful aspect of *Tel Quel*'s project, although it seems it is ultimately unproductive, by its very nature. It leads, however, towards a valorization of literature as an exceptional value outside the circuit of the exchange of values.

While this analogically based theory may be criticized for its reliance on an abstract model, the very thing it criticizes as a general equivalent, it does propose something quite radical in separating literature from value and exchange. Literature is not communication, neither does it have a social function. It is fundamentally a *dépense*, a radical loss, and it cuts across any posited economy. The commodity of literature, in the market, is also criticized from this perspective. Yet the theory relies more heavily on Bataille's notions of the general economy than on Marx, since, as Kristeva notes, Marx did not have the tools to analyse the productivity previous to the economy.[25] Marxism remains within the economy in this sense, and Marxism's fracturing in *Tel Quel* is a result of the pressure of the violent forces outside the structure of the economy. 1968, a cultural revolution of sorts, was a *dépense* of vital energies, unaccountable within the economies either of the PCF or of structuralist theory. Here historical time follows the time of theory's self-destruction, for it is almost as if Marxism is annexed to this violent form of expenditure in order for it to be internally ruptured.

Epistemological Break

Baudry and Goux's analogical Marxism is paralleled in a different way by Kristeva, who articulates her emerging semiology with Marxist theory.[26] The 'pre-sense' productivity of language is proposed by Kristeva to be more profoundly analysed by Freud in *The Interpretation*

---

[24] Id., 'Numismatiques II', *TQ* 36 (winter 1969), 59: 'c'est une pensée non phallocentrique, non centralisée, une pensée encore impensée du réseau ... une pensée du texte que rien ne saurait intituler. D'une manière générale "les possibilités de l'existence humaine peuvent être dès maintenant situées au-delà de la formation des sociétés monocéphales" ' (quoting Bataille).

[25] J. Kristeva, 'La Sémiologie: Science critique et/ou critique de la science', in *Théorie d'ensemble*, 88: 'Cette productivité antérieure à la valeur, ce "travail pre-sens", Marx n'a ni l'intention ni les moyens de l'aborder.'

[26] Ibid. 80–94.

of Dreams. So the hinge of the analogy between literary productivity and production in the Marxist sense turns instead to psychoanalysis. Already, Marxism is being overtaken by Freud. This recourse to Freud and psychoanalysis to account for lacunae in Marxism will increase, chronologically, to the point where Marxism is dropped as a privileged reference and psychoanalysis becomes a more explicit interest. This pattern is endemic to Kristeva's work, which very swiftly moves from linguistics and semiology towards *sémanalyse* (see below). The synthesis of *Théorie d'ensemble* is far from smooth, revealing at a deeper level conflicts and gaps. In the context, Marxism appears somewhat as the lame duck of theory, and psychoanalysis, catalysed by Lacan, gaining in theoretical prominence. Projects of psychoanalytical politics are nevertheless put forward, in *Tel Quel* and in the context, to halt this tendency.[27]

Kristeva's other major proposal is of an epistemological nature.[28] It is to do with the history and structure of knowledge. She proposes that, while structuralist and semiological linguistics, until her work, had focused on communication, there is a leap to be made to the productivity of language before the sign and its split into signifier and signified. This productivity she terms *signifiance* or *pratique signifiante*, which suggests the movement by which meaning is produced. The leap in question is termed an epistemological break and is proposed to be equal to, and as radical as, that of Marx in the shift of perspective from value to production. The two sciences of semiology and Marxism are not alike only in this way, however. Both are epistemologically distinct from the previous systems of knowledge in that they do not rely, Kristeva suggests, on an ideology, but constantly redefine their object and terminology. They are sciences that are also critiques of science; science is viewed as a circle, while semiology, and Marxist theory, open this circle to productivity. The notion of the epistemological break is taken from Althusser, and it reveals the extent to which *Tel Quel*'s Marxism derives and depends on Althusser's reworking of Marxism. *Tel Quel*'s Marxism is inextricably, it seems, wedded to the career of Althusser at this point. If Althusser's project is read as essentially flawed, as it has been read,[29] then such is the case also for *Tel Quel*. The implication of Althusser also involves *Tel Quel* with a proliferating number of groups

---

[27] See esp. A. Verdiglione (ed.), *Psychanalyse et politique* (Paris, 1974).
[28] See J. Kristeva, 'La Sémiologie'.
[29] See G. Elliott, *Althusser: The Detour of Theory* (London, 1987).

and movements such as *Cahiers pour l'analyse*, the film-journal *Cinéthique*,[30] and the Italian Marxist Maria-Antoinietta Macciocchi.[31] But the Althusserian frame is essentially unproductive, for Althusser's Marxism is ultimately structural, eliding any consideration of subjectivity. It conflicts with the trans-economic theory of Kristeva, which already favours a psychoanalytic approach to meaning. The tenacity of the reference to Althusser, however, conditions *Tel Quel*'s Marxism at least until the end of the decade.[32]

Ideology

What we have identified in the work of Sollers as a perspective that sees social discourse as inherently false and neurotic is developed in the Marxist theory of *Tel Quel* as a critique of ideology. The notion of ideology was, after Gramsci, one of the major developments in Marxist thought in the post-war period. Althusser's essay 'Les Appareils idéologiques de l'État'[33] was a pivotal point in this respect. The notion of ideology permitted a link between cultural practice and political practice, and many movements, reviews, and intellectuals would focus on this question.

At first Althusser's notion of ideology as 'imaginary relation', paralleling Lacan's imaginary identification with an ideal ego, and as 'interpellation' was endorsed in *Tel Quel*. Literature was seen as a privileged place for this interpellation of the subject, as it affirmed notions of

---

[30] *Cinéthique* was formed in 1968. It would include contributions by Sollers, Pleynet, Kristeva, and Baudry up until 1971: P. Sollers, 'Cinéma, inconscient, sacré', *Cin.* 5; M. Pleynet, 'Le Front gauche de l'art', *Cin.* 5 and 'Le Point aveugle', *Cin.* 6; J.-L. Baudry, 'Cinéma, effets idéologiques produits par l'appareil de base', *Cin.* 7/8; J. Kristeva, 'Cinéma, pratique analytique, pratique révolutionnaire', *Cin.* 9/10. See also J.-P. Fargier, 'Vers le récit rouge', *Cin.* 7/8, on a film produced by J.-D. Pollet and Sollers in the early 1960s, *Méditerranée*, also 'Le Mai qui fait parler', *Cin.* 9/10 and 'Les Pratiques artistiques dans le Marxisme-Léninisme', *Cin.* 11 1971. See 'Cinéma, littérature, politique', *TQ* 44 (winter 1971), for a manifesto signed by *Tel Quel*, *Cinéthique*, and *Cahiers du Cinéma*. For an account of this tangential history, and its influence on British film theory, see S. Harvey, *May '68 and Film Culture* (London, 1978).

[31] Macciocchi had corresponded with Althusser in 1968–9, and pub. the correspondence in Italy as M.-A. Macciocchi, *Lettere dall' interno del P.C.I* (Milan, 1969). Her first contacts with *Tel Quel* would be in 1971.

[32] Sollers refers to Althusser in 'Survol/Rapports', *TQ* 36 (winter 1969) and in the first version of 'Sur la contradiction', *TQ* 45 (spring 1971), but by its second version, in the book *Sur le matérialisme* (Paris, 1973), the approach is critical. Kristeva's article in *Cinéthique*, cited above, is critical of Althusser's conception of ideology.

[33] Pub. in *La Pensée*, the PCF philosophy journal, in 1970 and in L. Althusser, *Positions* (Paris, 1976).

identity, human nature, character, representation. Analyses of literary texts, such as Barthes's *S/Z*, were undertaken from this perspective.[34] As such a privileged site, however, literature could also become a space of the subversion of ideology, particularly in undoing notions of representation and identity and in exposing the production of the text. This emphasis on the means of production would also be carried over into other areas of cultural practice, such as film; articles by Baudry and Pleynet in the review *Cinéthique* looked at the apparatus of film as ideologically determined.[35] This would have a profound effect on film theory, particularly in Britain, where periodicals such as *Screen* or *Camera Obscura* would publish translations of these key texts.[36] In painting, the semiologist J.-L. Schefer would publish important work on the structuring of viewpoint, in *Tel Quel* and in the book *Scénographie du tableau*.[37] Through the link between the Althusserian theory of ideology and literary creation, both classical and subversive, *Tel Quel* became the reference point for a movement across the arts, whose focus was the text in its ideological relations.[38] Analyses of a more abstract kind were also present. Sollers affirmed Althusser's position on theoretical practice that: 'On ne peut parvenir à la connaissance des objets réels concrets qu'à la condition de travailler aussi et en même temps sur des objets formels abstraits.'[39]

---

[34] R. Barthes, *S/Z* (Paris, 1970). Barthes's text came out at the same time as Althusser's essay, but it was not limited to the Marxist theory of ideology, being focused more on a reading strategy that depends less on theory and more on subjectivity, that will be developed into a more playful approach with *Le Plaisir du texte* (Paris, 1973). Barthes's *L'Empire des signes* (Paris, 1970), pub. at the same time, but in a different editorial context (Skira), would also suggest this more subjective orientation. It is not completely distinct from the *Tel Quel* context, however, including a long quotation from Sollers's essay 'Sur la contradiction' on oriental calligraphy.

[35] See n. 30.

[36] See Society for Education in Film and Television, *Screen Reader*, i: *Cinema/Ideology/Politics* (London, 1977).

[37] J.-L. Schefer, 'Note sur les systèmes représentatifs', *TQ* 41 (spring 1970) and *Scénographie d'un tableau* (Paris, 1969). Other analyses of painting and the ideology of the history of art were present in Marc Devade's analytic, 'Sur une peinture chromatique', *TQ* 41 (spring 1970). Devade was a member of the painting group Supports/Surfaces and editor of its journal *Peinture, cahiers théoriques*, which entertained vital relations with *Tel Quel* from its creation in 1970. M. Pleynet's book *L'Enseignement de la peinture* (Paris, 1971) analysed the history of modern painting (since Cézanne) and its ideology in a way parallel to *Tel Quel*'s 'monumental' history of literature. Pleynet would also champion the Supports/Surfaces group in catalogues and contributions to *Peinture, cahiers théoriques*. See e.g. *Quelques problèmes de la peinture moderne: Louis Cane* (Paris, 1972).

[38] See particularly, J.-L. Baudry, 'Le Texte de Rimbaud', *TQ* 35–6; Pierre Rottenberg, 'Une lecture d'Igitur', *TQ* 37 (spring 1969); P. Thévenin, 'Entendre/Voir/Lire' (on Artaud), *TQ* 39–40, (autumn 1969–winter 1970).

[39] Sollers, 'Survol/Rapports', *TQ* 36: 6.

Theoretical practice, the elaboration of a theory that would account for the ideological situation and inscription of texts, propose methods of demystificatory analysis and subversion, also became a large part of the review's activity. Articles by J.-L. Baudry, J.-J. Goux, and J. Risset approached the question of ideology in a theoretical way, while other texts in the review applied the theory to specific objects.[40]

However, in *Tel Quel* the Althusserian conception of ideology soon began to reveal fundamental flaws from the emerging perspective of Kristeva's exploration of the genesis of signification. Again, this can be seen as a critique of structuralism by a more dynamic theory of its energetic basis, which it excludes. Althusser's ideology was essentially a structural apparatus which interpellated or imposed itself on the subject in various ways. A conception of subjectivity, process, and language was left out of the question. At the beginning of the 1970s, after the 'moment of Althusser',[41] Kristeva, and Baudry, in 'Pour une matériologie', developed a notion of ideology as inscribed in signifying practice and in the constitutive development of subjectivity. The symbolic—social and cultural discourse—is inherently and internally imaginary and ideological. The debate over the question of ideology as interpellation or as inscribed in signifying practice would be a source of much enquiry in the early 1970s. A series of interchanges in *Tel Quel*, between Marie-Claire Boons, later of the Maoist group Yenan, and Bernard Sichère, a fellow-traveller of *Tel Quel*, reflects this tension.[42]

If ideology is inherent in signifying practice, how is it possible, *Tel Quel* asks, to develop counter-ideological strategies? *Tel Quel*'s publishing activity of the time implies a number of responses: through revealing the ways ideology is inscribed in signifying practices, in theoretical analyses of the question, through an emphasis on the materiality of signifying practices, and through reference to other signifying systems. The triple strategy of the theoretical, the textual, and the political is reflected here. The last point, the analysis of non-Western signifying systems, implies an increasing interest in Chinese thought, which, articulated with politics, leads inevitably towards the shift to an overt

[40] J.-L. Baudry, 'Pour une matériologie', *TQ* 44–5 (winter–spring 1971); Goux, 'Numismatiques' *TQ* 35–6,; J. Risset, 'Lecture de Gramsci', *TQ* 42 (summer 1970). The last text in particular approached Gramsci's conception of the specificity of cultural practice and analysed his reading strategies in ways pertinent to *Tel Quel*'s textual theory.

[41] Cf. Elliott, *Althusser*, ch. 1.

[42] Bernard Sichère, Marie-Claire Boons, 'Enseignement, répression, répression et révolution; Le Mouvement étudiant; le révisionnisme à l'école', *TQ* 50 (summer 1972); Bernard Sichère, 'Sur la lutte idéologique', *TQ* 52–3 (winter 1972–spring 1973).

Maoism.[43] At the same time, Derrida had been publishing long and dense articles in the review which showed the basis of Western metaphysics in the philosophy of Plato to be undermined by a thinking of difference and absence.[44] The ideological target of this philosophical critique, as for Sollers in a number of contributions to the Groupe d'études théoriques,[45] was an idealism seen as repressive of a subversive and textual materialism.

May 1968

In this context of theoretical practice and the alliance with the PCF, the events of May 1968 are completely unexpected. The immediate analyses of the events in *Tel Quel* and by Sollers in *La Nouvelle Critique* repeat the analyses of the events by the PCF, that is to say, that they were a spontaneous, *petit-bourgeois* revolt that essentially undermined the class struggle and the primacy of theory.[46] *Contestation* replaced revolution. The ideology of imagination and spontaneity is criticized as a voluntarist idealism or *rousseauisme* which masks the true role of the party, the Leninist dictum of the necessity of the party and Marxist science, and the Althusserian postulate of the autonomy of theory and its guiding role.

Tel Quel's immediate reaction is to affirm the primacy of the party and the importance of theory. Although from a Marxist-Leninist point of view, the criticisms of the student events are just, objectively the PCF's role in the events was to act as a barrier between the demands of the students and the workers on one hand and between the workers and the government on the other, to pose reformist demands before the

[43] Articles on this question in *Tel Quel* of this period include: L. Mäll, 'Une approche possible du "sunyavada" ' (on the Buddhist notion of negativity), *TQ* 32 (winter 1968); R. Barthes: 'Lecon d'écriture' (on Japanese puppet theatre), *TQ* 34 (summer 1968); Chang Tun Sen, 'La Logique chinoise', *TQ* 38 (summer 1969); Sollers's translations of poems by Mao Tse-tung in *TQ* 40 (winter 1970). The publication of A. Artaud's 'Notes pour une "Lettre aux Balinais" ', *TQ* 46 (summer 1971) suggested how the interest in the East was mediated through the thought of Artaud and Bataille.

[44] See J. Derrida, 'La Pharmacie de Platon', *TQ* 32–3 (winter–spring 1968), and 'La Double Séance', *TQ* 41–2 (spring–summer 1970). Both essays are repub. along with Derrida's 1970 essay on Sollers's novel *Nombres* (Paris, 1968), 'La Dissémination', and a liminary 'Hors livre', in the book *La Dissémination* (Paris, 1972).

[45] See P. Sollers, 'Sur le matérialisme', I, II, and III, in *TQ* 55–6 (autumn 1973–winter 1973) and in id., *Sur le matérialisme*. In fact, the articles were given as *exposés* to the Group much earlier than their actual publication.

[46] 'La Révolution ici maintentant', *TQ* 34 (summer 1968) and 'Mai '68', in the same issue, p. 94; and Sollers, 'Contestation ou révolution', *La Nouvelle Critique* (June 1968).

government and give in at the first opportunity, thereby effectively betraying the long-term interests of the workers and students by settling for short-term wage increases.[47] *Tel Quel*'s reasons for mistrusting the student revolt and those of the PCF are not the same, but the alliance prevents any proper engagement with the events. This creates a certain amount of implicit tension in their relations, since *Tel Quel* is tending towards Maoism, which affirmed the importance of ideology and of the Cultural Revolution, of which 1968 was a version. At the same time, however, *Tel Quel* nominally asserts the necessity of the party as central to any revolution. But 1968 revealed the PCF to be resistant to a spirit of vitality and programmed into the history of *Tel Quel* a move to a more culturally oriented, heterogenous, and open Marxism.

The effect of the events of 1968 on *Tel Quel* are also implicated in a polemical conflict with Jean-Pierre Faye, who left the committee at the end of 1967. The involvement of the review with Derrida, to whose work Faye was rather antipathetic, and the arrival of Kristeva, whose work essentially bypassed the formalist emphases of Faye, are factors determining Faye's departure, as well as Faye's distinct position with regard to the other committee members. New committee members Jacqueline Risset and Pierre Rottenberg were brought in immediately before Faye's departure, constituting a majority around Sollers. Perhaps as a result of the publisher Seuil's desire to oust *Tel Quel* from the position of independence and ascendancy which it had attained, a review was created around Faye, titled *Change*. Other figures involved included the poet Jacques Roubaud and the Chomskyan linguist Mitsou Ronat. *Change* and Faye were to enter into lively but acrimonious and slightly banal polemics with *Tel Quel* up to the end of the decade.[48] A number of intellectuals would either side against *Tel Quel* with *Change* or be appropriated by *Change* in its reactive desire to oppose *Tel Quel*. From 1967, the forces opposing *Tel Quel* in the context, including J.-P. Faye

[47] For an account of the events sympathetic to the students, see P. Seale and M. McConville, *French Revolution 1968* (Harmondsworth, 1968) and C. Posner (ed.), *Reflections on the Revolution in France: 1968* (Harmondsworth, 1970).

[48] J.-P. Faye pub. a letter in the PCF newspaper *L'Humanité* in 1969 critical of Derrida's apparent Heideggerian affinities, associating them with Nazism, to which *Tel Quel* would respond in an editorial of autumn 1969 (*TQ* 39). A series of texts in *TQ* 43 (autumn 1970) ('Vérité d'une marchandise: Le Bluff *Change*') by Sollers, Pleynet, and Thibaudeau, with supporting letters by R. Barthes, M. Roche, and P. Flamand, the director of Seuil, respond to Faye's attacks on Sollers and suggestions that *Tel Quel* had been associated with the extreme Right during the Algerian war, in an interview with Jean Ristat pub. in the Swiss journal *La Gazette de Lausanne*. The interview, and one with Sollers in which he attacks Faye and *Change*, are repub. in J. Ristat, *Qui sont les contemporains?* (Paris, 1975).

and *Change*, the review *Action poétique*, the 'neo-Surrealist' Alain Jouffroy, director of the art review *Opus international*,[49] begin to become more explicit and active, leading to the strategic displacements and analyses of the review in response to the pressure of the opposition.

One example of such a polemic was directly influenced by the 1968 events. The Union générale d'écrivains was created by a large group of writers; it occupied the Hôtel Massa, the traditional base of the Société des Gens de Lettres.[50] A confrontational debate, between Sollers and Faye, took place, Faye arguing for a redefinition of the social function of the writer, Sollers opposing such a commitment. Apparently, Sollers was defending the position of the PCF, but more implicitly proposing that the writer could have no social function as such. In fact the leftist and utopian politics that emerged after 1968, crying for a disalienated, unified society, could not be further away from the exceptional, essentially asocial literary aesthetics of *Tel Quel* even in its Marxist period. While the apparent reasons for *Tel Quel*'s disenchantment with 1968 are generally part of the lack of response on the part of intellectuals in general,[51] its position with regard to the utopian leftism that emerged from it is consistent with its literary theory.

The summer 1968 issue of *Tel Quel* opens with a text entitled 'La Révolution ici maintenant' which cannot in any way be taken as an endorsement or celebration of the events of May.[52] It emphasizes the necessity of a theoretical practice. The 'here and now' refers to the text at hand, not to the utopian future. It stops short of saying 'la révolution sera textuel ou ne sera pas', but this is its implication. It also signals the creation of the Groupe d'études théoriques and is signed by the

[49] A. Jouffroy's 'posthumous reconciliation' of Bataille and Breton, Breton and Aragon, would be criticized in 'L'Art de boucher les trous', *TQ* 44 (winter 1971).

[50] See P. Combes, *La Littérature et le mouvement de Mai 68* (Paris, 1984), 47–54.

[51] A major exception was J.-P. Sartre, who, in the journals *Le Nouvel Observateur*, *La Cause du peuple*, and *L'Idiot international* (run by ex-*Tel Quel* director J.-E. Hallier), had proposed affirmative readings of the events, and who had taken to the streets himself and *pris la parole* in favour of the students.

[52] Contrary to the thesis of K. Reader in *Intellectuals and the Left in France since 1968* (London, 1987), 10. The title of the text, 'La Révolution ici maintenant', contrasts with the Surrealist, Trotskyist motto 'La révolution d'abord et toujours', suggesting a critique of utopianism. The text immediately following it is G. Bataille's unpub. 'La "vielle taupe" et le préfixe *sur* dans les mots *surréaliste* et *surhomme*', in which Bataille criticizes the 'icarian revolt' of the Surrealists as *petit-bourgeois* idealism. The diverted target, for *Tel Quel*, is the utopianism of May 68. In articles following Bataille's text, 'La Grande Méthode' and 'Le Savoir formel', Sollers and D. Hollier respectively underline the distance between Bataille's Marxism and that of the Surrealists, so that the issue reactivates an older polemic to justify its ideological position of the moment.

committee, and by other prominent figures in the context, such as Pierre Boulez. The group, perhaps the most immediate result of the 1968 events, was a public, extra-mural forum for the dissemination of a theory of the text, produced by *Tel Quel*.[53] Sollers, Kristeva, Baudry, Pleynet, Goux, and Derrida would give important papers, which are published in the review, taking up most of its space for the next few years, alongside other texts.[54] The group, run by Sollers, was directly modelled on Bataille's Collège de sociologie, a community with a public front, 'presqu'une société sécrète derrière', as Sollers puts it.[55] Through this corridor, *Tel Quel*'s force of effect in the context is increased. The militancy is, however, in the name of theory rather than action. It is an attempt to enable theory, *le savoir*, to have an effect in a public space, to widen the interaction of the review with the context.

The role of *Tel Quel* in the events of 1968 is minimal. The revolution of the review at this stage is theoretical and textual, not in the street. The effect of the events of 1968 cannot, however, be limited to the field of political alliances and of Marxism, since it was an insurrection that had a profoundly organic effect on the whole country. For Sollers, writing in 1976, 1968 was also an eruption, an irruption, of a vital language, inside a dead language.[56] The dead language was the language of authority, of the apparatus (state, university, as well as party). 1968 was the irruption of the political signifier into everyday life, of an admittedly somewhat confused theoretical discourse into the situation. As well as being, perhaps, an 'inflation' of the sign,[57] this was a condensation—of a political signifier with desire—articulated by the play of signifiers across the surfaces, written or auditory, of 1968. As an insurrection in language, of the signifier, 1968 cannot fail to have an organic effect on an organism whose determining activity is the production of texts. At a level below the strategic, the *Tel Quel* writers are affected organically. This is marked in Sollers's *Lois*, for example,

[53] The group met regularly in a location in the Rue de Rennes, charging a nominal admission fee. It attracted large numbers, too large to fit into its venue, including intellectual stars such as Lacan, Deleuze, and Klossowski.

[54] The first text is Sollers's 'Survol/Rapports'. Following it were: Baudry's 'Le Texte de Rimbaud'; Goux's 'Numismatiques'. J. Kristeva's 'L'Engendrement de la formule'; Rottenberg's 'Une lecture d'Igitur'; Thévenin's 'Entendre/Voir/Lire'; Derrida's 'La Double Séance'; Sollers's 'Lénine et le matérialisme dialectique' and 'Sur le matérialisme', I, II, and III; Baudry's 'Pour une matériologie'; M. Pleynet's 'Lautréamont politique'. (See initial refs. for dates of publication in the review.)

[55] Sollers, interview with author, Paris 1990.

[56] P. Sollers, *Délivrance* (Paris, 1977), 49.

[57] Cf. J.-M. Benoist, 'L'Inflation du signe', in id., *Marx est mort*.

by a switch to a more rhythmical, vital, Célinesque, and Joycean
language, in which the political signifier is brought to the forefront,[58]
also in Pleynet's *Stanze*, in which the political erupts in the text in an
insurrectionary fashion.[59] The level that holds back or delays this
irruption, however, is the alliance with the PCF. The tension in this
alliance, from 1968 to 1971, is determined by the contradictory relationship between the resistance of Marxist orthodoxy and the vitality of the
letter in the practice of the writers in question. When this breaks, the
vitality becomes evident at the strategic level, in the hysterical slogans
of the tracts of the Mouvement de Juin 1971.[60] The holding-back of this
vitality has a counter-effect, in a sense, in the somewhat hysterical
character of the review's Maoist pronouncements (see Chapter 5).

   1968 also has a profoundly fragmenting effect on the Left in France.
The next few years saw a proliferation of groups of various shades of
Marxism or Maoism. The *Cahiers pour l'analyse* group, for example, would
split, and some of its members would enter into the militant Gauche
prolétarienne movement, only to emerge from it later, disillusioned with
the Left in general. The same pattern is detectable with other Marxist
groups. The spontaneous irruption of everyday life of 1968 ruptured the
serenity of the structures that had been the focus of the previous years,
engaging an intense and extremely energetic political hysteria which
could only perhaps be analysed ten years after the events, leading to a
general lassitude. Political events and disclosures in the USSR and in
China also condition this loss of faith. However, 1968 produces, as if
reactively, an intensification of a theoretical leftism which constantly
strives to account for the spontaneity of the events and of the situation.
In *Tel Quel* this intensification of theory in its political articulation takes
the form of an expansion of the review's perspective to take in philosophy, particularly that of Marxism: dialectical materialism.

The Investigation of Dialectical Materialism

The second phase of *Tel Quel*'s theoretical Marxism, after the synthesizing analogy based on the critique of exchange, is an investigation of the
philosophical basis of Marxism. This often reaches levels of complexity

[58] P. Sollers, *Lois* (Paris, 1971) (see Ch. 4).

[59] M. Pleynet, *Stanze* (Paris, 1973), in which fragments of *actualité*, including newspaper
cuttings, interrupt the already fragmented poetic text. See pp. 58, 73, 88, 92.

[60] The journal of the Mouvement de Juin 1971, which lasted for about four issues,
collated reports of a Maoist and anarchist nature from universities around France; it also
pub. material in *Peinture, cahiers théoriques*.

which appear impenetrable, but it pushes Marxist theory to its limits by emphasizing heterogeneity, plurality, and negativity as excessive of any structure or system. The events of 1968, the heterogenous irruption of desire, are undoubtedly related to this transgressive approach. It leads first to the break with the party and then to the internal subversion of the structure of Marxism as such, which will take longer to produce its effects. The effect of the philosophical investigation, as Sollers suggests in the introduction to a collection of his articles on Marxist philosophy of 1974, *Sur le matérialisme*, is scandalous, since a group of writers outside the university, the ENS, and the party were proposing to have something to say about philosophy.[61] *Tel Quel* was trespassing on the terrain of the inner temple of philosophy. In another sense, the linking of literature to Marxism, the postulation that literature's negativity or its desire was somehow implicated in the Marxist dialectic, was scandalous in the eyes of the Marxist intelligentsia. *Tel Quel* consequently finds itself occupying an extremely marginalized, yet enormously influential position. It undoubtedly plays a decisive part in the demise of the left-wing intellectual option in the 1970s.

Tel Quel's semantic materialism was already evident in the stress on the materiality of the text. In the Marxist period this is accentuated by references to materialist philosophy. In the article 'Sade lisible', Pleynet shows how part of the sub-text of Sade is the philosophical materialism of the time.[62] Bataille's 'La "vieille taupe" et le préfixe "sur" ' proposed a 'base materialism' which Jean-Joseph Goux referred to as 'acephalic'.[63] Sollers's articles from 1968 develop the basis of materialism towards the philosophical investigations of 1970 onwards. In 'Survol/Rapports(Blocs)/Conflit' he affirms the necessity of '[une] position materialiste de base', referring to Lacan's emphasis on the signifier and on the letter, on language at an infrastructural level.[64] In other words, language

---

[61] Sollers, *Sur le matérialisme*, 5.

[62] M. Pleynet, 'Sade lisible', in *Théorie d'ensemble*, 350: 'Une théorie est au travail dans l'œuvre de Sade qui à quelque niveau que ce soit ne laisse jamais passer une occasion de revenir sur ce qui pourrait le trahir (rousseauisme, déisme républicain). Cette théorie qui peut être entendue comme une conséquence en extension systématique de la pensée matérialiste du XVIIIᵉ siècle, demande à être lue à partir de cette multiplicité de textes qu'elle fait fonctionner.'

[63] See Goux, 'Numismatiques', *TQ* 36 (winter 1969), 60: 'une organisation sociale polymorphique, acéphale'.

[64] Sollers, 'Survol/Rapports', *TQ* 36: 5–6: 'Théorie du langage matérialiste, les deux termes qui la spécifient dans le champ lacanien (*Signifiant, lettre*; signifiant toujours préalable, lettre toujours détournéée') sont à inscrire comme principes minimaux d'une position de départ.'

is part of the determinative production of the real. Later this will be affirmed in the statement 'la matière pense', the title of an article by Pleynet on Artaud.[65] *Tel Quel*'s materialism is a semantic materialism, proposing the determining activity of language upon the real, rather than a perspective from which language and meaning is determined by nature. Neither is meaning separated from the material level of language; Derrida's work, displacing the signified as another signifier, proposing the trace as the fundamental movement of language and the production of meaning, permits a view in which meaning itself is an aspect at the level of the materiality of language.

Sollers accentuates this in his article of autumn 1969 on Derrida, 'Un pas sur la lune', where he writes: 'La pensée de la trace serait fondamentalement matérialiste.'[66] However, in this move towards the investigation of dialectical materialism, Sollers effects a shift from Derrida's *différance* to the more Hegelian notion of contradiction which creates problems with the Derridean aspect of the theory.[67] The explicit investigation of dialectical materialism is begun with Sollers's 'Lenine et le materialisme philosophique'.[68] Sollers proposes a number of key points: materialism is not opposed to idealism, but is a third position, including the opposition.[69] Materialism, as a position removed from polemical oppositions, in fact enables *Tel Quel* to 'act pragmatically according to the context'.[70]

The second point is the identification of Hegel, the summit of idealist philosophy, as a major pivotal figure for Marxist philosophy,[71] which programmes a focus on Hegel in the theory of the review. The investigation of Hegel is fed through a Bataillean perspective of abstract

---

[65] M. Pleynet, 'La Matière pense', *TQ* 52 (winter 1972) and in P. Sollers (ed.), *Artaud* (Paris, 1973).

[66] P. Sollers, 'Un pas sur la lune', *TQ* 39 (autumn 1969), 8.

[67] Derrida's 'Hors livre' in *La Dissémination* develops a critique of Hegelian contradiction, while affirmatively referring to Sollers's article 'Lénine et le matérialisme dialectique'. While Derrida will implicitly become more distant from *Tel Quel* for political reasons, his suggestion of the relevance of the Democritean concept of *rhythmos*, a differential rhythm underlying any substance, seems consistent with Kristeva's *chora* (see Ch. 4).

[68] Sollers, 'Lénine et le matérialisme philosophique', *TQ* 43 (autumn 1970) and in id., *Sur le matérialisme*. This *TQ* issue also features the enlargement of the subtitle 'Science/littérature', present since 1967, when Kristeva's first article was pub. (issue 29), to become 'Littérature/philosophie/science/politique', irritating *La Nouvelle Critique*, which rebuked *Tel Quel* for its pretension to philosophy or politics.

[69] See Sollers, 'Lénine et le matérialisme philosophique', in id., *Sur le matérialisme*, 97.

[70] 'agir pragmatiquement selon le contexte', Sollers, interview with author, Paris, 1990.

[71] Sollers, *Sur le matérialisme*, 100: 'la logique du matérialisme sort de l'idéalisme poussée au bout'.

negativity, that is, a *dépense* prior to any structure or position. The form
and mediation of this negativity, and its relation to Freud's death-drive,
will also be a major focus of *Tel Quel*'s theory in this period, again
suggesting that the principal elements of interest are extraneous to
Marxism as such. Despite the problems created by the effacement of
difference under contradiction, which is developed in this essay, the
move towards a view of negativity before structure enables also an
elaboration of a view of the subject, which Derrida's perspective, up to
this point, has avoided. As soon as it is proposed as fundamental,
however, contradiction becomes problematic. Sollers identifies in
Lenin's philosophy 'une pluralisation, une hétérogénéisation de la
contradiction'.[72] This problematization of the dialectic will be pushed
further in Sollers's later essay on the reformulation of the dialectic by
Mao Tse-tung, 'Sur la contradiction'.[73]

Kristeva's contributions to the sessions of the Groupe d'études
théoriques and to the review also develop an investigation of materialist
philosophy and of the Hegelian dialectic. In 'Matière, sens, dialectique'
she argues against a view of negativity as a pure force that could be
diverted into a negative theology, opposing to this a view of negativity
as the heterogenous movement of matter.[74] The Bataillean connotations
of this heterogeneity are evident. They suggest that it is the effects of
the heterogenous and the plural that are more important than the logic
of Marxism. Yet the necessity of the dialectic is also affirmed. There has
to be a law, a subject position, an analytic approach to this heterogeneity rather than a celebration of its effects as a 'pure negativity'.[75]
This prefigures the move towards psychoanalysis as an attempt to
mediate or to merge the negativity in discourse, and the later stress on
ethics. At this point, however, Kristeva's work is an important moment
in the hollowing-out of the philosophical basis of Marxism and part of
the counter-ideology of materialism of *Tel Quel*.

Sollers's interest in China and in Maoism ran parallel to the
dialogue with the PCF, a constant ambiguity in this relation. The
publication of translations of poems by Mao in 1970, by Sollers, was a
gesture of extreme importance not only in threatening and pushing the
Tel Quel–PCF relation, but also for Maoism in France in general.[76]

---

[72] Ibid. 105–6.
[73] 'Sur la contradiction', *TQ* 45 (spring 1971) and in id., *Sur le matérialisme*.
[74] J. Kristeva, 'Matière, sens, dialectique', *TQ* 44 (winter 1971) and in ead., *Polylogue* (Paris, 1976).
[75] See ead., *Polylogue*, 281–2.
[76] 'Dix poèmes de Mao Tse-tung, lus et traduits par P. Sollers', *TQ* 40 (winter 1970).

Strategically, it is evident that in articulating *Tel Quel*'s textual theory with Mao's poetry and Chinese thought, Sollers is already pushing for a break with the PCF, 'pour tendre la politique du PCF', as he puts it.[77] Theoretically, the more interesting moment is Sollers's essay 'Sur la contradiction' in *Tel Quel* in 1971. It is basically a commentary on the essay 'On Contradiction' which was perhaps Mao's fundamental contribution to Marxist philosophy. Establishing this commentary is a way of philosophically preparing the ground for the shift of 1971; it is also a major, if dated, document in relation to French Maoism.[78] Sollers describes how Mao proposed a pluralization of contradiction. There was a distinction, for example, between antagonistic contradictions and non-antagonistic contradictions. This allows Sollers to claim that some contradictions or conflicts are only apparent—such as the conflict in Marxism between humanism and economism, or idealism and materialism. In fact they are viewed by Sollers as mutually dependent; the true antagonistic contradiction is between this duality and a third position, 'le tiers exclu', enclosing this duality.[79] *Tel Quel* exploits this third position in its intellectual strategy. So any resistance to *Tel Quel* from within the oppositional discourse of politics can be countered from a removed position outside it. 'You can't understand me, because you don't know what I know.' This dialectical structure is that of theoretical terrorism. Accusations of terrorism against *Tel Quel* are justified, but the terrorism results more from the inherent structure of a theory premised on the dialectic.

Sollers also affirms Mao's 'specificity' of contradiction. Contradictions are determined by their situation, their context, hence the necessity and benefit of acting, as Sollers says of *Tel Quel*, 'pragmatiquement, selon le contexte'. This might lead to the conclusion that it is Sollers's thought which finds itself expressed in political form in Maoism. Mao's pluralization of contradiction may moreover be a movement away from Marxism. If contradictions are plural and heterogenous, the 'determination in the last instance' which is the cornerstone of Marxist theory, particularly for Althusser, becomes unworkable. In other words, Mao (and Sollers) pluralize and complicate the original Marxist philosophy to such a degree that it becomes an abstract, strategic imperative of 'acting according to the context from a displaced position', affirming the strategy of the review. The notion of determination by the infrastruc-

---

[77] Sollers, interview with author, Paris, 1990.
[78] A fact recognized by Ristat in *Qui sont les contemporains?*, 148.
[79] Sollers, 'Sur la contradiction', in id., *Sur le matérialisme*, 74.

tural level of human relations is abandoned, if it was ever affirmed to begin with.

The essential position of *Tel Quel* can be seen to be fundamentally non-Marxist on a more general level. If Marxism is a fundamentalism which insists that all antagonisms are mediated through that of the class struggle, the economic determining in the last instance, Maoism moves towards the abandonment of this last instance by an insistence on the specificity of each contradiction, an irreducible plurality not solvable by the resolution of a fundamental antagonism. *Tel Quel*'s Maoist phase reflects an uneasy tension between fundamentalism and pluralism. Pluralism insists on the essential irreducibility of antagonisms. Later, this will be rephrased as a violence inherent in any social contract. The emphases of *Tel Quel*'s theory propose a force of negativity constantly at work undermining any essence or structure, that does not sit easily with the Marxist stress on the state and production. Kristeva's insistence on the surplus of the heterogenous over structure, or Bataille's negativity, or Freud's death-drive beyond the economy of pleasure, propose an irreducibility of conflict. Inasmuch as Marxism presents the possibility of a resolution of this plural irreducibility through that of an essential antagonism, it can be seen as a totalitarian illusion. Maoism is also implicated, despite its pluralizing philosophy. The value of *Tel Quel*'s Marxism is in presenting, subtly, the uneasy alliance of fundamentalism with pluralism and the gradual merging of the first into the second.

Sollers's essay 'Sur la contradiction' can be seen as the last fundamental analysis of Marxist philosophy that is not tending towards its abandonment. In effect the period from 1971 onwards sees the effects of this philosophical investigation emerge in *Tel Quel*'s publications and its strategy, identifying this time as the dissolution of the theoretical frame of Marxism set up between 1967 and 1971. Marxism is also fundamentally undermined through a parallel investigation of Freudian theory and an articulation with psychoanalysis.

TEL QUEL AND PSYCHOANALYSIS

In the late 1960s, psychoanalysis was a discourse in the ascendant. The *Écrits* of Lacan were a standard reference for many writers of theory across disciplines, and Lacan's seminars at the ENS were attended by an increasing number of intellectuals, including Sollers, Kristeva, and Baudry from *Tel Quel*. Other psychoanalytic groups tended to derive an impetus from Lacan's École freudienne de Paris; the person of Lacan is the focus, the symptom, one might say, for all the psychoanalytic groups. This renaissance led to the establishment of a number of important periodicals. *Cahiers pour l'analyse*, already running, published Lacan's 'La Science et la vérité' in 1966 and important work by J.-A. Miller on the *suture* and on structural causality, attempting a theory of the subject that would fit with Althusser's structural emphases.[80] The EFP review *Scilicet* was set up in 1967 as a forum for Lacan's work and that of other members of the group, whose contributions were anonymous, according to the master's decree. *Scilicet* would publish Lacan's 'Radiophonie', in which Lacan replied to questions posed to him in a radio interview, and 'Pour une logique du fantasme', a text of part of one of the seminars, where the writer had recourse to formal logic to understand and conceptualize the functioning of the unconscious.[81] The reference to logic was an increasingly important aspect of Lacanian analysis at the time. Lacan was searching for a formalizable discourse that would represent, on 'another scene' (than that of speech), the work of the unconscious. Psychoanalysis was attempting to propose itself as a science. Later in the decade, in the wake of 1968, a department of psychoanalysis was set up at the newly created and controversial University of Vincennes, under Serge Leclaire. It would be the focus of lively polemics at the end of the decade and the beginning of the 1970s.[82] The teaching of psychoanalysis, as a science, was also part of this general tendency. Psychoanalysis was therefore of strategic value for *Tel Quel* in ousting any tendency towards psychology and in parallel to its science of the text. That there could be a science of either the literary object or the literary subject was in radical opposition to a discourse of poetic effusion and intuition, in opposition to the psychologism identified earlier by Foucault. The Marxist, Althusserian primacy

[80] J. Lacan, 'La Science et la vérité', *CPA*, 1 (winter 1966); J.-A. Miller, 'La Suture, éléments de la logique du signifiant', *CPA* 1, and 'Action de la structure', *CPA* 9 (summer 1969). *Suture*, describing the way the subject figured in the signifying chain as a lack, was not unlike Kristeva's notion of the *sujet zérologique* (see below), while the latter essay elaborated a concept of causality inherent in structure rather than agency.

[81] J. Lacan, 'Radiophonie' and 'Pour une logique du fantasme', *Scilicet*, 2/3 (1970).

[82] Sollers would intervene in the debate between Leclaire and Lacan, on the side of Lacan, in 'De quelques contradictions', *TQ* 38 (summer 1969), having earlier criticized the recuperative enterprise of Vincennes in a veiled fashion: 'Une nouvelle gestion du symbolique se met en place et, bien entendu, pas dans n'importe lequel sens économique. Nous pouvons désormais le vérifier à tous les niveaux, nous ne manquerons pas de nous attacher éventuellement à le démontrer, cette distribution dût-elle se dérouler sur *vingt scènes* à la fois' (Sollers's emphasis), *TQ* 36: 3.

of theory also plays a part in this recourse to science. At the same time, science as such is criticized as excluding or 'foreclosing' (the concept comes from Freud via Lacan) the place of the subject. It will give way in the 1970s to a focus on ethics, particularly in the work of Kristeva.

Tel Quel's use of Lacanian theory is in some senses separate from the review's strategic support of Lacan. This support was established in 1969, when Lacan's seminar at the ENS was suspended by the director, Robert Flacelière. Outraged, Sollers, Kristeva, and others occupied the director's office, having to be forcibly removed. There are reports of Sollers 'carrying Lacan's suitcase' at moments when Lacan found himself apparently without support. Sollers's (unfounded) suspicion of Derrida's indifference in the 'Flatulencière' affair, as Lacan named it, may have led to a distancing in their relations. However, Lacan's seminar was simply displaced to a lecture hall in the law faculty near the Panthéon, and his popularity increased. The effect was to strengthen the links between Sollers and Lacan and to provide the possibility of a dialogue. Lacan would send Sollers a copy of the *Écrits* dedicated with the words, 'On n'est pas si seuls après tout'.[83] The dialogue would not, in fact, occur until much later, and even then it is blocked on certain crucial points (see Chapter 4).

Within the Lacanian school, meanwhile, there were productive developments and interesting polemics, the onset of the fracturing of Lacanian theory. Serge Leclaire, a member of the EFP, but not exactly under Lacan's thumb, would write a more practical and cure-oriented version of analysis in his publication *Psychanalyser* in 1968. A group of analysts from the EFP, G. Rosolato, J. Clavreul, P. Aulagnier-Spairani, F. Perrier, J.-P. Valabrega, published in 1969, in the 'Champ freudien' series at Seuil, a collective work on *Le Désir et la perversion*, which was a valuable contribution to an area of potential interest for *Tel Quel*. Rosolato would publish in 1969 his *Essais sur le symbolique*, after having resigned from the EFP in protest at Lacan's dictatorship. He was followed in 1969 by Aulagnier-Spairani, Perrier, and Valabrega, who set up a new group, Le Quatrième Groupe, with a periodical, *Topique*. Now there were four groups, each with a review, and apparently differing perspectives. *Tel Quel*'s strategic loyalty remains with Lacan, as their criticism of Leclaire's efforts at Vincennes shows, while theoretically, there are references to work by Rosolato and to earlier psychoanalysts

[83] The dedication is reproduced in *TQ* 90 (winter 1981), 2.

such as Ferenczi, and of course Freud.[84] Outside the EFP, J.-B. Pontalis would set up the *Nouvelle Revue de psychanlyse* in 1970, published by Gallimard, producing special issues on subjects such as 'La Mort', or 'Le Mal', with contributions by analysts of different persuasions. A new angle was introduced at this time, that would tend towards a different approach, tangential to Lacanian theory, in Deleuze and Guattari's work, when Louis Wolfson's book *Le Schizo et les langues* was published in 1970. Other works crucial for this time included: André Green's earlier reading of tragedy, *Un œil en trop* of 1965, particularly valuable as an articulation with literature, missed by *Tel Quel*; J. Chasseguet-Smirnel's collective work on feminine sexuality, *Nouvelles recherches sur la sexualité féminine* (1964), again ignored; and Pontalis's collection of articles *Après Freud* (1968), some of which concern writers like Leiris and Henry James.

This suggests that alongside Lacan's person there were a proliferating number of trends and perspectives that tend to be overlooked in histories of the period.[85] While this is undoubtedly healthy for French psychoanalysis in general, the focus on Lacan himself, on his person, tends to overshadow the work alongside him, and this tendency is equally pertinent in *Tel Quel* and in assessments of it as a synthesis of Lacan and Althusser. *Tel Quel*'s interest in psychoanalysis, while it nominally refers to Lacan as master, in fact derives its impetus from other areas. Lacanian theory in *Tel Quel* is fragmented because it is essentially only a strategic, nominal support. It is initially via the work of Derrida that Freud is at first approached.

Between Derrida and Lacan

Tel Quel's interest in psychoanalysis in its earlier years was, up to a point, pre-Freudian; it was an interest in dreams rather than in the science or practice of psychoanalysis. However, with the first extensive analysis of Freud in the review, Derrida's 'Freud et la scène de l'écriture',[86] the previous interests take on a different tenor, since they focus on the dream as a writing, as opposed to a representation, looking at texts about dreams, and the writing of dreams. Derrida's essay initially

---

[84] e.g. P. Sollers, 'La Matière et sa phrase', *Crit.* 290 (July, 1971).

[85] With the major exception of E. Roudinesco's *La Bataille de cent ans: Histoire de la psychanlyse en France*, (Paris, 1986), which is a valuable source of information about the psychoanalytic context.

[86] J. Derrida, 'Freud et la scène de l'écriture', *TQ* 26 (summer 1966) and in id., *L'Écriture et la différence* (Paris, 1967).

defines the space of *Tel Quel*'s extension of its theory into psychoanalysis. This inscribes in *Tel Quel* a certain ambiguity, for such articles as Sollers's 'Le Roman et l'experience des limites' and Pleynet's 'Les Problèmes de l'avant-garde' had referred to the enterprise of Lacan as productive, while Derrida's essay defines an ambiguously non-Lacanian space, at the level both of its origins in a seminar run by André Green and of its theory. This initially establishes an important distance from the mainstream of Lacanian analysis; *Tel Quel*'s interest will be in the articulation of the unconscious and writing, or as a writing, rather than in the space of speech and intersubjective relations.

Derrida's intention in the article is to show how, although psychoanalysis remains within the closure of metaphysics criticized as logocentric, Freud opens out within it a subversive space, a 'scene of writing' that transgresses this closure. The essay traces the career of the metaphor of writing in Freud's texts from the *Sketch for a Scientific Psychology* through the *Interpretation of Dreams* to the short 'Note on the Mystic Writing Pad'. Implicit in this tracing is a critique of Lacan, whose *Écrits* had not yet been published. Neither is Lacan mentioned in the article.

Derrida's article displaces Lacan's focus on language in its proposition, through a reading of the concept of writing in Freud, that writing as *espacement* and difference is at work in the unconscious before verbal representations. The latter are linked to the pre-conscious and to the ego. Dreams suggest an *archi-écriture*, 'lithographie d'avant les mots, métaphonétique, non-linguistique, a-logique'.[87] This writing undoes the distinction between signifier and signified and is not readable according to any code. It is not a question of 'la consécution linéaire irréversible, passant de point de présence en point de présence'.[88] Derrida writes: 'L'écriture générale du rêve déborde l'écriture phonétique et remet la parole à sa place',[89] and 'L'interêt de la psychanalyse pour la linguistique suppose qu'on "transgresse" le "sens habituel du mot langage" '. (Derrida quoting Freud).[90] In so far as Lacan's articulation of the unconscious as structured like a language is restricted to language based on *la parole* and on the Saussurean sign, Lacan is within the closure of metaphysics that represses a general writing. Lacan's emphasis on the signifier emphasizes a presence, rather than a difference, and Derrida proposes generally that language is restricted to the level of the

[87] Id., *L'Écriture et la différence*, 307.
[88] Ibid. 321.
[89] Ibid. 323.
[90] Ibid.

pre-conscious. This critique, which is reiterated in *Tel Quel*, is, however, discordant to an extent with other references in the review. Michel Tort's references to Lacan in his essay on Sade[91] are to some extent taken up in Derrida's identification of a closure, as are, perhaps, Barthes's emphases on the code in the same issue.[92] Lacan, on the other hand, does not propose any metalanguage of difference before language or the symbolic. Difference is an effect of language rather than language being an effect of difference, writing. An oscillation between these two positions is readable in the history of *Tel Quel*'s theory, which gradually gives way to an effacement of difference under contradiction in the Marxist period, and then to a view of language as 'infinite virtuality'.[93] Difference and a general writing are effaced by a faith in the exceptional power of the voice.

The subject is also taken up in Derrida's critique of the space of logocentrism: 'A l'intérieur de cette scène (de l'écriture) la simplicité ponctuelle du sujet classique est introuvable.'[94] Derrida also suggests, in a note, that *archi-écriture* is an effacement of the subject and the proper name, recalling Sollers's emphasis on writing as thanatography and on the question of the name. Even in so far as Lacan's interventions are a subversion of the subject, remaining centred on the question of the subject, Derrida's article is a critique of Lacanian theory. But analyses closer to *Tel Quel*, by Baudry and Kristeva, will take up the question of the subject, a subject specifically of literature, to elaborate a theory of the subject that will eventually displace the Derridean emphases and envelop the Lacanian space. It is possible to refer, therefore, to *Tel Quel*'s psychoanalysis, or its literary psychoanalysis, as evolving between Derrida and Lacan, and essentially via Kristeva.

Derrida also sketches out in this essay the foundations of the area in which *Tel Quel*'s theory and its articulation with psychoanalysis is specifically implicated. The question of difference or *différance* is linked to Freud's death-drive. Difference, Derrida proposes, is a movement that defers a 'dangerous investment'[95] through the constitution of a reserve (*réserve*). *Dépense* is deferred through repetition. Life defends itself against death through an economy of difference, repetition, reserve, in which repetition and *différance* appear as the working of death in life, the

[91] M. Tort, 'L'Effet Sade', *TQ* 28 (winter 1967), 75.
[92] R. Barthes, 'L'Arbre du crime', ibid. 34.
[93] Pleynet, 'L'infinie virtualité des langues', interview with author, Paris, 1990.
[94] Derrida, *L'Écriture et la différence*, 335.
[95] Ibid. 300.

death drive. *Dépense* is also superimposed on to writing, as an expending that is not fixed in any particular value. Sollers's *Logiques* and the analyses of Bataille had already prefigured the economy as a deferral of *dépense*. Derrida's identification of *différance* with *dépense* and the death-drive identifies the principal space of *Tel Quel*'s articulation with psychoanalysis as the dynamic between the primary drives and their secondary representations, the pre-symbolic and the symbolic. Kristeva's work in particular will focus on this dynamic. However, Derrida warns against proposing an original life that then comes to protect itself;[96] the concept of primacy is to be rethought, since it is the trace or the difference, between life and death, that is primary, a fact that undermines the notion of origin. Derrida links this to Freud's concept of the *nachträglich* (translated as *à-retardement* [97]), a rethinking of temporality which is of fundamental importance for the review, and for our consideration of it. The *après-coup* transforms the temporality of *Tel Quel*'s theory, and Derrida's input is crucial for this fact.

While indicating the ambiguity of the space of *Tel Quel*, between the primary and the secondary, or between Derrida and Lacan, Derrida's text also identifies important areas of enquiry, such as the question of scenic space, *scène*, as opposed to one of representation. It suggests the elaboration of a psychoanalysis of literature as a focus on 'le devenir littéraire du littéral',[98] that is, an analysis of the literary signifier and its specificity. That Derrida indicates the specificity of literature as the space of the letter, *le littéral*, paradoxically identifies the relevance of Lacan, as Sollers will indicate in 'Survol-Rapports (Blocs)/Conflit', Lacan's insistence on the instance of the letter is part of a materialist theory of language.[99] Kristeva's reading of Saussure's 'Anagrammes' is also productive in this area.[100] *Tel Quel*'s extension of its theory into psychoanalysis takes place in this space of writing and of the letter, and Derrida's essay is programmatic here.

Baudry's essay 'Freud et la "création littéraire" ',[101] extends the critique of Lacan that we have brought out of Derrida's article. It is

[96] Ibid. 362.
[97] Ibid. 303.
[98] Ibid. 340.
[99] See n. 64.
[100] See J. Kristeva, 'Pour une sémiologie des paragrammes', *TQ* 29 (spring 1967). The review will later pub. excerpts from Saussure's unpub. 'Anagrammes', ed. by Jean Starobinski, in *TQ* 37 (spring 1969): J. Starobinski, 'Le Texte dans le texte, extraits inédits des Cahiers d'anagrammes de F. de Saussure'.
[101] J.-L. Baudry, 'Freud et la "création littéraire" ', *TQ* 32 (winter 1968) and in *Théorie d'ensemble*.

telling within the history of the review, because of its distinction between two aspects of Freud. The first is centred on *The Interpretation of Dreams*, with the unconscious proposed as a general writing by Derrida, and this will be the Freud celebrated in *Tel Quel* in this period, but the second, with which Baudry is specifically concerned in this essay, is the emphasis on the author and 'literary creation' of Freud's analysis of literary texts. Baudry shows how Freud's view of literature is entirely taken up in a view of literary creation determined by the ideology of representation, expression, the subjectivity of the author, and a distinction between reality and imagination that is constantly undermined by the more radical insights of the writing of the unconscious. So the Freud relevant to *Tel Quel* is essentially a Freud read through Derrida. Implicitly, Baudry initiates in *Tel Quel* the argument that psychoanalysis is blocked when it comes to writing about literature, which will be developed, notably by Sollers, in the 1970s. Psychoanalysis cannot understand the literary text, and its attempts to do so miss the essential radicality of literature, since literature moves beyond the space with which analysis is primarily concerned. Psychoanalysis can, however, suggest parallels between the functioning of the unconscious and that of the literary text. Lacan's reading of Poe, which is later suggested as an exception,[102] is not referred to, probably as yet unread by the writers of *Tel Quel*. On the other hand, writing, literature (Baudry refers to Lautréamont) can reveal to psychoanalysis its transgression in literature, through a parallel and an extension of the concept of writing into the concept of the unconscious.

Baudry identifies the limitation of psychoanalysis as its obsession with the subject as centre. The Freudian distinction between reality and imagination, or between real dreams and literary dreams, which emerges in Freud's analysis of Jensen's *Gradiva*, derives from the persistence of the reference to the subject, the position of the author. We can see that Lacan's psychoanalysis is at the same time within this problematic and a transgression of it, since it seems centred on the question of the subject while it is a 'subversion du sujet' and of its positioning within language. Again, the philosophical background here is the situation of difference in or outside language that we have proposed as the area of an oscillation in *Tel Quel*'s theory.

---

[102] e.g. by Shoshana Felman in 'La Chose littéraire, sa folie, son pouvoir', *TQ* 80–1 (summer–autumn 1979) (an interview with Sollers), and by Stuart Schneidermann in 'Lacan et la littérature', *TQ* 84 (summer 1980).

In a final section of the article, Baudry also suggests that desire is an effect of representation:

Ne pourrait-on pas dire que le désir lui-même est un effet de la représentation, d'une mise en présence, et que dans la mesure où il est toujours désir de quelque chose . . . il est engagé dans la pensée téléologique du sens.[103]

From this analysis we can infer that the problematic of desire is relevant to the restricted economy of *la parole*, the focus of Lacan's enterprise, while writing, implicitly, is more relevantly linked to the problematic of the death-drive and *dépense*. Desire and the phantasm are 'impropre ou inutile', in Baudry's terms, for the question of writing as textual production.[104] This rejection of fantasy seems to cut out a whole area of enquiry relevant to literature, in favour of its more extreme moments. *Tel Quel*'s engagement with psychoanalysis, premised on Derrida's stress on writing, is partial, since it elides any analysis of representations, particularly visual representations, and of elements such as fantasy. Lacan's analysis is suggested, implicitly, as restricted in its focus on desire and the logic of the phantasm. Baudry links this restriction again to the central question of the subject; for writing as for sexuality it is not a question of the subject and his or her desire but of inscription and *dépense*, and this in turn is identified as Freud's 'beyond the pleasure principle'. The question of the subject is effectively effaced under that of writing, at this stage, but in *Tel Quel*'s later emphases it will be reintroduced in specifically psychoanalytical terms in the work of Kristeva, who can be seen as playing a decisive role in the mediation of the review between Derrida and Lacan and elaborating a dialectic between the subject and the 'non-subject' or the 'not yet subject'.

Perversion, Play, Après-Coup, *and Infinite Analysis*

Two specific areas where *Tel Quel*'s theory and practice of the text hinges on psychoanalysis and may derive some theoretical justification in Freud are those of the neurosis/perversion opposition and of play. It is a question here of a Freud upon whom *Tel Quel* has retroactively projected the characteristics of radicality. In Sollers's *Logiques*, the text as a perverse permutation opposed social discourse as neurosis. The text and neurosis are mutually exclusive, as Baudry suggests.[105] The text is

---

[103] Baudry, 'Freud et la "création littéraire" ', in *Théorie d'ensemble*, 173.
[104] Ibid.
[105] Ibid. 159–60.

seen as a play, an aspect Baudry implies was one of Freud's more radical insights which were not developed. He refers, in compensation, to Nietzsche's thought as having a more consistent emphasis on *le jeu*, or Bataille's *volonté de chance*, potentially subversive of rational, serious thought. Here, play and reality are not opposed, as for Freud. Play is not thought as fantasy but as a permutation that produces the real. A significant aspect of *Tel Quel*'s counter-ideology is a privilege given to the ludic and the permutational, determining thought and writing, rather than being a product of it. This emerges both in the theory (the reading of Sade) and in practice (the reference to the I Ching of *Drame*). The aleatory aspect which Baudry sees as hinted at in Freud may however be more determined by *Tel Quel*'s theory itself. It is essentially a critical approach to Freud's concern with the subject and fantasy.

A further point of juncture with Freud is on the notion of the *après-coup*. In the same article, Baudry identifies Freud's insight that the phantasm always carries a trace of its origin. This is a justification of the idea that any writing is already a retroactive reading of another text. The temporality of the *après coup*, which we can ally with the Derridean trace, is behind the general notion of intertextuality that functions in *Tel Quel*'s theory. In this sense there is no original moment of creation, an insight that Baudry also finds in Freud, in his analysis of the psychoanalyst's reliance on the concept of representation. Following an analysis of Michel Tort in *Cahiers pour l'analyse*,[106] Baudry suggests that variants of representation are operative at all levels of Freud's topology; at the level of the pulsions, their unconscious representations (*Vorstellungen*) and symptomatic formations (*Darstellungen*). The topology appears as 'une représentation de représentation de représentation',[107] suggesting an infinite chain of representations that become signifiers, since no longer related to an origin. This suggests Freud's more radical insight, 'l'autre versant de la pensée freudienne',[108] of interpretation as the eternal *renvoi* (referral) of signifier to signifier, but representation, especially visual representation, is written out of *Tel Quel*'s version of Freudian theory, leaving a serious aporia, sacrificed for the ideology of the permutational.

[106] J.-L. Baudry, art. cit., *Théorie d'ensemble*, 166. M. Tort's article is 'Le Concept freudien de "Représentant" ', *Cahiers pour l'analyse*, 5.
[107] Baudry, 'Freud et la "création littéraire" ', in *Théorie d'ensemble*, 172–3.
[108] Ibid.

What Derrida and Baudry elaborate is an affirmative analysis of Freud and of Lacan at some particular moments of their work. The more orthodox and central aspects of psychoanalysis are bypassed by the focus on literature. *Tel Quel* does not attempt to elaborate a psychoanalytic theory of the text, but uses literature to point to radical and restricted, undeveloped moments in psychoanalysis. In the same way that Marxism is appropriated for its undoing, Freud is called upon so that the limits of his thought on literature can be suggested. The moment of theory is beset by internal contradictions which reveal the synthesis to be conflictual on every level.

Freud and the Dreamwork

Derrida's essay on Freud was published in the review in 1966, Baudry's essay on literary creation in 1968, by which time Derridean writing and Lacanian theory were both enlisted in favour of the synthesizing project of *Théorie d'ensemble*, inscribing the contradictions we have underlined. Freud is also enlisted in the rupture or epistemological break of knowledge at the end of the nineteenth century. But Freud is far more important than Marx for *Tel Quel*'s theory, a fact brought out in Kristeva's contributions to *Théorie d'ensemble*, which at certain points are obliged to refer to Freud to extend Marxist theory to the area of 'pre-sense productivity', or the production of meaning before exchange.[109] The Freudian unconscious and the notion of the dreamwork effectively open up this area.

Kristeva identifies Freud's unconscious as a production before the positioning of value and its exchange. 'travail antérieur au dire circulaire, à la communication'.[110] Freud's work on the language of dreams, particularly on displacement and condensation, opens up the area of a study of language considered apart from meaning. For *Tel Quel*, Freud's work is analogous to Marx's emphasis on use value and, in Bataillean terms, opens out the area of a *dépense* anterior to meaning. This productivity of language is termed, by Kristeva and others, *l'autre scène*, or a space different from that of meaning, the sign, representation, and communication.[111] Structuralist theory, with its emphasis on models of communication and structure, is also displaced by the stress on production.

[109] See n. 25.
[110] Kristeva, 'La Sémiologie', in *Théorie d'ensemble*, 86.
[111] Ibid. 90.

Interpretation or Reading

An important qualification must be added, however, to the comparison between the dream and writing, which identifies another area of Freud's importance and forestalls the objection that while *Tel Quel*'s theory denies interpretation, Freud privileges it. The latent content of the dream and language as text are not hidden behind or before the manifest content or language when it is seen as communication. For it to be so would be to affirm the ideology of representation and expression. The dissimulated production is inscribed in the text as *lacunaire*; it is already there, in the text, and is what enables the text to function. For Baudry it is an unreadable inscription effaced by meaning as exchange: 'Inscription non lisible tant qu'une écriture, par un redoublement de l'inscription, ne le donne pas à lire.'[112]

Productivity, figured as an absent letter, or *lettre volée*, is only readable once a reading uncovers or rewrites it, affirming the complementarity of reading and writing as emphasized by *Tel Quel*. This entails a new, non-representative, conception of the relation between a text and what it dissimulates. The productivity, the writing that determines the text is always already inside it, but in the mode of absence, silent. Freud's interpretation and Lacan's analysis, a reading of dissimulated signifiers or symptoms within the analysand's discourse, appear particularly relevant to *Tel Quel*'s analogy, although this parallel had already been pointed out by Althusser.[113] Freud appears as a pioneer of a new conception of reading which defines it as a *redoublement*, a doubling of the writing it reads. *Tel Quel*'s theory of reading is distinct from a method of interpretation, since writing and reading are supposed to be part of the same process, not part of an intersubjective dialogue. The reading writes or rewrites the already written text in such a way as to make apparent the inscription of the general, dissimulated writing that determines the text. Baudry writes: 'Lire apparaîtra donc comme un acte d'écriture et pareillement écrire se révélera être un acte de lecture—écrire et lire n'étant que les moments simultanés d'une même production.'[114]

The reading/writing will also read the inscription of ideology in the text, a crucial factor that distinguishes the text that remains within ideological closure from one that transgresses it. For *Tel Quel* Freud joins

---

[112] J.-L. Baudry, 'Écriture, fiction idéologie', in *Théorie d'ensemble*, 131.

[113] Cf. Althusser, *Lire le Capital*, i (Paris, 1965) and the article 'Freud et Lacan' *La Nouvelle Critique*, 161–2 (Dec. 1964–Jan. 1965) and in id., *Positions*, 36.

[114] Baudry, 'Écriture, fiction, idéologie', in *Théorie d'ensemble*, 131.

up with Marx as theorized by Althusser, in *Lire le Capital*, and with Lautréamont, in so far as their texts rewrite, double, and transgress, the inscription of the text in the ideology of literature. Freud appears, *après coup*, as an instigator of the reading/writing complementarity proposed by *Tel Quel*. The temporality of this projection, after the event, is characteristic of the operation whereby theory justifies itself by reference to previous systems, only to undermine these systems by the implantation or the uncovering of subversive elements within them. The same projection of the characteristics of a post-structuralist radicality on to Freud's work is operative here, but this retroactive reading itself is what is found in Freud. While Freudian and Lacanian analysis valorizes the moment of reading, rather than the original trauma, *Tel Quel*'s theory of reading justifies its own reading of Freud and Marx as opposed to any original intention in those authors. *Tel Quel*'s reading of Marx and Freud, like its history of literature, is a transformative reading that emphasizes a moment of creativity outside historical temporality.

Primary and Secondary Dépense

The articulation of the theory of the text to Freudian psychoanalysis is innovative and powerful in itself, but is problematic when it comes to the link to Marxism. As Kristeva suggests, Freud's analysis of the dreamwork makes up for an absence in Marx. Marx does not tackle the productivity anterior to the exchange-system of language that he criticizes, and this lack restricts the scope of Marxism. The problematic link lies in the relation between the unconscious, *dépense*, work and use value. Use value and work remain within the restricted economy that is analogous to the conscious and the pre-conscious, while *dépense* is an anti-economic principle. The unconscious writing, moreover, cannot be a *dépense* as part of a primary process, since writing is seen as a detour in response to a primary process or an excess of stimuli. There is a distinction between a primary excess, which in Bataille's terms would be the energy given without debt by the sun,[115] and a secondary *dépense*, in the detour away from this violence taken by writing and the unconscious. The unconscious as writing, in *Tel Quel*'s theory, is a deferred *dépense*, an infinite repetition and effacement. Production, meanwhile, can be associated with this secondary *dépense*, but only if the conscious elements of the subject of production and the aim of

---

[115] See G. Bataille, 'La Notion de dépense', in id., *Oeuvres complètes* i (Paris, 1970), and *La Part maudite*, ibid. vii (Paris, 1976).

production are abstracted. *Dépense* and production seem in all respects to be mutually exclusive. There is a certain idealization of work and production, in *Tel Quel*'s Marxism, which is forced on to the Freudian and Bataillean terms of primary process and excess. This element of excess will be the factor that pushes Marxism towards the limits of its structure, while the Freudian death-drive tends in any case to problematize the more economic Oedipal structure.

Fragments of Lacanian Theory

While *Tel Quel*'s initial engagement with Freud is filtered through Derrida's reading and hints at an articulation with Bataille, Lacan is only really present at this stage in fragments; there is no real theoretical engagement with the Lacanian theory of the primacy of the symbolic, or the mirror stage, or the symbolic/real/imaginary trinity. Goux's 'Numismatiques' had implicated in its structural model Lacan's theory of the phallus, comparing it to the capitalization of money as value in capitalism, but Goux's work is dissociable from the essential currents of *Tel Quel*'s theory.[116] Sollers refers to Lacan's 'materialist theory of language' in his work on the signifier and the letter.[117] This is significant in that it is over this question that a Derridean critique of Lacan will be elaborated.[118] The reference to the 'instance of the letter' is relevant for *Tel Quel* in so far as the signifier, the materiality of language, is thought to determine the production of meaning. Lacan's thesis that the subject is represented by a signifier for another signifier, referred to by Michel Tort in his essay on Sade,[119] is interesting for *Tel Quel* in its proposition of a subjectivity subject to the permutations of writing. However, the reference to Lacan's theory here does not express an absolute agreement between *Tel Quel*'s theory of the text and the entirety of Lacan's psychoanalytical theory or his theory of language as the irreducibly symbolic Other of human intersubjectivity. The interest in the signifier and the letter is followed through in a more extensive and transgressive way by Kristeva in her 'paragrammatism', derived from a study of Saussure's 'Anagrammes'. Kristeva's analysis does not treat the letter or

[116] After 'Numismatiques', *TQ* 35–6, (autumn 1968–winter 1969), Goux will not publish anything more in the review. His later books, *Freud et Marx: Économie et symbolique* (Paris, 1973) and *Les Iconoclastes* (Paris, 1977) develop the articulation of Marx, Freud, and Bataille.
[117] See n. 64.
[118] See J.-L. Nancy and P. Lacoue-Labarthe, *Le Titre de la lettre* (Paris, 1973), a reading of Lacan which was taken as a criticism by him.
[119] Tort, 'L'Effet Sade', *TQ* 28 (winter 1967), 75.

signifier as a presence but effects a shift to a process of *signifiance*, which combines the differential process of Derrida with a reformulation of semiology and the concept of the sign. The subject is implicated in this process, establishing Kristeva's intervention eventually as an approach to the trans-subjective rather than the split subject in Lacan or the abstraction of the subject in Derrida. Lacan is present strategically, as a reference in Sollers's essay, but Lacan's psychoanalysis is essentially bypassed. The Lacanian models of the vector, passing from signifier to signified and constituting the subject through a kind of shuttle or pulsation, and the logic of fantasy, can be read as structural models which the textual practice of the writers Jacques Henric (*Archées*, 1969) and Jacqueline Risset (*Jeu*, 1971) uses, but only to write across them, transgressing their structures.[120]

Tel Quel's engagement with psychoanalysis appears to be based essentially on the identification of the unconscious with a radical textual productivity. This initial engagement is very much determined by the specific context of the review's textual theory, its engagement with Derrida, but also by an open approach to the work of Lacan. Lacanian theory in its totality is not tackled. In the 1970s it will become more relevant to an ethics in the wake of Marxism, and Sollers and Lacan will engage in a *dialogue de sourds* over Joyce (see Chapter 4). *Tel Quel* will publish a limited amount of work by analysts, mostly on literature and increasingly over the question of sexuality.[121] The review's attitude to Freud remains an ambiguous mixture of criticism and an affirmation of his fundamental radicality. However, the engagement with psychoanalysis becomes increasingly mediated through the work of Kristeva. By

[120] The texts seem to propose a topology analogous to Lacan's real/symbolic/imaginary structure, effecting a demystification of the imaginary often figured as a screen, an opening of the symbolic, figured as a circle or sphere, to the real, figured as a ground or *vide*.

[121] Articles by psychoanalysts in *Tel Quel* (excepting J. Kristeva) are: M. de M'Uzan, 'Richesse', *TQ* 4 (winter 1961) and 'Aperçus psychanalytiques sur le processus de création littéraire', *TQ* 19 (autumn 1964); M. Tort, 'L'Effet Sade', *TQ* 28 (winter 1967); Luce Irigaray, 'Le V(i)ol de la lettre', *TQ* 39 (autumn 1969); M.-C. Boons, 'Automatisme, compulsion: Marque, remarque', *TQ* 42 (summer 1970); D. Sibony, 'A propos des mathématiques modernes', *TQ* 51 (autumn 1972); id., 'Bifurcations', *TQ* 54 (summer 1973); id., 'Premier meurtre', *TQ* 64 (winter 1975); G. Miller, 'A propos du fascisme français', *TQ* 64; A. Verdiglione, 'Notulae', *TQ* 64; A. Compagnon, 'L'Analyse orpheline', *TQ* 65 (spring 1976); D. Sibony, 'Premier meurtre II', *TQ* 66 (summer 1976); id., 'Écriture et folie', *TQ* 70 (summer 1977); id., 'Musical I', *TQ* 71–3 (autumn 1977); Schneidermann, 'Lacan et la littérature', *TQ* 84 (summer 1980). The only book by a psychoanalyst, excepting Kristeva, in the 'Collection Tel Quel' was D. Sibony, *Le Nom et le corps* (Paris, 1974). From the mid-1960s to the end of the decade, Lacan's name was on the list of forthcoming publications, but nothing was ever pub. In 1976 an editorial signalled the creation of a *cercle psychanalytique*, but apparently nothing came of it.

the 1970s new psychoanalytic references have emerged, which have an effect in the review. Lacan would, in the view of many, go off on an infinite digression on knots and topological problems, losing his previous cutting edge, while a new and crucial psychoanalytic context around feminine sexuality would become prominent, in the wake of 1968 and the influence of Derrida on writers like Luce Irigaray, Michèle Montrelay, Hélène Cixous, and Cathérine Clément. The moment of theory for psychoanalysis essentially passes outside *Tel Quel*, while its effects have a greater impact in the next decade, in the wake of theory.

THEORETICAL FICTION

Alongside the theoretical work, the review continued in the late 1960s to act as an experimental foyer for textual practice.[122] The 'Collection Tel Quel' also continued to function as a vital corridor for the publication of fictional works, novels and poetry, from within and outside the committee. The innovative textual practice of *Tel Quel* and its function as a forum for writing with a theoretical consciousness, pushing often at the limits of fiction in its usual sense and also at the limits of typographic structure and readability, is a vital element of the review's activity and its relation to the context during the time of theory.

The Novel in the Late 1960s

The context of fiction at this time is wide and disparate. Evidently, it is not possible to give a comprehensive survey of it, there will be obvious elisions. It is possible to delineate the broad trends and the emerging individualities of the period. The period is post-*nouveau roman*, in the sense that the lessons of this ideology of the novel had already been learnt and the writers were not, as a group, proposing a new departure. The individual *nouveaux romanciers* were still producing texts, but the *nouveau roman* as a phenomenon, despite the efforts of Jean Ricardou and the Colloque de Cérisy of 1971, was in a phase of decadence.

Robbe-Grillet published the novel *Projet pour une révolution à New York* in 1970. It extends the questioning of narrative, narrative temporality,

---

[122] Apart from excerpts from forthcoming novels and poetry collections, the review would pub. work by P. Rottenberg, Marc Robic, J. Henric, P. Boudon, C. Cabantous, C. Minière, S. Ivankov, J.-M. Soreau, M. Laugua, as well as unpub. texts by W. Burroughs, J. Genet, A. Artaud, F. Ponge, and A. Adamov.

and viewpoint, but it remains within the framework of narrative fiction, even while complicating it. The same notion of subversion without departure from an essential frame can apply to the work of Pinget (*Quelqu'un*, 1965; *Le Libera*, 1968; *Passacaille*, 1969). It is a fiction where the mechanism of narration has broken down (whence the opening phrase of *Passacaille*, 'Quelque chose est cassé dans le méchanisme'[123]) leaving the mechanics of narration open and to be read. This leads to a kind of detective work to find out what is happening. In *Passacaille* the phrase 'On ne sait jamais, prudence' is regularly repeated. The recourse to the detective story resulting from the breakdown of narration is an influential seam in the novel, but one essentially restricted to a complication of narrative structure and set within its limits.

Other *nouveaux romanciers* were also active. Sarraute wrote *Entre la vie et la mort* in 1968, perhaps the finest of her works, which explore the tense dialectic of speech and thought, interiority and 'others'. Claude Simon produced *Histoire* (1967), *La Bataille de Pharsale* (1969), *Orion aveugle* (1970), and *Les Corps conducteurs* (1971). With *La Bataille de Pharsale*, Simon moved towards a more textualized form of writing, that is, one where the writing is produced more at the level of its linguistic reality than as a representative relation to an objective reality filtered through a narrative consciousness. The influence of Ricardou, and through him of *Tel Quel*, may be evident here; Ricardou produced an important essay on the novel in *Critique*, focusing on the textual aspects.[124] However, Ricardou notes that: 'l'établissement du texte moderne se reconnaît notamment à ce qu'il métamorphose les procédures expressives traditionnelles en moyens de production'.[125] This metamorphosis seems restricted in relation to *Tel Quel*'s textuality, where aleatory structures and the material tissue of language provide a frame which the writing traverses, rather than using aspects of narrative as generative elements. With Simon, and with Ricardou (*La Prose de Constantinople*, 1965; *Les Lieux-dits*, 1969) a referential architecture is needed to weld the disparate fragments of text into a novel. The major difference between the texts of Robbe-Grillet, Simon, Pinget, Ollier, and Butor, and the *Tel Quel* texts seems to lie in this appeal to an architecture to provide coherence, while for *Tel Quel* the structure is a vestige that enables the aleatory,

---

[123] R. Pinget, *Passacaille* (Paris, 1969), 12.
[124] J. Ricardou, 'La Bataille de la phrase', *Crit.* 274 (Mar. 1970).
[125] Ibid. 226–7.

permutational play of the text, while writing and reading become its reality. The influence of the *nouveau roman* is confused with the emphasis on textual reality of *Tel Quel*, via Ricardou, but important differences remain.

While the *récit* remained important, however pluralized and complicated, for the *nouveaux romanciers*, a different perspective was adopted by writers whose focus was more on the way language mediated experience, its relation to itself, its relation to its negativity, or silence. The influence of the writing of Blanchot, who did not produce works of fiction in this period, but the philosophical *L'Entretien infini* (1969), itself an exemplary textual monument, was evident on the writer Roger Laporte, whose autobiographical series of novels (*Une voix de fin silence*, 1966; *Pourquoi*, 1967; *Fugue*, 1970; and *Supplément*, 1973) are about the experience of writing lived by the writer. The same meditation on the experience of writing is detectable in the work of Hélène Cixous, (*Tombe*, 1965; *Dedans*, 1969) moving towards a writing of femininity and of the female body. In its desire to escape the phallic postulation of meaning or presence it was a writing in the gaps, holes, and silences of language; it attempted to inhabit the silence to which femininity was relegated by a patriarchal discourse. While this writing may seem similar to that of *Tel Quel*, its postulation of a silence underlying language and deriving expression in its fracturing owed more to Blanchot's subtle influence.

While the *nouveau roman* problematized elements of plot and character while retaining them or a vestige of them, other writers subjected story to the play of language and game-like structures. The works of Perec (*Les Choses*, 1965; *Quel petit vélo*, 1966; *Un homme qui dort*, 1967; *La Disparition* 1969) proposed a ludic fiction in which the possibilities of linguistic form were explored, not without humour. *Tel Quel*, while close, in its focus on aleatory structure, to the *Oulipo* group to which Perec belonged, had a different, less humorous, approach to the ludic. While for Oulipo, play determines content, for *Tel Quel* the focus on play is determined by an ideology that sees this perverse permutation as in conflict with society's neurosis. *Tel Quel*'s innovative play is more austere, less comic, than that of writers like Perec. It also displays a less fetishistic regard for the surface-level idiosyncrasies of language, being more concerned with shifts at a fundamental level. In *La Disparition*, the elision of the *e* throughout the text is an arbitrary play at the level of the signifier, the surface of language; in *Tel Quel*'s fiction, play also functions to produce meaning.

Despite the prevalence in the novel of a concentration on form and the modalities of creation, there was an equally innovative but perhaps less marked turn to story and myth as a fictional element. The work of Michel Tournier (*Vendredi ou les limbes du Pacifique*, 1967; *Le Roi des Aulnes*, 1970) exemplifies this turn. Innovation is not diminished, but the novels of Tournier appeared as a return, after modernism, to a reference to myth as model. The *Tel Quel* novel occupies a central place, between the *nouveau roman* and its decadence and the Blanchotesque writings of figures such as Laporte, Cixous and others, while writers like Tournier were developing distinctive responses to the period. Other novelists, such as Modiano, Duras, Le Clézio, are less identifiable as aspects of a current. Their work is exceptional and original, but does not have the same experimental force of *Tel Quel*'s theoretical fictions.

Change/Tel Quel

It is also important to distinguish the texts produced by *Tel Quel* from another strand of what can be called theoretical fiction, the fictional productions of the rival group Change, set up by Jean-Pierre Faye after his departure from the committee in 1967. The texts of the Change collective, less numerous and relatively less well known, are similar in appearance to the *Tel Quel* novels, in their lack of proper names and their typographic disposition, but the perspective and ideology that informs them is distinct. Faye's novels from before the split were set in a psychological frame, which distinguishes them from the textual space of the novels of Sollers, Baudry, Rottenberg, and others, where it is more a question of a subjection to the effect of writing than a superimposition of psychology and writing. After *Analogues*, in 1964, Faye published *L'Écluse*, also from 1964, then a new edition of his first novel *Entre les rues* (1958), and then *Les Troyens* in 1970, followed by *Inferno: Versions* in 1975. The other novelists of the Change collective were Jean-Claude Montel, whose *Plages* appeared in Cayrol's 'Écrire' collection in 1968, then *Le Carneval* in the 'Change' collection run by Faye, in 1969. Another novelist, Philippe Boyer (later to contribute to *L'Infini* and to write a book on Proust), published *Mots d'ordre* and *Non-lieu* in 1969 and 1972 respectively. *Change* also published work by the writer Danièle Collobert, *Dire I–II* in 1972 and *Il donc* in 1976, after her first novel *Meurtre*, published by Gallimard in 1964.

Faye's novels are architectural in their structure, while those of Sollers or Baudry can be described as geometric. *L'Écluse* sets up an interplay between names, generated by the 'sluice' (*l'écluse*) as an internal division or doubling, 'une ville coupée en deux',[126] but, as in Faye's previous works, this is framed in a narrative and related to the psychology of identifiable characters. This anchoring in narrative and psychology of textual structure puts Faye's novels in an entirely different context from those of *Tel Quel*; it prevents the text from becoming the cause and effect of itself, establishing an obstacle between the experience of reading and the production of meaning, or writing. *Les Troyens* is subtitled 'Hexagrammes', signalling the *entrecroisement* of the six previous texts Faye had written.[127] This hexagrammatic structure is again related to the geography of a city and to the story of a narrator's search, and the narrative relates encounters with a number of named characters. Narrative is problematized and made intertextual and semi-autobiographical through the insertion of previous texts, but it remains a locus of reference and a generating principle. This reference and motive is absent from the novels produced by *Tel Quel*, which refer to their own functioning without going through a narrative frame, directly or metaphorically, and not with reference to a recognizable, particular reality or the psychology of a character. This might suggest a major difference to be in terms of abstraction and degrees of particularity in reference. The *Tel Quel* novel escapes referentiality through abstraction, thereby making the moment of reading more particular and singular, focusing on the materiality of the word or phoneme.

While Danièle Collobert's work was less novelistic, more related to an interior, subjective space, after the manner of Blanchot, J.-C. Montel's texts are similar to those of Faye in their anchoring of a textual writing, one that has a consciousness of itself, that refers to itself and essentially is about the experience of reading and inhabiting a text, to a particular narrative event or structure. They are less structured and framed than Faye's, and appear very much like *Tel Quel* texts such as Baudry's. They are nevertheless just the other side of a dividing-line that separates a text from a narrative carried by a text. The theoretical perspective that informs these novels is distinct from the theory of *Tel Quel*. The Change group appeals to a pseudo-Chomskyan theory of a deep structure underneath the surface of language effecting transformations and exchanges which then appear on the surface of language. The deep structure is proposed as essentially narrative. Change's fiction is decisively programmed by this linguistic theory, mainly the work of J.-P.

[126] J.-P. Faye, *L'Écluse* (Paris, 1964), back cover.
[127] Id., *Les Troyens: Hexagrammes* (Paris, 1970), back cover.

Faye and the Chomskyan linguist Mitsou Ronat.[128] For *Tel Quel*, on the other hand, the deep-structure model is not pertinent. The surface of the text hides nothing, its engenderment is effected more on the level of the materiality of the text, at the level of rhythms, phonemic patterns of repetition, metaphoric and metonymic patterns, and typography. The text is a surface without depth.

Enlarging Textual Space

After the initial entry of *Tel Quel*'s own textuality into an area where the works considered the linguistic space they inhabited, and the structure of that space, the second group of texts, produced between 1965 and 1971, enlarge and explore this space, articulating it with the areas of ideology, and of sexuality. The emergence of intertextuality is a crucial element, paralleled in theory in the work of Kristeva. The texts address their relations not only to previous works, but to social discourse seen as text, to ideology as it is inscribed there, and to the subjective tissue of the writer as subject. The *Tel Quel* novel from 1965 to 1971 can be described as an abstract textuality. This means effectively that it is impossible to take anything out of the texts that would account for the effect of their reading, to describe or analyse the texts. Their reading is anchored at the moment of the eye's traversal of the page, which echoes that of the pen. Part of what can be said about the texts is that they defy representation and explanation. They can be written 'about'; a writing can be generated from them that analyses itself. So in writing about these texts it is the experience of their reading that is being unthreaded. It is also possible to set out details of their structure and of their intertextuality—that is, how they relate to each other and to earlier and later texts—and to trace general movements of the theory of fiction and fictionalizing of theory they produce.

The works fall into three broad categories: novels written by committee members, novels from outside but published in the 'Collection Tel Quel', and novels published elsewhere which are relevant to this textual space, or are articulated with it in critical articles by *Tel Quel* writers. The publications concerned are:

1967 J.-L. Baudry, *Personnes*
1968 P. Sollers, *Nombres*

---

[128] *Change*'s theory is well represented in the two vols. relating to a 1973 conference at Cérisy, titled 'Changement de forme, révolution, langage'. See J.-P. Faye and J. Roubaud (eds.), *Change de forme* (Paris, 1975) and *Change matériel* (Paris, 1975).

J. Thibaudeau, *Imaginez la nuit.*
1969 J. Henric, *Archées*
1970 J. -L. Baudry, *La 'Création'*
P. Guyotat, *Éden, Éden, Éden*
E. Sanguineti, *Le Noble Jeu de l'oye.*
1971 P. Sollers, *Lois*; M. Roche, *Circus*;
1972 G. Scarpetta, *Scène*
N. Balestrini, *Tristan*; S. Sarduy, *Cobra.*

The three major novelists of the committee are Sollers, Baudry, and Thibaudeau, while in the 'Collection', Jacques Henric and Guy Scarpetta write novels informed by the perspective of *Tel Quel*. The works by Sanguineti and Balestrini are translated from the Italian by Thibaudeau and Risset respectively, annexed to the *Tel Quel* group, while deriving from a different context, that of the Italian *neoavanguardia* and the *Gruppo '63*.[129] The works by Maurice Roche, Pierre Guyotat, and Severo Sarduy (co-translated from the Spanish by Sollers and the author) are slightly different in their approach, but throw an interesting light on *Tel Quel*'s fiction in their form and through the comments of *Tel Quel* writers about them.

After the first series of texts, ending in 1965 with Sollers's *Drame* and Rottenberg's *Le Livre partagé*, this second group extends textual space to articulate it with politics, seen as a textual tissue, with ideology, seen both as myth (particularly explored in Baudry's *La 'Création'*, which focuses on creation myths) and also as a certain way of reading, and with biography, particularly in the case of Thibaudeau's two works, which explore the tissue of memory as it is fixed in the text. These novels have a certain baroque flavour, but the geometrical structures they often use as frameworks restrict this aesthetic, which emerges more in the less structured work of Sarduy or Maurice Roche. The novels also tend to appeal, in their articulation with ideology, to non-Western thought and culture. Sollers's *Nombres*, for example, is interspersed with Chinese characters which tend to block the reading process and brutally introduce the limits of Western ideology. It features quotations, unattributed, from works of Chinese thought. Henric's *Archées* appeals to Zen Buddhism, particularly to a work called *Zen in the Art of Archery* (1972) by E. Herrigel, to develop a non-expressive, non-causal way of conceiving writing, confronting this with the Western tradition of the medieval

---

[129] For a discussion of this context, see C. Wagstaff, 'The Neo-avant-garde', in M. Caesar and P. Hainsworth (eds.), *Writers and Society in Contemporary Italy* (Leamington Spa, 1984).

chanson de geste and the paintings of Uccello. Baudry's *La 'Création'* amasses and confronts creation myths, including Greek, Christian, Chinese, and Vedic Indian, with a discourse about literary 'creation' and its ideology. The texts do not represent a counter-ideology, but tend to write across the structures of ideology. The formal patterns and rhythms of the text establish cross-currents passing through the ideological and intertextual structures that are set up.

The texts of Maurice Roche and Pierre Guyotat can be seen as tangential to *Tel Quel* textuality; they both feature singular aspects that make them distinct from the texts of Sollers, Baudry, Thibaudeau, and Henric. Sarduy's *Cobra* falls into a different grouping of texts produced during the 1970s, more relevant to the parodic heterogeneity that emerged in that period.

Maurice Roche: Compact Form

Before *Compact* (1966) Maurice Roche had published only a short monograph on the Italian madrigalist Monteverdi,[130] which suggests the musical aspect of the novelist's work. The text appears as a score rather than a narrative. Given Monteverdi's crucial place in the transition from polyphony to single-line harmony in the history of music, and supposing an influence, the novel *Compact* can be read as a polyphony of voices tied together into the single form of the novel, its 'compact'. The voices do not form a stable harmony, but are 'compacted', drawing attention to the ideological function of the novel as a unification of multifarious experience. Roche's novel was first brought to Sollers's attention by Faye, and for a limited time Roche followed Faye into the Change collective, only to return to *Tel Quel* soon afterwards. All of Roche's texts are published in the 'Collection Tel Quel', from 1965. However, the connection with Faye is relevant in that, as with Sarduy and Guyotat, Roche's novel tells a particular story: a dying narrator bargains for his tattooed skin with a Japanese doctor. However, with all three writers, a vital element is a parodic, often black humour which will become evident in later texts by the *Tel Quel* writers themselves— Sollers's *Lois*, for example. Roche's work is a precursor of the parodic textuality which will become influential in the 1970s.

The various voices of the novel are the varying levels of the narrator's experience and memory, plus his dialogue with the doctor. A major

---

[130] M. Roche, *Monteverdi* (Paris, 1960).

aspect of the novel, beyond this polyphony, is its typographic disposition. It includes a number of typefaces, figuring the different voices or levels, drawings, formulas, type-spacings, sizes, pitches, musical scores, hieroglyphs, death's heads. The writing compacts drawing, music, and writing, and this tendency is intensified in Roche's later work. Although the novel is a theoretical fiction in the sense that it writes the theory of itself, and fictionalizes it in a narrative, the theory is dispersed and taken out of its discursive space through typographic fragmentation. Typographic subversion as a way of destructuring narrative will be influential on a series of *Tel Quel* writers and other movements.[131]

Pierre Guyotat: Limits of Readability

Guyotat's text of 1967, *Tombeau pour cinq cent mille soldats* is also distinct from *Tel Quel* novels in its particular story, a holocaust of slaves from a mythical Western capital, the Algerian war being an obvious political sub-text. A liminary note to the text signals editorial changes that had to be made to render the text more accessible, to establish 'une meilleure lisibilité éditoriale'.[132] Previously it was 'une masse sans alinéa'.[133] This compromise to readability and the opposing radicality of the writing indicates Guyotat's importance for *Tel Quel* through a confrontation of the limits of readability. After an interview in *Tel Quel*[134] and discussions with Sollers, Guyotat's practice was radicalized and theorized, so that his next book, *Éden, Éden, Éden*, explicitly confronts these limits, without compromise. The novel was also prefaced by Leiris, Barthes, and Sollers, establishing its links with *Tel Quel*.

The text confronts the limits of reading first in its form, 'une phrase unique qui ne finit pas'.[135] The one sentence of the book never closes the scene of the narration, but suspends it, with a semi-colon, colon, or oblique stroke. This non-closure will be particularly instructive and relevant to Sollers's unpunctuated novels *H* (1973) and *Paradis* (1981), which propose a different kind of non-closure. As Barthes suggests, this lack of closure, a continual metonymic repetition, focuses reading on 'ce

---

[131] See e.g. the work of M. Robic in *TQ* 31 (autumn 1967), the texts pub. later in the review by the adolescent Sophie Podolski ('Le Pays où tout est permis', *TQ* 53 (spring 1973), and the later work of the *TXT* group.

[132] P. Guyotat, *Tombeau pour cinq cent mille soldats* (Paris, 1967), 3.

[133] Ibid.

[134] Id., 'Réponses', *TQ* 43 (autumn 1970).

[135] R. Barthes, 'Ce qu'il advient au signifiant', in P. Guyotat, *Éden, Éden, Éden* (Paris, 1970), 8.

qu'il advient au signifiant', the materiality of the text. Materiality appears as the limit of readability, a pattern also evident in the poetry of Denis Roche.[136] Materiality is a limit, moreover, further on than any ideological limit or law. The text does not stop, formally and in its content, at any ideological or moral limit. The 'further on' is also present in the content of the narration itself, an extremely explicit and violent series of sexual and erotic permutations between soldiers, prostitutes, and animals in an unidentified, but possibly North African, desert. This confronts limits of readability which are ethical and ideological, or rather it goes beyond them. The fact that this permutation is written in a form that cannot pause or close prevents the text from becoming pornographic; like Sade, it is a writing that attempts to traverse all possibilities or combinations. The adventure is textual rather than representational.

The text is fairly important for *Tel Quel*. Apart from Sollers's introduction, which links Guyotat's writing to a continuation of Sade,[137] and an article in *Critique* ('La Matière et sa phrase', showing a maturity of psychoanalytic and linguistic knowledge[138]), Guyotat is particularly relevant for the review because of the scandal surrounding the work when it appeared in 1970. In October the Ministry of the Interior declared it illegal for the work to be sold to people under the age of 18, to be displayed, or to be publicized, invoking the law for the protection of minors. In short, the novel was censored. In November, Jérôme Lindon, director of Minuit, launched a petition protesting against the measure and the application of the law for the protection of minors, 'détournée de son sens'.[139] Among the first signatories were Sollers, Pleynet, Thibaudeau, and other *Tel Quel* members. The petition was later signed by most of the French intelligentsia of the time.

Tel Quel had previously published an excerpt from the novel, 'Bordels boucherie'[140] and an interview with Guyotat, originally refused by *Le Monde* and *La Quinzaine littéraire*.[141] In an interview with Catherine Clément in *La Nouvelle Critique* Guyotat affirmed that his membership of the PCF and his association with *Tel Quel* were meant to prevent any attempt at recuperation and to link his work to 'un dialogue scientifique

[136] See D. Roche, *Le Mécrit* (Paris, 1972).
[137] P. Sollers, '17 . . ./19 . . suggestions', in Guyotat, *Éden, Éden, Éden*.
[138] Sollers, 'La Matière et sa phrase', *Crit.* 290 (July 1971).
[139] See P. Guyotat, *La Littérature interdite* (Paris, 1972) and 'La Littérature interdite', *TQ* 45 (spring 1971).
[140] Id., 'Bordels boucherie', *TQ* 36 (winter 1969).
[141] Id., 'Réponses', *TQ* 43 (autumn 1970).

sur l'écriture'.[142] Writing as a practice susceptible to being theorized would prevent any inflation of the sexual. Guyotat is correspondingly affirmative about the novels of Sollers, Baudry, and Henric.[143] He would refer to Sollers's article 'La Matière et sa phrase' as a 'nouvelle phase analytique'.[144] The association would last; Guyotat would contribute to the Artaud conference of 1972[145] and publish texts in *Tel Quel* during the 1970s.[146] He continues to publish texts in *L'Infini*.[147] Theorization, therefore, is important in preventing exploitation at the sexual level, in imposing a scientific approach. Guyotat is important for *Tel Quel* in introducing a vital ideological aspect of the practice of sexuality in writing as use value, rather than as exchange value, which leads to a critique of the sexual ideology of the current culture.[148]

J.-L. Baudry, P. Sollers, J. Henric, J. Thibaudeau

The texts specific to *Tel Quel* are by Thibaudeau, Henric, Sollers, and Baudry. The chronological limits of this group of texts seems to be marked by the appearance of *Lois* by Sollers in 1971. If this group of texts articulate the formal space of a writing that writes on itself, its own generation and the experience of its creation, with the reading and inscription of ideology, still in a formalist mode, the next group of texts, inaugurated by *Lois*, shifts away from this tendency towards a more baroque, parodic, and anarchic textuality. The formalist moment wanes to give way to what can be read as a parody of structuralist writing. *Tel Quel* parodies itself, in a sense. This parody is equally present in a whole range of writers whose texts appear in the 1970s.[149] The textual moment of *Tel Quel*, the moment of a theoretical textuality, is limited to the brief number of texts we have mentioned. The work of Roche and Guyotat,

[142] Id., *La Littérature interdite*, 72.

[143] Ibid. 60, 65. See also discussion with J. Henric, 'Nouvelles "incongruités monumentales" ', in Guyotat, *La Littérature interdite*.

[144] Ibid. 90.

[145] P. Guyotat, 'Langage du corps', in Sollers (ed.), *Artaud*.

[146] In *Tel Quel*: 'J'écris maintenant . . .', *TQ* 63 (autumn 1975). He would also feature regularly in the review *Art press*, associated with *Tel Quel* through one of its editors, J. Henric.

[147] P. Guyotat, 'A la lueur de mon sexe', *L'Infini*, 1 (winter 1983) and 'Le Livre', ibid. 2 (spring 1983).

[148] See P. Sollers's comments in the discussion following Guyotat's 'Langage du corps' in Sollers (ed.), *Artaud*, 182: 'Guyotat vient de nous parler de la valeur d'usage de la sexualité et nous savons que cette sexualité pour un appareil social doit être absolument instituée comme valeur d'échange.'

[149] See e.g. the novels of Pascal Bruckner, J.-L. Benoziglio, J. Almira, Renaud Camus.

meanwhile, is a move towards a less structured, more hedonistic play with language. The events of 1968, the irruption of desire in a *parole de la rue*, are also a major influence. The self-parody of *Tel Quel*, carried by its texts, displaces the review from any fixed position and prevents any identification of a *Tel Quel* text as such.

But before this parodic element comes into play, the *Tel Quel* novels exhaust the limitations of an abstract, formalistic textuality. Structure tends to be either geometric, as in the case of Sollers's *Nombres*, or permutational, as for Baudry's *Personnes*. The latter novel structures itself around the various possible combinations of subject positions, (*je, tu, il, elle, nous, vous, ils, elles*) and their corresponding objects, the blocks of text corresponding to a place on a grid representing the possibilities, printed at the back of the novel. This permutative structure, across pronoun positions, tends to evacuate any possibility of subjectivity. *Je* becomes just one possibility among others. The writing also plays on the other meaning of the word *personne*, in French, signifying: 'no one'. The permutational writing engages a sacrifice of the subject, linked to Kristeva's theorization of the *sujet zérologique*.[150]

Sollers's *Nombres*, despite a similarly complex structure, has a more subjective approach, but again the experience of the subject is of his own sacrifice and *dépense*. *Nombres* was perhaps the most important of the novels in the context, because of the long and theoretically dense analyses of it made by Derrida and Kristeva.[151] It draws heavily on materialist philosophy, Marxist theory, and Chinese thought, through unattributed quotations, or *prélèvements* (samples), which function to throw the reading out of joint, establishing a continual oscillation between the reading of the text at hand and texts deriving from other sites. In *Le Plaisir du texte*, Barthes describes such oscillatory techniques as linked to *jouissance* rather than *plaisir*. The reading of the text is made more difficult by the fact that the text theorizes its own production, commenting on its own reading and structure, so that the position of judgement, of the reader, before the text, is enveloped by it. The effect is terroristic in that it leaves the reader no place other than that of the writing itself. The novel is also, because of this enfolding, a sacrifice of the reader, an aggressive decapitation of any value the reader might posit. This decapitation is also figured sexually, as a castration that

---

[150] See below. See also the interview with Baudry in Ristat, *Qui sont les contemporains*, 233–47, 'Pour une littérature matérialiste', for a discussion of Baudry's novelistic practice.

[151] J. Derrida, 'La Dissémination', *Crit.* 261–2, (Feb.—Mar. 1969); Kristeva, 'L'Engendrement de la formule', *TQ* 37–8 (spring—summer 1969) (see below).

enables the subject, writer or reader, to accede to a *jouissance* considered as essentially feminine (see below). So, while it appears as the most intensely theoretical of the novels, due to the weight of its complex generative structure and references, *Nombres* is also the story of a subjective experience, a sacrifice, sexual and existential, of the subject in the process of writing.

The relation between Sollers's *Nombres* and *Lois* illustrates the shift from formalism and theoretical fiction to heterogeneity and parody. While *Nombres* is generated by a geometric structure, representing theoretically the leap from the present into its generative past, *Lois*, in a first version, was based on the structure of the cube; but only vestiges of this structure remain in the published novel, exceeded by the polyphonic and joyful play of language as parody. *Nombres* is a more austere and serious novel, which aproaches the limits of reading in its complexity, but its content tends to go beyond formalism. It is a fiction that concerns and is concerned with its own origin in language, with the metaphors this can produce, but there is also an important seam of writing on the body and on sexuality. The novel can be read as an attempt to leap from the phenomenal present into the invisible, infinite, and material engenderment of the real, identified at the level of language. Beyond the formal grace of the novel there is a subjective and erotic drama in play.

Thibaudeau's works *Ouverture* and *Imaginez la nuit* (*Ouverture II*) are an autobiographical writing in that the narrator (if this term can be maintained, it is often replaced by the 'scriptor') traverses, in a series of blocks of text, each time interrupted in mid-flow, the tissue of his memory. But this is not an autobiography in the usual sense, since it is written in a *présent perpétuel*,[152] with a consciousness of the fact that while the tissue of experience and memory, of language, is 'writing itself', it is located and active at the moment of the pen's traversal of the page. There is a continual tension, a struggle, between the moment of writing, the consciousness of the body at that moment, and the temporal flux of the tissue that is created. The text often approaches paroxysms of this temporal struggle: 'Ici, je suis ici maintenant, ici assurément ici';[153] 'ici, je suis ici cependant'.[154]

The difference between the two parts of this *ouverture* relate to that between day and night. *Ouverture* concerned the tissue of waking life; the

---

[152] J. Thibaudeau, *Imaginez la nuit* (Paris, 1968), back cover.
[153] Id., *Ouverture* (Paris, 1966), 131.
[154] Ibid. 23.

second volume attempts to write the conflict of the more clandestine, obscure elements of experience and memory, but the two are formally similar in their effects. We may be able, in this second volume, to read the present position of the narrator as lying in bed in the darkness, from the references to 'la chambre', the walls, and so on, but there is a constant struggle between the vision of what is present and the imagination of what is not present to perception. What is present can only be imagined, with relation to the moment of writing. Vision and imagination are engaged in a constant oscillatory struggle, as we may read in the opening block:

Imaginez par conséquent la nuit, imaginez la nuit, imaginez voyez ce que doit être, profondeur et fraîcheur, dans cet angle, imaginez et voyez ce que c'est, les yeux ouverts, les deux yeux toujours depuis toujours ouverts, dans ces ténèbres d'abord impénétrables, voyez ce que vous imaginez, regardez, ce qui est, maintenant, malgré que par exemple l'ombre couvre toute la place, mais elle s'éclaircit enfin et s'élève et la nuit se colore là-haut de violet et de bleu vif et de blanc en somme inexplicables et vous remarquez ces franges vaporeuses plus pâles qui passent sur les murs, autour, et alors cette fois, quelle réalité, aussitôt. Imaginez bien sür[155]

This is evidently a poetic prose that does not necessarily respect the sentence structure of prosaic French, using repetition within the phrase to create a rhythm. The rhythmic, repetitive, and fractured character of the language in these novels is an element that tends to be overlooked when they are considered as theoretical fiction. They are also texts where poetic language contaminates the laws of syntax.

J. Henric's prose style is similarly subversive of sentence structure, but in a less fluid way than the writing of Thibaudeau. The text is interrupted by oblique strokes and citation marks, cutting the language into short fragments. It is also cut into a series of printed blocks. The metaphor that generates the text is that of the arrow-shot, referring to the Zen art of archery to displace the notions of the expression of a meaning and of authorship. The reading is an experience of fragment-ation, of continually coming up against a blockage in meaning. Theory, in some senses, tends to prevent the writing from becoming a seamless tissue, imposing an infinite hesitation at the moment of creation. The text is theoretical in its reference to philosophical or religious sub-texts and in the presence of *énoncés* cited from texts such as Marx, Herrigel, but also Mallarmé. These intersect with more poetic, metaphoric

---

[155] Thibaudeau, *Imaginez la nuit*, 7.

phrases to give an impression of heterogeneity. What we read is an oscillation, producing a fragmented image between the action of creation and the meditation of its implications. This results often in an opacity of Mallarméan quality:

Se mouvoir: Il va de repos en repos. Le devier a date (sur le terrain): se trouve ponctualisé à même l'herbe brulée/totalité/perfection/enveloppe la ligne. De/en: la succession égale descente/chaîne du discours (premières lignes des fortifications adverses?) (nul fossé: coupable imprécision)/se lance si nul trait ne l'a encore atteint/«vole littéralement au-devant du danger». L'opération présente les plus grands risques: l'enjeu est une rencontre décisive (de ligne en ligne différée (sur l'une le soleil repose, l'œil sur la suivante, et le sang?[156]

The writing is not easy to read; it is not a seamless presentation of theory or of a fictional space, but a prose fragmented and hesitant about its own derivation. It can be proposed that the hesitation and difficulty is due to a conflict, a lack of harmony, between theory and fiction, such that the one constantly undermines the other. In Sollers's *Nombres*, however, this conflict is more successfully harmonized, since the theory relates essentially to the experience of sacrifice of the subject, and derives from it. Theoretical fiction is a challenge for the reader both in terms of its difficulty, its terrorism, and the sacrifice that is implied within it.

Poetry: Marcelin Pleynet, Denis Roche, Jacqueline Risset

Tel Quel textuality was not limited to the novel in this period. Its influence in poetry, in the work of Marcelin Pleynet, Denis Roche, and Jacqueline Risset, is equally strong, if not stronger, in a context less determined by formal rules of genre and in some senses further from theory.

The late 1960s sees the stabilization of currents in poetry. If Char and Ponge can be seen as the exemplary figures of the two opposing currents of a lyricism of presence and nostalgia and a certain faith in the naming power of words, and a deformative, fragmentative approach to language, other figures remain distinct from this polarity. The writings of Leiris, Michaux, Artaud, and Bataille remain powerful and singular examples, and the influence of non-French poetry, such as that emerging from the USA, is an important factor, as the description of the earlier context suggests. However, currents can be identified, and it is

---

[156] J. Henric, *Archées* (Paris, 1969), 62.

in this context that the poetry issuing from, or close to, *Tel Quel* can be located. For the most part, these currents are associated with reviews. The review *L'Éphémère*, set up in 1966, became an important forum for poets whose work retained a faith in the power of language to name. Yves Bonnefoy, André du Bouchet, Jacques Dupin, and Philippe Jaccottet, poets whose first works were published in the late 1950s and early 1960s, found a voice in this review.[157] Bonnefoy's pronouncement 'La poésie doit sauver l'être, à lui ensuite de nous sauver'[158] seems to represent the approach to poetry of this review, which, however, never had the formal status of a group. Important works were published in the late 1960s by these poets: Bonnefoy's *Pierre écrite* (1965), Dupin's *L'Embrasure* (1969), du Bouchet's *Ou le soleil* (1968).

The review *Action poétique*, founded in 1955, became, in the late 1960s, a vital forum for poetry and theoretical or critical reflections on poetic language. Directed by Henri Deluy, it was associated, after 1967, with the review *Change*, because of the presence on both committees of the poet Jacques Roubaud. Roubaud's *E*, published in 1967, appeared not unlike the novelistic or poetic innovations of *Tel Quel* in structuring the text, a mixture of prose and classically formed poems, on the Japanese game of Go. However, Roubaud's involvement with the Oulipo group places this interest in a different context from *Tel Quel*'s appeal to the non-Western. While Roubaud is one of the most prolific and successful poets of the last thirty years, *Action poétique* and *Change* represented the current of a poetry which sought to produce some kind of action in the world, whence its title and the pioneering work the review effected in publishing translations of poetry from outside France, particularly poetry of resistance to oppressive power-structures.

If in the late 1960s these three currents can, quite arbitrarily, be identified (not forgetting the more traditional roles of the *NRF* and the review *Cahiers du sud*, which ceased publication in 1966), in the 1970s a proliferation of poetry reviews, or reviews publishing poetry among other texts, were to spring up. Some of them can be linked directly to the influence of these currents, such as the review *TXT*, run by Christian Prigent, whose work on Denis Roche links him to *Tel Quel*.[159]

---

[157] See R. W. Greene, *Six French Poets of our Time* (Princeton, NJ, 1979), 3–21, for a discussion of the opposing currents of *L'Éphémère*, plus its successor *L'Argile*, founded in 1973, and *Tel Quel*.
[158] Y. Bonnefoy, 'L'Acte et le lieu de la poésie', in id., *Du mouvement et de l'immobilité de Douve* (Paris, 1953), 88.
[159] See C. Prigent, *Denis Roche* (Paris, 1977), partially pub. as 'Le Groin et le menhir' in *Crit.* 325 (June 1974). Writers associated with the *TXT* group, Jean-Paul Verheggen and

The review *L'Argile* became the focus of the *Éphémère* current after the latter review was dissolved in 1972. *Po&sie*, run by Michel Deguy, cannot be affiliated so easily, despite Deguy's earlier involvement with *Tel Quel*. Deguy's own poetry falls uneasily between the Heideggerian current and the deformative approach. Jean Ristat's review *Digraphe* is also less easily locatable.[160] Other sites of publication would include the 'Orange Export' series, which would publish poetry by *Tel Quel* figures such as Pleynet, Rottenberg, and Risset as well as by writers such as Faye and Roubaud.[161] All of these reviews publish experimental work by poets influenced by the theoretical currents of the 1960s, and, of course, by the events of 1968. Poetry is at the same time more distant from the events, as it can present itself as a more abstruse and hermetic genre than the novel, and closer, since the subject and his or her experience is present in a less mediated manner. The deformation of the poetry of *Tel Quel*, Roche, and Pleynet, is accentuated after 1968; the pressure of political turmoil and of the signifiers of desire that were invested in the everyday after 1968 are influential factors.

Tel Quel poetry, after the departure of Deguy and Faye, is focused on three writers: Denis Roche, Marcelin Pleynet, and Jacqueline Risset. Less-published writers such as Rottenberg, and writers known more as novelists, such as Henric, would also publish poetic texts in the review.[162]

Pleynet's *Comme* was published in 1965, followed by a series of publications in the review leading up to *Stanze* in 1973.[163] Denis Roche, after *Les Idées centésimales de Miss Elanize*, brought out *Éros énergumène* in 1968, followed by his 'last' book of poetry, *Le Mécrit* in 1972. Jacqueline Risset would publish texts in the review from 1967 that would eventually appear in the book *Jeu* in 1971.[164]

Valère Novarina, as well as Prigent, would pub. work in *Tel Quel* in the late 1970s (see Ch. 4).

[160] *Digraphe* would fill the vacuum left by the loss of *Les Lettres françaises*, being affiliated to the PCF and run by the future editor of *Les Lettres françaises* when it was reborn at the end of the decade.

[161] See E. Hocquard, Raquel (eds.), *Orange Export Ltd 1969–1986* (Paris, 1986).

[162] P. Rottenberg, 'Dialoque, fatigue et désœuvrement', *TQ* 25 (spring 1966); id., 'L'Attraction universelle', *TQ* 30 (summer 1967); id., 'Ces pages que vouz trouverez quand vous serez de retour', *TQ* 33 (spring 1968); id., 'Récapitulation', *TQ* 34 (summer 1968); id., 'Mots de tous les jours', *TQ* 45 (spring 1971); J. Henric, 'A faire communiquer', *TQ* 30 (summer 1967).

[163] M. Pleynet, 'Poésie', *TQ* 33 (spring 1968); id., 'Incantation dite au bandeau d'or', *TQ* 40 (winter 1970); id., 'Dédicace', *TQ* 47 (autumn 1971); id., 'Travestilait', *TQ* 51 (autumn 1972).

[164] J. Risset, 'Récit', *TQ* 27 (autumn 1966); ead., 'Après récit', *TQ* 30 (summer 1967); ead., 'Jeu', *TQ* 36 (winter 1969); ead., 'Forme et événement I', *TQ* 44 (winter 1971).

Roche's introduction to *Éros énergumène*, 'Leçons sur la vacance poétique', its title parodically echoing du Bouchet's *Dans la chaleur vacante* (1961), immediately sets up an opposition between Roche's own work and a current of lyricism: 'le bas lyrisme'.[165] The latter is described as a 'nostalgie de l'espèce de transcendence immédiate qu'on attribue avec tant d'empressement à la création poétique'.[166] Rather than this superior imaginative lyricism, Roche proposes to 'défigurer la convention écrite'.[167] His poetry is a defiguration, or a destruction, that works on the material level of language, phonetic and typographic, to displace the notion of lyrical effusion, and to demystify and deconstruct the edifice of poetry. This operation is formally effected through the fragmented intersection of a number of narratives within the poem, each cutting across the other, making a linear reading impossible. The fragments are often taken from the most typically unpoetic sources such as *A Social History of Extracting* or *Custom Magazine*.[168] Poetic rules or conventions are perversely imposed to fracture meaning and prevent any lyrical continuity, while the conventions are also deliberately flouted to expose their arbitrary nature. The content of the poetry is often an 'energumenic' eroticism, an eroticism depending on pulsions, a 'matière à convulsion',[169] which Roche sees as antithetical to structure and order, convention. The pulsional violence of eroticism, disfiguring form, will lead on in *Le Mécrit* (1972) to a more sustained attack, which Roche signalled as a limit of poetry as such. *Le Mécrit* encounters limits of meaning in figurality in a series of texts taken from non-Western sources (Chinese and Etruscan, for example).[170] Given that Roche's texts are dedicated initially to a destruction of poetry and then tend to articulate with other areas such as photography,[171] this defigurative approach can be seen as a cul-de-sac, but at the same time, its negativity has had a wide influence.

Pleynet's approach differs considerably from that of Roche, principally in that he is not concerned with an abandonment of poetry. Pleynet's comments in interviews of the early 1970s about a sexual

---

[165] D. Roche, *Éros énergumène* (Paris, 1968), 12.
[166] Ibid.
[167] Ibid. 10–11.
[168] Ibid. 89.
[169] Ibid. 12.
[170] D. Roche, *Le Mécrit*, 90–4, 140, 142.
[171] See id., *Notre antéfixe* (Paris, 1978) and *Dépôts de savoir et de technique* (Paris, 1980) and a text from the latter in *Tel Quel*: 'Au delà du principe de l'écriture', *TQ* 67 (autumn 1976).

exploitation of the corpse of poetry, after a resignation from it,[172] seem to point to a critique of Denis Roche's *démission*, the latter having left the committee of *Tel Quel* after disagreements concerning the publication of his intervention at the Artaud colloquium in 1972.

However, the same defigurative approach to language can be seen in Pleynet's focus on the letter as the vital element in poetic language. As opposed to the poets of *L'Éphémère*, who locate in the word a naming power, Pleynet draws attention to the letter as an element of excess within the word that fractures it and generates the poem as a continual fragmentative reading of itself. This poetry, to be read 'à la lettre' ('seul la lettre y fait sens'[173]) has been the principal aspect of Pleynet's poetic work since *Comme*. The texts of *Stanze*, published in *Tel Quel*, one dedicated to Barthes in the 1971 special issue on him, another Pleynet's contribution to the Bataille conference, present the *débordement*, the exceeding, of a structure, by the effects of violence of the letter. That this structure is predicated on nine 'modes of production' suggests it is the exceeding of theory as structure and as economy that is at stake.[174]

That the letter is an element of displacement, fracturing the word through its evident repetition, and the generation of sense through this displacement, suggests a negative, deconstructive movement. Meaning is never presence, not anchored to the intention of a thought, but subject to the material play of language. On the other hand, meaning, particularly erotic meaning, stands out in the writing; islands of meaning resist the tendency to a pure permutative literality. This tendency is realized, but problematized in Pleynet's text 'Litanies', published in *Tel Quel* during the 1970s,[175] where the numbers 1 to 1,002 are written out, followed by 'mille et tre', a quotation from Leporello's catalogue of Don Giovanni's conquests in Mozart's opera. The last line immediately recasts the previous enumeration, transforms it from a purely formal punctuation into an erotic meaning, taking to a limit the tension between the letter and its sense. Denis Roche and Marcelin Pleynet's poetry have in common that they set into motion a tension and a dialectic between the letter, language's materiality, and its sense. However, while Denis Roche leaves *Tel Quel*, and his poetry moves towards other areas, Pleynet's work continues; the texts that are

[172] M. Pleynet, 'Norme et excès', in id., *Art et littérature* (Paris, 1976), 230.
[173] Id., *L'Amour* (Paris, 1982), 12.
[174] See Id., *Stanze* (Paris, 1973), 151–61.
[175] Id., 'Litanies', *TQ* 64 (winter 1975).

included in the collection *Rime* (1981), constitute in the review a powerful strand of creative writing alongside Sollers's *Paradis*.[176]

Jacqueline Risset's writing in *Jeu* cannot so comfortably be identified as poetry. Sections of the book were published under the titles 'Poésie et prose', 'Récit', 'Après récit', 'Jeu', and 'Forme et événement'. The text as a whole is a traversal of different orderings of language: the horizontally determined (but fragmented) continuity of the 'Récit', the vertical, poetic deformation of this in 'Après récit', its theoretical reading in 'Jeu' and 'Méthode'.

The text (novel or poem?) reads as a journey across language, in order to touch some kind of reality or real, to hollow out the imaginary and be able to attain the real (*le réel*) in Lacan's terms. The book can in fact be read as a fictional investigation of Lacan's logic of the phantasm.[177] This touching is attained through a writing on writing. As in Sollers's work, writing is a doubling of itself, incessantly retracing or hesitating over its own steps, attempting to clear itself of illusion, or simply to purify itself. It becomes a purifying exercise, tending towards a vacant point—'l'acte vide', as Sollers puts it.[178] The emphasis on language is an attempt to get beyond language, not as transcendence but as a point right on, *à même*, its limit, just on top of it, a point referred to in the theory as transfinite. Far from a linguistic play or a restrictive formalism, this is a writing of quasi-mystical intentions, but with an analytic approach.

Roche, Pleynet, and Risset share a deformative, investigative approach to poetic language where the tension between form and sense is very evident. After 1973, poetry becomes more singular and subjective. Roche having left the committee, poetic activity within the group is centred on Pleynet and Risset.[179] For poetry as for the novel, after the moment of theory, which results in a tension between poetic language and its analysis within the text, leading to the approach of limits of readability and complexity and often to the fragmentation and hesitating deferral of the writing, *Tel Quel*'s textuality develops into areas of

[176] See Id., 'A la mère', *TQ* 62 (summer 1975); id., 'Litanies', *TQ* 64 (winter 1975); id., 'Do it', *TQ* 69 (spring 1977); id., 'La Gloire du ciel', *TQ* 71–3 (autumn 1977); id., 'Pange lingua', *TQ* 77 (autumn 1978); id., 'Heavenly glory', (a trans. into Eng.), *TQ* 77 (autumn 1978).

[177] See n. 120.

[178] P. Sollers, 'La Pratique formelle de l'avant-garde', *TQ* 46 (summer 1971).

[179] J. Risset publishes poetry in the review after *Jeu* that is related to her feminine subjectivity: 'La Petite Marque sur l'estomac', *TQ* 70 (summer 1977) and 'Sept passages de la vie d'une femme', *TQ* 74 (winter 1977). Her next book of poetry, *Mors* (Paris, 1976), is pub. not by *Tel Quel* but by Flammarion.

parody, heterogeneity, singularity, and subjectivity. The 1970s sees the return of the singular subject, although it is not so much a question of a return but a subsequent stage in a journey through the internal history of language. This journey is paralleled in theory in the work of Kristeva, with the infant's transition into the subjectivity implied by language.

JULIA KRISTEVA: 'L'ÉTRANGÈRE'

The moment of theory, while resulting from the intersections and syntheses operated by *Tel Quel*, also takes its impetus from the powerful theory of Julia Kristeva, a force within the review. This theoretical force is carried through across the next decade, but with a trajectory that essentially breaks down the dynamic of theory into a more nuanced, oscillatory enquiry. This subversion of theory by writing and the heterogenous subject-matters in question, is a major aspect of the history of theory realized in *Tel Quel*.

Julia Kristeva first arrived in France from Bulgaria in 1965.[180] Through her compatriot Todorov she will attend Barthes's seminar at the École pratique des hautes études, and be introduced to Sollers by Genette. Sollers gave his paper on Mallarmé, 'Littérature et totalité', at this seminar. The juncture of *Tel Quel* and Kristeva's interests takes place at the intersection between semiology and linguistics and an avant-garde literary theory, a factor that will define Kristeva's intervention in the review. Kristeva's marriage to Sollers in 1968 is an unpredictable but happy coincidence; its effects, an intense and fruitful exchange, are enormously important. Sollers's novel *Nombres* is dedicated to Kristeva; his critical work owes much to both her semiological and psychoanalytic work, but the parallel of her femininity and her (questionable) feminism gives his writing on this subject a complexity that has not been fully recognized. Sollers's influence on Kristeva is equally strong; she is undoubtedly influenced by his sacrificial view of the subject and femininity before moving towards psychoanalysis, perhaps as a resistance to this influence. Sollers introduces her to Bataille's work, probably also to that of Artaud and to Chinese thought. The interchange remains productive and subtle up to the present, while the apparent themes of enquiry may have diverged.

[180] For a semi-autobiographical account of Kristeva's intellectual trajectory, see J. Kristeva, 'Mémoire', *L'Infini*, 1 (winter 1983) and the novel *Les Samouraïs* (Paris, 1990).

Kristeva initially worked with Lucien Goldmann on her thesis *Le Texte du roman*,[181] but this influence is very swiftly superseded in the reformulation of semiology in the articles collected in the book *Séméiotiké*, published by *Tel Quel*.[182] Kristeva's ambitious rethinking of semiology will have decisive effects in the context. Her force is linked by Barthes to her eccentric origins and to her sex.[183] This would have undoubtedly had a terroristic effect in a context dominated by male theory and theorists. But the force of her intervention in semiology, initially in serious reviews such as *Communications, Langages, Information sur les sciences sociales*, and *Semiotica*, is also due to the character and structure of this reformulation itself.

Critique of Semiology

In the mid-1960s structuralist linguistics and semiology were already installed in the academic world, at the marginal but powerful École pratique. The journal *Communications*, brought out by the group of researchers there, established linguistics and semiology within this context. Barthes's 'Éléments de sémiologie', published in this review, appears as a summation of this current.[184] Perhaps a summation of this kind already suggests the imminence of a superseding, or at least, a transformation of the main currents of the field. Roland Barthes, as the principal proponent of a semiological approach, published his *Système de la mode*, an analysis of the 'fashion system', in 1967. It would provide a jumping-off point for Kristeva in an article in *Critique*.[185] Linguistics, meanwhile, was also in a state of flux in the mid-1960s. The ascendant trend was structural linguistics, which, mediated through the influence of the Prague School and writers such as Jakobson, derived from Saussure. The functionalism of linguists like Martinet and Jakobson focused on the phoneme as the unit of structure, and on communication as the essential function of language. This current dominated the *Communications* group—for example, in the work of Greimas, whose

---

[181] ead., *Le Texte du roman* (The Hague, 1969); the text of this work is inserted partially in *Séméiotiké: Recherches pour une sémanalyse* (Paris, 1969) and in the article 'Du symbole au signe', *TQ* 34 (summer 1968).

[182] ead., *Séméiotiké*. Repub. in the 'Points' collection, with a new preface and the more Marxist texts taken out, in the 1980s.

[183] R. Barthes, 'L'Étrangère', in id., *Le Bruissement de la langue* (Paris, 1984), 197.

[184] Id., 'Éléments de sémiologie', *Communications*, 4 (1964), and in id., *L'Aventure structuraliste* (Paris, 1985).

[185] J. Kristeva, 'Le Sens et la mode', *Crit.* 247 (Dec. 1967).

Sémantique structurale appeared in 1966. However, by the mid-1960s a number of emerging discourses problematized this ascendancy. The USA context of linguistics had mostly resisted the Saussurean current; its dominant thinker was Bloomfield, whose behaviourist approach sought to explain linguistic behaviour independently of any internal factors. There were certain parallels with Saussure, but as many differences. The problems of Bloomfield's approach and that of Zelig Harris, influenced by it, were the spur for the elaboration of a new approach by Noam Chomsky. His generative linguistics sought to account for the transformational and potentially infinite character of language, evading the faults in the previous linguistics of closure and a certain stasis. The critique of the static nature of structure and the proposition of generative, transformational mechanisms were close to Kristeva's critique of structuralism in France, but differed from it radically, in that Chomsky proposed an innate linguistic competence in the subject. Kristeva could not opt for this essentialist path. Chomsky's work (translated into French during the 1960s[186]) was nevertheless a new departure that had an enormous influence, not least on the Change group run by J.-P. Faye, who left *Tel Quel* soon after Kristeva appeared on the scene.

Alongside the transformation effected by Chomsky's influence, the work of Émile Benveniste was also of crucial importance in its effect on the context of linguistics.[187] Benveniste would articulate Saussure with Freudian psychoanalysis, introducing aspects such as a theory of the subject, of negation, of the nominal phrase (deviating from the Cartesian subject–object norm) and an emphasis on rhythm.[188] These tended to undermine and nuance the static edifice of structure. In these factors, and in its enquiry into the philological roots of certain words in Indo-European and Sanskrit, which were of interest for *Tel Quel*'s critique of the Western ideology of language, Benveniste's work was a crucial reference for the writers of *Tel Quel*, particularly Kristeva.

Kristeva's initial intervention in the intellectual context is a critique of semiology which reformulates it along different, non-structural lines. This reformulation is also a critique of linguistics, from the point of view of translinguistic practices—that is, practices that take place across

---

[186] N. Chomsky, *Structures syntactiques* (Paris, 1969) and *Aspects de la théorie du syntaxe* (Paris, 1971). See also N. Ruwet, *Introduction à la grammaire générative* (Paris, 1967).
[187] See E. Benveniste, *Problèmes de linguistique générale* (2 vols.; Paris, 1966 and 1974).
[188] See ibid. i for these essays.

language but are not identifiable with it.[189] Literature, as one such
practice, is of fundamental importance. Kristeva's project is a critique
of science from the perspective of its excess, of language from the
perspective of literature.

Semiology, for Barthes, uses the methodology of linguistics, and must
also approach its object through language. It is also, paradoxically,
transgressive of linguistics. This paradox is explained by the fact that,
while semiology uses the methods of linguistics and enounces itself in
language, it addresses itself to what the Soviet semioticians of Tartu, to
whom Kristeva refers as an alternative to Chomsky, term 'systèmes
modelants secondaires';[190] these are what Kristeva also calls 'pratiques
sémiotiques' or 'pratiques translinguistiques', which, while they may
have a linguistic base, add to this a complementary system which
dislocates and subverts the norms of communication, exchange of
meaning, and expression that linguistics assumes as its object of study.
Semiology is then in a position to return its critical gaze on to linguistics.

In 'Le Sens et la mode', a review of Barthes's *Système de la mode*,
Kristeva asserts that structuralism, which borrows from linguistics its
method and models, is efficient in its demystifying effect, but reaches a
point of saturation, a tautological limit, since the structure of the
exchange of meaning via the sign that semiology employs is analogous
to the exchange system of commodities in the economy. Semiology can
become, on the other hand, a science of signs that, through the study
of signifying practices different from, or complementary to, language,
can demystify the structuralist ideology. The condition of semiology's
capacity to effect this return on its linguistic origins, however, is that it
escapes from the closed circuit of exchange that the sign assures, moves
away from exchange, either linguistic or monetary. Kristeva is producing this analysis at the time of *Tel Quel*'s Marxism, annexing her
emerging science to Marxist theory. It is also an epistemological
critique. Kristeva sees the semiology of Peirce and Saussure as coextensive with this exchange mechanism. Kristeva's semiology, conversely, will
study the semiotic practices in question as a production of meaning. To
this end they are referred to as practices or as texts. Structuralist
semiology, a reified expression of society's system of exchange, meets its

---

[189] See Kristeva, 'Le Sens et la mode', *Crit.* 247 (Dec. 1967), 1006.
[190] ead., 'L'Expansion de la sémiotique', in ead., J. Ray-Debove, and R. Umiker (eds.),
Essais de sémiotique (The Hague, 1971), 32. See also J. Kristeva, 'La Sémiologie aujourd'hui
en URSS', *TQ* 35 (autumn 1968).

own image in what it studies and can effect a move away from this on the condition that it shifts its gaze on to the production of meaning.

The study of semiotic practices as translinguistic, effected not in the units of language but in its relations and in its spaces, and not reducible to language, not the sum of its effects, makes possible semiology in its critical mode. 'Systèmes modelants secondaires', the translinguistic, semiotic practices, are the exteriority of linguistics that semiology traverses to turn its gaze on to linguistics. For Kristeva, poetic language is the privileged area of this research.

This diagonal, transversal approach was already present in *Tel Quel*, and Kristeva is undoubtedly influenced by such articles as Sollers's 'Dante et la traversée de l'écriture'. *Tel Quel*'s fiction had also focused on the production of meaning, or writing, rather than accepting *tel quel* the meanings offered to it by culture and history. Previous and parallel to Kristeva's arrival, the review is also the foyer for semiological or semi-semiological researches preceding those of Kristeva or contemporary with her work;[191] her activity also makes *Tel Quel* into an important site for the reception of more marginal moments in linguistics and semiology.[192] The review can be seen as an incisive point where semiology joins a radical practice of writing; it is the 'other' of the more sober foyers of semiology such as *Communications, Langages*, and, later, *Poétique*.[193] Kristeva, as well as Barthes, provides the link between the two

[191] See G. Genette, 'Une poétique "structurale"', *TQ* 7 (autumn 1961); id., 'Proust palimpseste', *TQ* 12 (winter 1963); id., 'Le Travail de Flaubert', *TQ* 14 (summer 1963); id., 'La Rhétorique et l'espace du langage', *TQ* 19 (autumn 1964); id., 'La Littérature comme telle', *TQ* 23 (autumn 1965). See also, by Genette, the two vols. of *Figures*: i (Paris, 1966) and ii (Paris, 1969). T. Todorov will contribute to *TQ* 27 (autumn 1966) an important article, 'Choderlos de Laclos et la théorie du récit', introducing the linguistics of J. L. Austin into France. See also R. Jakobson' 'Du réalisme artistique', *TQ* 24 (winter 1966); id., 'Glossolalie', *TQ* 26 (summer 1966) (an issue subtitled 'Linguistique/Psychanalyse/Littérature'); id., 'Une microsopie du dernier spleen dans les Fleurs du Mal', *TQ* 29 (spring 1967); id., 'Un exemple de termes migratoires et de modèles institutionnels', *TQ* 38 (summer 1969), reprinted in *TQ* 41 (spring 1970), due to typing errors in the first publication.

[192] See her presentation of 'La Sémiologie aujourd'hui en URSS', *TQ* 35 (autumn 1968), with articles by V. V. Ivanov, 'Structure d'un poème de Khlebnikov'; and a collective work by I. M. Lotman, A. I. Syrkine, V. N. Toporov, B. L. Oguibenine, V. V. Ivanov, and E. S. Semeka, on 'Le Nombre dans la culture'. She also prefaces Mäll's 'Une approche possible du "sunyavada"' with her own 'Distance et anti-représentation', in *TQ* 32 (winter 1968). In *TQ* 37 Starobinski's 'Le Texte dans le texte', on Saussure's 'Anagrams', is related to Kristeva's work. In the 1970s her work and that of her associates in linguistics and psychoanalysis in university seminars will be pub. in the collective works, *La Traversée des signes* (Paris, 1975) and *Folle vérité* (Paris, 1979).

[193] *Poétique* will be founded in 1970, pub. at Seuil, and run initially by the editorial team of Genette, Todorov, Cixous, and J.-P. Richard. It is resistant to the context of *Tel Quel*,

areas, and her work should be seen, not as an extension of scientific research into the textual, politicized arena of *Tel Quel*, but as a militant invasion of the areas of semiology and linguistics by a representative of the review's radical textuality in theory.

Kristeva's appeal to an outside of linguistics also implies a consideration of the subject. While structuralism foreclosed the question, unable to account for its role in language and for the pre-linguistic in general, and appealed to innateness or 'interpellation' in the case of Althusser, Kristeva articulates linguistics with psychoanalysis in order to provide a theory of the relation between the linguistic and the pre-linguistic. If Kristeva's thought is initially allied to Althusserian Marxism in its positing of the epistemological break, the limitations of this soon give way in Kristeva's work to a *sémanalyse* that undermines the Marxist epistemology. This pattern is reflected in the general trends in thought at the time. The scientific impetus of thought running through the late 1960s, and through *Tel Quel*, eventually gives way to a psychoanalytically dominated approach, mediated through the analysis of the place of the subject, and through this to an ethics. Semiology essentially elided the subject in its insistence on models, and so, in a different mode, does Derrida's *différance*. The project of *sémanalyse*, of the analysis of language and meaning from a space before or outside them, defines Kristeva's relation to psychoanalysis. She will look at the subject, posed by Lacanian theory, from the perspective of the archaic, pre-linguistic pulsions which incessantly traverse it; this traversal is read by Kristeva as being particularly pertinent to literature and poetic language.

The Logics of Poetic Language

The reintroduction of the subject is effected via Kristeva's elaboration of a logic of poetic language into a theory of literature, which she elaborates in her first book, *Séméiotiké* (1969). It is a crucial and characteristic aspect of Kristeva's and *Tel Quel*'s articulation with science and with psychoanalysis that it is effected via a theory and practice of poetic language; science is transformed through literature.[194]

publishing nothing by Sollers, Kristeva, or other members of the committee, but open to texts by Derrida and associates such as P. Lacoue-Labarthe and J.-L. Nancy.

[194] From the point of Kristeva's first article in the review, 'Pour une sémiologie des paragrammes', in *TQ* 29 (spring 1967), the review will bear the subtitle 'Science/Littérature', which can be read, seeing the oblique stroke as a bar, as suggesting the subversion of science by literature. This postulation is justified by a gloss on the next subtitle, 'Littérature/Philosophie/Science/Politique', which is said to represent an 'exposition

Refusing the Chomskyan avenue, and opting at one moment for the alternative transformational linguistics of Saumjan and Soboleva of the Tartu school,[195] and at other moments for the numerical models and set theory offered by modern mathematics, Kristeva offers a proliferation of alternatives to the structuralist approach. The complexity and scope of her references to linguistic, mathematical, and logical models tend to blur the focus of her approach at times. *Séméiotiké* is distinguished by an exuberance in the proliferation of theories and models; this may be a function of the epistemological status of her approach as critique of science or of the dispersed origins of the articles that make up the book. Kristeva does not propose any fixed scientific model but rather a plurality of models that are progressively effaced in the production of theory. This underlines how her relation to science is always one of transgression. The basic gesture, the shift to a transversal process, remains constant.

This move is possible through the study of a system complementary to language. Kristeva studies poetic language; her contribution to semiology or to the theory of linguistics derives from this determining instance. A decisive part of this theory is the relation of poetic language to the language of communication and denotation.

The Russian formalists set out to define the specificity of literature in relation to linguistics, and emphasized the fact that literature could not be reduced to language;[196] in Kristeva's terms, it was translinguistic. However, in setting out the idea that literature was a deviation from the norm, however subversive of that norm, the formalists essentially provided a variant of the idea that literature was a supplementary decoration in relation to the language of communication, an aspect Kristeva identifies and criticizes.[197] Jakobson's analysis of poetic language as an emphasis on the message was also restricted in this sense. This view holds sway in *Tel Quel* for a certain time, but its limitations begin to appear when formalism is superseded by the Derridean critique of structuralism. Implicitly, if literature is considered as a supplement to normal language, for Derrida the characteristics of literature must

---

analytique vers sa cause', (*TQ* 43 (autumn 1970), 3). In other words, while politics rests on a science (historical materialism) which rests on a philosophy (dialectical materialism), literature is the 'repressed' aspect of philosophy. Cf. P. Sollers, 'Thèses générales', *TQ* 44 (winter 1971). The word 'Art' will be added to the subtitle in 1979, which remains in *L'Infini*.

[195] See Kristeva, *Le Texte du roman* (The Hague, 1969), 40.
[196] See T. Todorov (ed.), *Théorie de la littérature: Textes de formalistes russes* (Paris, 1965), 32.
[197] See Kristeva, 'Pour une sémiologie des paragrammes', *TQ* 29 (spring 1967), 55.

already be in normal language. Moreover, the view that literature is a deviation leads to a certain stasis in the political and ideological practice of literature. Kristeva provides, in her first article in *Tel Quel*, 'Pour une sémiologie des paragrammes', a complex alternative view of the relation of poetic language (which replaces the concept of 'literature') to language, based on the notion of the infinite. The aim to define a logic of poetic language, and the scientific way in which this is presented, suggest the forceful, terroristic nature of Kristeva's intervention, displacing any faith in the poetic effusion of a gifted subject.

Kristeva's main point of departure in this text is Saussure's 'Anagrammes', which were originally published, edited, and commented by Jean Starobinski in the review *Mercure de France* in 1964.[198] Unpublished extracts appear in *Tel Quel* in 1969, indicating a strategic desire in the review to integrate the more radical moments of linguistics, the margins of linguistics, into its project. Saussure had attempted in these texts to analyse certain Latin poems as double, that is, as having hidden within them the name of a chief or a god, an anagram which was dispersed in the text; this was nevertheless determined by the intention of the author. Saussure's intention was not subversive. It is Starobinski who initially poses the basis of further enquiry: 'Pourquoi ne verrait-on pas dans l'anagramme un aspect du processus de la parole—processus ni purement fortuit ni pleinement conscient?'[199] In the passage from Saussure's writing to Kristeva's, Saussure's theory has been considerably altered from its basic premises. This shift is not acknowledged explicitly, but Kristeva seems to suggest that Saussure's original intention is not complicit with hers by shifting the terminology from 'anagram' to 'paragram'. The shift from 'ana-', which signifies an anteriority or a substructure that is under or behind the text at a removed level, to 'para-', which captures the idea of dispersal or dissemination across or alongside the text, results in a view of the paragrammatic not as the intentional effect of an author but as an indication of the inescapably double nature of poetic language.

The paragrammatic level of the text insists in the relations and spaces of the text, having the radical effect of opening up the linearity of communicative, denotative discourse, which Kristeva calls the *pheno-text*, the text as phenomenon, to a volume of *signifiance*, of meaning as a process. *Signifiance* is infinite, because not fixed by denotation or the sign;

---

[198] J. Starobinski, 'Les Mots sous les mots', *Mercure de France* (1964).
[199] Id., 'Le Texte dans le texte', *TQ* 37 (spring 1969), 31–2.

it is a volume or space of generation or engenderment, which Kristeva calls the *geno-text*. The radicality of Kristeva's theory here is to break the linearity of denotative language by outlining this space, complementary to communicative language, as a generative volume. In more poetic terms, she introduces silence and volume into the linearity of discourse.

A fault as serious as seeing poetic language as a deviation from normal language would be to see the *geno-text* as an independent level that could exist on its own, without the mediation of communicative language, as in Surrealist automatic writing. The *pheno-text* is the necessary support and relaunching (*relance*) of the *geno-text*. Kristeva's point is that if denotative, communicative language is formalizable according to a logic that goes from '0–1', that is, according to a logic of identity, of the sign, where identity is a limit and negativity is its privative opposite, poetic language operates according to a logic that goes from '0–2', where 0 is significant and 1 is transgressed.[200] Kristeva sets out in numerical formulas the transgression of identity and unity involved in the relation of the infinite text of process to the text as phenomenon. Transgression of identity, of '1', can be seen as a motor for *Tel Quel*'s theory and practice of the text.

According to the logic of transgression, denotative, communicative language is contained within poetic language. The poetic text, Lautréamont for example, is a destructive, negative traversal of the culture of identity, but it is also its reordering, its transformation. This transformation is further specified by Kristeva by the notions of the transfinite and of intertextuality.

The Transfinite: Intertextuality

In order to specify the relation of poetic language to communicative discourse in 'Pour une sémiologie des paragrammes' Kristeva introduces the mathematical notion of the infinite, and the transfinite, a term taken from the mathematician Georg Cantor (1845–1918), whose texts were published in the review *Cahiers pour l'analyse* and whose presence in the literary journal *Tel Quel* would have been part of the current scientific flavour of thought. Cantor's breakthrough was a new way of conceiving infinity. If we think of the infinite set of numbers, and try to identify the last number of this set, we come up against a difficulty. Cantor's invention was to think of the last number of this set as the 'next' number

---

[200] See Kristeva, 'Pour une sémiologie des paragrammes', *TQ* 29 (spring 1967), 59.

in the sequence. This number is defined as 'transfinite', neither within the set nor outside it. The transfinite number is an element 'immediately superior' to the sequence of normal numbers in the infinite set, or it is, in J.-L. Houdebine's terms, a limit exterior to, and not interior to, the set concerned.[201] In different terms, there is a limit that is always already transgressed. We can recognize the logic of Bataille's transgression here, the transfinite being attained through a jump or a break of the interior limit that transgresses it. While the transfinite is actual, not transcendent, it cannot be judged real by the logic of identity, it is real according to an epistemologically different logic of the trans-subjective or the translinguistic. The transfinite point is 'just outside' what is already there, a point at the limit, right on it, à même. Literature, and literary theory, is read in Tel Quel as a transformation of the phenomenal, of language, from this point. The task of semiology or analysis is to analyse the finite in relation to the transfinite. Through its prefix 'trans-' it is cardinal in the theory of literature of Tel Quel.

Poetic language, for Kristeva, is a transformative movement across discourse, that opens it out and realizes the infinite potential of language as such. This is at the same time an affirmation (an opening-out) and a negation. Literature is viewed as a negativity that works across language. In Séméiotiké Kristeva looks at negation (particularly in the essay 'Poésie et négativité'[202]) as the essential relation of literature to language, and therefore to itself.

The transfinite, negative perspective informs much of Tel Quel's approach to the text. A text is often analysed according to its relation to the infinite. Is it open or closed, transgressive or transcendent? The definition of literature, for Tel Quel, may well be based on its capacity to transform closed systems by opening them to the infinite. From this perspective, L'Infini is a more fitting title; it suggests the essential basis of the theory of Tel Quel.

This logic is behind the notion of intertextuality. Intertextuality refers to the fact that the writer reads the anterior textual corpus as a rewriting, a redistribution, of that corpus. The notion is complicated by the fact that the 'anterior textual corpus' comprises the subject's insertion into the social text. Je therefore rewrites himself or herself. Through the rereading/rewriting of the anterior textual corpus the writer inserts the text into history:

---

[201] J.-L Houdebine, 'L'Expérience de Cantor', L'Infini, 4 (autumn 1983), 89.
[202] J. Kristeva, 'Poésie et négativité', in ead., Séméiotiké.

Le texte littéraire s'insère dans l'ensemble des textes: il est une écriture-réplique (fonction ou négation) d'un autre (des autres) texte(s). Par sa manière d'écrire en lisant le corpus littéraire antérieur ou synchronique l'auteur vit dans l'histoire, et la société s'écrit dans le texte.[203]

Writing is a participation in, and an aggression towards, the anterior textual corpus; Kristeva also refers to Mallarmé's dialectic of *réminiscence* and *sommation*. This was emphasized in *Tel Quel* before Kristeva—the participatory nature of reading was always stressed. What the notion of intertextuality means is not only that any text is related to the totality of other texts, as to a network or series, but that writing reorganizes literature as a whole in traversing and transgressing it, reorganizes also the text of identity (the subject) and of society (history). Intertextuality proposes a vision of literature as transformative of itself and of the world.

Scenic Space

Kristeva's theory also proposes a different, non-linear conception of textual space, of the inner space of literature. The text is a negative space, articulated with other texts, and transformative. It is also a volume, it ruptures the linearity of representation, and becomes what we could call a scenic space. The text becomes a *scène*, not a static, removed spectacle, but a space of a practice across, whence the use of the term *transcénique*.[204] *Signifiance* is not a single linear event but a practice in space. Meaning seen as a volume spatializes signification; it becomes theatrical or gestural. Its writing is a *scénographie*, a writing of the gestural.[205] The transcenic, as proposed by Kristeva, Baudry, and Sollers, is the passage, (*traversée*) of *signifiance* in volume across the space of the text, but only observable from the point of view of a *scène*, as a representation, such as the phenomenal, present-tense level of Sollers's *Nombres*. This explains the importance, beyond the theatre as spectacle, of Artaud's writing, and Mallarmé's conception of writing as gesture in space, of his *Le Livre* as a theatrical presentation of writing. One may see an emphasis on the scenic space in *Tel Quel* as another instance of the 'other scene' similar to the celebration of the non-Western. Barthes's article on the Japanese Bunraku puppet theatre, J.-L. Schefer's book *Scénographie d'un tableau*, applying the argument to pictorial space, Guy

---

[203] ead., 'Pour une sémiologie des paragrammes', *TQ* 29 (spring 1967), 58.
[204] J.-L Baudry, 'Le Texte de Rimbaud II', *TQ* 36 (winter 1969), 50.
[205] Kristeva, 'L'Engendrement de la formule', *TQ* 38 (summer 1969), 67.

Scarpetta's novel *Scène*, are just a few explicit instances of this.[206] It is an 'other scene' in that it substitutes for the theatrical space of representation and spectacle, which had been criticized in the work of the situationists, a scenic space as volume and as generation that is linked with the 'other scene' of Eastern thought in the Japanese *Noh* plays, the Mexican *Tarahumaras*, and Chinese and Indian theatrical practices, as Kristeva suggests.[207] These other spaces become increasingly important in French thought; *Tel Quel*'s focus on them is an important influence.

In the novels of *Tel Quel*, linear plot-development is replaced by a scenic space, which often relies on a structure such as the square or the cube, or a repetitive and revolving structure such as the permutation of pronouns or the seasons of the year. Scenic space also implicates 'trans-scenic' practices such as dance (for example, the work of Merce Cunningham and Trisha Brown) and in some senses, music. It has the powerful effect of linking the previously contemplative practice of literature to a more sensuous practice where reading and writing are seen as activities implicating the body in a passage across a space. Reading becomes a dance, in which the voice in the body traverses the space of the page. In 1963 Sollers had already written: 'le mouvement que j'évoque tient de la danse, de la nage'.[208]

Towards the Subject of Process: The Non-Subject

It is possible to see in Kristeva's book *Séméiotiké* a progression from the earlier texts towards the last, 'L'Engendrement de la formule'. Formalization and semiology, repeated in various modes across the book, give way in the last text to a more extensive approach, signalled by the shift from *sémiologie* to *sémanalyse*, and occasioned by the radicality of its object, *Nombres*. Sollers's text can be seen to effect a shift in Kristeva's theory; it widens and becomes more sensuous and corporeal. Sollers's novel provides the pivot on which Kristeva's work swings into a new period. We can detect in this text an increase in references outside Western culture. There is also a major new departure in the introduction of the problematic of the subject, the body and sexuality, not absent in other texts, but not emphasized.

---

[206] See Barthes, 'Leçon d'écriture', *TQ* 34 (summer 1968); Schefer, *Scénographie d'un tableau*; Guy Scarpetta, *Scène* (Paris, 1972). The blurb for Scarpetta's novel includes the following phrase: 'Scène: texte écrit comme en retrait du théâtre et le traversant cependant'.

[207] See J. Kristeva, 'Le Geste, pratique ou communication', in ead., *Séméiotiké*, 32.

[208] P. Sollers, *Logiques* (Paris, 1968), 20.

We noted earlier the relevance of Lacan's subversion of the subject for *Tel Quel*, and the potential opposition between Lacan's emphasis on the symbolic and Derridean *différance*. The Derridean perspective, elaborated by Sollers in *Logiques*, informs Kristeva's theory of the place of the subject as a *mise à mort* and in the postulation of a pre-symbolic process only readable in the symbolic. But Kristeva avoids the failure of Derridean theory to provide a coherent account of the subject by the insistence on the trans-subjective dimension. This at the same time includes Lacanian psychoanalysis. Implicitly, Lacanian theory ceases to be relevant (as a description of the subject) in the space of the text, as it applies to the subject of discourse and communication, and the text, in Kristeva's view, transgresses the realm of discourse. Although split, the subject of discourse remains in the zone of identity; in Kristeva's theory the subject is thought as coextensive with the sign, and is therefore transgressed by the paragrammatic level of the text, the level before or beyond the sign. As such, the Lacanian unconscious, which is equated with the symbolic as Other, is coextensive with the realm of discourse:

cette zone se présente plutôt comme une assise solide de la parole que comme une sortie à travers la parole, puisque c'est d'un point de vue privilégié de la parole logique (ici non-poétique) et de son sujet, que le concept d'inconscient est forgé en tant que modèle opératoire qui assume le rôle de residu où se jouent des opérations qui ne sont pas dans la parole.[209]

The subject of discourse is a subject complicit with the logic of identity, and the unconscious is added as the zone of the other, anything that logic cannot cover, in order to situate it within the domain of the subject. Kristeva therefore demands a concept of the subject that escapes from the domain of logic and speech, and a corresponding concept of the unconscious. The first is sketched in this first phase, the second is not analysed until later, with the notion of the *sujet en procès* and the 'semiotic'.

The notion Kristeva uses to refer to the transgressive subject is *le sujet zérologique*, a term borrowed from the linguist Linnart Mäll to refer to the Buddhist notion of *sunyavada*, which signifies zero or *le vide*.[210] It is interesting to note how a notion significant to Kristeva's theory derives from an Eastern culture through the refractive lens of a Soviet writer.

---

[209] Kristeva, *Séméiotiké*, 212.

[210] See Mäll, 'Une approche possible du "sunyavada" ', *TQ* 32 (winter 1968) and Kristeva's article on it, 'Distance et anti-représentation', in the same issue.

The fact that Mäll's text appears in *Tel Quel* again indicates to what extent the review integrates an 'other scene' in its publishing practice. The *sujet zérologique* or *le non-sujet* appears when the denotative level of language is reduced to zero. It is a subject beyond the sign:

Ce 'sujet' zérologique est extérieur à l'espace gouverné par le signe. . . . Le sujet zérologique (on voit à quel point le concept de 'sujet' est déplacé ici) ne dépend d'aucun signe même si nous, à partir de notre espace rationnel, ne pouvons le penser qu'à travers le signe.[211]

The subject is characterized by negativity, a negativity not identifiable within Western culture. However, since the subject-sign is transgressed by the text, the text contains the subject, the *sujet zérologique* is only approachable through the subject of discourse, as the paragrammatic is impossible without the denotative and communicative, which it nevertheless annuls. The text is a continual oscillation or transgression, between the subject and the *vide*:

Si cet espace 'vide' où se meut le sujet zérologique est le pôle opposé de notre espace logique, dominé par le sujet parlant, alors la pratique sémiotique poétique, avec ses particularités, devient le lieu où se joignent ces deux pôles dans un incessant mouvement de l'un vers l'autre.[212]

The text annuls the subject. In this conception, the subject is at the same time included in the text, constructed by it and annulled by it. It is not a question of a text without a subject; the subject is a necessary condition of the text. Lacanian theory is relevant up to a point, but beyond it a new conception of subjectivity is needed, which Kristeva goes on to investigate in her later work. Evidently, the shift towards psychoanalysis is determined by the limitations of linguistics and the demands of the theory that Kristeva elaborates.

The Fallen Subject

This theory of the subject is further developed in Kristeva's analysis of Sollers's *Nombres*, a point where Sollers's textual work feeds into her theory and transforms it also in a movement towards psychoanalysis. According to Kristeva's reading of *Nombres*, the structure of the text, the *pheno-text*, is a 'fall-out' of the process of generation. The *geno-text* is an infinite engendering process that denies fixity, while the *pheno-text* is an

[211] Kristeva, 'Distance et anti-représentation', in ead., *Séméiotiké*, 213.
[212] Ibid.

accidental incidence. *Signifiance*, in other words, is: 'comme [une] opération dont la structure n'est qu'une retombée decalée'.[213] The *pheno-text* is an *objet chu* or a *déchet*. The *geno-text* does not know the subject: 'il est son autre ouvrant en deça et au-delà de lui. Lieu hors-subjectif et hors-temporel (le sujet et le temps n'apparaissent que comme des accidents de ce vaste fonctionnement qui les traverse.'[214]

The subject of the text, the *je* of the text is also an *objet chu* or a *déchet*. In *Nombres*, *je* is a posited site, an *infini-point* in Kristeva's terms, of an otherwise unlimited process of meaning. The subject can therefore be seen as the place of a sacrifice.[215] The *geno-text* sacrifices its *engendrement* for the fixity of the *pheno-text*, its volume for the facial surface of the *je*. Sacrificed and fallen, the subject is also a lure (*leurre*). In determining the *pheno-text* and the *je* as *déchet* and sacrifice Kristeva is looking at the passage from the *geno-text* to the *pheno-text*, the movement is from the process to its incidence. In the movement in the opposite direction, which is the movement of reading, from phenomenon to generation, incidence to process, the subject is a lure. This is meant not at all in the sense it has for Lacan, which is as an imaginary mirror, an identification with an ego or imago, but as a ruse to entrap the subject, or the reader, in the infinite process of germination, the signifying process. For, if the text is an *objet chu*, a *déchet* it is also a *relance*, a point of relaunching of the process. This constant relaunching of the subject and the structure back into the process of meaning is attributable to the surplus of meaning over the subject and identity. The text as surplus of *signifiance* over the level of denotation is figured as a *dépense*, in which the subject is consumed, burned, or annulled. In other words, the surface level of the text, with its subject *je*, lures the reader into the process of meaning through a surplus of meaning over identity: 'la signifiance résorbant le corps du sujet'.[216] The Bataillean resonance here, working through Sollers's text, is obvious in Kristeva's formulations. *Signifiance* is a process of expenditure as an annulling, unfixed volume of sense expiating itself.

This surplus or *dépense* is articulated by Kristeva with *jouissance*. The surplus of the *geno-text* in the *pheno-text* makes the work an *objet de jouissance*. The reading of it is a passage, a leap (*saut*) from *déchet* to *jouissance*. *Jouissance* is a loss of the body, a sacrifice of the body. It annuls

[213] Kristeva, 'L'Engendrement de la formule', *TQ* 37–8 (spring—summer 1969), 37: 35.
[214] Ibid. 38.
[215] Ibid. 59.
[216] Ibid. 57.

the subject, and its absence enables the positioning of identity. Kristeva writes that *jouissance* is 'ce dont le manque permet de dire corps'.[217]

Kristeva is beginning in this article to sketch out a conception of textuality, not limited to *Nombres* but inspired by it, which sees it as an affair with death, sacrifice, and *jouissance*. The sacrifice of the subject to the infinite corresponds to the earlier mathematical notion of the jump to the transfinite. Kristeva is extending the models of previous analyses into more corporeal and subjectively oriented areas, marking a shift from an emphasis on epistemology to an ethics of the body. This has repercussions in the area of sexuality.

The Silent Woman

There is a view of sexual relations in her analysis of *Nombres* that may foreshadow later developments in Kristeva's theory. In *Nombres*, *je* is doubled by *elle*, not as another person, but as a function of *je*: ' "Elle" est une fonction de "je", une case de son jeu.'[218] The pronoun *elle*, in the novel, stands for the ability of the subject to experience sacrifice vicariously, through the death of a female counterpart. *Elle* in the novel may be either an abstract representation of femininity, or a part of the subject which emerges after the castrations which the writing portrays. In other words, *elle* is the representation of the female death through which the *jouissance* of the *je* is possible. Kristeva writes:

'Elle' renverse sa jouissance qu'il reçoit comme miroir de sa propre mort. Jouissant de sa mort, 'elle' assure la représentation de sa jouissance à lui, et lui donne cette representation de jouir qui déracine de la subjectivité.[219]

Sollers had already sketched out this vicarious sacrifice of femininity in his essay on Dante as 'la traversée de la mère'.[220] Kristeva sees *elle* as 'une mère folle'.[221] The sacrifice of femininity, enabling the writing of the infinite, involves a passage through the mother, a transgression of the incest taboo, since the sacrifice in question is fundamentally sexual. Paradigmatic texts in this respect are Dante's *Vita Nuova*: the death of Beatrice enabling the writing subject to accede to the poetic voice, and Bataille's *Ma mère*, involving a more sexualized

---

[217] Ibid. 67.
[218] Ibid.
[219] Ibid. 69.
[220] Sollers, *Logiques*, 60.
[221] Kristeva, 'L'Engendrement de la formule', 69–70.

transgression. In both cases, femininity is sacrificed to enable the passage beyond a fixed identity of the male subject. Kristeva writes: 'La possession de la Mère—d'"elle"—est par conséquent la première transgression de l'unicité de "je", le premier acte indispensable à son excentrement.'[222]

Although this may foreshadow further developments in Kristeva's work, it is worthwhile at this point posing the question: to what extent is this notion of femininity specific to Sollers's text and to a masculine representation of femininity, working through Kristeva's text through the internal corruption that texts effect on one another? The Dantesque, Bataillean, and Sollersian view of femininity presented here as an escape-path from the phallocentricity of masculine identity and sexuality, in other words of femininity as an extension of masculinity through which the latter can represent its death and *jouissance*, suggests that women 'do not exist' except as a negativity. This is very similar to Lacan's view of femininity as the (non-)locus of non-localizable, unobservable *jouissance*.[223] This view of femininity, and the frequency with which it appears in avant-garde representations of the feminine, is certainly questionable in so far as the female is always the non-person, the non-existent, the silent. Femininity has no voice in this topology. This may be redressed by Kristeva's later valorization of maternity as a way women can enter social discourse, but essentially the same notion of femininity as excluded from language dominates. A not negligible aspect of *Tel Quel*'s conceptual activity exists around the question of sexuality, treating the notion of the phallocentric and repressed homosexual nature of society, woman as object of exchange or sublimated version of the male ego, and the repression of an originary matriarchy as aspects of this conceptualization of femininity. The transgressive and sacrificial view of literature, historically speaking, also implicates a reassessment, or at least a problematization, of the place and role of femininity. This is present in Hölderlin, Nerval, Baudelaire, Proust, Joyce, Kafka. It is often the figure of the mother which is in question. It may be objected that this is conditioned by a lack of assessment of the place of women in literature, and a lack of consciousness of the canon as an exclusively male pantheon, a lack of awareness of literature as implicated in a masculinist sexuality. In that this vision seeks to open phallic identity to femininity, it presents itself as a liberation, but in

---

[222] Kristeva, 'L'Engendrement de la formula', 70.
[223] See J. Lacan, *Le Séminaire*, xx: *Encore* (Paris, 1975), 69.

specifically masculine terms. *Écriture féminine* seems also to be based on the same premisses, perhaps because of the influence of Lacan. What might seem necessary is an acknowledgement that there is a writing by women which is neither silent nor phallocentric. A special issue of *Tel Quel* in the 1970s goes some way towards this,[224] but innovative writers such as Virginia Woolf, Gertrude Stein, Djuna Barnes, or indeed Margeurite Duras, to name only the writers who come immediately to mind, are not extensively considered in the review.

Kristeva's 'L'Engendrement de la formule' introduces some notions of subjectivity and non-subjectivity that seem to go beyond or outside the Lacanian subject of discourse, to posit a (non-)subject of sacrifice and *jouissance*. Kristeva's notion of the subject remains, however, to an extent within a Freudian/Lacanian space in that it distinguishes between a subject and non-subject; the subject is the subject of discourse or is not at all; in Lacanian terms, it is in the symbolic, split by desire and lack, or is not a subject. A later step, after the publication of Deleuze and Guattari's *Anti-Oedipe* (1972), and *Tel Quel*'s focus on Artaud and Bataille, is the consideration of a pre-verbal, pre-Oedipal subject, subject to pulsions of what Kristeva terms the 'semiotic'. Here it is a pre-symbolic area, more relevant to the work of Klein and Freud than to Lacan, that is investigated. Kristeva simultanously implies Lacanian thinking in the history of *Tel Quel* and moves beyond it.

Kristeva's intervention has been interpreted as contributing an essential scientific impetus to the theory of literature developed in *Tel Quel*. As stressed above, the limitations of this approach are soon bypassed through her movement towards a psychoanalytically oriented approach, which eventually becomes an ethics. Kristeva effectively creates a new psychoanalytic topology and a new way of looking at ethics through her analysis of the literary text and the subjectivity of the writer. Literature transforms science and the ethics that it evolves into. Her involvement with *Tel Quel*, articles in the review, books in the 'Collection', contributions to conferences and to the Groupe d'études théoriques, is undoubtedly a major catalysing element, towards theory and then psychoanalysis. She will officially join the committee in 1970. Her presence associates the review with an academic context, giving it a certain analytic force. The team or partnership of Sollers and Kristeva, although always implicit and never referred to as a personal

---

[224] See 'Recherches féminines', *TQ* 74 (winter 1977). Viviane Forrester's article, 'Féminin pluriel' looks specifically at literature.

involvement, is a parallel attack on different fronts which is a major factor in the passages of persons across the time of theory.

The time of theory for *Tel Quel*, from about 1967 and lasting into the next decade, is a time of synthesis, the pulling together of elements that had been fermenting for a long time, but which only became prominent in the mid-1960s. *Théorie d'ensemble*, and other articles such as Sollers's 'Survol/Rapports(Blocs)/Conflit' attempted to weld the currents of Althusserian Marxism, Lacanian psychoanalysis, Kristeva's semiology, Derridean *écriture* together with the theory of literature and the fictional and textual practice produced in the review itself. This welding has been shown to be unstable, subject to subversion by its own principles. The Marxism of *Tel Quel* was projective and undermined by a principle of excess; *Tel Quel*'s reference to Lacan is only nominal and strategic, undermined by Derrida's influence which is already on the way to being displaced by Kristeva's emerging theory. Historically, it is a synthesis that cannot last. As a theory that proposes a transformation of knowledge by an untheorizable, resistant element, it undermines itself; in Paul de Man's terms, from a different but in many ways parallel context, a 'theory of the impossibility of theory'.[225] The events of 1968 cause a tremendous shift, precipitating the dispersal to extremes and eventually the dissolution of the dominance of leftism in intellectual France. They also determine the emergence of a new theoretical current of reflection on a vital, energetic force seen as unsystematic and unstructured, in the work of Deleuze and Guattari and Lyotard. The conflict between desire, unmediated force, and the Lacanian emphasis on the irreducibility of symbolic representations, will set the stakes for the theoretical debates of the next decade, in which the focus will be essentially on the subject.

Tel Quel both precipitates this movement and is caught up in it. Both Kristeva's and Sollers's work are meditations on the place and nature of the subject of literature, implicating a major engagement with psychoanalysis. Broadly speaking, if the 1960s is the time of a theoretical Marxism, the 1970s sees the dissolution of theory through its articulation with psychoanalysis and a theory of literature based on the exception. The history of *Tel Quel* in the 1970s takes place after the time of theory, in its wake, but in a sense this is also the time in which the consequences and implications of *Tel Quel*'s theory of literature are fully realized.

---

[225] P. de Man, *The Resistance to Theory* (Manchester, 1986), 16.

4 Theory's Wake

THE DISSOLUTION OF MARXISM

Theory after Theory

The synthetic theory proposed by *Tel Quel* in *Théorie d'ensemble*, based on an Althusserian epistemology that emphasized that real objects could only be understood after working on abstract objects, was to some extent a closed system. This closure is perhaps inherent to theory in general, but particularly to that premised on any kind of radical break of shift away from the usual structure of knowledge. It is possible to project this shift into history and to see it as a paradigm shift, linked to the evolution of knowledge, but this anchoring in historical time does not account for the distinct temporality of theory itself. In effect, while structuralism proposed closed structures, excluding dynamic aspects such as the subjective and the notion of process, post-structuralist theories, like those of Kristeva, proposed a different kind of closure, through the emphasis on a leap outside what was known to a position at the limit. Theory becomes terroristic in postulating this position outside, transforming the discourse within the circle. After structure, theory becomes sublime, through its analysis of what is seen as unspeakable or unrepresentable, reintroducing a force outside discourse within discourse, which transforms it. Another way of looking at the possibilities after theory, instead of this dialectic of the discursive and the pre-discursive, might be to hesitate infinitely at the limit, to oscillate around it, at its fracture or hiatus. If the second option is present in the work of a group of writers around Derrida, who emerged as prominent, to form a kind of philosophical hegemony, in the late 1970s,[1] the first option seems to be that of *Tel Quel* and Sollers. The theory after theory of *Tel Quel* is premised on this sublime dialectic of the transformation of discourse from the perspective of what it has excluded, or what appears

---

[1] This hiatus may be recognized textually, as in J. Derrida's *Glas* (1974), or discursively, as e.g. in the collective work by S. Agacinski, J. Derrida, S. Kofman, P. Lacoue-Labarthe, J.-L. Nancy, and B. Pautrat, *Mimesis des articulations* (Paris 1975).

at its limit. If in the early 1970s this dialectic is still linked to social revolution, through the review's Maoism, it eventually becomes more focused on singularity; the position at the limit, rather than being seen as an abstract force that could be part of a social dialectic, becomes an exception. The history of *Tel Quel* in the 1970s traces this movement. Theory after theory refers not only to a historical temporality, then, but to a moment after the closure of the theoretical system, or to a moment before it in the case of Kristeva's focus on the pre-symbolic. As well as being a wake, in the sense of a time after the death of something and the repercussions of a traversal, it is a renaissance, an awakening to the possibilities of this space after. The resonances of the wake are especially pertinent in that the decade sees a concentration on the texts of Joyce in *Tel Quel*.

June 1971

The alliance between *Tel Quel* and the PCF, engaged in 1967, came to an end in 1971, when the review broke with the party to become overtly Maoist. This was the result of internal tensions both on the side of the party and within the review, but it was precipitated by a number of events. Within *Tel Quel*, the philosophical investigation of dialectical materialism, the adding of the subtitle 'Philosophie/politique' to 'Science/littérature' on the review's covers irritated the editors of the PCF cultural journal *La Nouvelle Critique*, for whom this indicated a trespass on their own ground. *Tel Quel* defended its right to trespass; it would follow its own philosophical evolution and the positions this demanded in politics, not that of the party.[2] The tendency of the investigation of dialectical materialism was moreover explicitly towards Maoism, and Sollers's essay 'Sur la contradiction' could only have been read as a provocation by PCF intellectuals.

The PCF saw, for its part, that it need not exclusively follow *Tel Quel* when it came to the theory and practice of literature. The rivalry of *Tel Quel*, *Change* and *Action poétique*, exemplified at the second Cluny colloquium organized by *La Nouvelle Critique*, 'Littérature et idéologie', offered an opportunity to play one group against another.[3] Previous polemics,

---

[2] See 'A propos d'une note de *La Nouvelle Critique*', *TQ* 46 (summer 1971).

[3] *Tel Quel*'s interventions in general took the form of a critique of Surrealism, e.g. in P. Sollers's 'Thèses générales', *TQ* 44 (winter 1971), an edited form of his intervention. This is followed in issue 46, (summer 1971) by a critical focus on 'neo-Surrealism'. At the conference, meanwhile, Kristeva was attacked by Mitsou Ronat of the Change group, and the *Tel Quel* group threatened to leave at one point unless some kind of admonition were

specifically concerning Derrida's relation to Heidegger and the early politics of *Tel Quel*, engaged by J.-P. Faye, and against Kristeva's linguistic theory by Pierre Lusson, Jacques Roubaud, and Mitsou Ronat, made the situation more tenuous.

Within *Tel Quel* tensions arose between a group favourable to Maoism, essentially led by Sollers, and PCF members Ricardou and Thibaudeau, who were increasingly distant from the kernel around Sollers. This led to a crisis in 1971, when Ricardou and Thibaudeau left the committee. If, as we have suggested, *Tel Quel*'s Marxism is fundamentally transgressive of the basis of Marxism itself, this crisis and shift is inevitable, part of the mechanism of the review. The crisis is forced through by this transgressive logic. The effect of the events of 1968, the PCF having shown itself resistant to the spontaneous desire which erupted then, and the position of Althusser within the party while his pupils broke with it, also favoured this shift. In moving away from the party, *Tel Quel* is also distancing itself from the structural impasse of Althusserian theory, as the later criticism of Althusser suggests.[4] In fact, this effect of fracture and dispersal is part of a more general tendency in the context. Some members of the *Cahiers pour l'analyse* group, for example, would launch themselves into groups of Maoist orientation, such as the Yenan or Gauche prolétarienne groups, favouring subversive action rather than intellectual intervention, a disruption of the university rather than a position within it.[5] The University of Vincennes, created after 1968, would be a focus for this disturbance.

The precise chronology of the split with the PCF depends on events which appear as expedient ways of forcing through a crisis already demanded by the trajectory of writing in *Tel Quel*, after 1968 emerging with a less structural, more desirous and pulsional energetic force, as analyses of the texts will show. Satellite periodicals of *Tel Quel*, such as *Cinéthique*, to which Sollers, Pleynet, Kristeva, and Baudry contributed articles and with which *Tel Quel* signed a manifesto in 1969 against *Change* and the review *Positif*,[6] were already intimating a critique of the

made. It was, and the group stayed, but the tensions between the review and the PCF were increased.

[4] See P. Sollers, *Sur le matérialisme* (Paris, 1974), 140–1.

[5] Judith Miller, Lacan's daughter, would become a focus of this activity when she was expelled from the University of Vincennes for openly declaring her intention to subvert the structures of the institution.

[6] See 'Cinéma, littérature, politique', *TQ* 44 (winter 1971).

PCF.[7] At first this critique is rebuked in *Tel Quel*,[8] but later an editorial will note: '*Cinéthique* a eu raison de se révolter.'[9] The members of the poetry and theory periodical *Promesse*, Jean-Louis Houdebine and Guy Scarpetta, would also join with the Maoist group internal to *Tel Quel*, around Sollers. Their interview with Derrida, published in the book *Positions*, suggests that the estrangement from Derrida results from his unwillingness to commit himself to *Tel Quel*'s Maoism.[10] In 1970, a periodical was created specifically devoted to the plastic arts, but also including theoretical articles, entitled *Peinture, cahiers théoriques*. It was the organ of a group of artists known as Supports/Surfaces, including Marc Devade, who joined the committee of *Tel Quel* in 1971, Louis Cane, Daniel Dezeuze, and Claude Viallat. It also regularly included, in the last pages, polemical interventions and Maoist slogans of an increasing extremism, against the PCF. The committee of *Tel Quel*, being still run along democratic lines and therefore containing elements (Ricardou and Thibaudeau) resistant to Maoism, the internal kernel around Sollers makes itself felt in satellite periodicals, which reinforce the tendency towards the shift. There is a certain surplus or excess that overflows the review and appears in related sites of publication, and this tendency is continued throughout the decade.

The event which most explicitly precipitated the crisis of 1971 was the polemic over the book *De la Chine*.[11] In 1971 the Italian Communist and correspondent of Althusser, Maria-Antonietta Macciocchi, after a trip to China published a best-selling book (with Seuil) which was essentially a eulogy of Maoism. This was anathema to the Italian Communist Party (PCI), and she was not renominated for the post of deputy in Naples which she held. Apart from the polemic within the PCI, this had repercussions in France, when at the annual 'Fête de *L'Humanité*', a Communist speech-day, the sale of the book was forbidden. Sollers made an intervention and was criticized by a party luminary, Étienne Fajon, in the presence of Aragon. The Macciocchi book became a

---

[7] See 'Les Pratiques artistiques dans le Marxisme-Léninisme', *Cinéthique*, 11 (1971).

[8] 'Une analyse unilatérale', *TQ* 45.

[9] 'Déclaration', *TQ* 47 (autumn 1971), 139.

[10] See J. Derrida, *Positions* (Paris, 1972), pub. by Minuit, not in the 'Collection Tel Quel' at Seuil. See pp. 85–90. Derrida states his resistance to elaborate a position on Marxism 'tant que les conditions n'en sont rigoureusement élucidées' and says that this analysis, on his part, is 'encore à venir'. His recent *Spectres de Marx* (Paris, 1993) may be the long awaited response.

[11] M.-A. Macciocchi, *De la Chine* (Paris, 1971).

focus, and a convenient hinge on which *Tel Quel*'s political allegiance would turn.[12]

Around the same time, in an article on 'Lautréamont politique', Pleynet had polemically intervened over the 'posthumous reconciliation' of Breton and Aragon, which earned a critical reply from *La Nouvelle Critique*, since Aragon was the most respected Communist intellectual who, after all, had helped to launch Sollers's career. A certain amount of resentment over this apparent betrayal might have been a factor in the split. In a note following this critical response, *Tel Quel* indicates its readiness to follow its own line, whatever the consequences.

The result of all these polemics was the creation of the 'Mouvement de Juin 1971', the Maoist kernel of *Tel Quel*. Over the summer, the offices of the review were covered in Maoist *dazibao* or slogans, reminiscent of the graffiti of 1968. The situation was such that the next issue, a special issue on Barthes, announces the formal split with the PCF and the suspension of the Groupe d'études théoriques.[13] The review is declared to be in crisis. Given this situation, it was not surprising that Ricardou and Thibaudeau should resign,[14] and the first issue of the next year is a double issue fully devoted to 'La Pensée chinoise', including interventions by Sollers, Macchiocchi, and left intellectuals Michelle Loi and Charles Bettelheim over the *De la Chine* polemic.[15]

Hysteria/Analysis

From this point, *Tel Quel* will be overtly critical of the PCF and of socialism, of the alliance of dogmatism and revisionism which it neologizes as 'dogmatico-révisionnisme', seeing Stalinism and right-wing

[12] P. Sollers would contribute a letter of protest to *Le Monde* in Sept. The book is reviewed critically in *La Nouvelle Critique* (Nov. 1971) under the title, '*De la Chine* ou les racines de la sinophilie occidentale'.

[13] 'Positions du mouvement de Juin 1971', *TQ* 47: 133–41.

[14] See J. Thibaudeau, *Interventions: Socialisme, avant-garde, littérature* (Paris, 1972), 204.: 'J'ai quitté la rédaction de *Tel Quel* en décembre 1971, n'ayant rien pu publier dans la revue.' Thibaudeau declares in an interview pub. in *Nouvelle Clarté*, in 1971, his intentions to publish an analysis in *Tel Quel* of the review's turn to 'l'anticommunisme'. It was not pub., hence Thibaudeau's resignation.

[15] See *TQ* 48–9 (spring 1972), 'La Pensée chinoise'. M.-A. Macciocchi, 'Réponse à *La Nouvelle Critique. De La Nouvelle Critique* ou des racines de la sinophobie occidentale'; C. Bettelheim, 'Note de lecture sur l'article "De la Chine et des racines de la sinophilie occidentale" '; P. Sollers, 'De la Chine'; M. Loi, 'De la collusion idéologique des "sinophobes" '.

revisionism as two sides of the same coin.[16] Until 1976, many articles will appear concerning Chinese culture, thought, or politics. The culmination of this activity was the trip to China in 1974 of Sollers, Kristeva, Barthes, Pleynet, and François Wahl. In the French context *Tel Quel* enters a period of political and cultural extremism, the acute moment of which is the Artaud and Bataille conference of 1972. This position earned it a reputation for political radicalism of a somewhat hysterical nature. At the same time, however, the theoretical and fictional work it continues to produce is not restricted to this political faith, and tends to push it forward to different positions. For example, it will focus on the texts of Joyce, on the question of sexuality and of femininity. The political shifts are always determined by the internal theoretical and literary orientation of the review. The departure of Ricardou and Thibaudeau can be seen as equally determined by differences over literary practice, an adherence to the *nouveau roman* on the part of Ricardou, a resistance to leaving behind a certain formalistic perspective on the part of Thibaudeau. The committee, after their departure and the addition of Kristeva and Marc Devade in 1970, is essentially as it will remain for the rest of the decade: Sollers, Pleynet, Kristeva, Baudry, Rottenberg, Risset, Devade, Denis Roche. Devade's presence is essentially as a link to *Peinture*, which will publish articles by Sollers, Kristeva, Pleynet, and Baudry during the decade. The review also gains a wider circle of contributors: Houdebine and Scarpetta from *Promesse* regularly publish work in *Tel Quel*. Jacques Henric, who will be involved from its creation in 1972 with the review *Art press*, also friendly to *Tel Quel*, is another regular contributor. Bernard Sichère and Philippe Muray are notable among those whose names still appear in the contents pages of *L'Infini*. While Derrida became estranged after 1971, Barthes is still a valuable ally and close friend. Pierre Guyotat and Maurice Roche will also be in proximity. The departures from the committee during the decade are less the result of internal polemics than of the individuals concerned following their own interests. Denis Roche, Baudry, and Rottenberg will all leave the committee during the 1970s (in 1973, 1975, and 1979 respectively), the three contributing little during the years before their departure, leaving the kernel of the review,

---

[16] Cf. 'Positions du mouvement de Juin 1971', *TQ* 47: 137: 'Résumons: l'erreur est d'avoir pensé qu'il existait une contradiction antagoniste entre dogmatisme et révisionnisme. Or, tout prouve de plus en plus que cette contradiction secondaire est en fait non-antagoniste, que ses deux pôles, dans un espace homogène, convergent vers le même but: dépolitisation des masses, sclérose idéologique, restauration du capitalisme.'

around Sollers, Kristeva, Pleynet, and Risset. Denis Roche takes up a position at Seuil as editor of the 'Fiction et cie' series, his poetry moving towards an articulation with photography. Baudry, while involved with the review *Digraphe* run by Jean Ristat, takes up a university position outside Paris. Rottenberg continues to write poetry, published by the innovative 'Orange Export Ltd' series. The dispersal of the *Tel Quel* group suggests the dissolution of the synthesizing theoretical tendency of the late 1960s and the individualization of theory in the review, anchored in the singularity of the practice of the novel (Sollers), of poetry (Pleynet and Risset), of art criticism (Pleynet), of psychoanalysis (Kristeva), or of translation from the Italian in the case of Risset. Kristeva and Risset's femininity will also lead to developments in the review. Theory, in its wake, becomes, in its origin and its concerns, exceptional, singular, a theory of the exception or of literary singularity, which is a post-theory or a theory-after-theory, essentially and continually moving towards its own dissolution.

The Maoist period of *Tel Quel*'s political allegiance sees the theoretical austerity of the time of the alliance with the PCF mutate into a more spontaneous, heterogenous production. While the theory itself tends to emphasize a heterogenous force of negativity, at the Artaud and Bataille conference particularly, rather than the structural synthesis of *Théorie d'ensemble*, the political interventions of the review become more linked to real events, such as the *coup d'état* in Chile and the assassination of Allende, strikes at the Lip factory in 1973, electoral gains for the Right, the alliance between the PCF and the PS (Parti socialiste), all condemned and analysed in short editorials.[17] At the same time there is a hysterical tone to the extreme radicalism of the Mouvement de Juin 1971, which itself published some short tracts, collections of interventions from Maoist and anarchist groups around France; this tone appears, with hindsight, as a strategic radicalism, in order to 'épater le bourgeois' and to force the context in certain ways.[18] The editorial and political pronouncements of the review are couched in a Maoist *langue de bois*; while they were forceful in the context, they appear slightly dated now. This often determines how *Tel Quel* is stereotyped in the French intellectual context.

[17] See 'Éditorial', *TQ* 53 (spring 1973); 'Editorial', *TQ* 56 (winter 1973); 'Éditorial', *TQ* 57 (spring 1974); 'Éditorial', *TQ* 58 (summer 1974); 'Éditorial', *TQ* 59 (autumn 1974); *TQ* 61 (spring 1975).
[18] Cf. 'Position du mouvement de Juin 1971', *TQ* 47: 141: 'A bas le dogmatisme, l'empirisme, l'opportunisme, le révisionnisme! Vive la véritable avant-garde! Vive la pensée-maotsetoung!'

The repetition of the slogan 'Vive la pensée-maotsétoung' (the contraction suggesting more popular speech) in the review and its satellites up to 1976 is a caricature that hides the more fundamental transgression of the Marxist system. In some senses these are empty signifiers, performative *énoncés*, connoting a turn to a more spontaneous relation to language and its pulsional base. Their hysteria is accompanied, however, by an analytical position, which the editorials do not cease to affirm, that will eventually lead to the abandonment of these signifiers, the body of Maoism, or of Mao, as a referent or an upholstering point of *Tel Quel*'s thought. The special issue on Barthes of autumn 1971 inscribes an ironical critique of this revolutionary political hysteria at the outset of the Maoist period. Barthes writes that: 'le langage politique est lui-même fait de stéréotypes' and that 'le stéréotype est triste, car il est constitué par une nécrose du langage, une prothèse qui vient boucher un trou d'écriture'.[19] Writing, the pleasure of the text in Barthes's terms, always runs through or across this stasis, leaving the empty signifiers behind. Barthes's perspective, influenced by Lacan, is that any position in language is a position within the law; as soon as one speaks, one is on the side of the law. Political hysteria only reaffirms the law, and other methods have to be adopted: 'une autre intelligibilité'.[20] This other rationality, Barthes suggests, is that of writing, which is *atopique*; it cannot be assigned a place.[21] The history of *Tel Quel*'s Maoism is the story of the deterritorialization of the topos of Marxism, of China, by the *dérive* of writing.

The analytic traversal of Maoism, the extent to which it is not fixed, is also suggested by its insertion in the fictional practice of the writers of the review. Sollers's *Lois*, produced around the time of the split with the PCF, shows him creating a work which already puts the Marxist system within the parodic envelope of a euphoric writing. An encounter with the text of Joyce is significantly cited by Sollers as one of the determining motifs of this novel.[22] The Maoist *langue de bois* is here parodied and transformed into a heterogenous tissue. For example: 'Away! Prolétaires de tous les pays, unissez vous. Ne vous laissez pas faire moumou. Pas de fleurs en mots, de petits cadeaux. Gare au réviso. Vous tous des nations pillées . . . '[23]

[19] R. Barthes, 'Écrivains, intellectuels, professeurs', *TQ* 47. 8. Cf. also P. Sollers, 'R.B.', ibid. 20: 'L'hystérique est l'anti-R.B.'.
[20] Barthes, 'Écrivains, intellectuels, professeurs', *TQ* 47: 4.
[21] Ibid. 17.
[22] P. Sollers, *Vision à New York* (Paris, 1981), 112–13.
[23] Id., *Lois* (Paris, 1971), 83.

The writing of *H*, in which the signifier of Maoism in its form of Chinese ideograms is dropped, and *Paradis* will show the unfixing of any political signifier and a movement towards other signifiers, specifically towards the religious signifier as the prophetic matrix of signification. Pleynet's *Stanze* also traverses the system of Marxism, in that its structure is based in the Marxist or Maoist schema of the nine modes of production, which the poetry tends to exceed. After *Stanze*, Pleynet's poetry, written in the margins of the continuation of *Stanze*, is a more fragmented text in which the violence of 'l'expérience singulière'[24] makes itself felt, particularly in the text 'A la mère', published in the review in 1975.[25] The political allegiance to Maoism, in this period, is paralleled, and will eventually be displaced, by the excess of a 'joyeuse pratique critique d'analyse', as Pleynet puts it, in the fiction.[26] This fact is forgotten if the shift away from Maoism in 1976 is seen as an abrupt reversal conditioned by external events.

Chinese Thought and Politics

Immediately following the special issue on Barthes is a double issue focusing on 'La Pensée chinoise', which, apart from its political determinations, is important in analysing the links between the theory of writing of *Tel Quel* and Chinese philosophical thought, already suggested in Sollers's *Logiques*. The interest in China presents a complex interplay of political and cultural factors. On the one hand the review wishes to ground its political allegiance to Maoism in aesthetic and philosophical concerns. The Chinese conception of *espace-temps* is related to *Tel Quel*'s spatialization of narrative temporality, in such novels as *Drame* or *Nombres*. Chinese 'graphic language' is linked to the textual practice of the review, which problematizes representation and privileges inscription, and often structures the text around spatial motifs.[27] François Cheng and Julia Kristeva sketch out a view of the Chinese language and Chinese poetry that relates them to the revolution of poetic language Kristeva sees in Mallarmé and Lautréamont.[28] The Western

---

[24] M. Pleynet, 'L'Expérience singulière', preface to id., *Rime* (Paris, 1981).

[25] Id., 'A la mère', *TQ* 62 (summer 1975).

[26] Id., *Stanze* (Paris, 1973), 155.

[27] See J. Needham, 'Le Temps et l'homme oriental'; Ion Banu, 'Philosophie sociale, magie et langage graphique dans le Hong-fan', *TQ* 48–9.

[28] Cheng-Chi-Hsien (François Cheng), 'Analyse du langage poétique dans la poésie chinoise classique' and J. Kristeva, 'Compte rendu', *TQ* 48–9.

philosophical *episteme* of subject-object is annulled in Chinese poetry, according to François Cheng, in favour of an interiorization of the external world. Kristeva argues that in this poetic practice the subject is traversed and exceeded by the heterogenous force of *signifiance* that is brought into play, a dialectical operation which is linked to the textual practice of *Tel Quel*.

While the similarities between the more radical moments of literature and Chinese signifying practices are striking, because both present an outside of Western culture, the links between the aesthetic and the political are tenuous. There is a marked over-investment in the ideological at the expense of political analysis, so that there is a certain amount of wishful thinking in *Tel Quel*'s Maoism; it projects an ideological justification on to a political reality that diverts from it. The Chinese culture investigated by the review is, for example, almost without exception based on ancient modes of thought and takes no account of the modern cultural reality of China. On the other hand, if we accept that *Tel Quel*'s Maoism is a transgression of Marxism, then the misappropriation of political reality is not as relevant as the massive introduction, effected by the review, of a wealth of erudite knowledge about China into the arena of intellectual debate in France.

It is also true that the Maoist period sees a greater emphasis in the review on political questions. A large number of articles appear from sinologists who offer favourable reports of the political reforms since the Cultural Revolution.[29] While the projective wishful thinking of *Tel Quel* has much to do with its disastrous misreading of the political reality in China, it also has a lot to do with the disinformation supplied by these erudite sinologists, Jean Daubier, Jean Chesneaux, Macciocchi, and others. Their insights were at the expense of a considerable blindness. Reports of a less positive tone were also emerging, such as Simon Leys's *Les Habits neufs du Président Mao*, published by Champ Libre, which also published the situationists, in 1971, and Jean Pasqualini's *Prisonnier de Mao* in 1973. China's entry into the United Nations in 1971 and Nixon's visit to China in 1972 intimated that China's foreign policy was more

---

[29] See J. Daubier, 'La Chine aujourd'hui', *TQ* 50 (summer 1972) and 'Idéologie, pouvoir et gauchisme en Chine populaire', *TQ* 54 (summer 1973). Daubier is the author of an account of the Cultural Revolution and editor of the important periodical *La Nouvelle Chine*. See also Jean Chesnaux, 'Yanan', *TQ* 61 (spring 1975). A more phantasmatic and subversive approach is present in Susan Sontag's article, 'Projet d'un voyage en Chine', *TQ* 54. If Maoist China is recognized as a fantasy, the political hysteria resulting from it could then have been analysed as such.

conciliatory to the West than the ideology of Maoism suggested.[30] So for a long time, from 1971 to 1976, *Tel Quel*'s political pronouncements are determined by a disastrous misinterpretation of events in China on to which are projected an ideology specific to France.

Critique of Marxism

Tel Quel's Maoism is a critique of the Marxist system. This explains to an extent the eventual communication between *Tel Quel* and the *nouveaux philosophes*, many of whom were ex-Maoists and whose critique of Marxism emerges from that ground. There is also a marked continuity between *Tel Quel*'s Maoist critique of Marxism, which, however, retains the reference to the class struggle, and the work of a writer like Jean-Marie Benoist, whose *Marx est mort* came out in 1970, elaborating a critique of Marxism from the perspective of a Bataillean emphasis on heterogeneity, but without the vestiges of a nominal Marxism-Leninism. The works of Deleuze and Guattari, of Lyotard, and to an extent Foucault, which were published in the early 1970s were also developing a critique of the Marxist system as repressive of desire. The Lacanian emphasis on the law, in *Tel Quel*, resists this postulation of the spontaneous expression of revolutionary desire, which is criticized in the review. The early 1970s would also see the elaboration of a critique of Althusser, by Jacques Rancière in particular, in *La Leçon d'Althusser* (1974) and by Althusser himself in *Réponse à John Lewis* (1973) and *Éléments d'autocritique* (1972). The positions these books presented are severely criticized in the editorial sections of *Tel Quel*. The review would publish articles critical of the Marxist system, but from within, from the perspective of the cultural revolution of Maoism. The period sees a focus on Gramsci by Macciocchi, articles on socialism and women by Dominique Desanti, on the early socialism of Fourier, and analysis by N. Poulantzas of Fascism.[31] There are a number of articles concerning Marxism in its relation to China.

---

[30] China's foreign policy is defended by K. Mavrakis in 'La Politique internationale de la Chine', *TQ* 50 (summer 1972).

[31] M.-A. Macciocchi, 'Pour Gramsci', *TQ* 54, also 'Les Patrons de Gramsci', *TQ* 61 (spring 1975), and her book *Pour Gramsci* (Paris, 1974), an important theoretical biography; D. Desanti, 'A propos de Flora Tristan', *TQ* 53 (spring 1973) and 'Les Socialistes et les femmes', *TQ* 61 (spring 1975); Catherine Francblin, 'Le Féminisme utopique de C. Fourier', *TQ* 62 (summer 1975); N. Poulantzas, 'Note à propos du totalitarisme', *TQ* 53.

Donald Lowe, for example, concludes in his examination of Marxist thinking on the East, that Marxism is Eurocentric.[32] Marx and Engels inherited the Hegelian conception of China as historically stagnated because it did not fit into the plan of the dialectical development of historical materialism. Hegel's focus on rationality as 'the real' was inherited by Marx and Engels, resulting in a blindness to the non-Western.

The concepts of the state and of class consciousness are similarly criticized by Kristeva.[33] She notes how the state is a set or totality that blocks the force of revolutionary negativity. Part of Marx's radical discovery, she asserts, is that the state, seen as a totality that would envelop negativity, is an illusion: 'L'État comme ensemble de tous les ensembles est une fiction.'[34] She further criticizes the similar Leninist idea that the state can systematize a totality of individual wills. Moreover, Marx did not see that the illusion of the state as 'ensemble de tous les ensembles' prevented the posing of the existence of the infinite. She attacks Marxism for its closure of the consideration of infinity, which poetic language explores. Moreover, the concept of class consciousness is shown to be limited in its applicability only to totality and to production. Marxism never goes beyond the sphere of production, and the revolution of the proletariat only leads to the perfecting of this system. Even as early as 1972, the Marxist system, for Kristeva, is repressive and limited in its focus on production.

A crucial point where the system of Marxism is displaced by other elements of *Tel Quel*'s interests is the question of the subject. Kristeva's 'subject in process' takes account of a heterogeneity and negativity that the subject posed by Marxism denies. She implies that Marxism is a humanism in its philosophical derivation from Feuerbach, which forgets about Hegelian negativity: 'le Marxisme écarte la négativité hégélienne'.[35] Marx puts forward an 'unification subjectale'[36] of this negativity that transforms the subject into a unified atom rather than a process.

In his article on Bataille at the 1972 conference, Sollers similarly proposes the subject as 'la question rongeante non résolue' that goes

---

[32] D. M. Lowe, 'Marx, Engels et la Chine', *TQ* 56 (winter 1973).
[33] J. Kristeva, 'La Révolution du langage poétique', *TQ* 56.
[34] Ibid. 39.
[35] J. Kristeva, 'Le Sujet en procès', *TQ* 52 (winter 1972), 59, also in ea'd., *Polylogue* (Paris, 1976) and P. Sollers (ed.), *Artaud* (Paris, 1973).
[36] Ibid.

beyond dialectical materialism.[37] The emphasis on the subject as excessive with regard to the systemic is already susceptible to being developed into a stress on singularity or on the exception. Of course this passes through psychoanalysis, which is the most consequential consideration of the place of the subject, considered here as a 'subject in process', rather than the *sujet unaire* posed by Lacan, or the absent subject that Derrida's trace effaced. It is Lacanian psychoanalysis, rethought from the perspective of poetic language by Kristeva, that appears as the most promising area. While a Lacanian analytic approach is affirmed, the review takes a critical position towards Althusser and Derrida, whose work is suggested as eliding the question of the subject. While the former is criticized for the deflection of the place of the subject in a 'procès sans sujet', the latter is seen as idealist in celebrating a 'substance' of difference previous to the materiality of language. The Derridean moment and the Althusserian moment of *Tel Quel* give way to a Lacanian moment, but always within the framework of the transformative effect of literature and implicitly criticized in Kristeva's work.

Artaud/Bataille: The Subject as Knot

Only half a year after the strategic break with the PCF, *Tel Quel* organized a colloquium, the second specific to the review itself, at Cérisy-la-Salle, under the title 'Vers une révolution culturelle: Artaud/Bataille'. The proceedings of the conference, which took place in July 1972, were partly published in *Tel Quel* itself, in *Peinture, cahiers théoriques*, and then completely in two volumes published by the 'U.G.E 10/18' series which normally brought out the Cérisy conference texts. One notable omission was Denis Roche's tape-recorded contribution on Artaud, 'Artaud refait', which Roche would include as part of his 1976 'novel', *Louve basse*. Disagreements over this publication led to Denis Roche's departure from the committee in 1973. As the two separate volumes, on Artaud and Bataille, were and are among the few critical texts to focus on these authors, they have become a privileged site of the encounter of *Tel Quel*. In fact, the conference can be seen as a crucial moment, when *Tel Quel* makes its presence felt in the context, and a moment of definition of the approach of the review in that period.

[37] P. Sollers, 'L'Acte Bataille', in id. (ed.), *Bataille* (Paris, 1973), 13. The article is also pub. in *TQ* 52.

The title 'Vers une révolution culturelle' indicates the Maoist orientation. In fact, although there is a certain projection of the cultural revolution of Artaud and Bataille's writing on to the reality of Chinese politics (particularly in the contribution 'Artaud travaillé par la Chine', by Henric, who, having left the party, overtly situates revolutionary faith in China), the conference for the most part focuses on less explicitly political terrain, such as sexuality, the family, writing. In his preliminary address Sollers locates the essential knot of the conference, and the theoretical work to come, as the question of the subject, entailing an analysis of sexuality, the family, *le savoir* in its relation to the subject, of madness and writing.[38] This widens the focus of *Tel Quel* and brings it into closer contact with, or on to the ground of psychoanalysis. At the same time, explicitly situating the conference after 1968, the problem of theory and its appropriative capacities is posed. Sollers states that theory needs to begin with these questions, with the question of the subject posed by Artaud and Bataille, but that it also tends to thin out or water down these questions.[39] He also affirms that 'il faut penser l'impensé de Marx et Freud après eux'.[40] It is this afterwards (*après*) that defines the conference. Theory is opened up by the question of the subject, and this question, 'l'enjeu même de la dialectique',[41] also opens up and problematizes Marxist and Freudian theory, 'after theory'. Kristeva begins by proposing her long theoretical article on 'Le Sujet en procès', itself opening up the Lacanian and Hegelian *sujet unaire* to the negativity of the pulsional pre-verbal subject, as 'une invasion de la neutralité théorique positiviste par l'expérience même du sujet de la théorie'.[42] The conference appears as a site of vital contradictions, between science or theory and the subjective, a theory of the subject *troué*, holed or opened by experience. The terrain of enquiry of the subject and sexuality is superimposed on to, or condensed with, the philosophical and political, and the contradictions that result will force through developments in the review's history in the next half-decade. Sollers's answer to the question 'Pourquoi Artaud, pourquoi Bataille?' is, characteristically and aptly, 'Pour faire bouger des contradictions'.[43]

[38] P. Sollers, 'Pourquoi Artaud, pourquoi Bataille?', in id. (ed.), *Artaud*, 9–12.

[39] Ibid. 10: 'La théorie elle-même ne peut plus se faire sans partir d'eux (Artaud et Bataille), faute d'être frappée d'insignifiance, le plus souvent nous dirons même qu'elle s'élabore surtout en les délayant.'

[40] Ibid. 11.

[41] Ibid.

[42] Kristeva, 'Le Sujet en procès', in Sollers (ed.), *Artaud*, 43.

[43] Sollers, 'Pourquoi Artaud, pourquoi Bataille', 9.

While Kristeva's contribution, as underlined, theoretically treats the question of the subject before theory, before *le savoir*, Sollers's 'L'état Artaud' problematizes any envelopment of the subject in *le savoir* by producing a discourse from the law of the signifier—that is, in anchoring the production of *énoncés* in the displacement of letters, for example, from 'le pli' to 'le gli' to 'le cri'. 'Le gli', Sollers's critical target, appears to be the repressive, appropriative qualities of commentary:

Qui intronise le gli, l'émet, l'émane, le diffuse et le reproduit? Qui se fait en lui, le prend, le projette? Qui l'a décidé, qui l'a dit? Qui reste là pour en assurer le redit? C'est le gli qui se prend pour cri. Qui voudrait être gli dans le cri pour pouvoir commenter le cri. Et par conséquent en faire de l'écrit.[44]

Theoretical production is held to the materiality of language. In Pleynet's contribution on Artaud the contradictions between experience and 'le code du savoir' are more evident, since Pleynet begins by saying that essentially he has 'nothing to say' about Artaud, resulting in a text which pulls commentary towards reading; his commentary on the 'theatre' of Artaud eventually falls into a reading, or a writing that cannot be integrated with a discourse of knowledge or theory. For example: 'démontrer une sorte d'affinité mystérieuse entre la viande de pourceaux et la nature de la peste malaise physique tache rouge tournant au noir tête poids fatigue aspiration magnétique'.[45]

Moreover, the real erupts in the text in capitals, as Pleynet notes that while he was writing, a riot erupted in a street near him.[46] Just as Sollers's contribution sometimes has the same stylistic form as his novel *Lois*, so Pleynet's text, this political irruption in particular, recalls his book *Stanze*, which appeared in the following year. His contribution on Bataille was in fact a canto of *Stanze*, retitled 'L'Orestie' after a Bataille text.[47] Pierre Guyotat's text on Artaud, 'Langage du corps', describes his practice of writing while masturbating with the other hand, 'l'autre main branle'. Barthes's text on Bataille is structured as a series of fragments with titles in alphabetical order, to assure 'un degré zéro de l'ordre', prefiguring his *Roland Barthes par Roland Barthes*.[48] There is an infiltration of theory by the creative practice of writing, and vice versa, which tends to undermine the pretension of theory to closure and to the positivist neutrality Kristeva refers to. In the context the conference

[44] Id., 'L'État Artaud', in id. (ed.), *Artaud*, 14.
[45] M. Pleynet, 'La Matière pense', in Sollers (ed.), *Artaud*, 149.
[46] Ibid. 138.
[47] M. Pleynet, 'L'Orestie', in Sollers (ed.), *Bataille*, 106–119.
[48] R. Barthes, 'Les Sorties du texte', ibid. 39.

appears as a moment when *Tel Quel* defines its specificity, without the necessity of reference to Derrida, Lacan, or Althusser. Kristeva's work becomes the principal theoretical reference, displacing these three figures all at once. It is also 'post '68' in the focus on the subject, on sexuality and the family (there are references to anti-psychiatry and David Cooper, the English anarchistic anti-psychiatrist[49]). A new reference, but one accompanied by criticism, is to Deleuze and Guattari's *Anti-Oedipe*, to a more fluid, anti-structural psychoanalysis.[50] In the 1970s, *Tel Quel* develops its theory and its fiction independently, and towards the dissolution of the system of Marxism and Freudian analysis, elaborating, as Sollers states of Bataille, 'un système du non-système'.[51] The conference is a point of departure and of definition, of a theory after theory.

Heterogenous Fiction

The novel in the 1970s is a mixture of the continuation of already established trends, such as the *nouveau roman*, the work of Duras, Perec, or Tournier, and the emergence of new trends, such as *écriture féminine* or the 'postmodern' novel. The latter, in France, in the work of writers like Raphael Pividal, Jean-Luc Benoziglio, Pascal Bruckner, or Renaud Camus, engaged in a Barthesian playfulness, entertaining a parodic relation to the crisis of modernity. *Tel Quel*'s fiction, after the anonymous formalism of the late 1960s, becomes more individualized, more related to the itinerary of each writer, but all the same a general tendency can be identified towards a more heterogenous, violent, and humorous form of writing. While Jacques Henric and Guy Scarpetta produce novels (*Chasses*, 1975 and *Scène*, 1972) more in line with the theoretical advances of *Tel Quel*, and more essentially within the formalist tendency, the main figure of this period is Sollers, whose *Lois* and *H* come out in quick succession in 1971 and 1973, and whose work shows a remarkable development. Also of indirect importance are the novelists Maurice Roche and Severo Sarduy, particularly the latter, whose work *Cobra* (1972) co-translated by the author and Sollers, can be cited as an influence on the work of the latter.

Sarduy's *Cobra* is similar to *Lois* in its parodic approach to intellectual seriousness. Theory is treated parodically and joyfully, in terms of

---

[49] See Sollers, 'L'État Artaud', in id. (ed.), *Artaud*, 15.
[50] See Kristeva, 'Le Sujet en procès', ibid. 44.
[51] Sollers, 'L'Acte Bataille', in id. (ed.), *Bataille*, 11.

references and style.[52] It is also postmodern, in one sense, in its reframing of modernist theory as content, within a narrative frame. It is a post-' 68 novel in its appeal to popular culture, jazz and rock music, drug culture.[53] Maurice Roche's *CodeX* (1974) is the final part of the trilogy of novels begun with *Compact* (1966) and *Circus* (1971) in which a narrative is deformed by a heterogenous and polyphonic typography. *CodeX* begins with the question: 'comment crever proprement'.[54] The writing of the book is related to the question of death and mortality. In later texts, the theme of death and the macabre predominates.[55] Writing becomes a meditation on, and a gesture against, the death of the writer, but in a spirit of black humour, not unlike that of Denis Roche in his 1976 text *Louve basse*.

The work of Sollers, Roche, and Sarduy, as well as *Le Mécrit* by Denis Roche and Sollers's preface for it,[56] mark a definite turn towards heterogeneity. Typographically, a heterogenous visual text is accentuated in Maurice Roche's work, while *Lois* is a more fragmented, percussive, and punctured text. The difference is not only visual, however; it is also aural. *Lois* introduces as a major element the exclamation mark as the instance of a percussive rhythm, like a sharp tap on the tympanum. With *Lois*, Sollers had introduced a fiction that works as much on the level of sound and of rhythm as on a conceptual level. Written mostly in decasyllabic phrases, the text of *Lois* is humorously scanned by a repetition of sounds, principally the past participle ending in é, *alliteration, and rhyme*.[57] This writing forces contractions and neologisms, a more popular form of French, its antecedents being Rabelais or Villon rather than Mallarmé or Blanchot.[58] There are vestiges of a structure based on the cube, but they are related to a first

[52] See S. Sarduy, *Cobra* (Paris, 1972), 36: 'Oui, car par un phénomène d'*I. p. s*, (Indefinitely proceeding sequences, of course) qu'il n'est pas scilicet d'analyser, Cobra n'était pas déjà sortie de son premier show de la nuit', and p. 38: 'elles s'étaient arraché les cils postiches et les ongles, elles avaient roulé sur le sol, elles étaient restées telquelisées'.

[53] Ibid. 107–20, 'Eat Flowers'.

[54] M. Roche, *Codex* (Paris, 1974), 11.

[55] For a consideration of the texts of M. Roche, see J. Paris, *Maurice Roche* (Paris, 1989).

[56] P. Sollers 'L'Aréopagite', in D. Roche, *Le Mécrit* (Paris, 1972). Sollers's text is written in the same 'Rabelaisian' style as his novel *Lois*, parodying 'le coup du poète', (p. 14), an attack on the ideology of poetry and its idealism.

[57] See Sollers, *Lois*, 6: 'lui donc détaché libre mais encore ramassé crispé'.

[58] The neologizing tendency produces an aurally and orally delicious poetry; see Sollers, ibid. 14: 'Propulsé pulsif depuis les mimines! Dévié des accouches emmêlimétaux! Échomance! Bébête fonçant sous feuillage! Humouisseux baveux brûlant tous les feux!' It is a text in which onomatopoeia becomes a subversive principle within meaning, as recognizable in the following: 'broum schnourf scrontch clong pof pif clonck' (p. 107).

version of the novel, an excerpt of which appeared in *Tel Quel*.[59]
Between the two versions a process of destructuring, of heterogenization
occurs, so that in the final version, structure appears at the level of
rhythm and intertextuality, rather than being an arbitrarily imposed
spatial motif. In the next novel, *H*, structure is replaced entirely by
rhythm, in an unpunctuated text, without interruption by *le blanc* of the
page. The possible causes of this change are an encounter with the texts
of Joyce, principally *Finnegans Wake*. The death of Sollers's father may
also have unfixed, in the writer, a respect for the signifier; in *Lois* the
signifier is fractured, the (apparently) paternal culture of France is
demystified and violently parodied, while it is suggested to be more
inherently maternal than paternal.[60] *H* can be seen as an attempt to
recover the memory of the father, to trace a filiation.[61]

The content of the novel *Lois* also marks the introduction of sexuality
and the family as a major theme. The first section, for example,
intertextually enveloping Hesiod's *Theogeny*, Freud's originary horde of
Totem and Taboo, and Plato's *Laws*, tells the story of 'l'éducation de la
verge élévaginée permettant d'affirmer la communauté',[62] the castration
of the father by the sons in the thrall of the mother, or Mother Nature:
'Le fiston, si je comprends bien, depuis le ragin, lui sélectionne sec le
queue et les couilles, et les jette, dit le vieux, au hasard, au loi, tandis
que maman, couverte de sang, jouipisse comme une jument'.[63]

There is a force of humour and obscenity in *Lois* that was absent from
Nombres and which will again be transformed in *H* and *Paradis* into a
more serene form of social paranoia. The book is also a sustained attack
on French culture, *la francité*,[64] on philosophical and intellectual seriousness, a relentless parodying of myth and mystery forced by a work on

---

[59] P. Sollers, 'Lois', *TQ* 46 (summer 1971). A few diagrams relating to the structure of
the first version are reproduced in M. Pleynet's article 'Dès tambours', *TQ* 57 (spring 1974),
and in Pleynet, *Art et littérature* (Paris, 1977), 62.

[60] See Sollers, *Vision à New York*, 100–14 for a consideration by Sollers of the genesis of
Lois.

[61] See Sollers, *Vision à New York*. Sollers recalls his spontaneous reading of a passage
from Eckhart over the grave of his father, giving rise to an insight that writing would
permit a kind of voice from beyond the grave, 'des voix qui sortent de l'écriture' (p. 111).
The death of the father opens up, Sollers continues, the possibility of a 'résurrection dans
le langage' (p. 112), which can be seen as enabling the ascendant writing of *Paradis* (Paris,
1981).

[62] Id., *Lois*, 6.

[63] Ibid. 10.

[64] Ibid. 54–5: 'c'est le franc de france et de francité, c'est le franchitecte de l'enfranciré'.
The Chinese ideogram on the front cover of *Lois* signifies 'loi' but is also the root for the
Chinese word for France.

the tissue of language. It evidently has a certain effect on the theory and strategy of *Tel Quel*, suggesting that the resistance to the review is often a sign that this parodic level of humour has been misunderstood.

The most immediately noticeable aspect of *H* is the absence of punctuation. This absence is only apparent, only a typographic, visual absence, paradoxically enabling the resurgence of a punctuation latent in the text, related to its rhythm and its tone, in other words to its aural and oral reading. Punctuation, in other words, lives in the tissue of the text, and its imposition as a skeletal structure becomes irrelevant. This follows a trajectory already suggested by *Lois*. After the formal, Proustian prose of *Une curieuse solitude* and *Le Parc*, the spatially structured form of *Drame* and *Nombres*, the text works more at the level of the structure internal to language: rhythm and tone. Sollers's novels follow a general tendency towards an open form, ending eventually with the encyclopedic, mobile form of the novels from *Femmes*. *Lois* is perhaps the text in which punctuation intervenes most violently, in the incidence of the exclamation mark, a puncturing of the tissue of the text and the subject rather than its structuring.[65] After this violent *punctum*, suggesting a moment when the subject, writer or reader, is wounded and projected into the empty silence, *le vide*, after writing, *H* and *Paradis* are written in an ascendant, paradisaical form.[66]

The puncturing or wounding of the subject of the writing in *Lois*, perhaps engaged with the death of the father and the attack on the maternal tissue of culture, enables the re-emergence of an autobiographical subject in *H*. *H* is a new departure in Sollers's writing and in the fiction of *Tel Quel* in the introduction of an autobiographical mode. It is followed or paralleled in the poetry of Pleynet after *Stanze*, and of Risset after *Jeu* and in the novels of Maurice Roche and Jacques Henric (*Carrousels*, 1981). It prefigures the emergence of an autobiographical content in French fiction of the 1980s; but while the autobiographies of Robbe-Grillet, Sarraute, and others[67] were perceived as a break with the previous experimental work, Sollers's autobiography is produced from and through the tissue of writing. Parallels to Sollers's textual

[65] The exclamation mark also provides a link between the parodic text and the political pronouncements of the review, the oft-repeated phrase 'Vive la pensée-maotsetoung!' ending with the same mark and featuring a similar contraction to those of *Lois*.

[66] For a consideration of the relation between *Lois* and *H* (Paris, 1973). See P. Sollers's discussion with M. Pleynet and J.-L. Houdebine, 'Littérature et révolution: Vérité de l'avant-garde', in Pleynet, *Art et littérature*, 111–12.

[67] See n. 38, Ch. 2.

autobiography can, however, be recognized in the work of Perec and Roger Laporte.

After the formalist moment and its limit in *Lois*, *H* begins a traversal of biography, a reinterpretation of life from the perspective of writing, enabling the writer to occupy the position of the writer before or after experience as such. Autobiography is not present in the sense of a relation to events in a life, but is an experiencing of life through the experience of literature. This production of an autobiographical tissue in language needs a signifier, or a series of signifiers, to generate itself or to knot itself around. This tends to be a name or a figure related to the name of the writer. *Lois* already deformed the proper name in order to produce sense, an immersion of the name in the generative tissue of meaning which is crucial to Sollers's aesthetic. The deformation of the name in *Lois*, in *H*, becomes a tracing of its history, or of the possibilities of its signification, which generates sense, and specifically autobiographical sense. For example, in the first few pages of *H*, the writing produces a meditation on the name of the writer. Beginning with a section in which the writer addresses the question of the beginning of a new novel, its invocation to writing, as it were, the intention is expressed to: 'transformer le filtre se verser le philtre'.[68] The subject as writer will be transformed. 'Philtre' leads on, through a repetition of syllables, to 'j'ai ce phi flottant sur les lèvres'.[69] The writer's (true) first name—Philippe—is generated in the text, leading to 'l'autre infans', to infancy (via a reference to Freud's essay on Leonardo), and then, logically, to the father. The father ('octave') produces the figure eight: 'si le huit revient sans fin quand je marche si je pense facilement à la liturgie si un son m'apparaît toujours accompagné surmonté ça vient du prénom impossible en même temps latin de mon père non tu ne trouveras pas je l'écris octave exactement comme in octavo'.[70] The figure eight provides a juncture with a description of the signature (another vital element among Sollers's concerns) of the father, including the family name 'joyaux', which leads to a memory of a schoolmaster's parodying that name: 'ce joyaux que voulez-vous ce joyaux n'est pas une perle'.[71] The name 'joyaux' is also immersed in the internal signifying pulsion of language: 'on y entend à la fois jeu joie juif jouissance'.[72] 'Philippe' is then subjected to a similar analysis, producing a historical series, from 'philippines' (named after Philippe Magellan), the Greek father of Alexander, Greek place-names, calling this a 'passeport dans le monde

---

[68] Sollers, *H*, 9. [69] Ibid. [70] Ibid. 10. [71] Ibid. [72] Ibid.

grec'.[73] The Greek passport enables access to the name 'Sollers', 'surnom d'ulysse de sollus tout entier intact ars ingénieux'.[74] The reading of *H* is an immersion in a stream of meaning produced by the 'law of the signifier' and by a rhythm of sense internal and inherent to language, which Pleynet refers to as 'le battement du sens'. In this context, the subject of autobiography can be said to be immersed in, or subjected to, the writing, rather than being in a position of authorial control over the events of a life.

As the law of the signifier produces sense from the raw material of language, as it were, and reinterprets biography, it also brings on to the scene, or engages in its mechanism, other texts. The effect of intertextuality, where *H* runs parallel to other texts, at times citing them or commenting on them, has been marked by Kristeva in her article 'Polylogue',[75] and by Jean-Louis Houdebine, particularly a section where Hölderlin is present, in his article 'Le Chant (ou sens) vivant des langues'.[76] Perhaps the most notable text *H* brings into focus is the Bible, or that of religion, but in a less explicit way than in *Paradis*. In the opening section, Sollers relates the memory of his father to the Catholic liturgy. A page further on, remembering his nakedness on a beach, the writing presents: 'aussi dans la bible on a le même mot hébreu pour nu rusé éveillé'.[77] Further on we read 'je suis précisément sur le point de me faire catholique'.[78] The religious signifier intervenes at regular intervals in the text, without being integrated into a system, as in *Paradis*. *H* appears, as Sollers suggests, as the *brouillon* or sketch-book of the next novel,[79] principally in that the religious text is brought into focus, but is not integrated into the mechanism of the writing, perhaps still in conflict with the Maoist tendency, which also emerges at intervals.

The religious signifier is engaged not arbitrarily, but through the logic of the writing. After the demystification of *Lois*, *H* appears as the desperate meditation of an asocialized subject, perhaps a paranoid subject, writing from a position beyond social discourse and analysing

---

[73] Ibid.
[74] Ibid. 11.
[75] J. Kristeva, 'Polylogue', *TQ* 57 (spring 1974), and in ead., *Polylogue*.
[76] J.-L. Houdebine, 'Le Chant (ou sens) vivant des langues', *TQ* 57, and in id., *Excès de langages* (Paris, 1983). Kristeva and Houdebine's essays are pub. in a special issue on Sollers, including also articles on Sollers's novels by Barthes, Pleynet, and Stephen Heath, and the first excerpt of *Paradis*.
[77] Sollers, *H*, 11.
[78] Ibid. 16.
[79] See P. Sollers, 'La Coupole', in id., *Théorie des exceptions* (Paris, 1986), 201.

it. *Drame* and *Nombres* appear tangential to discourse as the realm of the spectacle, while *Lois* is a frontal attack. The subject of paranoia, outside the cohesion of language as social link, having deformed language, its guarantee, becomes an empty subject, only a *filtre* for the writing, whose biography is also evacuated by the writing. The text includes the *énoncé*, 'j'écris pour faire le vide'.[80] After this *vide*, which Sollers had emphasized in an article on Risset's text *Jeu*,[81] the only possibility, apart from silence or psychosis, is ascendance, realized thematically in *Paradis*, engaging the position of a subject before or after social discourse, as Sollers states, before the Fall or after redemption.[82] This position is logically one of prophecy, suggested in *H* and more developed in *Paradis*. Prophecy, a voice (*H* ends with the word 'voix', *Paradis* begins with it), before discourse but programming it, naturally engages the religious signifier.

It is evident that *H* serves as an experiment from which emerge a number of elements more successfully worked through or staged in *Paradis*. The fundamental aspect is the production of thought or meaning from the inherent logic of the signifier. What emerges then is a prophetic and socially paranoid voice, producing an analytic traversal of social discourse. This has effects in Sollers's theory, which after *H* become more closely welded to the production of fiction. *H* also brings religion into focus for the review, not as a reaction against the Left, but as the ground of social and political discourse, which it rests on without acknowledging the fact.

In the context, *H*, although an important stage, appears over-shadowed by *Paradis*. A special issue on Sollers of 1974, while including articles by Barthes, Kristeva, Pleynet, Houdebine, and Stephen Heath on *H* and *Lois*, also includes the first excerpt of *Paradis*, which will be published serially in each issue of *Tel Quel*, with the significant exception of the 'Recherches féminines' issue of 1978, up to its publication as a book in 1981. I will look at *Paradis* retrospectively in a final section on fiction, but it is important to note how the novel and its serial publication alters the status of the review. It is now more firmly linked to a singular literary production, while also publishing the poetry of Pleynet at regular intervals. It is producing one of the major fictional

---

[80] P. Sollers, *H*, 14.

[81] Id., 'La Pratique formelle de l'avant-garde', *TQ* 46.

[82] See id., 'La Coupole', in id., *Théorie des exceptions*. Listing the questions that conditioned *Paradis*, Sollers writes (p. 200): 'Pourquoi le français n'a-t-il pas traité de l'entrée dans le monde d'avant la chute et la faute, ou dans celui d'après la chute et la faute—de la Rédemption?'

works of the period, temporally spanning almost the whole decade, recording, in a certain sense, the evolution of thought, fiction, and theory in that period. Fiction parallels and accompanies theory, generating it and also producing new interests in the texts and images published alongside it.[83] Far from running into a cul-de-sac, Tel Quel's fiction, in the work of Sollers, develops new and innovative forms which themselves lead to what has been seen as the ultimate experimental novel of the period.

Contradictions: Politics and the Subject

Tel Quel's theory of the early 1970s appears as a compacting of contradictory discourses, forced together in order to precipitate developments in the context and in the review itself, in order to transform theory itself. The contradiction between system and subject is the most explicit symptom of this period. However, the system and the subject are not proposed as two separate sides of a dialectic, but forced on to one another; the review attempts to work out a politics based on the subject of excess; Sollers cites as programmatic Bataille's dictum: 'Il faut le système et il faut l'excès.'[84] There are two opposing developments that emerge from this superimposition: the elaboration of an ethics based on the subject of excess, and the projection of a utopian politics of the subject on to the political reality of China, requiring a certain leap of faith that Maoism would not fall back into the Marxist structure.

The politics Kristeva puts forward, for example, is a utopian anarchism that seems to admit from the start the impossibility of its resolution. According to this philosophy, the negativity at work in the subject in process is also in society, and becomes a revolutionary force when liberated from stasis in such atomic institutions as the family or the state. But as the psychoanalytic reference becomes more subtle, more based on the notion of cure, this utopian politics will give way to an ethics in Kristeva's work. From the perspective of cure, the negative excess of the subject has to be integrated within the symbolic, within the

---

[83] During the 1970s Tel Quel's appearance changed somewhat, with the introduction of numerous images accompanying the texts, particularly Paradis. These include pictures of Sollers himself, of his ear (suggesting the importance of the aural reception of the text), and of religious icons more often than not from non-Western contexts (Chinese, Indian, or Islamic).

[84] P. Sollers, 'Intervention', in id. (ed.), Bataille, 10.

law, rather than the law being subverted by it. This tendency is already present in Kristeva's work, as is suggested by her 1971 essay on Barthes, where she writes:

L'objectivation du désir pour l'écriture exige du sujet (de la métalangue) le double mouvement d'adhésion et de distance dans lequel il bride son désir de signifiant par la sanction d'un code elle-même dictée par une ethique (utopique?): insérer dans la société une pratique qu'elle censure, lui communiquer ce qu'elle ne peut pas entendre, reconstituer ainsi la cohésion et l'harmonie du discours social par nature brisé.[85]

The reference to social cohesion and harmony appears as less radical than the Maoist politics associated with *Tel Quel*, but if we also read Kristeva's view that society is essentially paranoiac, essentially oppressive in the imposition of a common discourse, then this emphasis on cohesion, the integration of elements of violence outside it, appears more complex. It poses the necessity of an ethics of the transformation of the law to account for its excess. The question of femininity also enters into this debate, since women appear as the silent guarantors of the common discourse that in reality oppresses them. Kristeva's reference to Maoism then appears as in conflict with the emerging ethics of her work, proposing literature as in some way curative, rather than as a subversive avant-garde.

Le Voyage en Chine: *Phantasy and Fragmentation*

Given the theoretical redundancy of the system of Marxism, undermined by the negativity of the subject of process, it appears that *Tel Quel*'s continued allegiance to Maoism in China is based on the premise that Maoism itself is a transgression of Marxism, while remaining at the same time the truth of Marx's thought. Such is the view proposed by the numerous articles on China and on Maoism that appear in the review. As we suggested above, this is a phantasmic projection conditioned by disinformation and an over-investment in the ideological level. The irruption of the reality of the Chinese situation, partly in the trip to China in 1974 and completely with the death of Mao and the arrest of the Gang of Four in 1976, ruptures the membrane of this phantasy. The trip is not a true encounter with the reality or real of China, since this is an opaque reality; as Barthes points out, it is not

---

[85] J. Kristeva, 'Comment parler à la littérature', *TQ* 47: 28.

subject to a hermeneutics.[86] Still, it may have had an effect in fragmenting the cohesion of the group phantasy of revolutionary Maoist China. Each individual reacts to the experience differently, as Pleynet's journal of the trip, *Le Voyage en Chine*, published in 1980, confirms.[87] We can identify this as a symptomatic moment when *Tel Quel* ceases to function as a group and becomes a community of individuals.

François Wahl's critical article in *Le Monde*, entitled 'La Chine sans utopie', forces the review to realize the phantasmatic, projective effect China has; they fault Wahl for just this, arguing that the criticism of Maoism as utopian prevents an analysis of the real in China.[88] Sollers invests further hope in the 'Criticize Confucius/Lin Piao' campaign, seeing it as an anti-metaphysical widening of the scope of Maoism and a move towards the extinction of the state.[89] This was far from being the case; the campaign enabled a reinforcement of the power of the state to counter Lin Piao (extreme left) radicalism. This was disastrous because of the events that followed; the death of the moderating Zhou Enlai, Mao's increasing retirement from politics, and the rise of the Gang of Four on the extreme left. However, despite the continued ideological projection, Sollers also insists on questions of aesthetics and sexuality that dissociate his interests from the system of politics. Aesthetics and sexuality are emphases that slide underneath the shift in strategy of *Tel Quel* away from Maoism. Sollers describes, of his encounter with China: 'un dynamisme du geste, de la transformation', 'une autre façon d'être dans l'espace, dans le geste, la langue, le sens'.[90] In effect, what remains of the adherence to Maoism is an attachment to the skeletal body of Maoism, of Mao himself, (suggested by the fascination with the Chairman's swim across the river Yangtze), the final term of which will be his death, and the assumption or cadaverization of this body. In

---

[86] See R. Barthes, *Alors la Chine?* (Paris, 1974). This pamphlet was seen as a 'no comment' by Barthes on his trip to China, emphasizing, instead of the political angle, an *assentiment* (assent) to experience.

[87] Pleynet reports (interview with author, Paris, 1990) that, due to the subjectively oriented, apparently apolitical, nature of the book, no publisher accepted it at the time, and its publication was delayed. Pleynet and Kristeva both report that Barthes would stay in the bus they travelled in, taking photographs through the window, rather than follow the others to visit the places they were taken to.

[88] 'A propos de "La Chine sans utopie" ', *TQ* 59 (autumn 1974). For an informative account of *Tel Quel*'s Maoism and trip to China unconnected to its theory or its creative practice, see Ieme van der Poel, *Une révolution de la pensée: Maoisme et féminisme à travers Tel Quel, Les Temps moderne set Esprit* (Amsterdam, 1992).

[89] P. Sollers, 'Quelques thèses', 'La Chine contre Confucius', and 'Mao contre Confucius', *TQ* 59 (autumn 1974).

[90] Sollers, 'Quelques thèses', ibid. 18.

other words, the end term of *Tel Quel*'s Maoism will be the death of Mao and the adherence to that corpse as a signifier, as opposed to the possible, but utopian, transcendence of the system, of Marxism and Maoism alike.

Sollers also programmes the demise of the Maoist current in *Tel Quel* by articulating its fate with the question of women and of sexuality. He asks the question: do women exist other than as objects of exchange in China?[91] Kristeva's book *Des Chinoises* (1974) only gives a partial answer, but the gesture of shifting the whole question into the arena of sexuality is effective in withdrawing the political and philosophical investment of *Tel Quel* from Maoist China.

The trip to China was a rupture of phantasy and the emergence of the real, of its otherness, tied into the question of its other theatre of gesture. This reality also implicates the status of women. Perhaps not coincidentally, Kristeva's response to the trip to China is articulated with the terms of her engagement with the feminist movement Psych et po, a radical splinter-group of the MLF (Mouvement de libération des femmes). This engagement is a failure in communication for both parties; Kristeva's approach, which recognizes the ubiquity of power in signifying practice, conflicts with that of the militant Psych et po group. Kristeva's perspective is non-feminist in her disagreement with the notion of a feminine essence or an aggressive affirmation of femininity as revolutionary in itself. To this extent, Kristeva's book *Des Chinoises*, published by *Des femmes*, the publishing house run by Antoinette Fouque and Psych et po, is highly contradictory and not necessarily representative. It is partly determined by the utopian anarchism we identified earlier, partly by the gradual emergence of her psychoanalytical and ethical concerns. Since I proposed these to be already present in Kristeva's work, *Des Chinoises* seems like a return to an old problematic.

Kristeva's essential thesis in the book is that feminism and Maoism alike are a critique of phallocentric patriarchy. She bases this on the thesis that non-Confucian (i.e. Taoist and Buddhist) sexuality was based on a true genitality which was not restricted to the dominance of the phallus. True reciprocal genitality also short-circuits the Oedipus complex; it is a 'traversée d'Oedipe'. The book itself runs historically through the early matriarchy, the repression of women in Confucianism, the laws of the Jiangxi Soviet, favourable to women's rights, and their emergence in the Cultural Revolution and especially in the

---

[91] P-Sollers, 'Quelques thèses', 10.

'Criticize Confucius' campaign. The historical part of the book is preceded by a theoretical critique of 'monotheism', the religious conception of women, and an analysis of the psychoanalytical discourse on female sexuality. However, Kristeva separates the psychoanalytical part of the book from the historical part, stating that this is in order to guard against a utopian projection of one on to the other. This dissociation invites a deconstructive reading that would see the psychoanalytical part of the book as a critique of the historical part. Indeed, while Kristeva pays lip-service to Maoism in the historical section, the psychoanalytical section criticizes patriarchal culture. The extent to which Maoism is patriarchal, to which Mao is or isn't a father, is another symptomatic point in the review's Maoism. It deflects the question of Maoism on to that of sexuality and the Freudian and Lacanian psychoanalytical terms of the Name of the Father, and programmes the abandonment of Maoism after the death of the father. Furthermore, it sets up Maoism for a critique of its approach to sexuality. While Taoism may imply a non-neurotic sexuality, the same is not necessarily true of Maoism.

Pleynet's articles on the trip to China look, typically, at the form of a discourse on China and his subjective response.[92] Pleynet's emphasis on the subjective response can be attributed to the degree of moderation and self-denial necessary for the role of the secretary of the review. The 'traversee d'abord subjective'[93] of his account shifts the emphasis on to the singularity of the writer, away from ideology. For Pleynet, China is an *outopos*, a utopia to the extent of its absolute otherness that cannot be recuperated in any place or topos. As we suggested earlier, the otherness of China as an experience allows the invasion of this lack of meaning, an impossibility of hermeneutics, by the ideology of Maoism. So *Tel Quel*'s trip to China appears as an oscillation between a recognition of its otherness and of the impossibility of interpretation, and the blanketing of this otherness by ideology. The ability to analyse the experience of this otherness only emerges painfully and slowly, and only after the phantasy has waned. This goes some way to explain why Pleynet's journal *Le Voyage en Chine* was only published six years later, in 1980, and only after the singular experience of the writer had become a recognized point of interest in the context.

[92] M. Pleynet, 'Pourquoi la Chine populaire', *TQ* 59 (autumn 1974) and 'Du discours sur la Chine', *TQ* 60 (winter 1974).
[93] Pleynet, 'Du discours sur la Chine', *TQ* 60: 31.

The Death of the Father: The Exception

The whole enquiry of *Tel Quel*'s Maoism from the trip to China revolves around the questions of whether the Chinese subject is neurotic or beyond neurosis, and whether or not Mao appears as a father. The first question is posed but is not analysed in *Tel Quel*. Although certain articles do approach the question of psychoanalysis in China, recognizing its complete absence,[94] the tools of a psychoanalytical treatment of the Chinese subject are not available. This blockage seems to have been displaced on to, and sublimated in, the experience of the Western subject of China; the accounts of Pleynet and Barthes recognize this anti-hysteria but can only analyse their own experience, which, in that they are subject to the Western neurosis, becomes a paradise projected on to an opaque reality.

Sollers addresses the question of Mao as father at the moment of Mao's death in 1976. An earlier article, by Éliane Escoubas, had recognized the importance for Maoism of the question of Mao's status as father or revolutionary subject.[95] Soller's thesis follows this in affirming that constructing a mausoleum for Mao, as was done for Lenin, meant the body becoming a corpse which elicits an exploitation, 'une jouissance du cadavre'.[96] By the act of mummifying Mao, his thought is turned into 'une lettre morte',[97] exhibiting how Marxism remains determined by Western religion, the dominance of the father. Here the ideological is determined by the writing of *Paradis*, which necessarily brought into focus an interest in religion. With the death of Mao, therefore, Maoism is turned into an oppressive, bureaucratic system which is supported by the exploitation of the corpse of the dead father, as Leninism turned into Stalinism by the same process.

At the same time, Sollers develops a critique of Marxism from the perspective of the subjectivity of the exception, that of the writer.[98] This is foreshadowed by the continual insistence on the subjectivity of the writer as transformative of the system, for example in the 1972 article on Bataille. The individual thought of Marx and Freud is affirmed by Sollers against its erection into a system. The terms are still those, however, of the dialectic; for Sollers the catastrophe of Marxism is that

---

[94] Chi-Hsi Hu, 'Mao-tse-toung, la révolution et la question sexuelle', *TQ* 59 : 68.
[95] E. Escoubas, 'L'École chinoise', *TQ* 61 (spring 1975).
[96] P. Sollers and M. Clavel, *Délivrance* (Paris, 1977), 141.
[97] Ibid. 139.
[98] This is presented in the discussions with M. Clavel, the 'nouveau philosophe avant la lettre', ibid.

it denies the negativity of the dialectic. 1968, for example, is the return of this negativity that survived in the artistic margins. This historical dialectic seems to be at odds with the emphasis on the exception of the writer. The emphasis for the moment, however, is on the subject as exception. Having passed through the Freudian/Lacanian dissolution of the subject as authority, the subject is now viewed by Sollers as the locus of a practice, of language or sex, which supports an individuality or an exception. The valorization of the exception against the systematic, the situationist spectacle, which becomes a reference for Sollers at this point, is a more radical turn than the turn against Marxism or even against Marx, which is fairly inevitable given the situation, as it emphasizes singular, individual practice as against theory, the group, the political project. *Tel Quel* therefore becomes in this view no longer a group with a project, a 'group-in-fusion' in Sartre's sense, but, in Sollers's view, a collection of singularities each of which forms an exception.

The dissolution of *Tel Quel*'s Marxism is determined as much by the internal logic of the thought and practice of the review as by the general disillusionment with the Left in France at this time. Contextual factors, such as the publication of Solzhenitsyn's *The Gulag Archipelago* (1974) and the Khmer Rouge invasion of Cambodia (late 1975), the rise of the *nouveaux philosophes*, the delayed after-effects of 1968, certainly play a major part in this process, but *Tel Quel*'s shifting allegiances are not wholly at the mercy of these factors. The emergence of the emphasis on the exception and of the Freudian or Lacanian thesis of the 'jouissance du père mort', together with the analysis of sexuality, effectively displace the political reference, allowing a widening of perspective, both globally and in the review's literary interests.

ETHICS: THE LAW AND ITS EXCESS

As the Marxist and Maoist terms of *Tel Quel*'s political engagement are undermined by an investigation of their philosophical basis, they are also paralleled by a powerful psychoanalytically based theory in the work of Kristeva, which tends to move towards an ethical perspective not identifiable with either system, although at certain moments it is projected on to Maoism. Kristeva's theory is detachable from the political emphasis, from the affirmation of Maoism, due to the very basis that makes such an emphasis possible, the aspect of practice that

Kristeva underlines. Practice is later developed into an ethics of literature that seems to contradict any political, totalizing effect, by introducing into the social the *jouissance* which is exploited in oppression. In other words, literature is on the way to a denial of politics and a constitution of an ethics of which Maoism was theoretically the project but of which, practically, it was a failure. That such a political approach would always fail seems marked from the start in Kristeva's writing.

The ethics that derives from Kristeva's view of the subject and the violence of the pre-verbal is a current as important in this period of the review's history as the literary theory of Sollers, with which it also entertains a productive parallel. To understand the mutations of *Tel Quel* across the decade, and the shift towards the present state of *L'Infini*, it is necessary to follow the development of Kristeva's initially linguistics-based theory towards psychoanalysis and an ethics based on the notion of the cure, before looking at its interaction with the context in *Tel Quel*.

Artaud/Bataille: The Semiotic

After the transformative moment of her text on Sollers's *Nombres*,[99] which seemed to suggest a movement towards a more dynamic approach to literature, Kristeva's articles, for example 'Matière, sens, dialectique'[100] and 'Objet, complément, dialectique'[101] presented a critical analysis of linguistics and of psychoanalysis from a perspective that emphasized heterogeneity as a negativity underlying discourse, which came to transform it in literature and art. Kristeva's contributions to the Artaud/Bataille colloquium reframe this dynamic in psychoanalytical terms, renaming this negativity in terms of the pre-Oedipal, 'semiotic' pulsions affecting the subject before insertion into language and identity. The subjectivity analysed was also significantly referred to as before the split subject inaugurated by Lacan's mirror phase, which his theory focused on. While emphasizing this pre-symbolic, affective pulsional base, Kristeva also stresses the necessity of the symbolic, the impossibility of simply escaping it or transcending it. Writing is described as a complex dynamic between language and its law, the symbolic, and the pre-verbal forces that traverse it, the semiotic.

In Kristeva's theory, the symbolic, which is coextensive with Lacan's field of the same name, is identified as language, inaugurated by a

---

[99] J. Kristeva, 'L'Engendrement de la formule', *TQ* 37-8.
[100] ead., 'Matière, sens, dialectique', *TQ* 44, also in ead., *Polylogue*.
[101] ead., 'Objet, complément, dialectique', *Crit.* 285 (Feb. 1971), also in ead., *Polylogue*.

specific moment. This is a *thetic* moment anterior to any discourse, a notion imported from Husserl's phenomenology.[102] The thetic is a moment of affirmation, within which operations of negation or denegation are carried out (here Kristeva refers to Frege and to Freud). Anterior to this thetic moment, the semiotic, labelled according to Kristeva's object of criticism the heterogenous (Bataille), the expulsive or *le rejet* (Artaud), negativity (Hegel), is at the same time foreclosed by the symbolic and is its condition, as it is the pulsional energy that the symbolic diverts to constitute itself, the negativity its affirmation excludes. However, extending this developmental model beyond the time of the infant, the semiotic comes to produce effects or affects in language. If syntax is part of the symbolic, it is already derived from the semiotic, which is already syntactically organized, in a sense, by the rhythm of pulsions across the body. This mobility is located, theoretically, in the *chora*, Plato's word for a nature preceding God.[103] Kristeva also refers in passing to Democritus' *rhythmos*, which Derrida had pointed out as prior to the Hegelian system.

Following Kristeva, this dynamic can be framed psychoanalytically. It specifically implicates Lacanian psychoanalytical theory as a closure. The semiotic is present in the anal and oral stages, in a sadism or aggression seen as the violence of *le rejet*, movements of expulsion or ingestion for which the work of Melanie Klein is relevant. The symbolic, with the cut-off point of the thetic moment, is also thinkable as a castration that inaugurates the phallus as a lack, an *object manqué*, then the metonymic law of desire and the Oedipal familial triangle. In the text, Kristeva explains, there is a dynamic between the symbolic and the semiotic that takes various forms but which involves a traversal, *traversée*, of the first by the second, a 'procès du sujet'.[104] The text is determined by the interplay of the dynamic between the two orders Kristeva proposes. The subject of literature traverses or exceeds the symbolic by introducing the violence of the semiotic, subverting the former and creating a new symbolic organization and a 'nouveau dispositif réel' that Kristeva identifies as innovation.[105] The mechanisms of this subversion and innovation differ for each author.

---

[102] ead., 'L'Expérience et la pratique', in Sollers (ed.), *Bataille*, and in Kristeva, *Polylogue*, 108–9.

[103] Kristeva, *Polylogue*, 57.

[104] Ibid. 56.

[105] Ibid. 68.

Having set out the two sides of this dynamic, Kristeva's writing oscillates between them. In 'Le Sujet en procès' (Artaud) Kristeva is confronting two theories of the subject, that of Lacan and that of Deleuze and Guattari in *Anti-œdipe*. The extent to which the theory of the subject of literature hinges on the psychoanalytical theory of the psychoses is affirmed by Kristeva's assertion that while Lacan's subject is paranoid, a unitary subject, *sujet unaire*,[106] determined by rejection of the Other, desire of the Other, triangulated into the familial Oedipus complex, there is a schizoid subject, that of Deleuze and Guattari, although not identified as such, which is afamilial, prior to the realm of desire, moved not by desire for a lack but by *le rejet*, a pulsional movement identified primarily with anality. In the essay on Artaud, Kristeva sets out a transgression of Lacan's symbolic order via the fluidity of Deleuze and Guattari, and the subject of literature is the site of this contradiction or practice.

She tends towards Deleuze and Guattari's position that desire is within the paranoiac realm of capitalist culture, and she affirms, for example, Artaud's focus on non-verbal gesturality as a limit of the avant-garde subversion of the symbolic. In the essay on Bataille, however, Kristeva emphasizes that an avant-garde that privileges negativity and misses the thetic moment falls into a celebration of negativity that is just the inverse of its own repression. It is 'l'envers solidaire de l'instance monothéiste',[107] a negative theology that fetishizes a fragmented body, 'le corps morcelé',[108] instead of the phallic, unitary body. *Anti-Oedipe*, with its references to Klossowski, suggests the kind of erotic fetishization in question. In the essay on Bataille, Kristeva proposes the opposing side of the dynamic, stressing Bataille's focus on desire in eroticism. This remains, however, a position that is *traversée*, exceeded or transgressed. Bataille is *transœdipe* rather than *anti-œdipe*.[109] The logic of analysis, *la méditation*, accompanies this transgression of the discursive.[110] Bataille's experience is of a constant recovering of the thetic moment in its continuous transgression by the semiotic. The phrase cited by Sollers 'Il faut le système et il faut l'excès' has a definite pertinence here.

---

[106] Kristeva, *Polylogue*, 55.
[107] Ibid. 107.
[108] Ibid. 108.
[109] Ibid. 123.
[110] Ibid. 117.

Artaud and Bataille are the two approaches to a contradiction between the two orders outlined by Kristeva. If the first approaches the limit of the avant-garde in dance, gesturality, and a non-verbal, hieroglyphic writing and in psychosis, the second privileges the logic of transgression in works of theory that meditate on *dépense*, while also limiting the transgression in literature to themes in a *récit*.

The subject of literature, therefore, is a subject traversed by affective pulsions relating to a space or time before language. Literature approaches the experience of psychosis, it is intimately linked to the subject of psychoanalysis but it is on the side of psychosis, rather than neurosis and desire. In the sense that psychosis appears as a limit of the psychoanalytic cure, the psychoanalysis that literature mobilizes is itself a psychoanalysis questioning its own foundations. Kristeva approaches psychoanalysis through the subject of literature and introduces a contestation of the psychoanalysis of the subject of discourse. The subject of literature is psychoanalysed, but also puts the theoretical writer, the analyst, in analysis, threatening the discourse of the latter with its excess.[111] This is the transference operated by the text. This transferential relation can be seen contextually, in the period in question, between *Tel Quel* and the work of Kristeva, and the theory of Lacan.

Before and after Lacan

Kristeva proposes an extension and a parallel of Lacanian theory.[112] Kristeva's analysis recognizes Lacan's symbolic order established by castration and identification, installing desire, but poses a traversal of this order by the dynamic that precedes it.[113] Kristeva returns to the infant before the Oedipal trauma, specifically before the father or the Name of the Father, where it is more a question of the painful separation from the fusional dyad of mother and infant. In this return she refers to the psychoanalytical work of Melanie Klein on infant psychosis,[114] from which Lacan had distanced himself in stressing the

---

[111] See Kristeva, in 'Polylogue' on Sollers's writing: 'H vous met en analyse,', in ead., *Polylogue*, 174.

[112] For an intelligent discussion of Kristeva's psychoanalytic theory, see J. Rose, *Sexuality in the Field of Vision* (London, 1986), ch. 6.

[113] See J. Kristeva, *La Révolution du langage poétique* (Paris, 1974), 43.

[114] See ead., 'Le Sujet en procès', in ead., *Polylogue*, 57. In the later article 'Noms de lieu', *TQ* 68 (winter 1976), she also refers to the work of D. W. Winnicott.

intervention of the father.[115] There is a particular dynamic in play here, between the mother–child relation as the archaic scene before the father's intervention and the domination of the father or his metaphor, or between an analysis dominated by meaning and one dominated by the affect, related to colour, rhythm, and image. However, this is not a return to the mother, for Kristeva also stresses the necessity of mediation through the symbolic field of human relations. Kristeva's theory occupies a difficult position; it is a theory which attempts to account for the terror prior to language, within language. It has been analysed as paralleling the mechanism of the sublime in this theoretical representation of what is properly unspeakable.[116] This terror and sublimity has profound implications for the relation of psychoanalysis to literature.

For Lacan, 'l'Inconscient, c'est la parole de l'Autre', 'Le sujet, c'est le signifiant pour un autre signifiant'; the subject of psychoanalysis for Lacan is the subject of speech, of language as discourse. The subject is a subject inasmuch as he is implied by speech. The subject of literature, analysed by Kristeva, is traversed by the excess that the relation of literature to language induces. In other words, the difference between literature and language is proportional to the subversion of the Lacanian subject implied by Kristeva, and the subversion of the ground of psychoanalysis by literature.

Kristeva does not, however, propose a subversion of psychoanalysis by suggesting that the difference between literature and language is simply the subversion of the symbolic by the pulsional. The relation is more nuanced, more of a transformation and an integration than a subversion. Literature is a successful traversal of the limit between symbolic and semiotic and a reorganization of the symbolic, its extension or transformation on a new basis. For if the relation between the law and what is 'before the law' were one of subversion, the subject would remain blocked in psychosis, in an inability to speak. Literature is not equivalent to psychosis; as Sollers suggests, the writer is a

[115] In an article in the *Écrits* (ii (Paris, 1971), 70), 'Du traitement possible de la psychose', Lacan had proposed the pre-Oedipal stages to be properly unanalysable, referring to Klein's work in this area: 'Ce schéma [the diagrammatic representation of the structure of the Imaginary] en effet permet de démontrer les relations qui se rapportent non pas aux stades précœdipiens qui ne sont pas bien entendu inexistants, mais analytiquement impensables (comme l'œuvre trébuchante mais guidée de Mme Mélanie Klein le met suffisament en évidence), mais aux stades prégénitaux en tant qu'ils s'ordonnent dans la rétroaction de l'œdipe.' The relation between Kristeva's theory of pre-symbolic and semiotic, and Lacan's postulation of a retroactive effect of the oral and anal stages, has yet to be properly worked out.

[116] S. Guerlac, 'The Sublime in Theory', *Modern Language Notes*, 106 (1991).

'Schreber heureux',[117] a subject who has passed beyond psychosis by reintegrating in language the experience of the transgression of the symbolic. Kristeva's essays on literature seem to propose judgements according to this ethics of transformation. A celebration of the pre-verbal leads to a kind of 'poetic femininity' in Bataille's terminology, and to fetishism,[118] while a writing wholly within the symbolic is affected by the violent return of the pulsions it has repressed.

Lautréamont/Mallarmé

After the Artaud and Bataille essays, and produced alongside Kristeva's more politically oriented work, which we will look at separately, the next major book is the monumental *La Révolution du langage poétique* (1974). It appears as a restatement of the basic premises of Kristeva's theory, in the first part, 'Préliminaires théoriques', the second section applying the theory to the texts of Mallarmé and Lautréamont. If Artaud and Bataille reflect each other by approaching the symbolic/semiotic divide from different directions, in the different organizations of the symbolic they propose, the same can be said of Lautréamont and Mallarmé, although in a more complex way. Kristeva proposes that, if Mallarmé undertakes a transformation of the syntactic guarantee of the symbolic, so that what she calls the semiotic *dispositif* is detectable at this level, with Lautréamont it is more a question of a reorganization of the position of the subject of writing and the relation to the anterior textual corpus, or intertextuality.[119] Mallarmé's transformation is essentially at the surface level of language; that of Lautréamont focuses on the logic of language and rhetoric. If Mallarmé's transformation is more formal in that his text approaches limits of coherence, Lautréamont's is never incoherent but reformulates the logic implied by language. The historical pattern present in *Tel Quel* from Sollers's 'Programme' is a reference here; the positioning of Mallarmé and Lautréamont as a revolution situated in history is still enounced as a history of the avant-garde. Furthermore, the dialectic of the text, between symbolic and semiotic, is still related to dialectical materialism as conceived by Lenin and Mao.[120] Later in Kristeva's work this dialectical structure will evolve into a less stable,

[117] P. Sollers, cited by J. Kristeva, in *Histoires d'amour* (Paris, 1983) 297.
[118] See J. Kristeva, 'D'une identité l'autre', *TQ* 62 (summer 1975) and in ead., *Polylogue*, 165.
[119] See ead., *La Révolution du langage poétique*, 207.
[120] Ibid. 179–82.

more painful dynamic or struggle around the border of identity. Kristeva's theory for Artaud/Bataille and Mallarmé/Lautréamont is enounced partly with a view to the collective project of *Tel Quel*, a theory of dialectical materialism, while it also undermines the foundations of Marxism as system. The focus on the excess or *dépense* tends to displace the Marxist emphasis on production. Moreover, as the collectivity of *Tel Quel* breaks up, and Kristeva is more and more engaged with psychoanalytic practice, necessarily more singular, the dynamic in question becomes less identifiable as a dialectic.

Céline, the Non-Verbal, Abjection

After the theoretical *magnum opus* of *La Révolution du langage poétique*, Kristeva's work becomes more varied and less structured as theory. It is no longer a theory of poetic language that determines the approach to the topic; the experience of the subject in question becomes more singular, differentiating the analysis and making the identification of a theory problematic. This coincides roughly with Kristeva's turn to the vocation of psychoanalysis, also marking a new turn in the character of her work. For Kristeva, it is 'sans doute hypersymptomatique'[121] that this turn should introduce Céline as an object of enquiry, a writer who, associated with anti-Semitism, is less easily insertable into a left avant-garde project. It is precisely as an exception that Céline is introduced. However, it is not only Céline who exemplifies the turn of Kristeva's concerns, but articles on varied subjects such as film, painting (Bellini and Giotto), dissidence, love.[122] This accelerates, gradually, a liberation of subject-matter that achieves fuller fruition with the later books, arranged thematically, on abjection, love, depression, alienation. However, all of these subjects are approached with reference to the common ground of psychoanalysis. It is Kristeva's profession of psychoanalyst after 1975/6 that most affects the exceptional quality of her work, given that a move from politics to psychoanalysis implies going from the group to the individual, who is in need of a cure, by way of a

---

[121] J. Kristeva, *Pouvoirs de l'horreur: Essai sur l'abjection* (Paris, 1981), back-cover rubric.

[122] ead., 'Ellipse sur la frayeur et la séduction spéculaire', *Communications*, 23 (1975), a special issue on film, and in ead., *Polylogue*, ead., 'La Joie de Giotto', *Peinture, cahiers théoriques*, 2–3 (Jan. 1972) and in ead., *Polylogue*, ead., 'La Maternité selon Giovanni Bellini', ibid. 10–11 (Dec. 1975) and in ead., *Polylogue*, ead., 'Un nouveau type d'intellectuel. Le dissident', *TQ* 74 (winter 1977); ead., 'La Dissidence comme réfutation du discours de gauche', *TQ* 76 (summer 1978); ead., 'Héréthique de l'amour', *TQ* 74 (winter 1977); ead., 'D'une identité l'autre', *TQ* 62 (summer 1975).

transference that implicates the body and the individuality of the analyst.

In the first essay on Céline, Kristeva presents a synopsis of her theory of the symbolic/semiotic dynamic. But rather than seeing the semiotic as a Hegelian negativity, its forces are considered to reside in infantile echolalia, rhythm, intonation, music.[123] The dynamic is also more specifically psychoanalytically framed as a transgression of the paternal law of the symbolic, towards the body of the mother. Kristeva reiterates that psychosis, the foreclosure of the Name of the Father, and fetishism, the refusal of the *jouissance* of the attainment of the mother's body by the positioning of a phallic mother, are the two limits bordering literature. The first results in a psychotic non-communicative babble, the second in an objectivization of the pure signifier.

Kristeva refers to Céline's style, in Barthesian terms the way the body is related to the writing, as the index of this transgression of the symbolic. Kristeva identifies the transgression in phrastic rhythms and obscene words and she adds that, in the case of Céline, it is not a question of a subversion of the rules of 'classical poeticity' but a confrontation of the body, the identification and rupture of the body, with the community.[124] To this extent the stylistic aggression of Céline recalls a crisis common to every ego. The problematic in question here is no longer of the political or theoretical project, variously Marxist or anarchistic, that finds in a monumental history of literature a channel for its cultural revolution, but of the crisis that is involved in the conflict between individual and community (already present in Kristeva's analysis of Sollers's *H* and in the 1971 essay on Barthes).

A liberation from the Hegelian terms of Kristeva's dynamic also permits an analysis of specifically non-verbal forms of art, representing in some senses a pure form of the semiotic, resulting in a mute fascination. The articles 'Ellipse sur la frayeur', 'La Maternité selon Giovanni Bellini', and the earlier 'La Joie de Giotto' (indicating that it is as much a question of different levels of Kristeva's interests as a temporal shift) are significantly published outside *Tel Quel*, in *Communications* and *Peinture, cahiers théoriques*. The first restates the semiotic/symbolic dynamic in terms of 'specular seduction' and 'la frayeur',[125] while the second celebrates Bellini's traversal of the *jouissance* of the mother through colour, opposed to Leonardo da Vinci's fetishization and cult

---

[123] ead., 'D'une identité l'autre' in ead., *Polylogue*, 159.
[124] Ibid. 166.
[125] 'Ellipse sur la frayeur et la séduction spéculaire', ibid. 379.

of the phallic mother.[126] The essay on Giotto describes the Scrovegni chapel frescos in terms of the emergence of the subject, of representation, from the luminous blue of the sky.[127] Perhaps a sign of the limits of the affirmation of the semiotic in literature or of the *traversée* is the fact that Kristeva is led to focus on the non-verbal, where colour, tone, 'frayeur', 'terror' are ranged with the semiotic. The semiotic is no longer the affirmed moment of an avant-garde project, but a painful experience for the subject in crisis. The utopian support of the avant-garde becomes an ethics of the cure. This is implied in the political movements of *Tel Quel*. In the 'Pourquoi les États-Unis' discussions, Kristeva explicitly marks this turn when she emphasizes as an aspect of the US avant-garde, the non-verbal: dance, painting, film.[128] The turn away from the project of the European avant-garde is a turn from the 'revolution of poetic language' that as a symptomatic limit turns to the non-verbal as a moment of crisis for a community.

The subject of literature, revolutionary in the cases of Artaud, Bataille, Lautréamont, Mallarmé, in the case of Céline is an exception, a singularity. This shift, as we suggested, implies further shifts in the semiotic/symbolic dynamic. Hegelian negativity as a potential utopian revolutionary force evolves into a form of terror. In 'Polylogue' Kristeva writes of: 'la violence qui me ronge . . . dissout l'identité et les cellules',[129] 'silence violent, pulsion, vide heurté et à ce rebours parcours de la jouissance',[130] 'gaieté déchirée de la douleur'.[131] Terror, as the unspeakable proximity to the mother and the violence of stimuli without a language through which to filter them, displaces a philosophical concept of the unrepresentable. In 'Ellipse sur la frayeur' Kristeva refers to Sollers's phrase in *Paradis*, 'Écrire relève de la terreur'.[132] Writing 'comes from' terror as well as saving the subject from it. This derivation and release are also applicable to Kristeva's theory, and to herself as subject of theory, so that Kristeva's work can be seen as sublime in its attempt to mediate and represent, within theory, what is properly outside it. Terror also engages a more psychoanalytic series of references. Terror as aggression is related to Freud's description of the auto-erotic sadistic pulsion that takes the ego of the subject as its object. The complex and

---

[126] 'La Maternité selon Bellini', ibid. 416.
[127] 'La Joie de Giotto', ibid. 399–400.
[128] P. Sollers, J. Kristeva, M. Pleynet, 'Pourquoi les États-Unis?', *TQ* 71–3.
[129] Kristeva, 'Polylogue', in ead., *Polylogue*, 175.
[130] Ibid. 193.
[131] Ibid. 198.
[132] Kristeva, ibid. 375.

detailed Freudian versions of the transition into childhood problematize the dialectic of semiotic and symbolic, so that from a certain point Kristeva's theory becomes more hesitant around the border between the two. When Kristeva writes of abjection a propos of Céline, this is prefaced by an analysis of infantile phobia, little Hans, and borderline cases of psychosis.[133] Abjection is related by Kristeva to a 'narcissisme primaire' where there is a fundamental ambiguity between the subject and the object, an ambiguity that results in violent affects of repulsion.[134] The 'narcissisme primaire' and the later description of a primary identification with the father, 'un père de la préhistoire individuelle',[135] pose different stages within the earlier dynamic; just as Sollers's analysis of contradiction problematized and ultimately untied the basis of Marxism, Kristeva's pluralization of her own theory makes it less relevant in the later works. This involves a certain liberation of the canon, which is recast to include, in the book on abjection, Dostoevsky, Borges, Artaud, Proust, Joyce, Kafka, Bataille, Sartre, Céline, and, most importantly, the texts of religion. The non-Hegelian terms of Kristeva's description of abjection are suggested by her introduction to the book, where she summarizes:

C'est dire qu'il y a des existences qui ne se soutiennent pas d'un désir, le désir étant toujours d'objects. Ces existences là se fondent sur l'exclusion. Elles se distinguent nettement de celles entendues comme névrosés ou psychoses, qu'articulent la négation et ses modalités, la transgression, la dénégation, et la forclusion. Leur dynamique met en question la théorie de l'inconscient, dès lors que celle-ci est tributaire d'une dialectique de la négativité.[136]

The abject is not a pre-symbolic abstract force that is effective in an anamnesis in the symbolic, but an oscillatory ambiguity in the subject, a crisis of subjectivity, that returns from a space before the constitution of the symbolic and the unconscious. Kristeva essentially opens up an area before the symbolic in which there is already a kind of subjectivity, but which is threatened by the pulsional within it. Her theory is discordant with that of Lacan, which exists within the thetic moment of the symbolic and proposes this as irreducible, as she identifies a subjectivity before the symbolic. In the book on abjection, therefore, Kristeva separates her analysis of *le rejet* that had emerged in the article on Artaud from the Hegelian notion of negativity, and this separation

[133] See Kristeva, *Pouvoirs de l'horreur*.
[134] Ibid. 54.
[135] See Kristeva, *Histoires d'amour*, 38.
[136] ead., *Pouvoirs de l'horreur*, 14.

also confronts Lacan in as much as his symbolic was implicitly within this system. The 'narcissisme primaire' and 'le refoulement primaire' that Kristeva identifies radically transform the relation of her work to Lacan, bringing it closer to other work such as that of André Green. Kristeva's specificity is, however, that she invariably takes the literary text as her object. While Kristeva moves towards psychoanalysis, but significantly away from Lacan, Lacanian analysis also becomes more important for *Tel Quel*, in a specific way which I will describe, after setting out the context of psychoanalysis in the 1970s.

The Lacanian Empire

The context of psychoanalysis in the 1970s is a curious combination of the establishment of the empire of the EFP under Lacan and its internal fragmentation, external criticism, and eventual dissolution. In some ways the EFP follows a trajectory similar to that of *Tel Quel*. Its dissolution comes just two years before that of the review, Sollers referring to it affirmatively in an article where he considers the 'permanent dissolution' of *Tel Quel*.[137] During the decade, psychoanalysis of the Lacanian school becomes more institutionally established, in terms of its publication and in the university. Lacan's seminars began to be published in 1973 under the control of J.-A. Miller at Seuil.[138] *Scilicet* continued to publish anonymous contributions from members of the EFP. Lacan's interview with Miller, *Télévision*, was published in 1973. The 'Champ freudien' collection, ostensibly run by Lacan at Seuil, also published important works. Maud Mannoni's *Psychiatrie et anti-psychiatrie* of 1970 was evidence of communication between the French Lacanian school and the British anti-psychiatry movement involving R. D. Laing, D. Cooper, and G. Bateson. Anti-psychiatry would gain a considerable influence in France in the decade, popularized in the libertarian atmosphere after May 1968, by Deleuze and Guattari's work, Guattari himself having trained as an analyst in the Lacanian school and being involved with the La Borde clinic, run along the same lines as Laing and Cooper's experiments in the UK. Another important publication in the 'Champ freudien' collection was Moustapha Safouan's *La Sexualité féminine* (1976), a Lacanian view of a problematic that was the focus of a particular concentration in the 1970s. On this subject Michèle

[137] P. Sollers, 'Le GSI', *TQ* 86 (winter 1980).
[138] See J. Lacan, *Le Séminaire*, xi: *Les Quatre Concepts fondamentaux de la psychanalyse* (Paris, 1973), followed by *Le Séminaire*, Livre XX 'Encore' (Paris, 1975).

Montrelay would publish an article in *Critique* in 1970,[139] while Luce Irigaray would produce a discourse on the question from a perspective linked to Derrida's work in her books *Speculum de l'autre femme* (1974) and *Ce sexe qui n'en est pas un* (1977).

Outside the EFP, from 1970, as well as Pontalis's *Nouvelle Revue de psychanalyse*, J. Laplanche would direct a review, *La Psychanalyse à l'Université*, and the review *Confrontations*, run by R. Major, would be a fruitful site of debate between philosophy and psychoanalysis. However, it is Lacan's influence that is predominant.

In the university, the Lacanian empire is established through the setting-up of a department of psychoanalysis at the University of Vincennes. Run initially by Serge Leclaire, this would be taken over by the Lacan-Miller tendency in 1975. After the crisis over Judith Miller's exclusion (see Chapter 3), in 1971 there was a further upset when Lacan was heckled by students at a lecture of 1971. He would reply to them: 'Ce que vous voulez, c'est un maître, vous en aurez un'. But by 1975, Lacan exercised complete control. The political connotations of his words to the students were elaborated in *Télévision* in 1974 in some comments on racism, seen as an infliction of a foreclosed *jouissance*. In the seminar *L'Envers de la psychanalyse* (1969–70) he had elaborated a theory of discourse and its relation to power in his model of the four discourses—of the master, the psychoanalyst, the university, and the hysteric.[140] This model of discourse, based on different relations of the subject to the object of desire, would be influential in introducing a political dimension, where political discourse could be analysed from a psychoanalytic perspective.[141] *Tel Quel*'s psychoanalytical politics, the group's analytic position on political discourse, would be a particular instance of this tendency during the 1970s. The affirmative view of Gérard Miller's book *Les Pousses-au-jouir du Maréchal Pétain* (1975) is particularly marked by it.

As well as the distinct psychoanalytic current emerging in the work of Deleuze and Guattari, proposing a closer articulation of the political and the psychoanalytic through the notion of a generalized schizophrenia, and the deconstructive readings of Derrida and his associates,[142]

[139] M. Montrelay, 'Recherches sur la fémininité', *Crit.* 278 (July 1970).
[140] See J. Lacan, *Le Séminaire*, xvii: *L'Envers de la psychanalyse* (Paris, 1991), pp. 31–99.
[141] See particularly, Barthes, 'Écrivains, intellectuels, professeurs', *TQ* 47, where Barthes takes up and enlarges Lacan's suggestions.
[142] G. Deleuze and F. Guattari, *Anti-Œdipe: Capitalisme et schizophrénie* (Paris, 1972) and *Kafka: Pour une littérature mineure* (Paris, 1975); J. Derrida, *La Carte postale de Socrate à Freud et au delà* (Paris, 1976); J.-L. Nancy and P. Lacoue-Labarthe, *Le Titre de la lettre* (Paris, 1973).

Lacan was criticized in less complex ways in books by François Roustang (*Un destin si funeste*, 1976) and François George (*L'Effet 'yua de poêle*, 1979). But the major crisis was internal, due to the conflicts arising from the dominance of the 'absolute master' and the rise of a younger generation. At the end of the decade, the EFP would be dissolved by Lacan, who created a new movement for those loyal to him, 'La Cause freudienne', only to die at the age of 80, almost a year later. Despite the internal conflicts and the external differences, Lacanian psychoanalysis largely replaced the earlier context of the PCF as the most vital institutional area of intellectual activity of the time. At the same time, however, Lacan's theoretical tangents, knots and bottles, were ruinous for the theoretical respectability of his word. Lacanian theory also dissolves, but in a different way from that of *Tel Quel*. Again, there is no real meeting between the two; Lacan was supposed to accompany the group to China, but bowed out at the last minute. Within the context of Lacan's empire, *Tel Quel*'s psychoanalytic engagements will be dissident.

The Italian Connection

Lacanian psychoanalysis was originally overshadowed in *Tel Quel* by a Derridean critique, by Derrida himself, Baudry, and later Luce Iriga-ray.[143] In the 1970s the necessity of disengaging from both Althusser and Derrida isolated Lacanian psychoanalysis as the most promising area in the context for *Tel Quel*. Furthermore, Kristeva's emerging concentration on the subject, a subject beyond that of Lacan, implicated Lacanian psychoanalysis. It was accepted as relevant, but transgressed by the excess of poetic language. The early to mid-1970s sees an increasing engagement with Lacanian analysis in *Tel Quel*, but also an increasing interest in Freud's later work, for example on religion.[144] However, the Lacanian connection is pursued obliquely, as so many of *Tel Quel*'s strategic movements. *Tel Quel* is connected with the Italian context in a number of ways, not only through links with the *neoavanguardia* and the Feltrinelli publishing house around writers Sanguineti and Balestrini, but also through M.-A. Macciocchi. So it is not altogether surprising

---

[143] Luce Irigaray, 'Le V(i)ol de la lettre', *TQ* 39 (autumn 1969).
[144] An article by Hubert Damisch, 'Le Gardien de l'interprétation', *TQ* 44–5 (winter–spring 1971) looks at Freud's *Moses and Monotheism*. Daniel Sibony's 'Premier meurtre', *TQ* 64 (winter 1975) and 66 (summer 1976), also analyses Freud's later work.

that part of *Tel Quel*'s investigation of psychoanalysis in the 1970s passes by way of the new Italian Lacanian school set up by, among others, Armando Verdiglione. An aspect of *Tel Quel*'s shift away from Marxism implicated Italy through Macciocchi and her hero Gramsci. So, if *Tel Quel*'s Marxism at one point passes from France (the PCF, Althusser) to Italy, the same mechanism of displacement is detectable with psychoanalysis. Although the links and friendship between *Tel Quel* and the École freudienne de Paris and other groups (such as the Societé psychanalytique de Paris) are active and strong, this never becomes fixed as an alliance between the groups, because of the tendency to flee institutional ties that *Tel Quel* maintains and the theoretical limitations of Lacanian theory as suggested by Kristeva. The adventure of *Tel Quel* with the Italian psychoanalytical empire of Verdiglione is permitted by a displacement of the centre—Paris—of analytical discourse, to other sites. Italy as a site of debate is significant for the historical fact of Fascism but also because religion, specifically Roman Catholicism, is a dominant ideological force and *Tel Quel*'s concerns with femininity and sexuality are particularly pertinent in this context. At the same time, Verdiglione was a particularly 'Parisian' intellectual, mobilizing an important array of intellectual forces through the organization of conferences and publications, until his eventual downfall, due to financial mismanagement and devious strategy in the early 1980s. Sollers, Kristeva, and Pleynet will attend and give papers at a number of conferences organized by Verdiglione, which are then published in the review, or in translations of the Italian periodical *Vel*, directed by Verdiglione. Many of the important theoretical interventions of Sollers are determined by the themes of Verdiglione's conferences or issues of *Vel*, such as 'Psychanalyse et sémiotique', 'Matière et pulsion de mort', 'Sexualité et politique', 'Dissidence de l'inconscient et pouvoirs', 'La Folie', 'La Semblance'.[145] It is largely in this context that a psychoanalytic ethics is elaborated in *Tel Quel*.

---

[145] See A. Verdiglione (ed.), *Psychanalyse et politique* (Paris, 1974); id. (ed.), *Matière et pulsion de mort* (Paris, 1975); id. (ed.), *Dissidence de l'inconscient et pouvoirs* (Paris, 1980). The articles in the review deriving from these conferences include: P. Sollers, 'A propos de la dialectique', *TQ* 57 (spring 1974) and in Verdiglione, *Psychanalyse et politique*; J. Kristeva, 'Sujet dans la langue et pratique politique', *TQ* 58 (summer 1974) and in Verdiglione, *Psychanalyse et politique*; P. Sollers, 'Lettre de Sade', *TQ* 61 (spring 1975) (also in id., *Théorie des exceptions*), and id., 'D'où viennent les enfants?', *TQ* 65 (spring 1976); M. Pleynet, 'La "Folie" thétique', *TQ* 65 (spring 1976) and in id., *Art et littérature*; P. Sollers, 'Dostoïevskï, Freud, la roulette', *TQ* 76 (summer 1978) and 'Le Sexe des anges', *TQ* 75 (spring 1978).

Jouissance *and Fascism: The Ethical Function of Literature*

The first interaction of *Tel Quel* with Verdiglione appears as a confrontation of psychoanalysis and politics, at a 1973 conference in Milan, under the title 'Psychanalyse et politique'.[146] Sollers and Kristeva gave papers among other important contributors such as Guattari, Serge Leclaire, and Maud Mannoni. The stakes for *Tel Quel* were a confrontation of Marxism and psychoanalysis. For Sollers, for example, Marxist materialism ignores the importance of the subjective. The 'motivations affectives' that are thereby repressed are exploited, transformed into religion by idealism.[147] This exploited excess is defined as fascism, which turns *jouissance* into massacre. Sollers identifies a possible cause of this situation in the lack of a law that can account for *jouissance*. While the emphasis on fascism may be a face-saving exercise to smooth over the crisis of Marxism, there is a basic structure here that we can recognize: a subjective excess or *jouissance* returns on an economy that represses it. The oppositional or repressive relation between the law and excess is criticized in favour of a transformative or cohesive relation between the two. Literature, as excess, has an ethical function in reintegrating excess into the symbolic order.

Kristeva enounces a similar problematic, but she also recognizes the difficult situation of this ethics. It is not a politics, for the political is the communal, and the community is held together by a 'common measure' in discourse.[148] Excess is radically alien to the common measure. The semiotic or the heterogenous remains threatening to the linguistic community which forecloses it. This foreclosure of excess results in its return as a mythical or political force, as religion or as fascism. What religious or rational monologism represses reappears in the guise of a violent substance, fascism: 'le retour du refoulé dans le monologisme religieux et politique'.[149] The ethical function of literature, then, is to 'faire passer dans le langage ce que le monologisme refoule',[150] to transform discourse through the introduction of its excess. This analysis also situates Sollers's interest in religion as a critique of monotheism; his emphasis on Catholicism emphasizes its short-circuiting of the logic of monotheism through the Trinity.

---

[146] See Verdiglione (ed.), *Psychanalyse et politique.*
[147] Sollers, 'A propos de la dialectique', in Verdiglione, *Psychanalyse et politique*, 29.
[148] Kristeva, 'Sujet dans la langue et pratique politique', *TQ* 58 (summer 1974) and in Verdiglione, *Psychanalyse et politique*, 61.
[149] Ibid. 66.
[150] Ibid.

Violence and Cure: Social Illusion and Truth

Literature's 'ethical function' is a kind of cure, analogous to that of psychoanalysis, engaging the subject in a transference: Kristeva's article on Sollers's novel *H* reflects this problematic. After the formalistic emphases of her article on *Nombres*, 'Polylogue' is far more concerned with the question of the subject, but the writing on Sollers produces a political consideration in Kristeva's article. She insists on the fact that the violence that is repressed by 'Yalta', by the constitution of the 'free world', returns as fascism.[151] In fact the 1970s saw a worrying emergence of fascism in developing countries such as Chile and Portugal, but also within Europe, specifically in Italy, so that Kristeva is responding to events and linking them to the ethics sketched out above. To the extent that the world of Yalta represses the violence necessarily inherent in the community, 'L'euphorie communautoire ment'.[152] A discourse on the community, based on a psychoanalytic problematic, that sees it as involving a fundamental violence, and as an illusion when it excludes this violence (a focus of René Girard's work, later affirmed in the review) will be an important element of *Tel Quel*'s politics from this moment, 1973, to the present.

Kristeva's perspective is in many ways similar to that of Sollers. The social is viewed from the point of view of an exception and thereby seen as an illusory spectacle; politics is the discourse of the illusion, of *la réalité*, given that phenomenal reality as such is illusory and spectacular, while literature, or the madness of subjects 'on the borderline' becomes *le réel*, or in Kristeva's later terms *le vréel*.[153] A transcendent, vertical truth is proposed as conflicting with the phenomenal, horizontal semblance of social discourse. Literature is the truth of a society based on a communal lie. The value of art lies implicitly, for *Tel Quel*, in its ability to tell the truth, and this notion is a constant from the opening 'Déclaration' of 1960 to *L'Infini* now.

However, this fundamental approach is differentiated in the practices of the writers involved. Kristeva's psychoanalytical approach tends towards the cure of an individual in analysis and therefore recognizes the difficulty and pain of the transformation involved on a subjective level, while Sollers has a more radical, paranoid vision of the social as spectacle and illusion, and of literature as Messianic truth. Since it is

[151] Kristeva, 'Polylogue', in ead., *Polylogue*, 175.
[152] Ibid. 175.
[153] J. Kristeva, 'Le Vréel', in ead. (ed.), *Folle vérité* (Paris, 1979).

Sollers who dominates the review, it is the latter perspective that dominates *Tel Quel* in its last years, implicating an interest in religion, particularly Catholicism, alongside Pleynet's vast and continual analysis of painting. Kristeva's analytic practice remains a constant pole of interest in the review, as a late special issue on 'Actualité de la psychanalyse' attests.[154]

Elements of Excess: Transgressive or Transcendental?

In the mid-1970s, publications in the context begin to outline the same dynamic of a return of excess on discourse. The works of the *nouveaux philosophes* criticize the *maîtres-penseurs* Marx and Freud, and, in the case of Clavel, turn to divine grace; Lardreau and Jambet's book *L'Ange* (1976) sets out a similar transgression of Maoism. However, *Tel Quel* does not immediately affirm this position, but recognizes a movement within Lacanian circles. G. Miller's book *Les Pousses-au-jouir du Maréchal Pétain* is an analysis of fascism as an inflicted *jouissance* that is critically celebrated in *Tel Quel*.[155] The book plays the role of a pivot between *Tel Quel*'s Maoism and its next phase of dissidence and a focus on the exception. The early works of the *nouveaux philosophes* do not, on the other hand, meet with such approval; Clavel, Glucksmann, Lardreau, and Jambet are criticized for characterizing the return of the excess on the system as a return of the transcendental.[156] A recurrent gesture resurfaces here: *Tel Quel* criticizes the transcendental while affirming the transgressive. The elements of excess are not posited as beyond the limits of the symbolic, but in a transgressive, transformational relation with them, such that the excess is to be reintegrated in rationalism rather than separated from it as a *deus ex machina*. Later, religion will be analysed from this perspective, and the *Nouveaux philosophes* movement evolves as other texts appear. There is a continuity between the rhetoric of *Tel Quel* and that of the *Nouveaux philosophes*, of transgression and

---

[154] 'Actualité de la psychanalyse', *TQ* 91 (spring 1982), including two articles by Kristeva, 'Abjet d'amour' and ' "Ne dis rien" '.

[155] See J.-L. Houdebine's review of the book, 'Aux couleurs de la France', *TQ* 63 (autumn 1975) and an interview, G. Miller, 'A propos du fascisme français', *TQ* 64 (winter 1975).

[156] See A. Compagnon and P. Roger, '*L'Ange* de Guy Lardreau et Christian Jambet', *TQ* 67 (autumn 1976). The response to Glucksmann is slightly more positive. See M.-A. Macciocchi, 'Marx, la cuisinière et le cannibale', and A. Glucksmann, 'Réponses', *TQ* 64 (winter 1975).

transcendence, after rationalism, that might explain the friendliness
between the two groups.

Crisis in Rationalism

Towards 1976, when the final disengagement from Maoism occurs, *Tel
Quel* articulates the crisis in its own strategy, brought on by the conflicts
between different emphases, as a 'crise du rationalisme'.[157] Rationalism
is in crisis to the extent that it cannot account for excess that returns on
it as violence or transcendentalism. This violence appears in the political
context of Italy, for example, with clashes between the anarchist
'Movement' and the authorities.[158] It also appears, as a return of the
repressed, in the rise of the feminist movement, and of a post-1968
subculture in general.[159] This recognition of a return of the repressed
and what is fundamentally a crisis in theory leads to a reformulation of
perspectives. The Maoist reference is about to be dropped, and the
review opts for an analytic position, which in fact it had already stressed,
and a widening of focus, in terms of geography, westwards rather than
eastwards, and thematically, to take in religion and art. In an editorial
section, the strategies to be adopted are detailed. First, the thinking of
'another limit' than that of rationality, which would be 'perméable à
une jouissance' needs to be elaborated.[160] This position recognizes the
necessity of a limit, a symbolic law without which fascism returns in the
real, but calls for its enlargement to take in the irrational or *jouissance*.
A 'new psychoanalytical rationality' and aesthetic practice are means to
this end. Secondly, the analysis of totalitarianism, which is explicit in a
number of articles in the review, must be continued.[161] Thirdly, the
history of religions, undertaken with the aid of psychoanalysis, is a

[157] 'Crise du rationalisme', *TQ* 65 (spring 1976).

[158] This was the focus of a book by M.-A. Macciocchi, *Après Marx, avril* (Paris, 1978),
pub. by the 'Collection Tel Quel'.

[159] The texts in the review by the adolescent Sophie Podolski, violent, scatalogical
scribblings with references to drugs and rock music, are a textual representation of this
jouissance. See S. Podolski. 'Le Pays où tout est permis', *TQ* 53 (spring 1973); '... et
toujours', *TQ* 55 (autumn 1973); 'Inédits', *TQ* 74 (winter 1977).

[160] 'Crise du rationalisme', *TQ* 65: 83.

[161] Analyses of fascism up to this point include: Poulantzas, 'Note à propos du
totalitairisme', *TQ* 53; a review of 'Les Staliniens' by D. Desanti, *TQ* 63; J.-L Houdebine's
review of Michèle Mattelart, 'Le Coup d'état au féminin' (on Allende's assassination in
Chile) *TQ* 63; S. Sontag, 'Féminisme et fascisme', *TQ* 63; Miller, 'A propos du fascisme
français', *TQ* 64; M.-A. Macciocchi, 'Sexualité féminine dans l'idéologie fasciste', *TQ* 66
(summer 1976). (The latter is an excerpt from a publication resulting from a seminar group
at Vincennes, where Macciocchi had a teaching position.)

necessity, as religion appears as what is repressed by rationalism. It is the last aspect which seems to have been most successfully carried out in the review in the late 1970s.

In general the review shifts its focus away from subversion and radical strategies in response to power, and towards analysing the forms of the law on which social discourse rests. The social is increasingly recognized as based on a fundamental violence, 'le mal radical'; here, not only the work of Freud and Lacan become relevant, but also that of René Girard, and the later *nouveaux philosophes*. Religion and psychoanalysis are fundamental to this enquiry. An increasing emphasis is the irreducibility of the symbolic and the impossibility of an unmediated relation to desire, sexuality, subjectivity. Lacan is affirmed, in other words, against Deleuze and Guattari, or the idea of a libidinal substance underlying the social which oppresses it.[162] These emphases programme the interests of *Tel Quel* from the mid-1970s, but on a deeper level the 'crisis of rationalism' editorial is simply the emergence on to an explicit strategic level of tendencies that had been present since the beginning of the decade and implicitly all through *Tel Quel*'s history, in that literature is seen as truth, the social as illusion. When Maoism is dropped as a strategic emphasis[163] the ethics derived from these concerns becomes explicit and merges into a politics. As I will suggest, a politics on this basis is a politics of dissidence. The shift to the USA is not so much a turnaround in political allegiances as the emergence of an already present theory into its application in a wider arena.

THE POLITICS OF DISSIDENCE

The dissolution of Marxism for *Tel Quel* produces a political vacuum, but an insistence on the ethics of the relation of the law to excess provides a link between *Tel Quel*'s excessive Marxism, pushed to its limit, and a politics based on the exception, elaborated from the point of view of the singular subject of literature. This politics is in itself an impossibility, since politics is the discourse of the communal, not of the exception, but a politics or ethics of the exception is articulated in *Tel*

---

[162] This perspective is affirmed in Scarpetta's '*Kafka* de Deleuze et Guattari', *TQ* 63 and his review article of D. Cooper's *Une grammaire à l'usage des vivants* (a translation of *The Grammar of Living* (Harmondsworth, 1974)), *TQ* 67 (autumn 1976).

[163] The shift is signalled in Sollers's discussions with M. Clavel in *Délivrance* and in a 'Note à propos du "Maoisme" ', *TQ* 68 (winter 1976).

Quel, under the name of dissidence. Dissidence can be seen as an ethics that derives from the insistence on the radical but transformative relation of excess to the law, and on the exception, particularly in literature. The politics of dissidence comes after the abandonment of the Marxist system as a reference, and occupies a precise historical period, from the issue on the USA in 1977 up to its mutation into an explicit emphasis on the exception. The temporal movement of theory, after the systemic and structural moment, passes through dissidence to reach the singular.

The Dissident Intellectual

'Dissidence' in French, given that this signifier itself proves to be an intersection in the texts, comes from the Latin verb 'dissideo', to be apart. This separation from the community is evident in *Tel Quel* on a number of levels, politically, psychoanalytically, philosophically, and in terms of the internal organization of the committee. Dissidence also refers to the particular phenomenon of the dissident writers of the Soviet bloc who are the subject of a consideration in *Tel Quel* and a special issue.[164] The appearance of Solzhenitsyn's *The Gulag Archipelago* in 1974 and the response to it produced a general affective shift in the context, away from the totalizing system of Marxism; *Tel Quel*'s position is analytic, stressing the literary aspects of the phenomenon of dissident literature, rather than its political function, although the two are closely linked.[165]

The issue on the USA marks a point of departure for the dissident movement of *Tel Quel*.[166] Before 1977 there are intimations of this interest, inversely comparable to the gradual withdrawal of support from Maoism. However, the 'new rationality' emphasis, the articles on Glucksmann, Miller, Desanti, the review of a Solzhenitzyn text do not explicitly enounce a politics of dissidence, perhaps since the determining instance at that point is the dissolution of the Marxist system. A series of critical articles on Marxism appears, including those by Houdebine

[164] 'Sur la dissidence', *TQ* 76 (summer 1978). A previous issue had included a series of texts by Czechoslovak writers, presented by Pierre Daix, arguing for freedom of expression. See *TQ* 58 (summer 1974): Günter Grass, 'La Liberté d'opinion de l'artiste dans notre société'; Antonin Liehm, 'Le Nouveau Contrat social et les intellectuels'; Pavel Kahout, 'Lettre au Ministre de la Culture tchèque'; Pierre Daix, 'Présentation'.

[165] *Tel Quel* had pub. a review of a short text by Solzhenitsyn, 'Le Chêne et le vœu', in volume 65.

[166] 'Pourquoi États-Unis?', *TQ* 71–3 (autumn 1977).

on Marxist views of language.[167] However, dissidence, although a specific phenomenon produced in the Soviet bloc during the regimes of Stalin and Krushchev, has a wider meaning and is relevant beyond the demise of Marxism. The disengagement from the Left of *Tel Quel* initially permits an enlargement of perspective, figured by an aerial picture of the world in the first pages of the USA issue. This implicates not only a shift away from the traditional French direction of the gaze eastwards, but also a widening of subject-matter to include, notably, religion and non-verbal art. The turn to the USA is not, as some have suggested, a radical turn to the Right, but is conditioned by aesthetic interests already present. Marcelin Pleynet had pioneered in France an interest in US abstract expressionism and abstraction. Both Sollers and Kristeva had already visited the States before the time of the special issue of 1977.[168]

This shift also implies a fairly radical change in the function of the intellectual, engaged in an impossible relation with the USSR or China. The function of the French intellectual can be seen to have undergone a change after 1968 to become, for example in the case of Foucault, more punctual. For *Tel Quel* this is reflected in the shift from a politics of opposition to an ethics of the transformation of discourse. The place of the intellectual in culture becomes a specific focus precisely because of the shift to the USA, a different context.[169] The enlargement of perspective permits a critical consciousness of the place of the intellectual and of the discourse of theory.

The position of the intellectual, as dissident in general, and more specifically from French culture, is also a focus of the interesting discussion between Sollers, Kristeva, and Pleynet, 'Pourquoi les États-Unis?' Although this is one of the few occasions when the three writers appear together in print, the discussion shows the dispersal of the group. The three speak from positions relative to the singular practice each is engaged in. Each has a different approach to the object of enquiry, the USA. Kristeva had already written in 'D'Ithaca à New York' (1974)[170]

---

[167] J.-L. Houdebine, 'L'Impasse du langage dans le Marxisme', *TQ* 68–9, (winter 1976–spring 1977).

[168] Sollers and Kristeva both contribute articles to *TQ* 69 on the States: P. Sollers, 'Deux interventions aux U.S.A'; J. Kristeva, 'Des Chinoises à Manhattan'.

[169] This is the subject of articles in the USA issue: Gregory Corso, 'Entretien'; N. Birnbaum, 'Politique étrangère et lutte sociale'; S. Hoffman, 'Les Américains et les Français'. See also, J.-P. Mathy, *Extrême-Occident: French Intellectuals and America* (Chicago, 1993) for a discussion of French intellectual responses to the States.

[170] J. Kristeva, 'D'Ithaca à New York', *Promesse*, 36–7 (spring 1974), also in ead., *Polylogue*.

about the experience of her trip to the USA in terms which indicate that for her at least, dissidence was already desirable. In terms which recall Barthes's article on her, 'L'Étrangère', she explains how the experience of *la voyageuse* is not to have a fixed Other, a 'chez-soi'.[171] This lack of stability is threatening; a terror of a lack of identity, (*atopie*). The subject, threatened by this *vide*, must make a pact with the law, must desire the law in order to ensure the continuity of identity that allows her to say *Je*, to assume the place of the subject of theory. Kristeva notes that while in France the status of intellectual discourse is antithetical to the law, in the States the law is somehow removed from discourse, not posed as a limit of language. As a result of this separation of law and language, transgressive discourse in the USA is split into a multiplicity of areas that are predominantly avant-garde and non-verbal, and have no effect on discourse, while the intellectual becomes a kind of specialist. This lack of transgression in language of the law, of discourse, is paralleled by a lack of role for intellectuals comparable to the situation in Europe: 'tout est libre mais rien n'est possible'.[172] The revolutionary role of the intellectual is non-existent and it is possible only to fill in the void left by the multiplicity of non-verbal art. The antithetical role of the intellectual, however, can only lead to a deadlock which favours the forced imposition of the law in fascism. While the plurality of non-verbal art in the USA and its analysis enables a mediation of *jouissance*, for the antithetical system it is either imposed or repressed. As a result the USA is valorized positively as a site of plurality. The turn away from the antithetical position of the intellectual also involves a departure from a community, to occupy a more mobile and open site, 'à l'écoute des discours de l'autre'.[173] This discourse of the dissident intellectual is important in its context in a French periodical, since it also achieves a performative status of a kind, while its dissident relation to the community of *Tel Quel* is suggested by its publication in *Promesse*. Already in 1974, Kristeva produces a consideration that prefigures the later focus on the USA, which largely reproduces the analysis of the earlier article. That this dissidence is accompanied by a self-consciousness of the place of the intellectual is further justified in Kristeva's important article of *Tel Quel* 74 (an issue entirely dedicated to 'Recherches féminines') entitled 'Un nouveau type d'intellectuel: Le Dissident'. Dissidence implies a movement away from, a separation, a self-consciousness that

---

[171] Kristeva, *Polylogue*, 495.   [172] Ibid. 508.   [173] Ibid. 513.

alters the place and function of the intellectual, and, implicitly, the review.

For Kristeva the Gramscian and Sartrean concepts of the intellectual derived from an opposition between individual and mass that was essentially determined by the Hegelian master/slave dialectic. This implicated also a belief in 'le mythe d'une société réussie'.[174] This utopian, Manichean stalemate resulted in a lack of mobility, plurality, and intellectual freedom. The whole question of dissidence can then be seen as a movement away from the Hegelian basis of French intellectual discourse, a far more profound shift than that from Left to Right or vice versa. The position of the dissident intellectual in relation to the law can also be seen to become eroticized, more subtle and nuanced, suggested by Kristeva's confession 'Je désire la Loi.'[175] While Pleynet already occupied a similar position in his art criticism, implying a certain freedom of analysis before the silent contemplation of painting, Sollers's position can be described as essentially parodic. Parody is a way of doubling the law without falling into an atopic void. It also implies a certain freedom and indifference to the law, evident in Sollers's fictional and theoretical work. Sollers's work appears in a sense 'beyond the law', suggesting its paranoia.

The 'fonction dissidente' of the intellectual as described by Kristeva also implies a different relation to the community. The intellectual becomes 'communautaire mais singulière',[176] addressing all, but heard by the individual. The stress on the individual is accompanied by a view of sociality as impossible, or inherently corrupt. The multiplicity of singularities means that society is inherently impossible; a vision of [les] ensembles sociaux comme impossibles'.[177] Again, society is seen as an illusion and an impossibility, conditioned by a violence that will in *Tel Quel* become increasingly rendered in religious terms as 'radical evil'. The sacred, as the basis of sociality not only in historical but also theoretical terms, is the ground on which this 'radical evil' is analysable.

The dissident function of the intellectual for Kristeva is therefore an openness to both sides of the law and to the multiplicity of singularities. She proposes that the rebel and the psychoanalyst do not fulfil this function, standing on opposite sides of the law. Only the writer can experience both aspects, as the transgressive dynamic of writing is an

[174] Kristeva, 'Un nouveau type d'intellectuel', *TQ* 74 (winter 1977), 3.
[175] ead., 'Héréthique de l'amour', *TQ* 74: 41.
[176] ead., 'Un nouveau type d'intellectuel', *TQ* 74: 4.
[177] Ibid.

experience of both sides. We can recognize the reaffirmation of the common denominator of literary creation and the transgressive pattern: the writer experiences the limits of identity and the subversion of the law in language that leads to: 'l'embrasement de l'être de la loi dans un vide-détente, paix, néant'.[178] The focus on dissidence turns out eventually to be another way of framing the dynamic of writing and valorizing literary creation as truth in relation to the social.

Maternity and Dissidence

Kristeva's own singularity is introduced in her consideration in this key article of the dissident aspects of femininity. She proposes that women are to some extent dissident, 'demonic', as they are outside discourse. The mother is the guarantee of a discourse that bases itself on a desire for the phallus, on the repression of castration. Sollers's vision of the repressed matriarchy as guardian of the law parallels this consideration. However, Kristeva revalorizes maternity in a positive sense. Maternity itself is an experience with psychosis, 'identité qui se scinde, se replie',[179] which passes through a difficult transference, to love. It is a passage from semiotic to symbolic which enables the occupation of a position within discourse and an experience of its traversal, in a similar sense to the logic of literature. Maternity allows 'une chance d'accéder à ce rapport, si difficile pour une femme, à l'Autre, au symbolique et à l'éthique'.[180] It allows a diffusion of the violence of the semiotic within 'le corps social'. Maternity effects a passage from the excluded singularity of the woman to the ethics of the community: 'La maternité est un pont entre singularité et éthique.'[181] Maternity becomes a kind of metaphor or allegory for feminine creativity.

This article is important for a number of reasons. First, it creates the possibility of a discourse on femininity that would not view it as 'masquerade' or as an identification with the phallic, defining the position of *Tel Quel* with regard to feminism. Secondly, it constitutes a fairly radical and controversial break with feminism that proposes maternity, usually taken as a sign of women's subjection, as a starting-point. *Tel Quel* becomes distanced from feminism as such and identified with a dissident feminism, a feminism dissident from feminism and a dissident feminism inasmuch as separate from male-dominated discourse. Thirdly, the move locates Kristeva's theoretical writing firmly in

[178] Ibid. 5.   [179] Kristeva, ibid. 6.   [180] Ibid.   [181] Ibid.

her own experience of maternity, and the article 'Héréthique de l'amour' (retitled 'Stabat mater' in the book *Histoires d'amour*), a text on representations of maternity typographically refracted and interrupted by an account of childbirth, ruptures the scientificity of theory by the diffusion of maternity Kristeva announces. However, this emphasis does not essentially conflict with Sollers's critique of matriarchy, as it is the mother as excluded, silent guarantor of the law that is his target, while Kristeva's writing through the experience of motherhood is its transgression. It is significant, therefore, that Kristeva refers to de Kooning's series of paintings 'Women' as the most truthful representation of creativity, via maternity, and reproduces a de Kooning painting alongside one by Piero della Francesca in the middle of 'Héréthique de l'amour', since the next issue contains Sollers's essay on de Kooning's 'Women' paintings in which he writes: 'Elles sont bêtes et irréfutables comme l'idée même de societé.'[182] Paternity, as a focus in Sollers's writing, does not come until much later, in his recent novel *Le Secret*.[183]

Motherhood, therefore, is dissidence, but it is also a possibility of ethics which is carried over by Kristeva into *L'Infini* and her later books on love, depression, 'etrangeté'. Kristeva's absence from *Tel Quel* during this last period (she publishes far fewer articles than Sollers or Pleynet and spends much time lecturing in the States) is symptomatic of her self-confessed intellectual exile ('Je parle une langue d'exil', 'L'exil est dejà, en soi-même, une dissidence'[184]). Dissidence can be seen as the condition of many French intellectuals since the 1970s (Derrida, Baudrillard, Lyotard) whose site of enunciation is often predominantly outside the hexagon, in the USA.

The Literature of Dissidence

The extended or metaphorical use of the term dissidence coincides with a general emergence of dissident literature in the French context, and with a specific focus on it in a special issue of *Tel Quel*. The issue also applies the notion of dissidence to areas such as literature and psychoanalysis. The fact that the first three articles derive from a 1978 Paris

---

[182] P. Sollers, 'Pour de Kooning', *TQ* 75 (spring 1978), and in id., *Théorie des exceptions*, 168.

[183] See id., *Le Secret* (Paris, 1992); the narrator's relations with his son 'Jeff'.

[184] Kristeva, 'Un nouveau type d'intellectuel', *TQ* 74: 7. From the US issue to *Tel Quel*'s dissolution, Sollers contributes around thirty articles, not including *Paradis*, compared to Pleynet's twelve and Kristeva's four.

conference on 'Dissidence de l'inconscient et pouvoirs' organized by
Verdiglione justifies the use of the phrase 'dissidence of psychoanalysis',
given Verdiglione's excentric status, and since Sollers's article poses the
limitations of Freudian theory with regard to literature, taking as an
example Freud's short article on Dostoevsky. For Sollers, literature
(Dostoevsky) undermines psychoanalysis, it is a negation that goes
further than Freud, 'une dépense au-delà de la dépense'.[185] The Oedipal
limitations of psychoanalysis, 'au nom du père-pour-la-mère'[186] are also
pointed out, while psychoanalysis is suggested to be blind to a non-
antagonistic filiation, 'le fils incluant son père'.[187] (This phrase suggests
the relevance of the Catholic Trinity and the Incarnation for Sollers's
thought.) Literature becomes a symptom of the limitations of psychoanalysis. Dostoevsky is a dissident in this sense, but also in the strong
thematics in his work of a radical evil, 'le fond du Mal'.[188] The same
philosophy of the impossibility of the social link is present in Sollers's
approach, played against the 'sociability' of Freud. Dissidence is linked
to this impossibility and to the disappearance of the writer from
sociality. The epigraph for the article, from Bataille's *L'Impossible*
proposes the writer as 'acceptant la disparition'.[189] Sollers's focus on *la
roulette* a propos of Dostoevsky, prefiguring a later emphasis on Pascal's
pari,[190] suggests that the disappearance in question is a form of sacrificial
ascendance, within language. In some sense the disappearance can also
be read as the dissolution of *Tel Quel*.

Pleynet's text, 'De l'inégalité sexuelle' also focuses on the impossibility
of community. If literature is a symptom of the sickness of society, as
dissident literature fundamentally was, 'Il ne saurait y avoir de communauté de symptôme.'[191] Literature is an experience of singularity, at odds
with social discourse. The stress on the singular experience of the writer
is an element of Pleynet's writing that continues throughout his work,
so that the focus here on dissidence as 'dissidere', separation and
singularity, is perhaps a 'return of the repressed' of the earlier formalist
and ideologically conditioned period and of Pleynet's moderating role

[185] Sollers, 'Dostoïevskï, Freud, la roulette', *TQ* 76 (summer 1978) and in id., *Théorie des
exceptions*, 70. The essay is also pub. in Verdiglione, *Dissidence de l'inconscient et pouvoirs*, under
the title 'État de la religion et religion de l'État'.
[186] Sollers, 'Dostoïevski, Freud, la roulette', in id., *Théorie des exceptions*, 64.
[187] Ibid.
[188] Ibid. 63.
[189] Ibid. 57.
[190] See Sollers, *Théorie des exceptions*, 202–3, 266, 283, and 'L'Analyse infinie', *L'Infini*, 1
(spring 1983).
[191] M. Pleynet, 'De l'inégalité sexuelle', *TQ* 76: 19.

as secretary, requiring a certain commitment to community. But here Pleynet stresses the illusion of community, specifically as concerns literature. Both psychoanalysis and literature shatter this illusion.

In the same way Macciocchi, in an article on Pasolini, murdered in strange circumstances in 1975, stresses his status as a writer and as dissident from the PCI. Sexuality also enters into the frame here; Pasolini was 'le dissident des dissidents' in his homosexuality, because of the 'nature intrinsèquement homosexuelle' of the community.[192] If society is based on a fundamental repression of femininity, its structure is intrinsically homosexual, and explicit homosexuality appears as an unbearable symptom of its unacknowledged reality, potentially subversive. This is a facile proposition, limited to the level of theory; *Tel Quel* was not involved with the homosexual rights movement in the 1970s. In *Femmes*, Sollers's aggressive heterosexuality is antagonistic towards figures such as Barthes and Foucault, or William Burroughs. Homosexuality, like feminine *jouissance*, is an element on the symbolic level, rather than a real or political choice.

Macciocchi reads Pasolini's work as a meditation on the generalized violence of power (most explicit in the film *Salo*) and a recognition that the law implies a radical evil. The thesis of radical evil inspires an exploration in the review of the status of the law in religion, Judaism, Christianity, and Islam, but also in literature; Solzhenitsyn is linked to Sade through this radical negation. Significantly, Kristeva had already, in 'Noms de lieu', linked the names of Sade and Solzhenitsyn, proposing that the radicality of their writing was the link between *jouissance* and horror.[193] As such it is not a new emphasis, determined by the interests of *Nouveaux philosophes* such as Philippe Nemo,[194] but an aspect already stressed in the work of Bataille and fictionally present in Sade.

In the articles by Sollers, Pleynet, and Macciocchi, the notion of dissidence acts as a knot that binds together a number of emphases that are effective in defining the character of the review from that point. In a sense the binding is a temporary measure to bring about this effect; dissidence is a self-contradicting notion that allows a subsequent dispersion. The term is also extended from its use to refer to writers of the Eastern bloc, and has a general relevance as a description of the period.

[192] M.-A. Macciocchi, 'Pasolini, assassinat d'un dissident', *TQ* 76: 28. Macciocchi also organized a seminar series at Vincennes on Pasolini to which Sollers and Pleynet both contributed. See M.-A. Macciocchi, *Pasolini* (Paris, 1981).
[193] Kristeva, *Polylogue*, 467.
[194] See P. Nemo, 'Job et le mal radical', *TQ* 70–71/3 (summer–autumn 1977).

The special issue on the subject does, however, focus on the specific phenomenon, with articles by Kristeva and Scarpetta, and texts by dissident writers I. Brodski, A. Siniavski, G. Konrad.[195] For Kristeva, dissident literature is a refutation of 'le discours de gauche'.[196] The latter, for Kristeva, is based on a Rousseauesque view of the people as *polis*, and of society as a contract, that excludes the individual and the irrational. The thesis of 'le Mal radical' is reiterated, here in terms of ethics: any ethics becomes totalitarian if not based on the recognition of the impossibility, the fundamental violence or evil, of social relations. Religion fulfilled this function, but in the present climate of the lack of religiosity, aesthetics contaminates the political as the return of the repressed. Solzhenitsyn, the explicit focus of Kristeva's article, writes a polyphonic, carnivalesque language with a multiplicity of subjects that reflects the realized paranoia of the totalitarian state, or any unified system. For Kristeva, the essence of society is paranoiac, based on a universal aggressivity. (This is close to the theory of Girard, who will be a subject of interest for the review.) So not only is the Gulag the truth of Marxism, but Marxism as totalitarianism is the truth of 'le lien social paranoiaque'.[197] The political pessimism of this position is countered by Kristeva's insistence on ethics despite the impossibility of any social link. Dissidence is linked to the same asocial, open, and mobile position of the intellectual, speaking from 'un lieu hors la contrainte sociale'.[198]

Politically, this seems to affirm the carnivalesque revolt of the Italian Movement, 'refusant la loi jusqu'au crime',[199] which is the subject of a book by Macchiochi.[200] For political discourse, dissidence is catastrophic. The dissident movement in a sense creates a political vacuum, since the possibility of the political, the *polis* is problematized. Implicitly, this suggests the fundamental relevance for *Tel Quel* of religion, as an ethics based on original sin, and literature as exceptional and as the exceeding of 'le lien social'.

Dissidence implies for *Tel Quel* the rejection of the very idea of a project and of the idea of a collective group called *Tel Quel*. *Tel Quel* as

---

[195] See G. Scarpetta, 'Dissidence et littérature'; I. Brodski, 'Poésie et dissidence'; A. Siniavski, 'L'Art est supérieur à la réalité'; G. Konrad, 'L'Autre littérature'; all in *TQ* 76 (summer 1978).

[196] Kristeva, 'La Littérature dissidente comme réfutation du discours de gauche', *TQ* 76.

[197] Ibid. 43.

[198] Ibid.

[199] Ibid.

[200] Macciocchi, *Après Marx, avril.*

a group ceases to exist in a proper sense with the emphasis on dissidence, if it was not already fractured by the shock of the trip to China and the USA focus. Dissidence also implies dispersion, and this dispersion is that of the review itself. In some senses the review's actual demise post-dates its dissolution, but it is this *post* which characterizes the period as in the wake of theory. After dissidence, after theory, and after the dispersion of the review comes a theory of the exception. The exception comes after dissidence in the sense that dissidence is a separation from, and the exception is a point radically different from, the body which is fragmented.

THE EXCEPTION IN LITERATURE

Theory of Exceptions

Sollers's theoretical work of the 1970s programmes many of the enquiries and contributions published in *Tel Quel*, and runs parallel to the work of Kristeva and Pleynet.[201] From the mid-1970s Sollers's theoretical articles dominate the review, accompanying the continuous publication of the novel *Paradis*. Although the form of the contributions tends to undermine the closure of theory, being written in an aphoristic, encyclopaedic style produced from the possibilities emerging from language, from the permutation of signifiers, it does present a system, a 'system of the non-systemic', as Sollers affirms.[202] The articles, for the most part collected in the 1986 publication *Théorie des exceptions*, present what can be called a theory of exceptions, a view of literature based on the exception and on singularity, analysing sexuality, religion, and psychoanalysis from this perspective. It is necessary to analyse the whole stretch of this theory, pointing also to its continuation in *L'Infini* in a

---

[201] The theoretical articles of M. Pleynet occupy a substantial part of the review. Many of his critical articles concern painting, assessed further on, but the articles 'La "Folie" thétique', *TQ* 65 (spring 1976) and 'La Compromission poétique', *TQ* 70 (summer 1977) are a no less innovative and interesting aspect of *Tel Quel*'s theoretical activity during the 1970s. Pleynet's main concern in the articles, and in his art criticism and poetry, can be summed up as the relation of the subject to whatever discourse he is engaged in, 'la question du procès constituant le rapport du sujet à la loi' (Pleynet, 'La "Folie" thétique', in id., *Art et littérature*, 20).

[202] Sollers, interview with author, Paris, 1992: 'votre formulation d'un système du non-système me paraît intéressante, parce que je pense que ce sujet de la littérature telle que je la pratique n'est pas un sujet du discours philosophique. Il se met en position de pouvoir l'intégrer'.

series of important discussions with Franz de Haes,[203] thematically, to grasp its historical development and relation to the history of *Tel Quel* and the way it programmes contributions by other writers. It is also necessary to underline that it runs alongside the continual production of *Paradis* that is a major factor in the review's history and style.

Le Dire pensant

While the theoretical writing of Kristeva starts from a scientific formalization and increasingly implicates the subject of theory in its writing, Sollers starts from writing to produce a theory. Theory is the thought that the practice of writing has created. While the writing of *Drame* and *Nombres* produces the theory of *Logiques*, and the writing of *Lois* produces *Sur le matérialisme*, the writing of *H* and *Paradis* produces the various articles that appear in *Tel Quel*, some of which are collected in *Théorie des exceptions*. The articles apply a logic derived from the practice of writing to the subjects in consideration. This logic is that of *le dire pensant*,[204] a theory in the course of being produced in language through the effects of the signifier, of the voice upon the letter. Sollers's non-fictional writing is always anchored, with a sometimes impenetrable amount of complexity, in the form of his writing, in his style. The production of theory through the language of a subject immersed in the space of language, of the voice, is fundamental to Sollers's work, and to his writing in *Paradis*. This theory, although fragmentary, is based on a logic, or system, which is coherent and communicable. It is not restricted to *Tel Quel* but is a long-term strategy on the part of Sollers, so the logic of dissolution that it sets in place is partly the cause of the dissolution and dispersion of *Tel Quel* and its eventual passage to *L'Infini*.

D'où viennent les enfants?

Sollers's articles confront psychoanalysis with literature. They examine, for example, a propos of the writers Joyce and Dostoevsky,[205] the extent

---

[203] These articles are collected in the recent publication P. Sollers, *Le Rire de Rome* (Paris, 1992).

[204] Sollers, interview with author, Paris, 1991: 'Il s'agit de formuler un discours du dire pensant qui se montre capable de traverser tous les discours, et de les ré-écrire'.

[205] P. Sollers, 'Joyce et cie', *TQ* 64 and 'Dostoïevski, Freud, la roulette', *TQ* 76 (summer 1978), both in *Théorie des exceptions*.

to which psychoanalysis is blocked in its attempt to analyse the subject of literature. Literature can itself turn a critical gaze on to psychoanalysis and analyse it, as it does in Kristeva's theory. Sexuality is the symptomatic area of this debate, so that Sollers's interest in these matters is conditioned still by a will to propose literature as a system theoretically in advance of theory. The debate is knotted around the question: 'D'où viennent les enfants?', the title of one of Sollers's articles.[206] The obvious answer, 'le corps de la mère',[207] situates the mother as the screen or blockage, the limit, of the phenomenal world. Already present in the earlier essay on Dante is the notion of the traversal of the mother, which Sollers also metaphorizes as 'sortir d'Égypte', linking the question to the history of religions.[208] The mother is the limit or the guardian that allows discourse and exchange to circulate, Sollers suggests in the article ' "Folie"-mère-écran'.[209] The circulation of signs, of language, is closed at its possible hole, by the screen of the mother. This proposes that it is a refusal of femininity that is the condition of social discourse, and it is what Sade and Joyce suggest in their work, according to Sollers's reading.[210]

Religion is the system that, for Sollers, most consequently thinks through the position of the mother. In 'Vers la notion de Paradis' Sollers considerably widens the frame of reference of his system by marking the engagement of a reading of the Bible that *Paradis* has forced through.[211] The reference to the Bible, to religion, and to the question of the sacred is the key to the development of Sollers's theory, applied to, and engaged by, the logic of the text. This articulation permits an elaboration of theory that is not closed within the necessity of reference to Marxism or psychoanalysis.

---

[206] Sollers, 'D'où viennent les enfants?', *TQ* 65.

[207] Ibid. 18.

[208] P. Sollers, 'Histoire de femme', *TQ* 88 (summer 1981), 36: 'tout le problème étant de savoir ce qui est arriver ou pas à sortir d'Egypte'.

[209] Id., ' "Folie"—mère-écran', *TQ* 69 (spring 1977). See also 'D'où viennent les enfants?', *TQ* 65: 19—'La mère occidentale est alors cet écran refermé, mommifié, repucelé, ravagé, revirginisée à l'envers.'

[210] Id., 'D'où viennent les enfants?', *TQ* 65: 19. 'Freud insiste: c'est de toute façon la féminité qui est refusée par les deux sexes.' See also id., 'Lettre de Sade' in id., *Théorie des exceptions*, 56: 'le fait qu'une femme se soit acharnée contre lui prouve qu'il excède bien, en ce point, ce qui de l'homme, en la femme, refuse la femme', and in 'Joyce et cie', *Théorie des exceptions*, 93: 'ce que Joyce "déplace" c'est très exactement la place de la paranoïa féminine.'

[211] Id., 'Vers la notion de *Paradis* II', *TQ* 75 (spring 1978).

Le 'Semblant'

Guaranteed by the limit of the maternal body and a closure of the infinite, social discourse appears as illusion and semblance. Sollers states categorically in 'Le Pape' that 'le monde est une illusion, un mensonge'.[212] Sollers proposes this realm of *le semblant* as the world that is defined by the common measure, the social: 'Le semblant est la texture de l'étant qui permet de penser que tous les noms sont équivalents.'[213] Sollers takes the term *le semblant* away from Lacan's idiosyncratic definition of it to bring it closer to the notion of the spectacle as proposed by Guy Debord. Kristeva follows Sollers's use of the term in 'Le Vréel', where she writes: 'Le langage est alors toujours du semblant, vraisemblable mais jamais vrai.'[214] *Le semblant* in Sollers's use of the term does, however, resonate with Lacan's usage in that for Sollers it affirms the idea of a common measure, of a collective unconscious or a cofraternity, a rationality, while for Lacan the same sense of consistency is connoted, an imaginary consistency fixed by the symptom, which paradoxically makes the subject different. Through this vision of the world as illusion, Sollers can be seen to occupy a specific place in a long tradition of moralists who argue for the illusory nature of the social, from Parmenides through Bossuet to Guy Debord.

For Sollers, sexuality is not liberating in itself; sexual reproduction is part of the realm of 'le semblant'. As Kristeva and Lacan affirm, sexual identity is an aspect of the symbolic, it is not pre-given. Sollers refers to 'le semblant de la reproduction de l'espèce',[215] and writes in 'Le Sexe des anges': 'Dans "Au commencement était le Verbe et le Verbe s'est fait chair" n'est pas forcément visible la place d'un sexe.'[216] Reproduction is an effect of language.[217] This joins with Lacan's proposition that 'there is no sexual relation'; sex does not stand as a biological fact outside language.[218] Sollers follows a tradition of thinkers who deny the

---

[212] Id., 'Le Pape', *TQ* 84 (summer 1980), also in id., *Théorie des exceptions*, 218.

[213] Id., 'Histoire de femme', *TQ* 88: 36. This text was a contribution to a 1981 Verdiglione conference on 'Le Semblant', (Milan, Jan. 1981).

[214] Kristeva, 'Le Vréel', in ead. (ed.), *Folle vérité*, 20.

[215] Sollers, 'Le Sexe des anges', *TQ* 75 (spring 1978), 87.

[216] Id., 'Histoire de femme', *TQ* 88: 36.

[217] See Id., 'La Trinité de Joyce', *TQ* 83 (spring 1980), 65: 'non seulement il n'y a pas de sexualité naturelle, mais ce qu'on prend pour sexe n'est jamais qu'un effet du langage'. See also the article 'Je sais pourquoi je jouis', *TQ* 90 (winter 1981) and in id., *Théorie des exceptions*. In Sollers's 1984 novel *Portrait du joueur*, the erotic scenarios with 'Sophie' are also predicated on this predominance of 'l'élément verbal', (p. 165).

[218] See J. Lacan, *Le Séminaire*, xx: *Encore* (Paris, 1975), p. 12.

existence of nature, and he has an immediate ally in Lacan. Nature is not the basis or substance of the world: the limits of my world are the limits of my language.

The Limits of Language

Wittgenstein proposed that the limits of language are the limits of the world.[219] Sollers proposes that whatever is posed as outside these limits becomes sacred or unthinkable. An important aspect of Sollers's thought is that language offers the possibility of an access to the infinite, an exit from the closure of *le semblant*. However, this infinite is proposed as being a possibility within language, rather than beyond it. If a limit of language is posed, what is beyond the limit appears as a transcendence separated from the real. Religion, as the discourse that most directly concerns this transcendence, is of fundamental relevance. What is posed as outside language, sex for example, is the condition of religion. If the mother is posed as the limit of language, the origin and limit of phenomena, there is a religion of the mother, which for Sollers is the condition of society. Catholicism is of explicit interest for Sollers as the religion that most consistently attempts to short-circuit this logic and the position of the mother as limit. Sollers's attitude to religion is not to see it as an affirmation of the sacred, but the site of its most consistent negation, that is, the site of the most consistent negation of the limits of language and the phenomenal. In 'L'Assomption' he writes: 'contrairement à ce que tout le monde pense, il ne s'agit pas d'affirmer dans cette logique quoi que ce soit mais de se livrer, à travers ce raisonnement, à une négation radicale'.[220]

Catholicism is, moreover, 'la négation même de toutes les religions', the Immaculate Conception a negation of the position of the mother as limit, of the closed exchange-system of procreation, the Assumption a negation of death.[221]

In a 1978 essay, 'Le Marxisme sodomisé par la psychanalyse elle-même violée par on ne sait quoi', both Marxism and psychoanalysis are signalled as limited in their attempt to impose a rule or a common measure and in proposing the exception as a deviation from the rule

---

[219] L. Wittgenstein, *Tractatus Logico-Philosophicus* (London, 1961), 56.
[220] Sollers, *Théorie des exceptions*, 224.
[221] Ibid. 225.

that proves it.[222] A different notion of the exception and of the subject is necessary. In the Trinity, and the Immaculate Conception, Sollers shows how Catholicism proposes a hole, (*trou*) in *le semblant*, enabling a transcendence in the real. The Virgin Mary is a hole in the realm of reproduction, the only real hole that is not blocked up by a phallus or fetish. The Virgin Mary is at the same time mother and daughter of her son, short-circuiting the position of the Mother as origin in a paradoxical knot, comparable to Lacan's Borromean knot of real, symbolic, and imaginary.[223] Catholicism's logic proposes a symbolic negation of death, in the Assumption or the Resurrection of Christ, of the Oedipal family, through the incarnation of Christ, and reproduction or sex in the 'effet BVM' (Bienheureuse Vierge Marie).[224] Catholic religion, as a negation of limits posed in the phenomenal world by death, reproduction, the mother or father, is of interest to Sollers as a theology that makes possible the superseding of a religious position as such. The religious signifier enters into writing to suggest the way literature also forces a way through the limits of the phenomenal, becomes infinite and transcendent of mortality, corporeality, sexuality. The logic of the Incarnation and sacrifice of Christ is directly relevant to the incarnation in the body of language, and the sacrifice of the body to writing. From this perspective, the body, and the phenomenal in general, becomes something that has fallen out of an infinite process, a *déchet*. The world is conditioned by negativity (Sollers points to the homophony between 'n'être' and 'naître'[225]), and, if this infinite process if foreclosed, by a fetishization of *le déchet*.[226]

Sollers's theory is consistent in many ways with the writing of theologians such as Pascal, Eckhart, Bossuet, and with Jesuitical thought. Sollers's education by Jesuits is perhaps not without consequence. In an essay entitled 'Éloge de la casuistique' of 1978, Sollers praises the Portuguese theologian Gracian for having recognized that: 'le langage, en ce monde, est en trop, est la figure même d'un excès qui

---

[222] P. Sollers, 'Le Marxisme sodomisée par la psychanalyse elle-même violée par on ne sait quoi . . .', *TQ* 75 (spring 1978), also in id., *Théorie des exceptions*.

[223] A key text in this respect is Dante's *Paradiso*, particularly the last canto: the lines 'vergine madre figlia del tuo figlio/Termine fisso d'eterno consiglio'. Sollers writes of these lines in 'Je sais pourquoi je jouis', in id., *Théorie des exceptions*, 289–90: 'La délibération "humaine" tourne ainsi autour d'un terme fixe qui est celui d'une vierge mère fille de son fils.'

[224] See Sollers, *Théorie des exceptions*, 224.

[225] See id., 'La Trinité de Joyce', *TQ* 83: 83.

[226] *Paradis* can be seen as an analytic and parodic traversal of a proliferation of fetishes and fetishizations.

indique, comme à l'envers, le trop-plein divin qui vide et gonfle en même temps les phenomènes'.[227]

Language is identified as a figuration of the divine which is a principle of excess within phenomena, such that: 'le verbe peut donc nous accompagner au-delà des fins de tout ce qui a été fait et se fera jamais'.[228] Sollers's system is close to that of Bataille in identifying a universal principle of excess, but distinctive in its faith, in the religious and other senses of the word, placed in the possibilities afforded by writing.

Sollers's theory, although it can be more accurately called a theory-after-theory in that it places itself beyond the closure of a system, is in many senses a remarkable vision not only of literature but also of art in general, as offering possibilities of verticality and transcendence within the real, and as a transformation of the usual patterns of thought. Its consistency and coherence are often overlooked when Sollers is seen as an archetypal intellectual obsessed with strategy and image. These aspects are subservient to the putting-forward of the logic described above. If Maoism is seen as a radical negation of the closure of the Marxist system, Sollers's interest in Catholicism is entirely consistent with it at the level of this logic. While Kristeva's thought shows a development throughout the 1970s, Sollers's non-fictional writing appears as a reiteration of a basic logic and its application to different areas. Repetition, in *Tel Quel* of the excerpts of *Paradis*, within that text of sounds and rhythm, and of a basic theory, is a particular aspect of Sollers's writing. This repetition punctures the closed time of theory and the linear time of history. Repetition is a problem for history, as Sollers suggests in an article entitled 'Le Tri':

Bien entendu, si on pose la question du temps, de cette soi-disant existence du temps entraînant un développement quelconque, on va être amené à se poser immédiatement ce problème de la répétition. *La* question, c'est en effet la répétition. Je me répète.[229]

For the proof of this, one has only to read in Sollers's most recent novel: 'De la répétition répétée dans la répétition des répétitions. Vous innovez, paraît-il, moi je me répète.'[230] This temporality of repetition

---

[227] P. Sollers, 'Éloge de la casuistique', *TQ* 77 (autumn 1978) and in id., *Théorie des exceptions*, 34.

[228] id., *Théorie des exceptions*, 37.

[229] See id., 'Le Tri', orig. in *Peinture, cahiers théoriques*, repub. in id., *Improvisations* (Paris, 1991), 196.

[230] Id., *Le Secret* (Paris, 1992), 51. The narrator is writing about the Pope.

takes a while to emerge, however, having to disengage itself from the avant-garde project that linked literature to political and theoretical utopias. When it does, in Sollers's work, in the 1970s, it sheds a retrospective light on the previous work, such as *Logiques*. The articles that appear in *Tel Quel* in the 1970s, and much of the work published in *Tel Quel* by associates such as Houdebine, Scarpetta, Sichère, and Muray, are applications of this repetitive logic of the exceptional. This implies a widening of the canon, to include not only writers associated with the avant-garde, but also writers such as Céline, Malraux, Hugo, and later in *L'Infini* a proliferation that seems to relate to no particular criteria, specifically revalorizing classical writers such as Bossuet, Saint-Simon, La Rochefoucauld. Religious texts, particularly those at the margins of monotheistic religions, including Catholicism as what Sollers calls a 'monotrinisme',[231] become objects of interest. Biography, as the study of the way the writer occupies the writing, also becomes relevant. An intersection of these interests, reactivating an emphasis already present, makes the work of Joyce a focus throughout the decade.

The Name of the Exception

In 'Le Marxisme sodomisé' Sollers proposes a new vision of the exception other than as that which confirms the rule. This is centred on the the the question of the name, a previous emphasis in 'La Science de Lautréamont'. Sollers writes elsewhere that: 'le semblant est la texture de l'étant . . . qui permet à penser que les noms sont équivalents'.[232] The name, as the mark of singularity, cannot be equivalent. Its reproduction, the handing-down of the name of the father, has to be interrupted to constitute singularity. This 'coup dans le langage' is effected by Lautréamont, Joyce, Sade, Dante, Sollers himself, who 'pass through the name' or the name of the father by an insertion of their name in the tissue of language, a *redoublement*.[233] Having evacuated the possible equivalences of the name, the writer can occupy the name as the mark of an exception, so that 'le nom, vocalement, sort du semblant'.[234] In 'Lettre de Sade' Sollers condemns the mutation of the name of Sade into an adjective, and the resultant repression of the fact that Sade lived and

---

[231] Id., 'Pourquoi je suis si peu religieux', *TQ* 81 (autumn 1979), and in id., *Improvisations*, 117.
[232] Id., 'Histoire de femme', *TQ* 88: 36.
[233] See id., 'L'Auguste Comte', *TQ* 79 (spring 1979) and in id., *Théorie des exceptions*.
[234] Id., 'Histoire de femme', *TQ* 88: 37.

died, that he existed as an exception.[235] The life of the writer is important as the event of this singularity in the real. In terms of the subject of literature, the passage through the name involves a realization that, as Nietzsche wrote: 'I am all the names of history.' In other words, the literary exception can only be constructed through intertextuality, through a traversal of all the possibilities of other texts in the text.

The literary exception is anchored in the singularity of a name. This would seem to propose a departure from the anonymity of the textual machine of *Tel Quel*'s earlier emphases, but it is in fact its extension beyond the limits of an avant-garde formalism, which was a stage on the way to the exception. The emphasis on the name is precisely due to the dissolution of the identity of the author. Sollers explains this mechanism in the article 'L'Auguste Comte': the writer passes through the alterity of the pseudonym (Lautréamont) and 'all the names of history' to be able finally to sign his own name, Isidore Ducasse.[236] Writing appears as a tripartite passage from the sacrifice of authorial identity through a reintegration of the multiplicity of discourses, their rereading and rewriting, to the subjectivity of the writer.

The investigation of the exception also leads to a consideration of community. Sollers says of the lives of the writers Lautréamont, Mallarmé, Joyce: 'c'est parce que toutes ces expériences sont très différentes les unes des autres que c'est la même'.[237] There is a kind of community of the exception in this sense, but 'c'est un espace qui ne fait pas communauté d'une facon égalisante'.[238] The names, Sollers, Pleynet, Risset, and so on, do not define a community in which the names are annulled under the weight of a common project, just as Bataille, Leiris, and Caillois retained their difference and their disagreements in the Collège de sociologie. This kind of community, a community of the name as exception, defines the character of the later *Tel Quel* and *L'Infini*.

The singularity of the name, what we could call the use value of the name, to revive an earlier analogy, is opposed to the capacity of exchange of language in general, or social discourse. The name of the social subject is a sign of an identity, as Sollers proposed, 'la mise en carte de l'identité sociale',[239] while the literary name is an exception. In

---

[235] See id., 'Lettre de Sade', *TQ* 61 (spring 1975).
[236] See id., 'L'Auguste Comte', in id., *Théorie des exceptions*, 117–18.
[237] Ibid. 121.
[238] Ibid.
[239] P. Sollers, *Logiques* (Paris, 1968), 60.

'L'Assomption' Sollers criticizes the mutation of the name into a part of
a social set, deconstructing the logic that passes from 'Tous les hommes
sont mortels' to 'Socrate est un homme' and 'Socrate est mortel'.
Psychoanalysis is also implicated here, since it makes of the exception a
case, as is evident in the use of the terms 'oedipal', 'sadistic', 'masochistic'. Implicitly, Tel Quel affirms singularity in opposition to the exchange of meaning or exemplification. The subject of literature
therefore becomes an exception by a passage through language, to the
point where he can occupy his name. This occupation refers not only
to the fact that when we use the word 'Shakespeare' we think as much
of a text, a body of language, as a historical individual, but also to the
physical occupation of the body by language. Writing is not a Derridean
impersonal process but a profoundly sensuous invasion of the body by
language, an inhabitation of the body by the voice, to the point where
the body becomes a name, an exception at the transfinite point of
language. The logic of the exception is not only theoretical, it is also a
physical experience.

The Body of the Exception

The body of the exception is an exceptional body, and it is analysed in
Tel Quel as such, for example by Philippe Muray in the aptly titled 'Le
Corps glorieux de l'écriture'.[240] Other analyses of this question are
undertaken by Scarpetta, on Artaud, and by Muray again, on Céline.[241]
Literature, Muray proposes, opens up the possibility of a 'résurrection
dans le multiple'.[242] We can recognize here the singularity that emerges
through the death of individuality and passage to multiplicity and
infinity. The theme of resurrection engages the question of the body of
Christ, precisely because it is a question of the resurrection and
disappearance of the body. Focusing on the Turin shroud as a figure of
this problematic, Muray proposes that the body of the writer is engaged
in a similar dissolution: 'Le verbe se faisant chair dissout jusqu'à la chair,
le corps ne tient plus le coup dans l'incarnation.'[243] The body becomes
'un corps glorieux', and is lived as an 'unsupportable reality' (or Sollers's
term déchet), the experience of Artaud appearing particularly relevant,

---

[240] P. Muray, 'Le Corps glorieux de l'écriture', TQ 80 (summer 1979).
[241] See G. Scarpetta, 'Artaud écrit ou la canne de St. Patrick', TQ 81 (autumn 1979);
P. Muray, 'Céline et la religion révélée', TQ 88 (summer 1981).
[242] Muray, 'Le Corps glorieux de l'écriture', TQ 80: 61.
[243] Ibid. 68.

because its reality cannot support the divine. This recalls what we have already signalled a propos of Sollers as the sacrifice of the body in the writing in a kind of Pascalian wager, between nothing and infinity. In 'Socrate en passant' Sollers also emphasizes how, for the writer, the body is a limitation to be transgressed. Writing passes beyond the body as *corps*, as corpse, and becomes *la chair* through the incarnation of language. Moving away from the fetishization of writing evident in Derrida's 1974 text *Glas*, the incarnation of language in the body is proposed by Sollers, Muray, and others, as activated by the voice.

This is the case in *Paradis*, from which Sollers gave readings which physically exhausted him. It is a writing that coincides with the voice, that reaches a point at the end of the phrase-unit that coincides with the stillness in the interstices of breathing, enabling a coincidence, incarnation, or occupation, of the body by the writing. A *vide* is the still point at which the circulation of signs and fetishes can be interrupted and enable a verticality. Sollers himself terms the passage beyond the circulation of *le déchet*, 'le trou noir' or 'le transphère', suggesting that the experience in question is also transgressive of the psychoanalytic exchange of *le transfert* or transference.[244] The body of the exception escapes from the circulation of *le transfert*, or extends it, to become transcendent, beyond the sphere, in writing. The metaphor of the black hole suggests how it is a question of exiting from the circulation of the phenomenal universe, whence Sollers's interest in the new physics in *Paradis* and in later works.

The Signature of the Exception: Intertextuality

The signature of the exception can only take place after the traversal of the infinity of texts, after intertextuality. In Houdebine's article 'La Signature de Joyce' the question of the passage to the singularity of the name is articulated as from the particular through the universal to the singular.[245] The signature is a 'transname', characteristically prefixed with 'trans-' to suggest the diagonal, neither purely vertical nor horizontal process, with which *Tel Quel* is concerned. Sollers had stated in 'Socrate en passant': 'Je suis ce sujet singulier qui s'interesse à la logique de l'universel.'[246] Joyce's 'wake', Houdebine explains, expresses the idea

[244] P. Sollers, 'Socraté en passant', *TQ* 83 (spring 1980), also in id., *Théorie des exceptions*, 275.
[245] J.-L Houdebine, 'La Signature de Joyce', *TQ* 81 (autumn 1979).
[246] Sollers, *Théorie des exceptions*, 280.

of the post-universal singularity that exists in a temporality of the *pressant*, the infinity of texts pressing behind the moment of writing, a temporality of the *dépense* of the anterior texts. The singularity of the exception, in other words, is a post-intertextual singularity. Implicitly, texts which are conscious of their intertextual relations with other texts and open to them, like Joyce, Lautréamont, or Borges, are of interest as versions of this logic.

Houdebine discusses the signature of Joyce as an infinite point coming after the multiplicity of discourses, laying out a structure for this *traversée* based on a word in *Finnegans Wake* 'me/ander/tale', reading the three parts as follows: i) 'le récit de moi comme autre'; ii) 'le récit de l'autre comme moi'; iii) 'l'Autre en moi, moi en l'Autre comme dit'.[247] First, alienation or sacrifice, then the interiorization of other texts, then the speaking, *le dit*, of both in the text. This coincides with what Sollers calls 'le passage du sujet à sa trinité',[248] hence the relevance of the Catholic dogma of the Trinity. This traversal is neither metaphoric nor real. It is not a question of a discourse that is consciously aware of copying all other languages—the *traversée*, moreover, exists within one language, although there are exceptions, of which Joyce is the obvious one—but of a writing that has no consciousness of itself as pure origin and does not close itself off from other texts, or any writing that can be read in these terms. It reveals itself as within the same general corpus (language) as the infinite texture of human interaction. Intertextuality is not limited to relations between texts but implies a vision of the interrelatedness of all human experience mediated in language. With this consciousness, the text comes after language, not as an end but as a continuing process to infinity: a 'publication permanente', as Lautréamont called his own *Poésies*. Borges suggested the same idea when he noted that every writer creates his own precursors.

The Exception and the Father

The subjectivity of the writer as exception also implicates a consideration of the relation to the family. Consistent with emphases since *Logiques*, it is a question of a passage through the mother or the blockage of this passage by the screen of the mother. If the mother is a screen, then the writer is blocked in the particularity of his own history. Viviane

---

[247] Houdebine, 'La Signature de Joyce', *TQ* 81: 61.
[248] Sollers, 'Le Tri' in id., *Improvisations*, 201.

Forrester's essay 'Marcel Proust: Le Texte de la mère' reads Proust as such a writer.[249]

There is an implicit psychoanalytical problematic behind the transgression of the familial structure of the writer. Behind the mother, it is the father who is desired, the father being not as for Lacan a Name of the Father, a single father who has to be continually killed to reiterate an initial sacrifice or murder, but a father of filiation. Filiation opens the subject to the infinity of past discourses rather than the closed structure of the family and reproduction. Sollers suggests in 'Pourquoi je suis si peu religieux' why the figure of Christ is paradigmatic for the writer. Christ joins the Father and Son together in one person. While the Virgin is at the same time mother and daughter of her son, in the Oedipal family, the mother intercedes between father and son to prevent the passage of the subject into the multiplicity of past discourses.[250] Kristeva's work is not in conflict with this; her affirmation in 'Héréthique de l'amour' that maternity is or can be the experience of a *traversée* of the law is itself a passage through the mother. Maternity here is an open experience, rather than a closure of *le trou* with the phallus of the infant. In her later work on love, excerpts from which appear in the last issues of *Tel Quel*, Kristeva also postulates an originary and imaginary father which seems consistent with the emphases of Sollers.[251]

From Kristeva's articles 'Noms de lieu' and even more so in the later 'Abjet d'amour', there is an inclusion of the psychoanalytic case. Analysis as a practice, rather than a site generating theoretical models, intersects with writing as a practice. It is this aspect of practice, necessarily deriving from the experience of a singular subject, that distinguishes Kristeva's analysis from the theory previously emphasized in the review. This emphasis on the singularity of psychoanalysis is stressed in an editorial note to a special issue 'Actualité de la psychanalyse':

Le discours analytique n'est-il pas, par son ancrage dans la sexualité, par l'irréductibilité de la pratique qui le porte, par sa marginalité nocturne inaudible aux fantasmes communautaires, un des rares lieux où s'énonce la sauvage singularité, insensée, de l'être parlant?[252]

---

[249] V. Forrester, 'Marcel Proust: Le Texte de la mère', *TQ* 78 (winter 1978).

[250] See Sollers, 'Pourquoi je suis si peu religieux', *TQ* 81 (autumn 1979), also in id., *Improvisations*, 121.

[251] See Kristeva, 'Abjet d'amour', *TQ* 91 (spring 1982).

[252] 'Actualité de la psychanalyse', *TQ* 91: 17.

Psychoanalysis, the practice and singularity of Kristeva, is affirmed against community, effective in the context in distinguishing *Tel Quel* from the community of Lacanian analysis. Psychoanalysis thereby achieves an analogous status to literature, with which it has certain points of intersection. Kristeva's articles in this issue approach the exception through a discussion of love, the subject of her next book, *Histoires d'amour* (1983). Love is at the same time approached through psychoanalysis and used to outline a psychoanalytical theory, an indication of the thematic approach, an approach based on the affect, of Kristeva's work since *Pouvoirs de l'horreur*. As a theme, love is effective in linking together the psychoanalytical transference and the singular experience of the writer, seen to an extent as a symptom that resists this transference.

Kristeva's theory looks at the passage of the subject, from the fusional dyad of infant and mother to the insertion into the symbolic, in terms of a primary narcissism. A primary identification with an imaginary father or 'father of imaginary prehistory' is the condition of the disengagement from the abject, the difficult oscillatory relation with the mother. The semiotic/symbolic dynamic is also rephrased here in terms of a passage from the pulsional or libidinal to representations or mnesic traces. Narcissism is the structure of the circulation between discharge, affect or the pulsional, and the representations which are investments around *le vide* of the subject, a concept borrowed from André Green.

The relations Kristeva sets out between the subject of love, the mother and the father can be superimposed on the familial relations proposed in the theory of the exception in literature. The appeal to the figure of the father is common to both, and both implicate a relation of love or transference in the transgressive movement of the exception. Kristeva shows how the mother can be a figure of terror, as in the experience of abjection, a figure of closure and painful ambiguity. On the other hand, she also shows in her article on maternity, 'Héréthique de l'amour', that there can be an open experience, a 'good' *jouissance*. From this perspective it appears that whether the mother appears as closure or as opening depends on the experience of the subject; the experience of Sollers imposes a view of the mother as 'bad'. However, it is true to say that many male writers, especially those analysed by *Tel Quel*, propose the same view of the mother; to this extent we can agree with the association of the transgression of literature with that of the mother, while bemoaning the lack of analysis of women writers or feminine sexuality in *Tel Quel*. It is also evident that Kristeva's proposition of an originary identification with an imaginary father bears many points of similarity with the focus on religion pioneered by Sollers.

Joyce Tel Quel

The theory considered above is derived and applied to a number of different texts, but perhaps the most complete exploration is of Joyce. Joyce appears as the writer who epitomizes *Tel Quel*'s view of literature during the 1970s. The different emphases of the *Tel Quel* theory of literature can be gauged through the analyses of Joyce. Joyce is the paradigm of the experience of the writer as exception, but the earlier articles on Joyce by Sollers and Stephen Heath stress the mechanism of intertextuality and the heterogenous.[253] The importance for *Tel Quel* of Joyce is retrospectively acknowledged by Houdebine in the very last issue of the review, in an article entitled 'Joyce tel quel'.[254] The interest parallels and intersects in some instances with the context. Lacan, Derrida, and Cixous have written on Joyce, but it is the first whose work is particularly questioned in *Tel Quel*.[255]

In the early 1970s the texts on Joyce play an important part in the affirmation of the exception of the writer against historically totalizing movements such as Fascism and Stalinism. Joyce appears as a symptom, to the extent that the political analyses and strategies *Tel Quel* effects occur partly through a concentration on his texts, and he points to what has been historically repressed: 'Joyce déplace en acte, en histoire, ce qui s'effectue de l'inconscient dans la langue.'[256] The textual effects that are marked here have a real political importance in that Joyce is a historical unconscious, a return of the repressed of Stalinism and Fascism that later analyses, by Sollers and Houdebine, will take up.[257] *Tel Quel* champions the exceptional values of Joyce's texts, mostly *Finnegans Wake*, against nationalism, through the concept of the plurality of languages—*l'élangues*, as Sollers neologizes.[258] *L'élangues* is deliberately

[253] S. Heath, 'Ambiviolences', *TQ* 50–1 (summer–autumn 1972) and 'Trames de lecture', *TQ* 54 (summer 1973); P. Sollers, 'Argument', *TQ* 54. The issue also contains a translation of a part of *Finnegans Wake* by Sollers and Heath. The following issue includes articles by Umberto Eco and J. Risset on Joyce.

[254] J.-L. Houdebine, 'Joyce tel quel', *TQ* 94 (winter 1982).

[255] See G. Lernout, *The French Joyce* (Michigan, 1990) for a discussion of the various perspectives, including that of *Tel Quel*, on Joyce.

[256] 'Joyce in Progress, Introduction', *TQ* 54 (summer 1973), 3.

[257] See J.-L Houdebine, 'Jdanov ou Joyce?', *TQ* 69 (spring 1977).

[258] Sollers, *Théorie des exceptions*, 90, defined as 'l'écriture comme multiplication des langues', p. 61.

distinct from Lacan's totalizing *lalangue*, promoting the multiplicity of languages that Joyce's *Finnegans Wake* celebrates. Joyce becomes almost synonymous with the capacity of literature to undermine politically totalizing systems, and to this extent the emphasis on Joyce is a political choice. This has effects in the review's interaction with the context. In discussing Deleuze and Gauttari's book on Kafka, Scarpetta plays Joyce against the authors' philosophical intentions. Likewise, discussing Lukaçs, Joyce is used as a stick to beat not only the representative of socialist realism, but also Brecht, who failed to recognize the value of the Joycean text.[259] The emergence of a critical discourse on Joyce appears as a continuation of the emphasis on the singular subjectivity of the writer that transgresses the political structures in which *Tel Quel's* Maoism is implicated. Joyce appears implicitly as the exception that returns on the rule to subvert and transform its system.

Joyce the Symptom

Joyce appears as a symptom for psychoanalysis and history, which points to what is repressed. This immediately poses the question of the extent to which the symptom is equivalent to the exception, enabling a comparison between the approach to literature of *Tel Quel* and of Lacan; particularly pertinent since the principal interaction between *Tel Quel* and Lacan over literature concerns Joyce. For Lacan, in an article of 1975, Joyce was 'the symptom' or *le sinthome*, the saint outside normal human relations.[260] The relation between language and literature is knotted around the question of the symptom by Lacan. If the subject of language, the subject as such, experiences a lack, *manque à être*, through his subjection to the other, that something is missing in his relations with the world or with the other, the symptom is what the subject wants to use to stop up this lack. If the subject in language is always prey to metonymic substitution, is always fading in the *fort/da* play of the signifier-subject-signifier vector or shuttle, the symptom is a bit, a thing that resists this movement and blocks up the hole where the subject disappears or fades. Moreover, if the substitution of meaning is a law, if every subject is prey to the unconscious, the symptom is what constitutes singularity, what makes the exception. For Lacan, the

---

[259] Scarpetta, '*Kafka* de Deleuze et Guattari', *TQ* 63 (autumn 1975), and 'Problèmes du réalisme de G. Lukacs', also *TQ* 63. Scarpetta's book *Brecht et le soldat mort* (Paris, 1979) was a similar debunking of the leftist perspective on literature from this position.

[260] J. Lacan, 'Joyce le symptôme', in J. Aubert (ed.), *Joyce avec Lacan* (Paris, 1987).

relation of literature to language is that the former equivocates between meaning and symptom, between the instance of the letter as metonymy and as 'dead letter', the letter as symptom, or 'litter' and 'letter'; Joyce is the symptom in that he introduces equivocation into language, that he installs an obstinate, unreadable letter within language.

The symptom or exception for *Tel Quel* is not a blockage of language but its opening to infinity. Lacan's approach identifies a blockage because it does not entertain the possibility of an infinite enunciation. Excess or *jouissance* for Lacan is silent, whereas for *Tel Quel* it is reintegrated into language to become an infinite enunciation. Superimposing Lacan's Borromean knot of symbolic, imaginary, and real on Sollers's Trinity, it is evident that while for Lacan the real is a silent, terrible shock, for Sollers is is a heterogenous tissue of meaning. The symptom becomes reformed as an infinity within language, a *débordement* or a surplus, a music. This is made explicit in Sollers's deformation of the term *jouissance* as *jouissens*.[261] The symptom is an exception that cannot (yet) speak.

Joyce and Transphenomenality

Joyce also symptomatically points to *Tel Quel*'s widening of focus to take in religion in the later half of the 1970s, particularly in the special issue 'Obscénité et théologie'.[262] This reiterates the vision of reality or phenomenality as illusion, enounced from the point of the exception. Joyce's thought on Catholicism, analysed in a discussion entitled 'La Trinité de Joyce', is an instance where Sollers's theological interests are applied to a particular text. The beginning of Ulysses is analysed as a conflict between Greek paganism and Jesuit Catholicism. In the former (for the character Mulligan) the mother is a substance, a 'mother nature', that should be venerated. Stephen Dedalus's refusal to kneel in front of his mother's deathbed is indicative, for Sollers, of his will to attain a distance from the matriarchy. Joyce's Catholicism is a refusal of the worship of a pagan, maternal substance, which Sollers's *Paradis* suggests is the condition of society. The linking of mother to nature suggests, moreover, the 'transphenomenal' aspect of *Tel Quel*'s theory in the sense that the maternal is linked to the phenomenal. Language and writing, as a passage to infinity, pass beyond or transgress the order of

[261] See S. Heath's translation of Sollers, 'Joyce et cie', *TQ* 64 (winter 1975), 5.
[262] 'James Joyce, obscénité et théologie', *TQ* 83 (spring 1980).

the phenomenal. What writing enables is access to the invisible, to something outside the order of the phenomenal. For Joyce, the critical experience of Catholicism, specifically of the Trinity, allows this passage in language through the screen of the phenomenal. This is consistent with the constant critique in *Tel Quel* of the visual and the representational, the spectacle, in favour of language and writing.

Again, the body is left behind, as *déchet*, in this passage across and beyond the phenomenal. The notion of 'le Verbe fait chair' is at the same time completely consistent with Kristeva's psychoanalytical theory, where the subject disengages from the maternal fusional dyad through an experience of abjection (in *Ulysses*, Stephen's disgust with the substance of his mother's body) and an identification with an imaginary father. Significantly, this identification is mobilized, for Kristeva, by the voice: 'Cette identification idéale au Symbolique soutenu par l'Autre, mobilise donc davantage la parole que l'image.'[263] The voice or *le souffle* intervenes in the body to transform it into an incarnation of the divine possibilities of language. The stress on the voice at the expense of the image reveals that the critique of the visual in *Tel Quel* is the negative side of an affirmation of language, nevertheless balanced out by Pleynet's analyses of visual art. The materialism of *Tel Quel* is not a fetishization of writing but an affirmation of the irrepressible role of the voice in human relations.

The question of transcendence and the theology that permits it are the essential subjects of the 'Trinité de Joyce' discussions which focus on the latter's inscription of the Trinity in his writings and the 'heresies' that deny the various dogmas of Catholicism. Joyce acts here as a symptom, in the sense that his writing is the platform for a discussion of wider issues that we have extracted as a theory of writing. Sollers's and Houdebine's discussion of Joyce is a productive reading of the text that produces an extension or a reiteration of a theory. Theory is not a set of dogmatic principles, a closure that postulates its only possible opening as a blockage, but a mobile production, a transference that operates from one text to another.

From Joyce to Jazz

This theoretical transference operates also for music, another widening of interests in *Tel Quel* in its final years. While Joyce acts as a nexus for

[263] J. Kristeva, 'Freud et l'amour: Le Malaise dans la cure', in ead., *Histoires d'amour*, 51.

a mobile theory of literary creation, this also programmes a series of other interests. The transphenomenal emphasis shifts from the focus on Joyce to that on jazz in a discussion of 1979. Sollers proposes that writing is in advance of jazz and music since the latter is still tied to the order of the phenomenal in an instrument, even though it strains to escape from it. The voice, a music not tied to an instrument but incarnated in the body, can give access, Sollers affirms, to the invisible.[264] Houdebine, in a further article on Joyce, included in his important book *Excès de langages* (1983) reiterates the dynamic of the phenomenal and the transcendent in terms of *visibilia* and *invisibilia*, while asserting that the symbolic is able to codify the invisible, transform *le vide* into the space of meaning.[265]

In the 'Jazz' discussion, Sollers had emphasized that writing can force a hole in the screen of the phenomenal. This leads to a consideration of the relation between the visual and the aural, important in the context since the decade saw a reassessment of the visual, in the work of Lyotard, among others, after the stress on language of structuralism. *Le trou* can be seen as an exit from the visible to the invisible through the medium of the voice and its music, through the ear. Sollers had stressed the importance of the ear as opposed to the eye for *Paradis*, and of the ear as the opening through which *le verbe* enters the body of the Virgin.[266] 'In his 'mythobiography', Sollers also emphasizes the importance of having a ruptured tympanum for his writing career.[267] While the relevance of the latter two points may be limited, it can be argued that *Paradis* also presents as radical a challenge to the eye, in reading, as it does to the ear. The visual impression of absolute unpunctuated continuity contrasts with the necessity for pauses in the aural appreciation of the text. Furthermore, much of the radicality of *Tel Quel*'s textuality pertains to typographic innovation; the texts of Denis Roche, and even more of Maurice Roche, are an important strand of *Tel Quel*'s textuality. While the affirmation of language as such privileges the ear, the materiality of language being affirmed through music and the voice,

---

[264] P. Sollers, 'Jazz', *TQ* 80 (summer 1979). Other contributions to the review on music include a discussion with John Cage, *TQ* 90 (winter 1981), and an interview with Stockhausen, *TQ* 75 (spring 1978).

[265] J.-L. Houdebine, 'Joyce: Littérature et religion', *TQ* 89 (autumn 1981).

[266] See P. Sollers, 'Vers la notion de *Paradis*', in id., *Théorie des exceptions*, 196: 'Ici l'œil s'efface dans ce dont se souvient l'orielle.' Cf. also 'Comment aller au Paradis', *Art press*, 44 (Jan. 1981).

[267] See Id., *Vision à New York*, 47: 'je me suis donné tout ce mal dans les oreilles pour affirmer ma propre conception du monde par l'oreille'.

this also involves a reinterpretation of the visual aspect of the text. The text is now less a representation, but appears more as a musical score.

Writing and Sex

The theory of the exception in *Tel Quel* is worked across a series of texts, Lautréamont, Joyce, Céline, Sade, Artaud, Balzac, Hugo, Malraux, continuing in *L'Infini*, and constituting an encyclopaedic approach to literature as a whole rather than a focus on a specific canon of writers. The dispersion of *Tel Quel* is also that of its subject-matter. But there is a constant theory at work, less in the sense of a unified body than a procession, another sense of the word theory which Sollers suggests in *Théorie des exceptions*[268] (see Introduction). The analyses are supported in the review by the publication of numerous documents relevant to the texts. In some instances these documents relate to the obscene, as with Joyce's letters and the publication of documents on Sade and their commentary by, among others, the venerated Sade scholar Gilbert Lely.[269] Sade's 'Récapitulations', for example, is a catalogue of masturbations which implicates sexuality and obscenity in the singularity of the writer. It suggests that sex is open to the same infinite permutations as writing. A 'comptabilité de la jouissance', as Pleynet terms it in an accompanying article, is what discourse cannot accept, what appears as obscene.[270] Joyce's letters to Nora are not a simple demand for gratification but a self-conscious filtering of sexuality through writing. Sollers's aptly named article 'Je sais pourquoi je jouis' proposes that the obscene is sexuality as the object of a *savoir*. What Sollers proposes is scandalous is that *jouissance*, and sexuality in general, is not a mystery but subject to a rigorous logic and analysis, to an aesthetic control. The obscene is what cannot be recuperated by a natural form of sexuality, as within the limits of reproduction, therefore putting in doubt the semblance of sexuality as natural and leading to the postulation that sexuality is an effect of language. This is the sense

[268] Id., *Théorie des exceptions*, 12: 'Quant au signification du mot *théorie*, on sait qu'il s'agit aussi d'une ambassade, d'une procession, d'une fête. Un défilé, ou plutôt une danse d'exceptions?'
[269] See J. Joyce, 'Lettres à Nora' and 'Lettres à Martha Fleischmann', *TQ* 83 (spring 1980); D. A. F de Sade, 'Récapitulations', and G. Lely, 'L'Almanach illusoire de M. de Sade', *TQ* 78 (winter 1978); D. A. F. de Sade, 'D'Alembert, Troubadours, Vaudois' and G. Lely, 'Un cahier inédit de D. A. F. de Sade', *TQ* 81 (autumn 1979).
[270] M. Pleynet, 'Sade, des chiffres, des lettres', *TQ* 78 (winter 1978), 36.

in which obscenity is linked to theology, as both imply that what was considered to be outside language, either natural or beyond it, is in fact logically within it, if it is opened up to its infinite potential.

Marcelin Pleynet and Painting

During the 1970s an important current of work is represented by writing on the visual arts, principally painting.[271] Alongside Sollers's *Paradis* and aphoristic articles, and Kristeva's psychoanalytic investigations, Pleynet's critical articles on painting form a trinity of perspectives within the review. In the 1960s Pleynet's essays on the US abstract expressionists, in *Tel Quel* and *Les Lettres françaises* had virtually introduced this current in painting into the French context. But apart from this journalistic activity, linked to exhibitions in Paris, Pleynet's theoretical work on painting is first represented in *L'Enseignement de la peinture* (1971). Like Sollers's *Logiques*, this was intended as an analytic, rational approach to modern painting, a 'système producteur', determined by the Marxist frame of reference which was that of the review at the time.[272] After this systematic, theoretical moment, Pleynet's articles are dispersed in various reviews, *Tel Quel* and *Peinture, cahiers théoriques* among them, and in subject-matter across the history of art. While the earlier theory was centred on Matisse, the later articles, collected in *Art et littérature* (1977) largely concern the American artists again, this time from a more theoretically informed perspective. The latter book also includes articles on the painters of the Supports/Surfaces group, a current within France. In the late 1970s the subject-matter becomes more linked to the activity of art history (although Pleynet is not, properly speaking, an art historian), with essays on Giorgione and Picasso. This activity is continued in *L'Infini*, and since then Pleynet has taken up the Chair of Aesthetics at the École normale supérieure des Beaux-Arts in Paris. His activity is one of an art historian, or writer in aesthetics, while the determining instance of this activity, his status as a poet, lies outside it.

This apparent separation belies the fact that Pleynet's experience of poetic language fuels and determines the writing on painting. This

[271] Articles on sculpture include P. Sollers, 'Via di levare' (on the sculptor Alain Kirili), *TQ* 79 (spring 1979) and Pleynet's article, 'Le Sujet invisible d'Alberto Giacometti', *TQ* 93 (autumn 1982). Sollers has also focused more recently on Rodin and Maillol.

[272] See M. Pleynet, *L'Enseignement de la peinture* (Paris, 1971), 7 and the article (also in the book), 'Contradiction principale, contradiction spécifique', *TQ* 43 (autumn 1970). The book was later repub., in the Seuil 'Points' collection under the title *Système de la peinture* (Paris, 1977), with the Marxist emphasis removed.

relation follows a specific evolution. While in the 1960s poetry had been initially separated from the activity of art criticism, reaching a limit in the systematicity of *L'Enseignment de la peinture*, it was in fact always underwritten by it. In the essay on Matisse in the latter book, Pleynet played on the syllables of the name 'Matisse', 'Ma' and 'tisse', to emphasize the aggressive, castrating activity of Matisse's 'system' of painting and its relevance to the later *papiers collés*.[273] This destructuring of the name and focus on the function of the letter, displacing meaning, derives from the experience of poetry.[274] However, after the moment of theory, the two become more closely linked. In *Rime*, Pleynet includes the inscription 'Col tempo' from a Giorgione painting he had commented on in his essay on Giorgione, published around the same time. The essays on painting lose the emphasis on systematicity and generate themselves from the experience of the subject before the painting.

Pleynet's critical activity can be said to be based in the relation of the writer to the discourse he adopts. While the experience of poetic language is of a subjection to the violent effects of the letter, the experience of writing on painting is one of a place impossible to occupy. In 'La "Folie" thétique', an article on the position of the subject relative to the law, commenting Freud's later works, Pleynet begins: 'Je dirai bien voici la place que je n'occupe pas, ou encore j'occupe la place que je n'occupe pas', and ends the article with a phrase he has cited as describing his position as critic: 'j'y suis de ne pas y être et d'y être je n'y suis pas'.[275] The activity of art historian or art critic is one which Pleynet occupies with a negative consciousness of the impossibility of occupying that place, of occupying any subject position in language. Painting is relevant to this place precisely because it is an extra-linguistic phenomenon which demands to be analysed in language. So Pleynet's true subject-matter in the articles on painting in *Art et littérature* is his own subjective position in relation to the discourse he is adopting, and by extension the subjective relation of the painting subject to language. This can be read explicitly in the essays on painting. In an essay on Motherwell, Pleynet writes: 'Qu'est-ce qui se dit de l'art, sous quelque forme que ce soit, si ce n'est du type de rapport que le porteur de discours entretient avec sa propre langue?'[276] On Cy Twombly, Pleynet

[273] Pleynet, *L'Enseignement de la peinture*, 90.
[274] *Provisoires amants des nègres* (1962) can be read as a meditation on the experience of the evacuation and loss of the name. In *Rime* (1981), however, the name produces meaning: 'd'où vient ce nom et sa semence plaît né/bien être de mon nom' (p. 81).
[275] Id., 'La "Folie" thétique', in id., *Art et littérature*, 19, 30.
[276] Ibid. 282.

writes: 'Du corps à l'écrit et de l'écrit par le corps il y va de cette jouissance et dans cette partie du corps où s'éveille la beauté.'[277] The study of painting necessarily involves a consideration of the body in its erotic relation to writing, foregrounded in the work of Twombly. Since painting is in its form pre-linguistic, this relation will necessarily involve the more archaic pulsions, oral and anal, which constitute a violence towards the subject and towards language, towards the writing subject in language. Pleynet's writing on art, his poetic language on art, while it may borrow the code of art criticism, borrows it conscious of the irreducibility of this violence. It is a writing which is determined by the experience of the 'thetic' madness of language, the necessity of having to occupy a place impossible to occupy. This experience is of poetic language.

Pleynet's writing on art, more present in *Tel Quel* in the 1970s, turns the review into a more widely focused forum of enquiry. This widening, and the closer link in Pleynet's work between criticism and poetry, reflect the development of the review after theory as a fracturing of system and emergence of the singular subject, with his or her experience, as the determining instance.

Textual Singularities

Alongside the theoretical and critical analyses of the literary exception, *Tel Quel* continues to publish creative writing of varying kinds. *Paradis*, the poetry of Pleynet and Risset, texts by Guyotat, Henric, Maurice Roche, Denis Roche, and Severo Sarduy represent the development of writers already associated with the review.[278] Barthes can be associated with these textual singularities to the extent that his work is present less as a contribution to theory or to a project, than as writing, a fact suggested by the more subjectively oriented themes that Barthes writes on. While also continuing to produce unpublished texts of the past, by writers such as Pound, Hölderlin, and Sade, the review also includes excerpts from current works by established writers such as Goytisolo and Burroughs.[279] In terms of literary creation, the review attains a much more heterogenous status during the late 1970s. It publishes

---

[277] M. Pleynet, 'La "Folie" thétique', in id., *Art et littérature*, 305.

[278] See Bibliog. for the 'Collection Tel Quel'.

[279] E. Pound, 'Cantos LXXXVI and LXXXVIII' and F. Hölderlin, 'Fragments inédits', *TQ* 68 (winter 1976); see n. 270 for Sade; J. Goytisolo, 'Variations sur un thème Fessi', *TQ* 65 (spring 1976); W. Burroughs, 'Cities of the Red Night', *TQ* 66 (summer 1976).

literature as literature, rather than as avant-garde project, rejoining in this later period its initial emphases on 'la qualité littéraire', but differently, having traversed the moment of theory. The review also acts as a showcase for new writing from outside. There is a mutual exchange with the *TXT* group, the review publishing texts by the writers Christian Prigent, Valère Novarina, and Jean-Paul Verheggen.[280] In the penultimate issue (93) there is an excerpt, 'Vice', from an early text by Hervé Guibert, suggesting how the review acted generously in promoting up-and-coming writers. There is a considerable interest in women writers, although not associated with *écriture féminine* or Antoinette Fouque's Des femmes publishing house, which was increasingly important. The texts by Viviane Forrester and Sophie Podolski relate to this interest.[281] The 'Collection Tel Quel' continues to bring novels or poetry out into the market; works by Viviane Forrester, Sarduy, Henric, and Maurice Roche are published in the 1970s, as well as the work of Sollers and Pleynet.

These texts appear as singularities, each bearing a specific force related to the subjective style of the writer. It is not possible to look at them in terms of a common approach to writing, although a perverse play with sexuality is a recurrent theme. Given that this is the case, it seems pertinent to focus on the most important, in terms of their exceptional and singular qualities.

The 'Collection Tel Quel' continues to publish the texts of Barthes, although the last one, *La Chambre claire* will be published by Skira in 1980. After *Fragments d'un discours amoureux* (1977), *L'Obvie et l'obtus* (1982), a series of texts on painting and music is published posthumously. In the review, after excerpts from *Roland Barthes par Roland Barthes* in 1975, Barthes's contributions seem to relate exclusively to the subjective orientation of the critic towards the text he is focused on, and more to the activity of writing itself, in a move towards fiction which never arrives at its destination. 'On échoue toujours à parler de ce qu'on aime', published posthumously, concerns Stendhal's relation to Italy; it is an extension, in a sense, of *Fragments d'un discours amoureux*, forming an important current of the analysis of love in the review, with Kristeva's

---

[280] J.-P. Verheggen, 'Vie et mort pornographique de Mme Mao', *TQ* 84 (summer 1980); V. Novarina, 'Naissance de l'homme de V.', *TQ* 85–6 (autumn 1980–winter 1980); C. Prigent, 'Voilà les sexes', *TQ* 86 (winter 1980).

[281] For S. Podolski, see n. 159. V. Forrester, *Vestiges* (Paris, 1978) (in 'Collection Tel Quel') and 'Vestiges', *TQ* 66 (summer 1976).

Histoires d'amour and Pleynet's *Rime*.[282] Both Barthes's and Pleynet's work relate in different ways to the question of the love of the mother. Barthes's focus in the article on Stendhal, 'la sorte d'aphasie qui naît de l'excès d'amour'[283] joins with Kristeva's article ' "Ne dis rien" ' in its theme, if not in its approach. Barthes's writing has become more personal and singular; Stendhal is not present as part of a canon of writers but as a writer loved by the critic. In the article 'Délibération', the last published during Barthes's lifetime, on the writing of the diary, the relation between writing and singularity, and more explicitly between singularity and the generalizing tendency of criticism, is the focus.[284] It is painfully ironic that the final non-posthumous text treats the way the singularity of the writer is inscribed in the writing, a last measure before the disappearance of the writer as a body. But already, identity is in question, the writing of the diary raises the question 'Suis-je?'[285] To turn the diary into a writing, rather than a narcissistic, self-affirming reflection, the subject must disappear in the writing. The last lines of the article are poignant: 'je puis sauver le Journal à la seule condition de le travailler à mort, jusqu'au bout de l'extrême fatigue, comme un Texte à peu près impossible'.[286]

If Barthes's texts seem to lead towards death as the disappearance of the writer, Sollers's *Paradis* opts for a more resurrectionary position, an ascendance. *Paradis* is, as suggested, a prophetic text. This is evident in a number of ways. First of all because it is written from a subject position outside social discourse, commenting on it and traversing it. How is this possible? Essentially because the *je* of the text is not an identifiable narrator or author, but a discursive shifter always placing itself at the genetic point of language. The *je* is not limited to one position but occupies all possible positions in language. This is evident in the permutative conjugations that recur throughout: 'j'y fus j'y étais j'y est je m'y fus j'y serai j'irai bien avant abraham lui-même'[287], 'je suis j'étaisuis je suitais je suirai suijrai suijerrai',[288] 'moi je dis ce que j'ai été chez je suis si je suis était votre cause vous m'aimeriez car c'est de je

---

[282] R. Barthes, 'On échoue toujours à parler de ce qu'on aime', *TQ* 85 (autumn 1980) and in id., *Le Bruissement de la langue* (Paris, 1984).

[283] Barthes, *Le Bruissement de la Langue*, 340.

[284] Id., 'Délibération', *TQ* 82 (winter 1979) and in id., *Le Bruissement de la langue*.

[285] Barthes, *Le Bruissement de la langue*, 412.

[286] Ibid. 413.

[287] Sollers, *Paradis*, 7.

[288] Ibid. 31.

suis que je suis sorti'.[289] Egocentric identity as such, on the other hand, is negated: 'je suis la négation du moi nous'.[290] Identity becomes subject to the permutations of language, so that the specific identity of *je* is evacuated, sacrificed to language, and *je* becomes a generalized subject position within language. As such, it is displaced from the locus of identity to that of language at its point of enunciation, 'je dis'. This position is precisely that of prophecy; it is, as Sollers proposes, an incarnation of the voice in the subject, at the point where, 'ça parla disant parle'.[291] Prophecy is enabled by an incarnation of the voice. The lack of visible punctuation, the continual suspension of the phrase at its end, and its *enchaînement* with the next means that the rhythm of the text has to coincide with the rhythm of the body, its breathing. *Paradis* demands to be read aloud, since the unbroken stream of the writing imposes too great a challenge for the eye alone. The visual terrorism of the text, allowing no space for the reader, necessitates an entry into its vocalization, its aural scansion, which itself effects the incarnation of the writing in the body. The reading of *Paradis* is a complex dialectic between *l'écrit*, writing as a visual fetish and a phenomenal *déchet*, and its ascension through the voice and the body to invisibility and infinity. The structure of *Paradis*, rather than the geometry of *Nombres*, is the trinity of writing/body/voice. The title signifies not only the joyous euphoria of the writing and its ascendant qualities, but also its traversal, through or across language or speech: 'para'—across, 'dis'—speech, or the speaking.

Paradis is also parody, an envelopment of discourse in a parenthetic irony. The prophetic text details the fetishistic limitations of social discourse from a parodic position: 'il s'agit d'exposer une fois pour toutes la merde universelle mise en toute la mort merde régnant sur sa croûte de lui déchirer son voile animé'.[292] An important aspect of this is the discourse on sex, subjected to a rigorous and obscene aggression in the text: 'et elle le prit tendrement pendant qu'il se cabrait chaudement et elle haleta faiblement pendant qu'il suffoquait ardemment et ils se touchèrent s'enlacèrent se mordirent et se confondirent et elles se parcoururent l'enluminure se sucèrent les commissures s'encrémèrent se hurlèrent'.[293] The family structure is also a target, as for Sollers's articles

[289] Ibid. 46.
[290] Ibid. 126.
[291] Sollers, *Improvisations*, 121.
[292] Sollers, *Paradis*, 164.
[293] Ibid. 123.

in *Tel Quel*: 'vouloir une queue à soi pour une femme signifie pour l'homme vouloir être femme à papa or pour être femme à papa il faudrait la perdre en impasse'.[294]

This parodic, paradisiacal text is also paranoid. It is a paranoia inserted in language but not stuck on its affective level. The paranoia is also only a doubling of the generalized paranoia of language and social discourse as such, pointed out by Kristeva. But the text is not only an incessant detailing of social fetishes, it oscillates between sections of parodic intent and epiphanic moments of ascendance, where the writing subject is 'emporté', carried away by the text. The text begins with such a sacrificial vision: 'voix fleur écho des lumières cascade jétée dans le noir chanvre écorcé filet dès le début c'est perdu plus bas je serrais les mains fermées de sommeil et le courant s'engorgea redevint starter le fleuve'.[295] The text is also readable as a dialectic between a temporality of history, of the simulations of social discourse, and a vertical time of ascendance, figured also by the difference between the horizontality of the writing and the physical and musical verticality of the voice.

Paradis has many points of contact with Sollers's theoretical articles and interventions, particularly on religion and sexuality, perhaps the two areas of principal interest, in that society, for Sollers, is inherently and secretly religious, and obsessed with sex to the point of making it a commodity. However, theory, in *Paradis*, is enounced not in the language of system and analysis, discursively, but in popular speech. The critique of exchange, the circulation of subjects in the inferno of social discourse is phrased, for example: 'plus je suis con plus je tourne en rond'.[296] This suggests something about the shift in Sollers's writing from *Paradis* to *Femmes*, which essentially determines the shift from *Tel Quel* to *L'Infini*. It is a move away from the separation of theory and creative writing, so that in *Femmes* we can read criticisms of text, theological meditations, and so on. *Femmes* was perceived as a radical shift in Sollers's writing, from experimentation back to tradition, a renunciation of formal innovation. In many ways this is accurate. *Femmes* is a novel with characters, a semblance of plot structure, punctuation, description. However, there is a continuity at a deeper

[294] Sollers, *Paradis*, 89.
[295] Ibid. 7.
[296] Ibid. 79.
[297] Ibid. 251.
[298] Ibid. 250.
[299] Ibid.

level; the same parodic vision of the social insists, punctuated by moments of epiphanic vision. The writing in *Femmes* is also interspersed with 'theoretical', critical sections which read in a similar way to *Théorie des exceptions*. The suspension of the phrase in *Paradis* is carried over into *Femmes* in the Célinesque technique of three dots at the end of the sentence. What has changed is that the vision of *Paradis* has simply been transposed into a narrative frame. Having been enounced in a euphoric, extreme form it is reinserted into a frame where it has a more internally subversive effect. It is the 'Inferno' to *Paradis*, or perhaps the 'Purgatorio'.

The shift is, moreover, prepared for in *Paradis*. In the final pages the narrator, 'il' walks through a city (Paris?) to the cathedral, where he gives to a priest 'un livre récemment imprimé'.[297] The book is put into a hole in the wall of the cathedral and cemented in. The shift from *je* to *il*, the deposition of the book, as object, in a sacred place, the previous transformation of the book by computer into 'une petite annonce bien chiffrée',[298] an argument with a publisher ('comment ça encore sans ponctuation oh non'[299]), prefigure and prepare for *Femmes*, where the narrator is paying a writer, S., who has written a book without punctuation, to write his book about 'women'. Rather than seeing the shift from *Paradis* to *Femmes* as a renunciation, it is more pertinent to see it as a shift in the mode of presentation. Written form, which in any case was increasingly viewed as a fetishistic limitation, is no longer the vehicle of the vision; form itself, as radicality, becomes represented in a narrative frame, or as object. It is a shift to a postmodern text in that its formal radicality is now represented at the level of content, or representation. By turning the avant-garde text into a 'lettre volée', or 'petite annonce bien chiffrée', a simple message which no one can see, the fixation of the avant-garde is outwitted. *Tel Quel*, almost carried by Sollers's *Paradis*, is implicated here. Rather than becoming in itself, as it obviously has for many people judging it, the epitome of the extreme avant-garde of the 1960s or of the political shifts of the context, either in a positive or negative way, its transformation into *L'Infini* is part of its permanent dissolution of itself.

5 Dissolution

The intellectual context of the late 1970s in France is to a large extent determined by the waning of left-wing radicalism. This 'agony of the French Left' results both in a lassitude due to the loss of a fixed system of values, and an opening-up of new and interesting areas of study. The *nouveaux philosophes*, as they were known, produced a discourse critical of the Marxist and Freudian systems, that hinged into religion. *Tel Quel* engaged in dialogue with some writers of this loose grouping. Other writers took more singular and tangential paths. Foucault, for example, after *Surveiller et punir* (1975), which can be situated as an early 'dissident' text in its critique of penal systems, began the monumental *Histoire de la sexualité*, tied into the more personal concern of homosexuality, in the late 1970s. Although there are no direct links with Foucault at this stage, *Tel Quel* does publish a eulogistic account of Foucault, written by Bernard Sichère, in 1981.[1] A will not to abandon the Left as a reference point seems also to have been a factor influencing a critical turn on the intellectual establishment itself, from a sociological perspective, in the work of Debray and Bourdieu.[2] Lyotard's *La Condition postmoderne* (1980) signals the loss of 'great narratives' and a pessimistic attitude to the present climate, present also in the work of Baudrillard. Within philosophy, there is on the one hand the continuation of the work of Derrida and Deleuze and Guattari, and the rise of an interest in a more restricted form of philosophical enquiry, centred on the review *Critique*, particularly the work of Jacques Bouveresse on analytic philosophy.[3]

Intellectually, the time is one of restriction and pessimism, the tailing-off of the theoretical euphoria of the previous years. This tragic tone is brought into sharp focus at the end of the decade when a series

---

[1] B. Sichère, 'A partir de Michel Foucault', *TQ* 86 (winter 1980).

[2] See R. Debray, *Le Pouvoir intellectuel en France* (Paris, 1979); P. Bourdieu, *La Distinction* (Paris, 1979). Bourdieu and colleagues created the review *Actes de la recherche en sciences sociales* in 1976.

[3] J. Derrida, *Éperons* (Paris, 1978) and *La Vérité en peinture* (Paris, 1978); G. Deleuze and F. Guattari, *Mille plateaux: Capitalisme et Schizophrénie* (Paris, 1980); J. Bouveresse, *Le Mythe de l'intériorité* (Paris, 1976); *Rationalité et cynisme* (Paris, 1982); *Le Philosophe chez les autophages* (Paris, 1984). See also a special issue of *Critique* on Anglo-Saxon philosophy: *Crit.* 399–400 (Aug.–Sept. 1980).

of events seem to mark a sense of ending. Barthes's death in 1980 after a car accident seems to have been partly willed after the loss of his mother. In the same year Lacan dissolved the École freudienne de Paris, precipitating another institutional crisis and marking the end of a psychoanalytical empire. Still in the same year, Louis Althusser, suffering from the mental depression that had haunted him for years, strangled his wife Hélène in their apartment in the École normale supérieure. In September of the next year came the death of Lacan. Other endings were more protracted; Foucault died of the Aids virus in 1985, his history of sexuality incomplete. This sense of a general dissolution of French intellectual life, influenced also by the partial emigration of many figures to the States, is double-edged, however, there is also a sense that theoretical discourses, philosophy in particular, can continue 'as if nothing had happened'. Meanwhile, the 'post' or the 'after' is pursued in different ways. In *Tel Quel*, there is a will to engage the dissolution completely, passing into the infinite after it, while paradoxically affirming at the same time a repetition and an innovative position. The title of a late article by Sollers, 'On n'a encore rien vu' is suggestive of this optimism with regard to the future.[4] This paradox is explained by the curious temporality of which *Tel Quel* is the vehicle. Dissolution becomes the focus of a discourse and a strategy in the review, so that it in a sense dissolves itself through a critical consciousness of its place in the context. The etymological sense of dissolution as analysis implies a critical attitude to the intellectual hegemonies of the time in philosophy and psychoanalysis particularly, still from the point of view of literature as exceptional truth.

DISSOLUTION AS ANALYSIS

Despite the critique of the relevance of the theory of psychoanalysis for the study of literature, it is still affirmed as a privileged site of the singularity of the subject and for its subversion of the discourse of rationalism, by Sollers, for example, in 'Le Cours de Freud'.[5] Lacanian analysis is praised for its continuation of Freud's essential discoveries, against projects of political community and against philosophy: Derrida,

[4] P. Sollers, 'On n'a encore rien vu', *TQ* 85 (autumn 1980) and id., *Improvisations* (Paris, 1991).

[5] Id., 'Le Cours du Freud', *TQ* 79 (spring 1979) and in id., *Théorie des exceptions* (Paris, 1986).

Deleuze and Guattari, Sartre, Merleau-Ponty, Camus. A psychoanalytical conference at Tbilissi, attended by various Lacanian and other
analysts, is perceived as the victory of psychoanalysis over Communism,
finally discovering it. The relation of psychoanalysis to art, however, is
proposed as fundamentally problematic.

It is moreover a dissident psychoanalysis that *Tel Quel* affirms through
its publications. Verdiglione continues to be important as the organizer
of a number of conferences separate from the institutional space of
Lacanian analysis. Addressing the question of psychoanalysis critically
are articles such as Serge Hajlblum's on psychosis, Jean-Jacques
Abrahams's on the 'tape-recorder man' affair publicized by Sartre in *Les
Temps modernes*, where a subject rebelled against his analyst, Max Graf's
'Réminiscences sur le Professeur Freud'.[6] The relation of psychoanalysis
to art is a specific interest of Sollers, particularly concerning Sade and
Joyce, while inspiring other publications in the review. Sollers's discus-
sions with Shoshana Felman on the subject of 'la chose litteraire'
exemplify this interest.[7] Felman and Sollers emphasize how psychoanalysis is dependent on literature. It takes the Oedipus complex from
Sophocles; 'la chose litteraire' informs and undermines psychoanalytical
theory. Literature can analyse psychoanalysis, and this is an operation
Lacan effects in the seminar on 'The Purloined Letter', according to
Felman. Similarly, if Joyce is a symptom, it is because 'la chose litteraire'
(the expression suggesting the unbearable, repressed status of literature
for the discourse of analysis) is a symptom of psychoanalysis. Stuart
Schneidermann, in 'Lacan et la littérature', also notes that 'la lecture
lacanienne de Freud est un détournement de textes'.[8] Lacan's reading
of literary texts is in a sense affirmed within his theory as a subversion
of theory, a hole in theory, presenting the possibility of a reading of
Lacan's reading of literature against his theory, an operation conducted
in Felman's book *La Folie et la chose litteraire* (1980). There is at the same
time an affirmation of Lacan and Freud, a Lacan within Lacanianism
and a Freud within the Freudian corpus, and a critique of psychoanalytical theory inasmuch as it is a rationality that excludes the madness

---

[6] Serge Hajlblum, 'Propriété et possession', *TQ* 63 (autumn 1975); J.-J. Abrahams,
'L'Homme au magnétophone', *TQ* 65 (spring 1976); M. Graf, 'Réminiscences sur le
Professeur Freud', *TQ* 88 (summer 1981).

[7] S. Felman, 'La Chose littéraire, sa folie, son pouvoir', *TQ* 80-1, (summer–autumn
1979).

[8] S. Schneidermann, 'Lacan et la littérature', *TQ* 84 (summer 1980), 46. See also id.,
Jacques Lacan: The Death of an Intellectual Hero (Cambridge, Mass., 1983), trans. P. E. Dauzat
as *Jacques Lacan, maître Zen?* (Paris, 1986).

of the literary thing. Literature analyses or dissolves psychoanalysis, itself a dissolution, and the institutional dissolution of the EFP by Lacan, welcomed by Sollers, reflects that of *Tel Quel*.

Theology after Theory

The time after theory, after the agony of the Left, is partly explored in *Tel Quel* in an interest in religion and theology. The relevance of theology is determined by historical as well as literary factors. Philosophy was seen not to have dissolved the question of the divine, and, having repressed this question, it implicitly rests upon it while resisting it. Theology appeared as the most obscene or scandalous emphasis with regard to the philosophical hegemony of the time. At the same time, theology is relevant in that its logic is seen to inform that of literary creation at a fundamental level. This re-emergence of religion resulting from an analysis of the bases of philosophy was an aspect that emerged particularly from the work of the *nouveaux philosophes*, writers such as Jean-Marie Benoist and Bernard Henri-Lévy, who were viewed with suspicion by the philosophical establishment. *Tel Quel* engages in a fruitful dialogue with these writers, affirming its position critical of this establishment.[9] This division is represented to an extent in the context, between the publishers Grasset, run by Lévy, and Gallimard, and the more theoretically and philosophically oriented Minuit and Seuil. The 'philosophical hegemony' identified by Sollers, Lévy, and Benoist, is represented by the restrictive interest in analytic philosophy of Bouveresse, Deleuze and Guattari, and Lyotard, all published by Minuit, and all the target of criticism in *Tel Quel*. Politically, as a strategic gesture, Sollers affirms the Pope as a figure, emerging from within a Communist country, coming to the head of the Catholic church, as the index of a historical crisis, and as 'le moins policier au niveau de la surveillance de l'exception possible'.[10]

At the level of content, *Tel Quel*'s interest in religion is also determined by its recognition of the fundamental violence inherent in any social link. Philippe Nemo's analysis of the book of Job, 'Job et le mal radical', is a prefatory statement of this interest linked to the emergence of the *nouveaux philosophes* or a philosophy of dissidence.[11] Later, *Tel Quel*

---

[9] J.-M. Benoist, 'La Normalisation', *TQ* 84 (summer 1980) and 'Une nouvelle critique . . .', *TQ* 85 (autumn 1980); B.-H. Lévy, 'La Preuve du pudding', *TQ* 77 (autumn 1978); id., 'C'est la guerre?' and 'Discours au mémorial', *TQ* 82 (winter 1979).

[10] P. Sollers, 'Pourquoi je suis si peu religieux', in id., *Improvisations*, 135.

supports and questions the work of René Girard, who proposes that society is essentially persecutory, founded as a result of the exclusion of an inherent violence and the sacrifice of a *bouc émissaire* or scapegoat.[12] His books *Des choses cachées depuis la fondation du monde* (1978), and *Le Bouc émissaire* (1982), elaborate his system and reiterate it in a similar way to Sollers's work. Significantly, Catholicism and the figure of Christ particularly are read by Girard as a way out of this fatality, a non-sacrificial theology. This has a certain resonance, as Sollers himself points out, with the vision of Christ as an incarnation, 'une parole vivante' short-circuiting the logic of *le semblant*.[13]

It is not only Catholicism that is the focus of *Tel Quel*'s interest in religion, but the other religions: Buddhism, Islam, and Judaism. Monotheism, however, is criticized, particularly by Sollers in the key text 'Pourquoi je suis si peu religieux'. Where religion is a focus it is the more marginal moments that come to the fore, from an analytic position. Martine Liebovici, for example, publishes a long study on 'La Position féminine dans la Bible';[14] Sarduy's novel *Maitreya* (1980) thematically addresses Indian mysticism; there are articles on Gnosticism, Judaism, Zen Buddhism, and considerations on Islamic mysticism by Jean-Marie Benoist.[15] The position remains analytic and non-partisan, and for the most part engaging with religion as text and in its relation to art.

Intellectual Self-consciousness and Dissolution

As with the shift to Maoism in 1971 and the shift away from Maoism in 1976, the end of *Tel Quel* is logically already programmed into its discourse. The objective reason for this dissolution is Sollers's writing of the novel *Femmes*, which was refused by Seuil. Its publication by Gallimard justifies the shift of the review, under a different name, to

---

[11] P. Nemo, 'Job et le mal radical', *TQ* 70–71/3, (summer–autumn 1977).

[12] See R. Girard, 'Quand les choses commenceront', *TQ* 78–9 (winter 1978–spring 1979).

[13] See Sollers, 'Pourquoi je suis si peu religieux', in id., *Improvisations*, 121.

[14] M. Liebovici, 'La Position féminine dans la Bible', *TQ* 74–6 (winter 1977–summer 1978).

[15] Gnosticism: see M. Olender, 'Le Système gnostique de Justin', *TQ* 82 (winter 1979); M. Tardieu, 'Épiphanie contre les gnostiques', *TQ* 88 (summer 1981). Judaism: M. Halter, 'Entretien', *TQ* 82; 'Sepher Yetsira, traduction de B. Dubourg'; B. Dubourg, 'L'Hébreu du Nouveau Testament', *TQ* 91 (spring 1982). Zen Buddhism: Dôgen, 'La Fonction-lune', *TQ* 94 (winter 1982). J.-M. Benoist, 'La Normalisation', *TQ* 84 (summer 1980).

Gallimard's subsidiary Denoël and later to Gallimard itself. Seuil being co-proprietors of the name *Tel Quel*, the name of the review is changed to the fitting *L'Infini*. Despite a change in the internal structure of the review, with Sollers named as 'directeur' alone, there is little difference between *L'Infini* and *Tel Quel* in its last period. The subtitle 'Littérature/Philosophie/Art/Science/Politique' remains the same; so do the range of articles and some of the contributors. *Tel Quel* does not so much end as change its name; its dissolution is not so much an event as a permanent state. But the closure of the review is prepared for by a consideration of its place in the context. Sollers's articles 'On n'a encore rien vu' and 'Le GSI' constitute an explicit self-consciousness that makes a distinction between 'Tel Quel' as an avant-garde, theoretical journal, and 'Tel Quel' as a mechanism of permanent analysis and dissolution.[16] On one side there is the avant-garde periodical that, for Sollers, was caught in the illusion of a belief in a social revolution, that was the illusion of all the avant-gardes of the twentieth century: Surrealism, Futurism, that the crisis of the West could be turned into a state of non-crisis. *Tel Quel* had traversed the adventure of the avant-garde in this sense. The avant-garde, and the group, are already a limitation on the possibilities of the exception. The link between social revolution and artistic revolution is illusory because it postulates a continuity between the logic of the exception and that of society, of the *polis*, which the analyses of *Tel Quel* propose as repressive: 'Mais il s'agit de revenir sans cesse sur des exceptions. Nous voulons éclairer l'histoiredu côté de l'exception et pas du côté de la règle ou de la communauté.'[17]

There is a self-conscious critique of a *Tel Quel* as avant-garde and revolutionary group that projects the 'new' *Tel Quel* into a different space. At the same time, however, Sollers emphasizes a continuity, an insistence, in *Tel Quel*, on the experience of literature. *Tel Quel* at the same time revolves and repeats, insists. The paradox of change and insistence is explained by a different way of looking at temporality. *Tel Quel* cannot be interpreted through the temporality of the book, of the text, as it is a periodical that exists in a historical dimension; it is always non-closed, open to its next issue. It disturbs an approach that identifies it as a closure. Neither, however, can it be read exclusively through a historical temporality in terms of events, with revolutionary and

---

[16] Sollers, 'On n'a encore rien vu', *TQ* 85 (autumn 1980) and in id., *Improvisations*; id., 'Le GSI', *TQ* 86 (winter 1980).

[17] Id., *Improvisations*, 181.

strategic turns, because the repetition and insistence of writing, either of
Paradis or the experience of Artaud, Bataille, Sade, or Dante, remains
constant and undermines the linearity of this eventual history. The
temporality of the book is undermined by that of history, which is
undermined by the temporality of literary creation. The publication of
Paradis in serial form in the review since 1974 makes this paradoxical
temporality explicit.

In the article 'Le GSI' Sollers approaches a more developed perspective on *Tel Quel*'s place in the context, in discourse. Sollers's proposition
in 'Le GSI' is that *Tel Quel, Paradis*, 'Sollers' constitute a space outside
the predictable circulation of discourses, that programmed by the
organism, invented by Sollers, called the GSI, the 'Gestion des surfaces
imprimées' or 'Giration du semblant illimité'.[18] The fictional 'GSI' that
may seem to fall within the predictable context of conspiracy theory, is
in fact a more interesting notion, an ironic fiction that proposes a view
of the real. The programming of discourses or *le semblant*, is total, with
a few exceptions. *Tel Quel* falls outside the circuit of the GSI, Sollers
proposes, for the following reasons. First, it is not identifiable in a fixed
place: 'l'expérience est telle qu'elle désoriente toute assignation de
place'.[19] Secondly, *Tel Quel* is in a situation of 'permanent dissolution',
not only in the sense that its committee members are constantly
dropping out, but also in its continuing analysis of literature, its *dépense*
of discourses. Thirdly, *Tel Quel* reproduces the memory of discourses, of
the GSI—that is, it desacralizes all the positions of its own discourse in
a traversal of all discourses, including that which is fundamental,
religion: '*Tel Quel* suit une évolution parallèle à celle de la constitution
de la mémoire GSI.'[20] This involves an experience of fiction in which
the place of the subject is exceeded, but which does not opt for
psychosis, madness, a position predicted by the GSI. Permanent dissolution is a more radical proposition. Evidently the publication of *Paradis*
is an important aspect of this displacement, but Sollers also recognizes
Lacan, Pascal, Lautréamont, Joyce as exceptions who might escape the
closed circuit of discourse, of *le semblant*. The time of literary creation,
its excess and *dépense* is a dissolution that falls outside the historical time
of the circulation of discourses; a *punctum temporis* which repeats and
insists.

This is a utopian and paranoiac view of the intellectual context and
the place of *Tel Quel*, but one which it is hard to disagree with. The

---

[18] P. Sollers., 'Le GSI', *TQ* 86. 10.   [19] Ibid.   [20] Ibid. 11.

responses of critics to *Tel Quel*, which are almost without exception predictable and programmable, seem to justify the view that its place is unidentifiable and misunderstood. Its dissolution is ultimately linked to the creative process of writing. Seuil can be seen to be less interested once the review left behind the discourse of theory to pursue its dissolution, after the disappearance of its umbrella figures Barthes and Lacan. Permanent dissolution is also in a sense a survival, and it is not surprising that the demise of *Tel Quel* coincides roughly with the death of one of its principal allies, Roland Barthes, and that of Lacan, with whom it had always entertained a mutually helpful but suspicious relationship. That this dissolution is permanent, not the burial of a corpse but its survival, is assured by the continuation of *L'Infini*, and of the writing of *Paradis*.

L'Infini

L'Infini's place in the context is similar to that of *Tel Quel*, affirming literature as a value higher than the philosophical, sociological, or theoretical. It has a vital role in publishing a wide range of texts from the history of literature, emphasizing their exceptional and radical status in the present. For example, the second issue of the review is a concentration on Dante, while an issue of 1989 focuses on Voltaire.[21] Other key publications include Goethe, the mathematician Cantor, Bataille, F. Scott Fitzgerald, Anaïs Nin, Freud, and Pasolini. It also has a more open approach than *Tel Quel* to contemporary foreign writers, publishing and analysing work by Kundera (special issue in 1984), Nabokov (special issue in 1988), Norman Mailer, Philip Roth, V. S. Naipaul, Edmund White, Léonardo Sciascia. In the French context, among its contributors are a number who were present also in the pages of *Tel Quel*: Pleynet, Kristeva, Risset, Guyotat, Sarduy, Sibony, Muray, Henric, Scarpetta. A group of contributors specific to *L'Infini*, whose fictional works were also published in the 'Collection L'Infini' run by Sollers, include Alain Nadaud, Pierre Bourgeade, Marc-Édouard Nabe, Dominique Rolin, Bernard Wallet, Emmanuel Moses, Gabriel Matz-neff. Bernard Wallet will organize a special issue on literature and eroticism in 1986, while Alain Nadaud organizes a special issue in 1987 subtitled 'Où en est la littérature?', publishing the work of many of the important writers of the present, such as Euqère Savitzkaya, François

---

[21] 'Dante', *L'Infini*, 2 (spring 1983); 'Voltaire', ibid. 25 (spring 1989).

Bon, Olivier Rolin, Marie Redonnet, François Rivière, and Danièle Sallenave.[22] In 1989 *L'Infini* published a special issue entitled 'Génération '89', a platform for writers of the new generation that was crucial in the context.[23] Sollers's *Paradis II* is published, again in serial form, up to 1987, accompanied by a series of important discussions between Sollers and Franz de Haes which focus for the most part on theology. After then Sollers's publications are mostly culled from his journalistic interventions in places like *Le Monde* and *Le Nouvel Observateur*, on writers such as Voltaire, Bossuet, Hemingway, Guy Debord, Parmenides, artists such as Rodin, Warhol, Courbet, and subjects such as 'la nouvelle censure' and the actress Glenn Close. This exhaustive cataloguing of exceptions, Sollers proposes, is moving towards an encyclopaedic project that traverses the whole history of literature.

L'Infini is almost totally dominated by Sollers. To this extent the tension that characterized the *Tel Quel* group, between the perspectives of Sollers, Kristeva, Pleynet, and others, a tension between individuals and ideas, is absent from *L'Infini*. *L'Infini* has not had to traverse the various crises of modernism and of theory that was the adventure of *Tel Quel*. It does not have the ideologies of structuralism, formalism, Marxism, Maoism to set up and dissolve. Its character is determined by a time after theory in literature, where theory itself has become displaced by a celebration of singularity and the exception in literature. *L'Infini* also exists in a period that has not seen the ideological swings and eruptions, centred on 1968, of the time of *Tel Quel*. The context of *L'Infini* is that of the spectacle, the dominance of the media, particularly visual, and of information; the ideological dominance of the media is in some ways coincidental with the creation of the review. It is published in a context of postmodernity, a context in which, as Lyotard puts it, the 'great narratives' have ceased to function. In postmodernity, reference and meaning become submerged in a proliferation of seductive, superficial visual systems, so that *L'Infini*'s assertion of the exceptional truth of literature is a constant and singular voice of dissent, sometimes accompanied by a parodic discourse within and on the discourse of the spectacle, as in Sollers's novels and his interventions in the media. This voice could only come into being, however, through the *traversée* of the time of theory of *Tel Quel*.

[22] 'Où en est la littérature?', *L'Infini*, 19 (summer 1987).
[23] 'Génération '89', *L'Infini*, 26 (summer 1989), under the responsibility of F. Berthet.

Chronology

1957–1959: Sollers meets Hallier, Huguenin, Coudol, Boisrouvray, Baudry, Matignon, Thibaudeau.

1957   Sollers's 'Le Défi' published by Seuil, praised by Mauriac.

Barthes, *Mythologies*.

1958   Sollers's *Une curieuse solitude* published, praised by Mauriac and Aragon.

Lévi-Strauss, *Anthropologie structurale*.

1960   Formation of review. 'Déclaration'. Sollers, 'Sept points sur Robbe-Grillet'. Publications by Ponge, Artaud, Simon, Pinget.

Huguenin and Matignon leave committee. Sollers and Hallier meet G. Bataille, who gives them a series of lectures from 1950 to publish. Contacts with Breton and Céline.

Sartre, *Critique de la raison dialectique*. Godard, *A bout de souffle*.

Death of Camus. 'Manifeste des 121'.

1961   Publications by Ponge, Bataille, Artaud, Robbe-Grillet, Pound, Hölderlin, Borges. Barthes, 'La Littérature aujourd'hui'. Sollers, *Le Parc*.

Affirmative letter by Sollers to Pleynet on Pleynet's poetry. Thibaudeau joins committee.

Foucault, *Histoire de la folie*. Ricardou, *L'Observatoire de Cannes*. Robbe-Grillet and Resnais, *L'Année dernière à Marienbad*.

Rauschenberg exhib. in Paris. *Communications* review launched. Death of Merleau-Ponty. OAS active in Paris.

1962   Publications by Pleynet, Michaux, Bataille, D. Roche, Eco, Butor. Pleynet, *Provisoires amants des nègres*.

Deguy and Ricardou join committee. Michel Maxence joins and leaves committee. Coudol leaves committee. Hallier leaves committee after attempting to gain complete control. 'Collection Tel Quel' begun with D. Roche, *Récits complets*.

Lévi-Strauss, *La Pensée sauvage*. Derrida, Introduction to Husserl's *L'Origine de la géometrie*. Deleuze, *Nietzsche et la philosophie*. Bataille, *Les Larmes d'Éros*.

Contacts between Derrida and Sollers. Death of Bataille. OAS *plastiquages*. Referendum in Algeria. Demonstrations in France.

1963   Publications by Pleynet, Olson, Faye, Baudry, D. Roche, Boulez. Robbe-Grillet, 'La Littérature aujourd'hui'. Sollers, 'Logicus Solus', 'Logique de la fiction'. Foucault, 'Le langage à l'infini'.

Pleynet, D. Roche, Faye, Baudry join committee. Deguy leaves.

Conference at Cérisy on 'Une littérature nouvelle?', chaired by Foucault. Foucault, 'Distance, aspect, origine'. Special issue of *Critique* on Bataille. Foucault, *Naissance de la clinique, Raymond Roussel*. Robbe-Grillet, *Pour un Nouveau Roman*.

First issue of review *L'Herne* (on Céline).

1964   Publications by Boulez, Sanguineti. Barthes, 'Littérature et signification'. Pleynet, 'La Pensée contraire', 'L'Image du sens'. Sollers, 'Pour un nouveau roman'. Barthes, 'Éléments de sémiologie'. Deleuze, *Proust et les signes*. Althusser, 'Freud et Lacan'.

Lacan founds EFP, begins seminar at ENS. *Socialisme ou barbarie* and *Arguments* reviews fold.

Evacuation of French troops from Algeria. Brezhnev replaces Krushchev in USSR.

1965   Special issues on Artaud, Dante.

Sollers, *Drame*. Pleynet, *Comme*. Todorov, *Théorie de la littérature*.

Barthes, 'Drame, poème, roman' (on Sollers). Althusser, *Pour Marx, Lire le Capital*. Picard, *Nouvelle critique ou nouvelle imposture?* Pinget, *Quelqu'un*. Perec, *Les Choses*. Ricardou, *La Prise de Constantinople*. Derrida, 'De la grammatologie'.

Julia Kristeva arrives in Paris. Sollers and Baudry at Lacan's seminar ('L'Objet de la psychanalyse'). Sollers meets Lacan. *Mercure de France* review folds.

Mao, *Little Red Book*.

1966   Pleynet, 'Les Problèmes de l'avant-garde'. Derrida, 'Freud et la scène de l'écriture'. Sollers, 'Littérature et totalité', at Barthes's seminar at École pratique. Thibaudeau, *Ouverture*. M. Roche, *Compact*. Genette, *Figures* I. Barthes, *Critique et vérité*.

Conference on Sade. Boisrouvray leaves committee. Pleynet in USA lecturing on Lautréamont. Sollers meets Kristeva.

Lacan, *Écrits*. Foucault, *Les Mots et les choses*. Benveniste, *Problèmes de linguistique générale*.

Review *Cahiers pour l'analyse* launched at ENS, publishes Althusser, Lacan, Derrida. Nadeau launches *La Quinzaine littéraire*.

Lacan's seminar: 'Pour une logique du fantasme'.

Chinese Cultural Revolution.

1967   Special issue on Sade. Sollers, 'Le Toit'. Kristeva, 'Pour une sémiologie des paragrammes'. Sollers, 'Programme'.

Pleynet, *Lautréamont*. Derrida, *L'Écriture et la différence*. Sollers, 'La Science de Lautréamont'.

Dialogues with PCF review *La Nouvelle Critique*. Contacts with PCF writers Daix, Houdebine, Scarpetta, Henric. Split in committee at end of year, Faye leaves. Risset and Rottenberg join. Adoption of 'Science/Littérature' subtitle. Marriage of Sollers and Kristeva.

Derrida, *De la grammatologie*. Barthes, *Système de la mode*. Debord, *La Société du spectacle*.

Student unrest in Strasbourg. Lacan's seminar: 'L'Acte psychanalytique'. Death of Che Guevara.

1968   Derrida, 'La Pharmacie de Platon'. Baudry, 'Freud et la "création" littéraire'. Kristeva, 'Distance et anti-représentation'. Publications by Bataille, Baudry, Goux. Sollers, *Logiques*, *Nombres*. *Tel Quel*, *Théorie d'ensemble*.

Review supports PCF policy on 1968 and no comment on Prague Spring. Groupe d'études théoriques created. Polemic over refusal to join Union générale d'écrivains.

Conference at Cluny with *La Nouvelle Critique*. Althusser, *Lénine et la philosophie*. Poulantzas, *Pouvoir politique et classes sociales*. Deleuze, *Différence et répétition*. Baudrillard, *Le Système des objets*.

Lacan's seminar, 'D'un autre à l'Autre'. *Scilicet* review created.

In May student demonstrations erupt in Paris. Sorbonne is occupied, creation of occupying councils. Unrest spreads after university cleared at end of May. General strike. Strike called off after negotiations between govt. and CGT union. University of Vincennes opens in Sept. with Foucault as director. Occupied immediately.

In August Prague Spring uprising crushed by Communist forces.

1969   Publications by Guyotat, Genet, Burroughs. Sollers, 'Survol/Rap-ports(Blocs)/Conflits'. Starobinski, 'Le Texte dans le texte'. Kriste-va, 'L'Engendrement de la formule'. Kristeva, *Séméiotiké*.

Polemic with Faye over letter in *L'Humanité* accusing Derrida of complicity with Heidegger's alleged Nazi sympathies. Sollers and Kristeva occupy office of Flacelière when Lacan's seminar at ENS is suspended.

Deleuze, *Logique du sens*. Foucault, *L'Archéologie du savoir*. Blanchot, *L'Entretien infini*. Cixous, *Dedans*. Simon, *La Bataille de Pharsale*.

Reviews *TXT* and *Cinéthique* created. Lacan's seminar at ENS suspended, moves to Law Faculty building near Panthéon. Lacan lectures at Vincennes where the students heckle him. Demonstra-tions and occupations at Vincennes. *Cahiers pour l'analyse* folds and some of its members join the militant Gauche prolétarienne.

Pompidou elected President. Lin Piao designated Mao's successor.

1970   Publications by Mao. Derrida, 'La Double Séance'. Sollers, 'Lénine et le matérialisme philosophique'. Baudry, *La 'Création'*. Kristeva and Marc Devade join committee. Review *Peinture, cahiers théoriques* created by artists of the Supports/Surfaces group. Polemics with *Change* over accusations of early right-wing tendencies by Faye in *La Gazette de Lausanne*. Leclaire's Department of Psychoana ysis at Vincennes criticized in *Tel Quel*. Addition of 'Philosophie/Po-litique' to subtitle. Guyotat, *Éden, Éden, Éden*. Polemic over its censure; a petition protesting against it is circulated and published in *Tel Quel*. Second Cluny colloquium, 'Littérature et idéologie'. Kristeva and Derrida criticized by members of *Change* and *Action poétique* at the conference.

Barthes, *L'Empire des signes*.

Review *Poétique* created by Todorov, Cixous, Richard, Genette. *Nouvelle Revue de psychanalyse* created. Lacan's seminar is 'D'un discours qui ne serait pas du semblant'. Judith Miller expelled from Vincennes for subversion. Further occupations. Foucault gives inaugural lecture at Collège de France.

US offensives in Vietnam.

1971   Kristeva, 'Matière, sens, dialectique'. Sollers, 'Sur la contradic-tion'. Pleynet, 'Lautréamont politique'. Special issue on Surrealism and Neo-Surrealism. Special issue on Roland Barthes.

Barthes, *Sade, Fourier, Loyola*. Sollers, *Lois*. Pleynet, *L'Enseignement de la peinture*.

Polemic with A. Jouffroy over Surrealism. *Tel Quel* signs manifesto with *Cinéthique* and *Cahiers du cinéma* against review *Positif*, but criticizes *Cinéthique* for its criticism of PCF. Mouvement de Juin 1971 created. Offices of *Tel Quel* covered in Maoist slogans. Pleynet criticizes 'posthumous reconciliation' of Breton and Aragon. *La Nouvelle Critique* publishes a note criticizing the review for its addition of 'Philosophie/Politique' subtitle and critique of Aragon. *Tel Quel* replies, defending its position. Sollers publishes letter in *Le Monde* protesting against interdiction of Macciocchi's *De la Chine* at 'Fête de *L'Humanité*'. Intervenes at festival. November issue announces formal break with PCF. Review declared in crisis. Groupe d'études théoriques suspended. Criticism of *Cinéthique*'s dogmatism. Thibaudeau and Ricardou leave committee.

Lyotard, *Discours, figure*. Sartre, *L'Idiot de la famille*. Macciocchi, *De la Chine*.

Lacan's seminar: 'Ou pire'.

Lin Piao dies in an air crash while ostensibly fleeing to the USSR. China admitted to United Nations.

1972   Special issue on 'La Pensée chinoise'. D. Roche, *Le Mécrit*. Derrida, *La Dissémination*. Sarduy, *Cobra*.

Polemical interchange in review between Sichère and Boons over question of ideology. Derrida's discussions with Houdebine and Scarpetta published in *Positions*. Conference on Artaud and Bataille. Review *Art press* launched.

Deleuze and Guattari, *Anti-œdipe*. Review *Digraphe* launched by Jean Ristat. *Les Lettres françaises* folds.

Lacan's seminar: 'Encore'.

Gauche prolétarienne dissolved. Death of Pierre Overney at an anti-government demonstration. Alliance between PCF and PS (Parti socialiste). Nixon vists China.

1973   Special issue on Artaud and Bataille. Special issue on Joyce. Sollers, *H*. Barthes, *Le Plaisir du texte*. Pleynet, *Stanze*.

Denis Roche leaves committee. Kristeva in the USA. Criticism of Hallier's *La Cause du peuple*, which ironically recalls early split with *Tel Quel*. Review condemns fascist coup in Chile and PCF–PS alliance in France. Texts fictionalize Overney's death. 'Psychanalyse et politique' conference in Milan, organized by Verdiglione.

Althusser, *Réponse à John Lewis*. Lacan, *Séminaire*, xi; *Télévision*. Foucault, *Moi, Pierre Rivière . . . .*

Lacan's seminar: 'Les Non-dupes errent'.

End of Vietnam war. Watergate scandal. *Coup d'état* in Chile. Allende assassinated. Strikes in France at Lip factories. Gains for Right in legislative elections.

1974   Sollers, 'Sur le matérialisme'. Kristeva, 'La Révolution du langage poétique'. Special issue on Sollers. First instalment of *Paradis*. Special issue on China.

Sollers, *Sur le matérialisme*. Kristeva, *La Révolution du langage poétique*. Macciocchi, *Pour Gramsci*. Kristeva, *Des chinoises*.

Editorials criticize Derrida and Althusser. In Apr. and May, Sollers, Kristeva, Pleynet, Barthes, and F. Wahl visit China, invited by embassy. On return letters in *Le Monde* by Barthes and Wahl. Sollers affirms 'Criticize Confucius' campaign in China. Verdiglione conference: 'Psychanalyse et sémiotique'.

Althusser, *Éléments d'autocritique*. Derrida, *Glas*. Irigaray, *Speculum de l'autre femme*. Solzhenitsyn, *The Gulag Archipelago*.

Lacan made director of Vincennes Psychoanalysis Dept.; seminar is 'RSI'.

Antoinette Fouque and others of *Psych et po* group create 'Des femmes' publishing house.

Coup d'état in Portugal. Giscard elected President. Legislation on abortion. Fascist violence in Italy.

1975   Sollers, 'Lettre de Sade'. Pleynet, 'A la mère'. Baudry leaves committee, having published nothing since 1972.

Barthes, *Roland Barthes par Roland Barthes*. Deleuze and Guattari, *Kafka*. Foucault, *Surveiller et punir*. Glucksmann, *La Cuisinière et le mangeur d'hommes*. Miller, *Les Pousses-au-jouir du Maréchal Pétain*. Lacan, *Séminaires*, xx: *Encore*. Cixous and Clément, *La Jeune Née*. Derrida, 'Le Facteur de la vérité'. Review *Actes de la recherche en sciences sociales* created by P. Bourdieu and others.

Lacan's seminar: 'Le Sinthome'.

In April Khmer Rouge invade Cambodia.

1976   Sollers, 'Joyce et cie'. 'D'où viennent les enfants?' Pleynet, 'La "folie" thétique'. 'Crise du rationalisme'. Kristeva, *Polylogue*. Review affirms G. Miller, criticizes Glucksmann, Lardreau, and Jambet. In discussions with Clavel, Sollers shows his disillusionment with Marxism and 'tragedy' in China. Letters by Sollers in

Le Monde. Verdiglione conference 'La Folie'. Sollers's first trip to USA, meets De Kooning. Kristeva practising psychoanalysis.

Foucault, *Histoire de la sexualité*, i. Derrida, 'La Carte postale'. Jambet and Lardreau, *L'Ange*. B.-H. Lévy, dossier on 'Les Nouveaux Philosophes'.

Lacan's seminar: 'L'Insu qui sait . . .'.

Zhou Enlai dies. Rise of Gang of Four. Riots in Tiananmen Square. Sept.: Death of Mao. Oct.: Arrest and trial of Gang of Four. 22nd Congress of PCF; 'dictatorship of proletariat' dropped.

1977   Publications by Barthes, Kristeva, Sollers. Special issue on the USA.

Barthes, *Fragments d'un discours amoureux*. Pleynet, *Art et littérature*. Sollers and Clavel, *Délivrance*.

Verdiglione conference on 'La Violence'.

Article by Sollers in *Le Monde* on B.-H. Lévy's *La Barbarie à visage humain*.

Glucksmann, *Les Maîtres penseurs*. Irigaray, *Ce sexe qui n'en est pas un*.

Lacan's seminar: 'Le Moment de conclure'.

1978   Special issue on 'Recherches féminines'. Special issue on dissidence. Part special issue on Pleynet.

Verdiglione conference on dissidence.

Macciocchi, *Après Marx, avril*. Derrida, *Éperons, La Vérité en peinture*. Girard, *Des choses cachées depuis la fondation du monde*.

Lacan's seminar: 'La Topologie et le temps'.

1979   Publications by Girard, Sade, Muray, S. Felman, Sollers. 'L'Auguste Comte', 'Jazz', 'Pourquoi je suis si peu religieux'. Pleynet publishes books on painting. Barthes, *Sollers écrivain*.

Rottenberg leaves committee, having published nothing since 1971. Subtitle 'Art' added.

Bourdieu, *La Distinction*. Debray, *Le Pouvoir intellectuel en France*.

1980   Barthes, 'Délibération'. Sollers, 'Socrate en passant', 'Le Pape', 'On n'a encore rien vu'. Special issue on Joyce.

Kristeva, *Pouvoirs de l'horreur*. Pleynet, *Le Voyage en Chine*. Eulogistic note after death of Barthes. Sollers welcomes dissolution of EFP.

Sollers, Benoist, and Lévy, in *Tel Quel*, criticize 'hegemony of philosophy' centred on *Critique*.

Barthes, *La Chambre claire*. Deleuze and Guattari, *Mille plateaux*. Lyotard, *La condition postmoderne*. Special issue of *Critique* on analytic philosophy. Lacan dissolves EFP. Barthes dies in hospital. Louis Althusser strangles his wife at ENS and is committed without a trial. Papal visit.

1981   Sollers, 'Le GSI', 'Pourquoi j'ai été chinois', 'Histoire de femme'. Publications by Muray on Balzac, Houdebine on Joyce.

Sollers, *Paradis*. Pleynet, *Rime*. Muray, *Céline*. Baudrillard, *Simulations*. Debray, *Critique de la raison politique*. Clément, *Vies et légendes de Jacques Lacan*. Lacan, *Séminaire, iii*. B.-H. Lévy, *L'Idéologie française*. Sept.: death of Lacan.

1982   Sollers, 'Je sais pourquoi je jouis', 'L'Assomption'. Special issues on Picasso, psychoanalysis. Publications by Malraux.

Barthes, *L'Obvie et l'obtus*. Girard, *Le Bouc émissaire*. Levinas, *Éthique et infini*.

1983   Final issue: publications by Muray on Hugo, Houdebine on Joyce and *Tel Quel*.

Sollers's *Femmes* published by Gallimard. *Tel Quel* shifts publisher to Gallimard and changes name to *L'Infini*.

Bibliography

PRIMARY SOURCES

Periodicals

Tel Quel, quarterly periodical, 1–94, (91 volumes), (Paris, 1960–83, Éditions du Seuil).

L'Infini, quarterly periodical (Paris, 1983–94, continuing, Éditions Denoël, then Gallimard).

Publications of the 'Collection Tel Quel'

BALESTRINI, N., *Tristan* (Paris, 1972).

BARTHES, R., *Essais critiques* (Paris, 1964).

—— *Critique et verité* (Paris, 1966).

—— *S/Z* (Paris, 1970).

—— *Sade, Fourier, Loyola* (Paris, 1971).

—— *Le Plaisir du texte* (Paris, 1973).

—— *Fragments d'un discours amoureux* (Paris, 1977).

—— *L'Obvie et l'obtus* (Paris, 1982).

BAUDRY, J.-L., *Les Images* (Paris, 1963).

—— *Personnes* (Paris, 1967).

—— *La 'Création'* (Paris, 1970).

BOULEZ, P., *Relevés d'apprenti* (Paris, 1964).

—— *Par volonté et par hasard* (Paris, 1975).

DAIX, P., *Nouvelle critique et art moderne* (Paris, 1968).

DERRIDA, J., *L'Écriture et la différence* (Paris, 1967).

—— *La Dissémination* (Paris, 1972).

FAYE, J.-P., *Analogues* (Paris, 1964).

—— *Le Récit hunique* (Paris, 1967).

FORRESTER, V., *Vestiges* (Paris, 1978).

GENETTE, G., *Figures*, i (Paris, 1966) and ii (Paris, 1969).

GINSBERG, A., *OM: Entretiens et témoignages 1963–1978* (Paris, 1981).

HENRIC, J., *Archées* (Paris, 1969).

—— *Chasses* (Paris, 1975).

—— *Carrousels* (Paris, 1981).

KRISTEVA, J., *Séméiotiké: Recherches pour une sémanalyse* (Paris, 1969).

KRISTEVA, J., *La Révolution du langage poétique* (Paris, 1974).

—— *Polylogue* (Paris, 1976).

—— *Pouvoirs de l'horreur: Essai sur l'abjection* (Paris, 1980).

—— (ed.), *La Traversée des signes* (Paris, 1975).

—— (ed.), *Folle vérité* (Paris, 1979).

MACCIOCCHI, M.-A., *Pour Gramsci* (Paris, 1974).

—— *Après Marx, avril* (Paris, 1978).

MURAY, P., *Céline* (Paris, 1981).

PLEYNET, M., *Paysages en deux* suivi de *Les Lignes de la prose* (Paris, 1963).

—— *Comme* (Paris, 1965).

—— *L'Enseignement de la peinture* (Paris, 1971).

—— *Stanze* (Paris, 1973).

—— *Art et littérature* (Paris, 1977).

—— *Rime* (Paris, 1981).

RICARDOU, J., *Problèmes du nouveau roman* (Paris, 1967).

—— *Pour une théorie du nouveau roman* (Paris, 1971).

RISSET, J., *Jeu* (Paris, 1971).

ROCHE, D., *Récits complets* (Paris, 1962).

—— *Les Idées centésimales de Miss Elanize* (Paris, 1964).

—— *Éros énergumène* (Paris, 1968).

—— *Le Mécrit* (Paris, 1972).

ROCHE, M., *Compact* (Paris, 1966).

—— *Circus* (Paris, 1971).

—— *CodeX* (Paris, 1974).

—— *Opéra bouffe* (Paris, 1977).

—— *Macabré* (Paris, 1979).

—— *Maladie mélodie* (Paris, 1980).

ROTTENBERG, P., *Le Livre partagé* (Paris, 1965).

SANGUINETI, E., *Capriccio italiano* (Paris, 1964).

—— *Le Noble jeu de l'oye* (Paris, 1970).

SARDUY, S., *Maitreya* (Paris, 1980).

SCARPETTA, G., *Scène* (Paris, 1972).

SCHEFER, J.-L., *Scénographie d'un tableau* (Paris, 1969).

SIBONY, D., *Le Nom et le corps* (Paris, 1974).

SOLLERS, P., *L'Intermédiaire* (Paris, 1963).

—— *Drame* (Paris, 1965).

—— *Logiques* (Paris, 1968).

—— *Nombres* (Paris, 1968).

—— *Lois* (Paris, 1971).

—— *H* (Paris, 1973).

—— *Sur le matérialisme* (Paris, 1974).

—— *Paradis* (Paris, 1981).

Tel Quel, Théorie d'ensemble (Paris, 1968).

THIBAUDEAU, J., *Ouverture* (Paris, 1966).
—— *Imaginez la nuit* (Paris, 1968).
—— *Mai '68 en France* (Paris, 1970).
TODOROV, T. (ed.), *Théorie de la littérature: Textes des formalistes russes* (Paris, 1965).
UNGARETTI, G., *A partir du désert* (Paris, 1965).

SECONDARY SOURCES

(For articles, excepting those in English and those not referred to in text, see footnotes.)
ADORNO, T., *Negative Dialectics* (London, 1973).
AGACINSKI, S., DERRIDA, J., KOFMAN, S., LACOUE-LABARTHE, P., NANCY, J.-L., and PAUTRAT, B., *Mimesis des articulations* (Paris, 1975).
ALTHUSSER, L., *Pour Marx* (Paris, 1965).
—— *Lénine et la philosophie* (Paris, 1968).
—— *Réponse à John Lewis* (Paris, 1973).
—— *Positions* (Paris, 1976).
—— et al., *Lire le Capital* (2 vols.; Paris, 1965)
ARON, J.-P., *Les Modernes* (Paris, 1984).
—— BALIBAR, E., and ESTABLET, R., *Live le Capital*, ii (Paris, 1965).
ARTAUD, A., *Œuvres complètes* (15 vols.; Paris, 1970–90).
AUBERT, J. (ed.), *Joyce avec Lacan* (Paris, 1987).
AUBRAL, F., and Delcourt, X., *Contre la nouvelle philosophie* (Paris, 1977).
AULAGNIER-SPAIRANI, P., CLAVREUL, J., PERRIER, F., ROSALOTO, G., and VALA-BREGA, J.-P, *Le Désir et la perversion* (Paris, 1967).
BACHELARD, G., *La Psychanalyse du feu* (Paris, 1938).
BANN, S., 'Introduction to Marcelin Pleynet: Painting and "Surrealism and Painting" ', *Comparative Criticism*, 4 (1982).
—— 'The Career of *Tel Quel*: *Tel Quel* becomes *L'Infini*', *Comparative Criticism*, 6 (1984).
BARNES, J. (ed.), *Early Greek Philosophy* (London, 1987).
BARTHES, R., *Le Degré zéro de l'écriture* (Paris, 1953).
—— *Mythologies* (Paris, 1957).
—— *Sur Racine* (Paris, 1963).
—— *Système de la mode* (Paris, 1967).
—— *L'Empire des signes* (Paris, 1970).
—— *Alors la Chine?* (Paris, 1974).
—— *Roland Barthes par Roland Barthes* (Paris, 1975).
—— *Sollers écrivain* (Paris, 1979).
—— *La Chambre claire* (Paris, 1980).
—— *Le Bruissement de la langue* (Paris, 1984).
—— *L'Aventure structuraliste* (Paris, 1985).

BARTHES, R., *Incidents* (Paris, 1987).

BATAILLE, G., *Œuvres complètes* (12 vols.; Paris, 1971–88).

BATTISTINI, J., *Trois présocratiques* (Paris, 1968).

BAUDRILLARD, J., *Le Système des objets* (Paris, 1968).

BAUDRY, J.-L., *L'Effet cinéma* (Paris, 1978).

—— *Proust, Freud et l'autre* (Paris, 1984).

—— *Personnages dans un rideau* (Paris, 1991).

DE BEAUVOIR, S., *Pour une morale d'ambiguïté* (Paris, 1947).

—— *Faut-il brûler Sade?* (Paris, 1951).

BENNINGTON, G., and DERRIDA, J., *Jacques Derrida* (Paris, 1991).

BENOIST, J.-M., *Marx est mort* (Paris, 1970).

—— *La Révolution structurale* (Paris, 1975).

BENVENISTE, E., *Problèmes de linguistique générale* (2 vols.; Paris, 1966 and 1974).

BLANCHOT, M., *Thomas l'obscur* (Paris, 1941 and 1950).

—— *L'Arrêt de mort* (Paris, 1948).

—— *La Part du feu* (Paris, 1949).

—— *L'Espace littéraire* (Paris, 1955).

—— *Le Livre à venir* (Paris, 1959).

—— *L'Entretien infini* (Paris, 1969).

—— *Faux pas* (Paris, 1975).

BLOOM, H., *The Anxiety of Influence* (New York, 1973).

BONNEFOY, Y., *Du mouvement et de l'immobilité de Douve* (Paris, 1953).

BOSCHETTI, A., *Sartre et 'Les Temps modernes'* (Paris, 1985).

DU BOUCHET, A., *Dans la chaleur vacante* (Paris, 1961).

BOURBAKI, N., *Éléments de mathématique: Théorie des ensembles* (Paris, 1968).

BOURDIEU, P., *La Distinction* (Paris, 1979).

—— *Homo academicus* (Paris, 1984).

BOUVERESSE, J., *Le Mythe de l'intériorité* (Paris, 1976).

BOWIE, M., *Freud, Proust, Lacan: Theory as Fiction* (Cambridge, 1987).

—— *Lacan* (London, 1991).

BOYER, P., *Mots d'ordre* (Paris, 1969).

—— *Non-lieu* (Paris, 1972).

BRETON, A., *Les Vases communicants* (Paris, 1955).

—— *Manifestes du surrealisme* (Paris, 1972).

BRITTON, C., 'The Nouveau Roman and *Tel Quel* Marxism', *Paragraph*, 12 (Mar. 1989).

CADAVA, E., CONNOR, P., and NANCY, J.-L. (eds.), *Who Comes after the Subject?* (New York, 1990).

CALVET, J.-L., *Roland Barthes* (Paris, 1990).

CAMUS, A., *L'Homme révolté* (Paris, 1951).

CASTORIADIS, C., *Le Socialisme bureaucratique* (Paris, 1973).

CÉLINE, L.-F., *D'un château l'autre* (Paris, 1957).

CHAR, R., *Recherche de la base au sommet* (Paris, 1955).

CHOMSKY, N., *Structures syntactiques* (Paris, 1969).

—— *Aspects de la théorie du syntaxe* (Paris, 1971).

CIXOUS, H., *Tombe* (Paris, 1965).

—— *Dedans* (Paris, 1969).

CLÉMENT, C., *Vies et légendes de Jacques Lacan* (Paris, 1981).

COBBAN, A., *A History of Modern France*, iii (Harmondsworth, 1965).

COLLIER, P., 'Georges Bataille: The Theory and Practice of Communication', Ph.D. thesis (London 1975).

COLLOBERT, D., *Dire I-II* (Paris, 1972).

—— *Il donc* (Paris, 1976).

COMBES, P., *La Littérature et le mouvement de Mai '68* (Paris, 1984).

DANTE, *La Divine Comédie*, trans. J. Risset (3 vols.; Paris, 1992).

DAVIES, H., *Sartre and 'Les Temps modernes'* (Cambridge, 1987).

DEBORD, G., *La Société du spectacle* (Paris, 1967).

—— *Considérations sur l'assassinat de Gérard Liebovici* (Paris, 1985).

—— *Commentaires sur la société du spectacle* (Paris, 1988).

—— *Im girus imus nocte et consumimur igni* (Paris, 1990).

—— *Panégyrique* (Paris, 1990).

DEBRAY, R., *Le Pouvoir intellectuel en France* (Paris, 1979).

DELEUZE, G., *Nietzsche et la philosophie* (Paris, 1962).

—— *La Philosophie de Kant* (Paris, 1963).

—— *Proust et les signes*, (Paris, 1964).

—— and GUATTARI, F., *Anti-œdipe: Capitalisme et schizophrénie* (Paris, 1972).

—— *Kafka: Pour une littérature mineure* (Paris, 1975).

—— *Mille plateaux: Capitalisme et schizophrénie* (Paris, 1980).

DERRIDA, J., *De la grammatologie* (Paris, 1967).

—— *Marges de la philosophie* (Paris, 1972).

—— *Positions* (Paris, 1972).

—— *Glas* (Paris, 1974).

—— *La Carte postale de Socrate à Freud et au delà* (Paris, 1976).

—— *Éperons* (Paris, 1978).

—— *La Vérité en peinture* (Paris, 1978).

—— Introduction to E. Husserl, *L'Origine de la géométrie* (Paris, 1962).

DESCOMBES, V., *Le Même et l'autre* (Paris, 1979).

DEWS, P., *Logics of Disintegration* (London, 1987).

DUCROT, O., and TODOROV, T., *Dictionnaire encyclopédique des sciences du langage* (Paris, 1972).

ECO, U., *L'Œuvre ouverte* (Paris, 1965).

ELLIOT, G., *Althusser: The Detour of Theory* (London, 1987).

ERIBON, D., *Michel Foucault* (Paris, 1989).

FAYE, J.-P., *Battement* (Paris, 1962).

—— *L'Écluse* (Paris, 1964).

—— *Les Troyens: Hexagrammes* (Paris, 1970).

FAYE, J.-P. *Inferno: Versions* (Paris, 1975).

—— and ROUBAUD, J. (eds.), *Change de forme* (Paris, 1975).

—— and ROUBAUD, J. (eds.), *Change matériel* (Paris, 1975).

FLETCHER, J., and Benjamin, A. (eds.), *Abjection, Melancholia and Love: The Work of Julia Kristeva* (London, 1990).

FOREST, P., *Philippe Sollers* (Paris, 1992).

FOUCAULT, M., *Maladie mentale et psychologie* (Paris, 1955).

—— *Histoire de la folie à l'âge classique* (Paris, 1961).

—— *Naissance da la clinique* (Paris, 1963).

—— *Raymond Roussel* (Paris, 1963).

—— *Les Mots et les choses* (Paris, 1966).

—— *Surveiller et punir* (Paris, 1975).

—— *Histoire de la sexualité, i: La Volonté de savoir* (Paris, 1976).

—— Introduction to L. Binswanger, *Rêve et existence* (Paris, 1954).

FOURNY, J.-F., 'La Deuxième Vague: *Tel Quel* et le surrealisme', *French Forum*, 2 (1987).

FREUD, S., *The Interpretation of Dreams* (London, 1976).

—— *On Sexuality* (London, 1977).

—— *On Metapsychology* (London, 1984).

—— *The Origins of Religion* (London, 1985).

—— *Essais de psychoanalyse appliquée* (Paris, 1933).

GEORGE, F., *L'Effet 'yua de poêle* (Paris, 1979).

GIDE, A., *Retour de l'URSS* (Paris, 1936).

GIRARD, R., *Des choses cachées depuis la fondation du monde* (Paris, 1978).

—— *Le Bouc émissaire* (Paris, 1982).

GLUCKSMANN, A., *La Cuisinière et le mangeur d'hommes* (Paris, 1975).

—— *Les Maîtres penseurs* (Paris, 1977).

GOLDMANN, L., *Le Dieu caché* (Paris, 1956).

—— *Pour une sociologie du roman* (Paris, 1964).

GOUX, J.-J., *Freud et Marx: Économie et symbolique* (Paris, 1973).

—— *Les Iconoclastes* (Paris, 1977).

GRANET, M., *La Civilisation chinoise* (Paris, 1929).

—— *La Pensée chinoise* (Paris, 1934).

GREEN, A., *Le Discours vivant* (Paris, 1973).

GREENE, R. W., *Six French Poets of our Time* (Princeton, NJ, 1979).

—— 'Poetry, Metapoetry, Revolution: Stages on Marcelin Pleynet's Way', *Romanic Review*, 68 (1977).

GREIMAS, A., *Sémantique structurale* (Paris, 1966).

GUERLAC, S., *The Impersonal Sublime*, (Stanford, 1990).

—— 'The Sublime in Theory', *Modern Language Notes*, 106 (1991).

GUYOTAT, P., *Tombeau pour cinq cent mille soldats* (Paris, 1967).

—— *Éden, Éden, Éden* (Paris, 1970).

—— *La Littérature interdite* (Paris, 1972).

HALLIER, J.-E., *La Cause des peuples* (Paris, 1973).

HAMON, H., and ROTMAN, P., *Les Intellocrates* (Brussels, 1981).

HARLAND, R., *Superstructuralism* (London, 1987).

HARVEY, S., *May '68 and Film Culture* (London, 1978).

HAWKES, T., *Structuralism and Semiotics* (London, 1972).

'Healing Words: Dr. Lacan's Structuralism', *Times Literary Supplement* (25 Jan. 1968).

HEATH, S., *The Practice of Writing*, (London, 1972).

—— *Le Vertige du déplacement* (Paris, 1974).

HEGEL, G. W. F., *The Essential Writings*, ed. F. G. Weiss (New York, 1974).

HEIDEGGER, M., *Introduction à la metaphysique* (Paris, 1967).

HERRIGEL, E., *Zen in the Art of Archery* (Paris, 1972).

HILL, L., 'Philippe Sollers and *Tel Quel*', in M. Tilby (ed.), *Beyond the Nouveau Roman* (London, 1990).

HOBSON, M., 'On the Subject of the Subject: Derrida on Sollers in *La Dissémination*', in D. Wood (ed.), *Philosopher's Poets* (London, 1991).

HOCQUARD, E., and Raquel, *Orange Export Ltd. 1969–1986* (Paris, 1986).

HOLLIER, D. (ed.), *Le Collège de sociologie* (Paris, 1979).

—— '1968, May', in D. Hollier, (ed.), *History of French Literature* (Harvard, 1989).

HOUDEBINE, J.-L., *Excès de langages* (Paris, 1983).

HUGUENIN, J.-R., *Une autre jeunesse* (Paris, 1961).

—— *Journal* (Paris, 1964).

IRIGARAY, L., *Speculum de l'autre femme* (Paris, 1974).

JAMBET, C., and Lardreau, G., *L'Ange* (Paris, 1976).

JOUFFROY, A., *Le Gué: Machiavel, Novalis, Marx et une conversation de P. Sollers avec A. Jouffroy* (Paris, 1977).

KERR, T., 'A Postmodern Novel', *Paragraph*, 12 (Mar. 1989).

KLEIN, M., *The Selected Melanie Klein* (London, 1986).

KLOSSOWSKI, P., *La Révocation de l'Édit de Nantes* (Paris, 1959).

KOJÈVE, A., *Introduction à la lecture de Hegel* (ARIS, 1979).

KOYRÉ, A., *Du monde clos à l'univers infini* (Paris, 1973).

KRISTEVA, J., *Le Langage, cet inconnu* (Paris, 1969 and 1981).

—— *Le Texte du roman* (The Hague, 1969).

—— *Histoires d'amour* (Paris, 1983).

—— *Soleil noir* (Paris, 1987).

—— *Étrangers à nous-mêmes* (Paris, 1989).

—— *Les Samouraïs* (Paris, 1990).

KUAPPI, N., *Tel Quel: La Constitution sociale d'une avant-garde* (Helsinki, 1990).

KUHN, T., *The Structure of Scientific Revolutions* (Chicago, 1970).

LACAN, J., *Écrits* (Paris, 1966).

—— *Écrits*, (Collection 'Points'), (2 vols.; Paris, 1970 and 1971).

—— *Le Séminaire*, xi: *Les Quatre Concepts fondamentaux de la psychanalyse* (Paris, 1973).

—— *Télévision* (Paris, 1973).

LACAN, J., *Le Séminaire*, xx: *Encore* (Paris, 1975).

—— *Le Séminaire*, xvii: *L'Envers de la psychanlyse* (Paris, 1991).

LA CHARITÉ, ff., *Twentieth Century Avant-garde French Poetry* (Kentucky, 1992).

LACLAU, E., and Mouffe, C., *Hegemony and Socialist Strategy* (London, 1985).

LACOUE-LABARTHE, P., and NANCY, J.-L., *L'Absolu littéraire* (Paris, 1980).

LAPLANCHE, J., *Hölderlin et la question du père* (Paris, 1961).

—— and PONTALIS, J.-B., *Vocabulaire de la psychanalyse* (Paris, 1964).

LAPORTE, R., *Une vie* (Paris, 1986).

LAVERS, A., *Roland Barthes: Structuralism and After* (London, 1982).

—— 'France: The End of the Terreur? The Evolution of Contemporary Critical Attitudes', *The Human Context*, 2 (1970).

—— 'The New Medecine of Organs', *Times Literary Supplement* (1 Feb. 1974).

—— 'In Revulsion is our Beginning', *Times Literary Supplement* (24 Oct. 1980).

—— 'On Wings of Prophecy', *Times Literary Supplement*, (1 May 1981).

LECHTE, J., *Julia Kristeva* (London, 1980).

LECLAIRE, S., *Psychanalyser* (Paris, 1968).

LEFEBVRE, H., *Critique de la vie quotidienne* (Paris, 1947).

—— *Fondements d'une société de la quotidienneté* (Paris, 1961).

—— *La Révolution urbaine* (Paris, 1970).

LELY, G., *Sade* (Paris, 1967).

LERNOUT, G., *The French Joyce* (Michigan, 1990).

LEVINAS, E., *Autrement qu'être ou au-delà de l'essence* (Paris, 1974).

—— *Éthique et infini* (Paris, 1982).

LÉVI-STRAUSS, C., *Introduction à l'œuvre de Marcel Mauss* (Paris, 1950), trans: F. Baker (London, 1987).

—— *Anthropologie structurale* (Paris, 1958).

—— *La Pensée sauvage* (Paris, 1962).

LÉVY, B.-H., *La Barbarie à visage humain* (Paris, 1978).

—— *Questions de principe deux* (Paris, 1986).

LEYS, S., *Les Habits neufs du Président Mao* (Paris, 1971).

LIPOVETSKY, G., *L'Ère du vide* (Paris, 1991).

LLEWELYN, J., *Derrida on the Threshold of Sense* (London, 1986).

'Logicus Sollers', *Times Literary Supplement*, 3484 (5 Dec. 1968).

LYOTARD, J.-F., *Discours, figure* (Paris, 1971).

—— *Dérive à partir de Marx et Freud* (Paris, 1973).

—— *Des dispositifs pulsionnels* (Paris, 1973).

—— *Économie libidinale* (Paris, 1974).

—— *La Condition postmoderne* (Paris, 1980).

MACCIOCCHI, M.-A., *De la Chine* (Paris, 1971).

—— (ed.), *Pasolini* (Paris, 1981).

MACEY, D., *Lacan in Contexts* (London, 1988).

—— *The Lives of Michel Foucault* (London, 1993).

MALLARMÉ, S., *Correspondance de Mallarmé*, 1862–1871 (Paris, 1959).

DE MAN, P., *The Resistance to Theory* (Manchester, 1986).

MARX-SCOURAS, D., 'The Dissident Politics of *Tel Quel*', *L'Esprit créateur*, 27 (summer 1987).

MASPERO, H., *Le Taoisme* (Paris, 1950).

MATHY, J.-P., *Extrême-Occident: French Intellectuals and America* (Chicago, 1993).

MAURIAC, F., *Nouveaux bloc-notes* (Paris, 1961).

MAURON, C., *Des métaphores obsédantes au mythe personnel: Introduction à la psychocritique* (Paris, 1961).

MAUSS, M., *Sociologie et anthropologie* (Paris, 1950).

MICHELSON, A., 'The Agony of the French Left', *October*, 6 (1978).

MOI, T., *Sexual Textual Politics: Feminist Literary Theory* (London, 1985).

MONTEL, J.-C., *Plages* (Paris, 1968).

—— *Le Carneval* (Paris, 1969).

MULHERN, F., *The Moment of Scrutiny* (London, 1979).

NADEAU, M., *Histoire du Surréalisme* (Paris, 1964).

NANCY, J.-L., *La Communauté désœuvrée* (Paris, 1986), trans. (and ed.) P. Connor as *The Inoperative Community* (Minneapolis, 1991).

—— *Une pensée finie* (Paris, 1990).

—— *The Birth to Presence*, eds. W. Hamacher and D. E. Wellbery (Stanford, Calif., 1993).

—— and LACOUE-LABARTHE, P., *Le Titre de la lettre* (Paris, 1973).

NEEDHAM, J., *Science and Civilisation in China* (6 vols.; Cambridge, 1954–86).

NICOLAS, A., 'Écriture et/ou linguistique', *Langue francaise*, 7 (Sept. 1970).

NIETZSCHE, F., *A Nietzsche Reader*, ed. R. J. Hollingdale (Harmondsworth, 1977).

PASCAL, B., *Pensées* (2 vols.; Paris, 1991).

PASQUALINI, J., *Prisonnier de Mao* (Paris, 1973).

PAULHAN, J., *Les Fleurs de Tarbes ou la terreur dans les lettres* (Paris, 1941).

PAUVERT, J.-J. (ed.), *L'Affaire Sade* (Paris, 1958).

PEREC, G., *La Disparition* (Paris, 1969).

PHILLIPS GRIFFTHS, A. (ed.), *Contemporary French Philosophy* (Cambridge, 1987).

PICARD, R., *Nouvelle critique ou nouvelle imposture?* (Paris, 1965).

PINGET, R., *Quelqu'un* (Paris, 1965).

—— *Passacaille* (Paris, 1969).

PLEYNET, M., *Lautréamont* (Paris, 1967).

—— *Quelques problèmes de la peinture moderne: Louis Cane* (Paris, 1972).

—— *Système de la peinture* (Paris, 1977).

—— *Transculture* (Paris, 1979).

—— *Le Voyage en Chine* (Paris, 1980).

—— *Spirito peregrino* (Paris, 1981).

—— *L'Amour* (Paris, 1982).

—— *Fragments du chœur* (Paris, 1984).

—— *Les Trois livres* (Paris, 1984).

—— *Giotto* (Paris, 1985).

PLEYNET, M., *Plaisir à la tempête* (Paris, 1987).

—— *Premières poésies* (Montpellier, 1987).

—— *Le Jour et l'heure* (Paris, 1989).

—— *Motherwell* (Paris, 1989).

—— *Les Modernes et la tradition* (Paris, 1990).

VAN DER POEL, I., *Révolution de la pensée: Maoisme et féminisme à travers Tel Quel, Les Temps modernes et Esprit* (Amsterdam, 1992).

PONTALIS, J.-B., *Après Freud* (Paris, 1968).

POSNER, C. (ed.), *Reflections on the Revolution in France: 1968* (Harmondsworth, 1970).

POSTER, M., *Existential Marxism in Post-war France* (Princeton, NJ, 1975).

POULANTZAS, N., *Pouvoir politique et classes sociales* (Paris, 1968).

POUND, E., *Les Cantos*, trans. D. Roche (Paris, 1986).

PRIGENT, C., *Denis Roche* (Paris, 1977).

RAGLAND-SULLIVAN, E., and BRACHER, M. (eds.), *Lacan and the Subject of Language* (London, 1991).

RANCIÈRE, J., *La Leçon d'Althusser* (Paris, 1974).

READER, K., *Intellectuals and the Left in France since 1968* (London, 1987).

'Rejoycing on the left', *Times Literary Supplement*, 3681 (22 Sept. 1972).

RICARDOU, J., *L'Observatoire de Cannes* (Paris, 1961).

—— *La Prise de Constantinople* (Paris, 1965).

—— *Les Lieux-dits* (Paris, 1969).

—— (ed.), *Nouveau Roman: Hier, aujourd'hui* (2 vols.; Paris, 1972).

RICHARD, J.-P., *Littérature et sensation* (Paris, 1954).

—— *Poésie et profondeur* (Paris, 1955).

RISSET, J., *Mors* (Paris, 1976).

—— *Dante écrivain* (Paris, 1982).

—— *Tel Quel* (Rome, 1982).

—— *Sept passages de la vie d'une femme* (Paris, 1985).

—— *Marcelin Pleynet* (Paris, 1988).

—— *Petits éléments de physique amoureuse* (Paris, 1991).

RISTAT, J. (ed.), *Qui sont les contemporains?* (Paris, 1975).

ROBBE-GRILLET, A., *Dans le labyrinthe* (Paris, 1959).

—— *Pour un Nouveau Roman* (Paris, 1963).

—— *Projet pour une révolution à New York* (Paris, 1970).

—— *Le Miroir qui revient* (Paris, 1985).

—— *Angélique ou l'enchantement* (Paris, 1988).

ROCHE, D., *Louve basse* (Paris, 1976).

—— *Notre antéfixe* (Paris, 1978).

—— *Dépôts de savoir et de technique* (Paris, 1980).

ROCHE, M., *Monteverdi* (Paris, 1960).

ROSOLATO, G., *Essais sur le symbolique* (Paris, 1969).

ROSE, J., *Sexuality in the Field of Vision* (London, 1986).

ROUBAUD, J., *E* (Paris, 1967).

ROUDINESCO, E., *La Bataille de cent ans: Histoire de la psychanalyse en France*, ii (Paris, 1986).

ROUSTANG, F., *Un destin si funeste* (Paris, 1976).

RUWET, N., *Introduction à la grammaire générative* (Paris, 1967).

DE SADE, D. A. F., *Œuvres complètes*, i and iii (Paris, 1986).

SAFOUAN, M., *Le Structuralisme en psychanalyse* (Paris, 1968).

—— *La Sexualité féminine* (Paris, 1976).

SARDUY, S., *Écrit en dansant* (Paris, 1965).

—— *Cobra* (Paris, 1972).

—— *Barrocco* (Paris, 1975).

SARRAUTE, N., *Le Planétarium* (Paris, 1959).

—— *Entre la vie et la mort* (Paris, 1968).

—— *Enfance* (Paris, 1983).

—— *Tu ne t'aimes pas* (Paris, 1989).

SARTRE, J.-P., *L'Existentialisme est un humanisme* (Paris, 1947).

—— *Qu'est ce que la littérature?* (Paris, 1947).

—— *Situations I* (Paris, 1947).

—— *Critique de la raison dialectique* (Paris, 1960).

—— *Situations VIII: autour de '68* (Paris, 1972).

SCARPETTA, G., *Brecht ou le soldat mort* (Paris, 1979).

—— *Éloge du cosmopolitisme* (Paris, 1981).

—— *Walkman* (Paris, 1988).

SCHNEIDERMANN, S., *Jacques Lacan: The Death of an Intellectual Hero* (Cambridge, Mass., 1983), trans. P. E. Dauzat, as *Jacques Lacan, maître Zen?* (Paris, 1986).

Screen Reader I (London, 1977).

SEALE, P., and McCONVILLE, M., *French Revolution 1968* (Harmondsworth, 1968).

SICHÈRE, B., *Le Nom de Shakespeare* (Paris, 1983).

SILVERMAN, H. J. (ed.), *Philosophy and Non-Philosophy since Merleau Ponty* (London, 1988).

SIMON, C., *La Bataille de Pharsale* (Paris, 1969).

—— *L'Acacia* (Paris, 1989).

SOLLERS, P., *Une curieuse solitude* (Paris, 1958).

—— *Le Parc* (Paris, 1961).

—— *Francis Ponge* (Paris, 1963).

—— *L'Écriture et l'expérience des limites* (Paris, 1971).

—— *Vision à New York* (Paris, 1981).

—— *Femmes* (Paris, 1983).

—— *Portrait du joueur* (Paris, 1984).

—— *Théorie des exceptions* (Paris, 1986).

—— *Paradis II* (Paris, 1986).

—— *Le Cœur absolu* (Paris, 1987).

—— *De Kooning, vite* (Paris, 1988).

SOLLERS, P., *Les Folies françaises* (Paris, 1988).

—— *Carnet de nuit* (Paris, 1989).

—— *Le Lys d'or* (Paris, 1989).

—— *La Fête à Venise* (Paris, 1990).

—— *Improvisations* (Paris, 1991).

—— *Le Rire de Rome* (Paris, 1992).

—— *Le Secret* (Paris, 1992).

—— 'A propos de l'avant-garde', *Peinture, cahiers théoriques*, 6/7 (1973).

—— 'La Révolution impossible', *Le Monde* (13 May 1977).

—— 'La Lettre volée de l'Évangile', in 'Dieu est-il mort?', *Art press*, 19 (1978).

—— 'Pasolini, Sade, Saint Mathieu', in M.-A. Macciocchi (ed.), *Pasolini* (Paris, 1981).

—— Introduction to P. Morand, *New York* (Paris, 1988).

—— (ed.), *Artaud* (Paris, 1973).

—— (ed.), *Bataille* (Paris, 1973).

—— and Binet, J.-L., 'Le Sang dit-il la vérité?', *Le Monde aujourd'hui* (12 Aug. 1984).

—— and Clavel, M., *Délivrance* (Paris, 1977).

—— and Kirili, A., *Rodin: Dessins érotiques* (Paris, 1987).

Starobinski, J., *La Transparence et l'obstacle* (Paris, 1958).

—— *L'Œil vivant* (Paris, 1961).

Sturrock, J., *Structuralism and Since* (London, 1979).

Suleiman, S. R., 'As is', in D. Hollier (ed.), *History of French Literature*, (Cambridge, Mass., 1989).

Sun Tse, *The Art of War*, trans. S. D. Griffith (Oxford, 1963).

Sur le passage de quelques personnes à travers une assez courte unité de temps, catalogue of an exhibition held at the Centre Pompidou in 1989 (Paris, 1989).

Thibaudeau, J., *Une cérémonie royale* (Paris, 1961).

—— *Interventions: Socialisme, avant-garde, littérature* (Paris, 1972).

Tournier, M., *Vendredi ou les limbes du Pacifique* (Paris, 1967).

—— *Le Roi des Aulnes* (Paris, 1970).

Turkle, S., *Psychoanalytical Politics* (New York, 1978).

Valéry, P., *Tel Quel* (2 vols.; Paris, 1941).

Vaneighem, R., *Traité du savoir-vivre à l'usage des jeunes générations* (Paris, 1967).

Verdiglione, A. (ed.), *Psychanalyse et politique* (Paris, 1974).

—— *Matière et pulsion de mort* (Paris, 1975).

—— *La Jouissance et la loi* (Paris, 1976).

—— *Dissidence de l'inconscient et pouvoirs* (Paris, 1980).

Wagstaff, C., 'The Neo-avant-garde', in M. Caesar and P. Hainsworth (eds.), *Writers and Society in Contemporary Italy* (Leamington Spa, 1984).

Winock, M., *Histoire politique de la revue 'Esprit': (1930–1950)* (Paris, 1975).

Wittgenstein, L., *Tractatus Logico-Philosophicus* (London, 1961).

WOLLEN, P., 'Bitter Victory: The Art and Politics of the Situationist International', in E. Sussman (ed.), *On the Passage of a Few People through a Rather Brief Moment in Time* (Boston, 1989).

WRIGHT, E., *Psychoanalytical Criticism: Theory in Practice* (London, 1984).

ZIZEK, S., *The Sublime Object of Ideology* (London, 1989).

Periodicals consulted: *Acéphale*; *Actes de recherche en sciences sociales*; *Action poétique*; *L'Arc*; *Arguments*; *Art press*; *Botteghe oscure*; *Cahiers du cinéma*; *Cahiers du sud*; *Cahiers pour l'analyse*; *Change*; *Cinéthique*; *Communications*; *Critique*; *La Critique Sociale*; *Diacritics*; *Digraphe*; *Documents*; *L'Éphémère*; *Esprit*; *Europe*; *L'Herne*; *L'Internationale situationniste*; *Les Lettres françaises*; *Littérature*; *Locus Solus*; *Mercure de France*; *Minotaure*; *Musique en jeu*; *La Nouvelle Critique*; *La Nouvelle Revue française*; *La Nouvelle Revue de psychanalyse*; *October*; *Paragraph*; *Peinture, cahiers théoriques*; *La Pensée*; *Po&sie*; *Poétique*; *Potlatch*; *Première livraison*; *Preuves*; *Promesse*; *La Psychanalyse*; *La Quinzaine littéraire*; *La Révolution surréaliste*; *Revue française de psychanalyse*; *Scilicet*; *Screen*; *Socialisme ou barbarie*; *Le Surréalisme au service de la révolution*; *Les Temps modernes*; *TXT*; *Yale French studies*.

Index

)